an a-z of
social
work
theory

T0349519

Sara Miller McCune founded SAGE Publishing in 1965 to support the dissemination of usable knowledge and educate a global community. SAGE publishes more than 1000 journals and over 800 new books each year, spanning a wide range of subject areas. Our growing selection of library products includes archives, data, case studies and video. SAGE remains majority owned by our founder and after her lifetime will become owned by a charitable trust that secures the company's continued independence.

Los Angeles | London | New Delhi | Singapore | Washington DC | Melbourne

an a–z of

social
work
theory

malcolm payne

Los Angeles | London | New Delhi
Singapore | Washington DC | Melbourne

Los Angeles | London | New Delhi
Singapore | Washington DC | Melbourne

SAGE Publications Ltd
1 Oliver's Yard
55 City Road
London EC1Y 1SP

SAGE Publications Inc.
2455 Teller Road
Thousand Oaks, California 91320

SAGE Publications India Pvt Ltd
B 1/I 1 Mohan Cooperative Industrial Area
Mathura Road
New Delhi 110 044

SAGE Publications Asia-Pacific Pte Ltd
3 Church Street
#10-04 Samsung Hub
Singapore 049483

Editor: Kate Keers
Assistant editor: Catriona McMullen
Production editor: Martin Fox
Copyeditor: Chris Bitten
Proofreader: Leigh C. Smithson
Indexer: Martin Hargreaves
Marketing manager: Camille Richmond
Design: Wendy Scott
Typeset by: C&M Digitals (P) Ltd, Chennai, India

Library of Congress Control Number:
2021930234

**British Library Cataloguing in
Publication data**

A catalogue record for this book is available
from the British Library

ISBN 978-1-5264-8726-1
ISBN 978-1-5264-8725-4 (pbk)

Contents

About the author

Malcolm Payne holds honorary professorial posts with Manchester Metropolitan University, where he was for many years Professor and Head of Applied Community Studies, and Kingston University London. He worked as a social worker and manager in probation, child and adult social care and in community, mental health and residential care development work in local and national voluntary organisations. Most recently he was director of psychosocial and spiritual care for St Christopher's Hospice, London, and policy and development adviser there. He has also worked in social work education in the UK, Finland, Poland and Slovakia. His publications include articles and papers on practice and theory in social work, on teamwork in interprofessional practice, and on practice and research in end-of-life care. Among his many books are *Modern social work theory* (5th edition, 2021[1990]), *Humanistic social work*; *What is professional social work?* (2nd edition, 2006), *Citizenship social work with older people*, and (edited with Emma Reith-Hall) *The Routledge handbook of social work theory* (2019).

About this book

This book is about the concepts and theory that inform social work and how it is done. It's a review of how psychological and social ideas have influenced social work and what consequences they have for social work practice. I give some brief examples to explain why these ideas matter to social workers, but not to suggest how you practise.

An important feature of this book is that it makes links between ideas. When Kate Keers asked me to put together an A–Z of social work theory, my first thought was: 'How can I make it useful to a social work student or practitioner?' The A–Z format allows me to explain and explore links connecting theoretical concepts that I haven't been able to do elsewhere. As well as links between ideas, I also connect practice theories with the concepts and process by which social work came to use them and with the people who have devised them or made them important, so that you can see why they are part of social work thinking. I have included both psychological and social ideas, because people in social work find a wide range of thinking useful.

Structure and features of the book

The chapters (entries) in this A–Z are succinct, getting straight to the heart of the concept or theory under discussion. I imagine a social work practitioner or student who hears or reads a mention of a concept or theory and wonders what it's about, so each entry starts with a brief explanation; but this is not a dictionary, so defining things is not the main aim. Entries referring to important concepts that you might want to follow up contain a fuller account of the idea and of debates about it and some further reading. They also mention connected ideas and names of people who created the idea or worked it up for use in social work, so you can turn to briefer entries that explain the situation in which this idea came up and the people who introduced it to social work.

Because the book is mainly for social workers, I've interpreted and limited the material mentioned here to be useful to them. You can follow up these entries through the references to take these theoretical ideas on and use them well in social work, and to find the full implications of ideas and theories for other purposes. It's not just for students, because we all hear about new things from time to time, and an important aim is to give you somewhere to make a start on looking for more explanation. If, as an outsider, you want to know about social work, you can pick up a good idea of the issues that social workers talk about and worry over.

Writing the entries, I have borne in mind what a social worker might use them for. I try, therefore, to give social work examples that show how a theoretical point affects what a social worker might do or think in practice. The entry may not fully represent the complexity of what can be a very sophisticated theoretical argument, and mainly focuses on social work, not on wider issues.

Inevitably (there's a word limit, and I've cut down what I originally wrote), I have not said everything I could say about any topic, and I have chosen both to discuss and to miss out things that other people would have thought important. You might want to know how I made the decisions about what I included. Here are the main points:

- The main practice theories that are currently in use that provide alternative perspectives on how you should do social work.
- Explanations of important concepts from those theories that you might find in social work writing and how they connect with the practice theories they come from.
- The main debates about the nature of social work and value systems that inform it.
- Usually very briefly, where these ideas came from in the history of social work and, less fully, other social sciences, to connect different ideas and sources.
- A few concepts from social policy and skills thinking where they inform debate about the nature of social work and its values; mainly policy and skills are off limits.

Good luck with your hunt for useful ideas.

Malcolm Payne
Sutton, London.

A

Acceptance is an ethical and practice principle in social work, mainly where social workers deal with people in interpersonal relationships. As an ethical principle, it requires social workers to value clients and their reality whatever their qualities and circumstances. It is the same with interpersonal connections to families, groups and wider populations in community settings, where different and sometimes conflicting personal identities need to be accepted; accepting one identity may be in tension with accepting another. This arises where, in a community for example, there are different interests among diverse ethnicities, or in a family conflict about an individual's sexuality. Acceptance derives from the moral principle of **respect for persons** because that principle means valuing a person's point of view and circumstances (Plant, 2009[1970]: 22).

As a practice principle, acceptance communicates to clients and others that people can be secure in understanding that they will be helped without being judged for any undesirable characteristics that they display. Hamilton (1951) says that this requires minimising clients' sense of being discriminated against, not emphasising hoped-for improvements all the time. We must also legitimate feelings that clients express and encourage participation and cooperation with clients and families, groups and communities. Later, Hamilton (1952: 29) argued that accepting **difference** was also important in acceptance. Timms (1983: 52–4) suggests that the principle is more than an attitude; social workers have a duty to continue to work with people who are hard to sympathise with. Part of this requires that they should avoid expressing rejection, condemnation or negativity about clients. Acceptance acknowledges that someone may be unchangeable, or the circumstances that led to objectionable behaviour were oppressive, and values human attitudes or actions because they meet a purpose for someone, even though they may appear objectionable. Cannon (1939[1933]: 102–3), writing in the 1930s economic depression, argued that social workers were involved with people **stigmatised** by social factors outside themselves. She suggests that this led social workers to tolerate personal difficulties and value individual achievement and interdependence rather than criticising failure and dependence. Biestek (1961: 67–88) regarded acceptance as one of the seven principles of the casework **relationship**.

Among problems with acceptance are the following:

- It is a **traditional social work** 'received idea' (Rojek, Peacock & Collins, 1988) supporting a **non-directive** style of practice like **counselling**. In this way, it encourages clients to reveal themselves and then puts them at risk of being judged.
- It may not help clients if we avoid confronting criminal or damaging behaviour.

- The principle lacks clarity about how to be accepting in practice and the consequences for clients and practitioners of doing so (Timms, 1989: 14–15).
- It may seem a patronising or arrogant attitude: 'I accept you, even though many would not.' Therefore, acceptance requires us to drop any sense of being superior because we're **helping**, recognising that helpers share an imperfect humanity with clients and others (Faatz, 1985[1953]: 98–106).
- Simply acknowledging and permitting people to express anger about oppression does not achieve social justice through social change against that oppression. It seems more like tokenism (Baines, 2017c).

Despite the critiques, acceptance is still present in social work as an approach to inter-personal relationships. For example, Miller and Rollnick (2013: 16–19) treat it as a basic principle in **motivational interviewing**, identifying four elements of it.

- Prizing clients' inherent worth and human potential.
- Offering clients accurate **empathy** by actively making the effort to be interested in and understand clients' views.
- Supporting clients' **autonomy** and right of self-direction.
- **Affirming** clients by communicating that we appreciate their **strengths** and efforts.

This account reminds social workers to experience their appreciative attitude (they cannot just put acceptance on, it has to be **authentic** or genuine) and also to communicate it.

Another recent account of acceptance as a practice principle is 'acceptance and commitment therapy' (ACT) (Boone, 2014), a form of **mindfulness** practice. The point here is letting go of struggle, accepting how things are and how you have reacted to issues that you face in your life, and then building new reactions to them. Wong (2014) describes 'radical acceptance' in which people learn to understand and accept imperfections in their lives, understand that things are often not 'either–or' choices but can be **reframed** through multiple perspectives to become 'both–and'. By recognising through awareness of when others are using power and privilege, we can accept what is happening and then find more satisfactory ways of reacting to it.

Accountability is the duty to explain and justify the reasons for actions taken by practitioners in the course of their work. Such a duty is more than responsibility, which refers more to a personal sense of 'duty to explain'. This is because accountability operates in the context of formal professional responsibilities and assumptions about structures of 'social accountability' (McGee, 2020). These may lead to accountability to an employing organisation, generally a social work agency, in a job role and as an employee, and also for compliance with professional standards set by a regulating body, or through membership of a professional association, or by personal commitment. Processes for accountability may, however, create a 'new accountability', when they lead to **proceduralisation** because of political and managerial distrust of professional **discretion** in decision-making (Banks, 2004: 149–94).

Professional and personal commitments may set more important standards than an employer when practitioners work in private practice or with colleagues. Accountability in such circumstances may be to a personal sense of responsibility, to an employer, to professional standards, to colleagues, to clients and others involved in a case, and to a community and the public interest (Shardlow, 1995).

McGee (2020) points also to possibilities for developing 'social accountability' in political and social structures in most societies, involving relations between citizens, corporations, organisations and the state. Attempts to introduce and increase the influence of structures that give citizens **voice** or **power** over decision-making can be important ways of working on accountability issues, and, presented carefully, may be hard for a democratic state to resist. Social workers can look at and try to stimulate factors that mobilise people to seek accountability from structures in society, for example when they perceive injustices, asymmetries in power, or poor responsiveness in service provision. They can also work collectively with clients to generate 'civic engagement' (McGee, 2020: 60) that gives **excluded** groups democratic muscle to influence decision-makers. Other ways of stimulating social accountability includes informing people about entitlements and opportunities and helping them claim and respond to them, to reduce the 'invisible power' of people's low expectations. Success in making **welfare rights** claims may be an important route for doing so.

Further Reading

Banks, S. (2004). *Ethics, accountability and the social professions.* Basingstoke: Palgrave Macmillan.

Action and activity

Action and **activity** are the basis for social work interventions in several practice theories. **Giddens'** sociology argues that society is created by the actions of human participants in it. It is therefore not an unchanging basis for social relations and social structures. The actions that create society are 'skilled **performances**', activities based on people's knowledge and understanding of how social relations operate in that society (Giddens, 1976: 160). **Bourdieu**'s conception similarly sees actions within social relations as expressing cultural influence and human preferences. Action therefore forms and changes social structures and relationships; these are not given to us, we create them (Lawler, 2013: 109–10). Ronnby's (1992) account of **praxis** argues in the same way that human and social work action creates the ideas, thoughts and **discourses** surrounding social phenomena.

'**Social action**' in sociology contests **liberal** economic determinism by making it clear that people act as they do because of others' influence in social relationships, not because of economic pressures. More recently, 'social action' describes collective action to achieve social change.

Many ideas about social work pick up **diagnostic theory**'s 'controlled and directed action' by clients towards their goals (McCormick, 1954). Staub-Bernasconi (1992, 2007) sees social work as an 'action science', helping people take action to respond to micro-experiences of suffering, discrimination and powerlessness by using their resources and entitlements. This brings **privatised** troubles into public action. Clients can make claims and raise rights issues within social and political debates from the bottom up. This is more effective than policy and professional help being developed from the top down (Askeland & Payne, 2017: 173–4).

Other social work theory emphasising activities includes the following:

- **Task-centred practice** theorises social work as action to complete tasks in a planned programme to resolve priority problems. This focus motivates people to deal with difficulties quickly and in a practical way (Reid & Epstein, 1972b).
- The social goals model of **groupwork** uses activities to enable people to experience interactions with others facing similar issues (Papell & Rothman, 1966).
- Polish **social pedagogy** uses activity in residential and day care and in interpersonal practice, to resolve people's issues. Activities help them learn to become 'acting **subjects**', able to take action to influence their situation (Marynowicz-Hetka, 2019a).
- 'Positive activity interventions' are a **cognitive behavioural** approach to reducing anxiety and depression using social skills approaches. They include ideas such as writing letters of gratitude, counting one's blessings, practising optimism, building opportunities and plans, performing acts of kindness, and meditating on positive feelings about others (Layous & Lyubomirsky, 2014).
- 'Experience-near' descriptions in narrative practice concentrate on **deconstructing** experience by looking at actions taken as events took place, the people who acted and the meanings attributed to the actions by people involved (Béres, 2014: 33).

The critique of action argues that just taking action or completing tasks is not enough to get results in social work; clients' mental effort is required. Action plus cognition in social relationships is needed to initiate and maintain social structures that will create change.

Not all practice theory emphasises activity and action. **Relationship**-based theory, for example, requires interpersonal influence rather than clients' activity. The **transtheoretical model** of behaviour change used in **motivational interviewing** suggests, contrary to task-centred practice, that significant behavioural change is not a rapid process, requiring prior contemplation and then a difficult and lengthy struggle. Behavioural **change** is just as difficult for social workers to achieve as **social change**. Completing a few actions or tasks will not, therefore, kick-start improvements as task-centred practice supposes. Similarly, **solution-focused practice**, though accepting that change might be rapidly achieved, focuses on clarifying people's objectives and motivation to achieve them, rather than simply carrying out various actions. Reid (1997) suggested balancing action-oriented with reflective and expressive social work. Most contemporary social work therefore integrates clients' **reflection** and rehearsal (as 'homework' or '**in vivo**' work) as actions between meetings with social workers.

Activism is campaigning vigorously in public arenas of debate to achieve a political or **social change**. Debate about activism in social work connects with questions about the role of political and **social action** as part of the **professionalised** social work role. Pearson (1973), in a famous paper, aligns social work activism with being 'misfits' alongside other groups that seek social change contrary to contemporary **managerialist** forms of social life. This aspect of social work may therefore always be in tension with social work **professionalisation**. American research suggests that social workers are more likely to be involved in political activism than people in other similar professions, but social workers with a strong 'client orientation' who participate in professional activities are more committed than practitioners whose main commitment is to their agency (Reeser, 1991, 1992). An Australian study (Gair, 2017) found that student social workers were prepared to participate, but were busy with other responsibilities and did not know how to pursue activism. They are helped by strong social awareness of the **intersecting** aspects of **social justice** and active reading about policy advocacy and macro practice (Morley, 2016; Nayak & Robbins, 2019).

Adaptation refers to people changing attitudes and behaviour to fit with social expectations. Frosh (1987: 88–94) argues that adaptation is a particular concern of American psychology, the source of much social work theory, but is absent or less strong in European psychologies. The emphasis on seeking forward-looking **change** in the more recent positive psychologies may help to redress the balance.

Social work might therefore be cautious about the psychological emphasis on people adapting to a new **self** or a new situation. A preventive or **social development** strategy could focus social work on preparation for both expected and unexpected changes, such as **disasters** like flooding, a major fire, an earthquake leading to disruption and loss of homes, famine, genocide, war or other human catastrophes. **Social pedagogy** or youthwork strengthens the **resilience** of communities for shifting the life experience of young people and the consequences for their family and community. Public and social care services could be adapted to be responsive when disasters with social consequences occur. An important focus is helping people where lack of social **support** or **poverty** makes them unable to adapt to the impact of serious events.

A theoretically important usage of **adaptation** is in **ecological systems theory**, in particular Gitterman and **Germain**'s **life model** of practice where supporting adaptation of environments or people to fit with each other is an important objective. **Crisis intervention, empowerment**, preventive, **resilience, social development**, interpersonal and **social change** practice may all be helpful in achieving this aim since ecological systems theories are generally **eclectic** in their use of theory.

Advocacy practice involves two different kinds of activity:

- Arguing or speaking for a cause, idea, proposal or way of doing things in policy and **social change**; this may include social **activism**.
- Speaking on behalf of or in the interests of a person or group of people, to help pursue their concerns and needs, or of arguing for or appealing against decisions about social care services, social work and welfare benefits.

While pioneers of social work were part of social reform movements (Dalrymple & Boylan, 2013: 21–31), **traditional social work** practice legitimated a consensus rather than an adversary or combative stance, and **professionalisation** contested partisan alignment (Ad Hoc Committee on Advocacy, 1969). So also did employee status, especially in government agencies. UK practice had two sources of advocacy practice: **welfare rights**, and advocacy for people with intellectual **disabilities** and **mental illness**, as part of the mental patients movement.

Social work advocacy may include:

- Case advocacy on behalf of clients with external agencies, including welfare rights advocacy to achieve or improve clients' welfare benefits and services.
- Cause, systemic or policy advocacy, concerned with achieving policy or social change.
- Representation of clients' interests in **agency** decision-making.
- Facilitating **clients' participation** and **representation** in agency and wider decision-making.

In representing clients' interests (as opposed to other representation), advocacy may be:

- Instructed where social workers represent clients' arguments, like a courtroom lawyer.
- Uninstructed, where social workers act on behalf of or support clients' interests in agency decision-making.

Many social workers step back from instructed advocacy, and instead facilitate specialised advocacy agencies. This is because all advocacy requires clarity about who the client is, and there may be multiple clients with conflicting interests in, for example, a family or community. Sometimes interests must be balanced among people who all have a right to the social worker's voice, for example between a child, birth parents and foster carers in contested childcare situations. Social workers' legal duties may also be a factor limiting advocacy roles. For example, in the UK the child's interest is paramount in many childcare decisions and parents' interests may go unrepresented in decision-making forums. Social workers may gain influence where their agency is the decision-maker, but this may exclude them from being an instructed advocate.

Advocacy agencies in the social work field provide different services.

- Client group advocacy for people such as children in public care, mentally ill people, older people, and people with intellectual or physical disabilities.
- Citizen advocacy where volunteers build relationships with people, often with intellectual disabilities, to support them in representing their interests in decision-making, for example at case conferences. The relationship is necessary so that the volunteer can communicate with and understand the person's interests.
- **Peer advocacy** is part of **peer support** often in mental health **recovery** services, and involves people with experience of the person's condition and services in that field to support their interests.
- Self-advocacy, providing people with training and support so that they can represent themselves in decision-making and in care processes.
- Best interests decision-making involves advocacy in decisions about what may be in the best interests of a client without mental capacity to make their own decisions. This is often provided in intellectual disability, mental health and older people's services. Best interests assessors and Independent Mental Capacity Advocates (IMCAs) in the UK are often private practice social workers.

Everyday social work representing clients' needs and advocacy service practice both use advocacy practice theory. The dimensions of advocacy are identified first, as follows:

- Purpose, whether you are speaking for someone or enabling them to speak.
- Perspective, whether you are aiming to persuade or give **voice** to a viewpoint.
- Focus, whether you are aiming to get change or some result for the client, or helping to express a position.
- Scope, whether your main aim is to meet an individual or family need or to represent collective concerns (Wilks, 2012: 22–6).

Many models of the social work advocacy process are **stage** theories (Bateman, 2006: 75; Wilks, 2012: 90–4), which identify a similar process:

- Analysing and defining the issue or problem to be addressed.
- Research and information-gathering about the issue and potential resolutions.
- Feedback to the client, interpreting the issues as aspects of advocacy.
- Negotiation and informal advocacy.
- Formal representation, litigation or appeal.
- Feedback and evaluation.

Expert consultation, peer support and professional supervision take place at each stage.

Practitioners need to consider the degree of assertiveness required and appropriate in each case. Social workers may feel forced to pull their punches in advocacy because they want a continuing relationship with the agencies or colleagues. Sometimes agencies may disapprove, forbid, not cooperate in or prevent forceful advocacy where this may damage inter-agency cooperation or disrupt internal decision-making or managerial authority. Dalrymple and Boylan (2013: 46) comment that the '**business**' model of many social work agencies, setting targets, managing **risk** and organising packages of care, raises the question of whether advocacy can remain part of social work practice.

Further Readings

Dalrymple, J. & Boylan, J. (2013). *Effective advocacy in social work.* London: Sage.

Wilks, T. (2012). *Advocacy and social work practice.* Maidenhead: Open University Press.

Affect and affect regulation

concern people's emotional states and how **emotions** are expressed in patterns of human behaviour. The theoretical issue is the balance in social work assessment and practice between a focus on emotions and rational thinking. Affect regulation, important in **attachment** practice and **neuroscience**, is about how people manage their emotions as they react to events in their lives and how they communicate or express them to others.

Affiliation

is a sense of connection with another person or organisation; for example, we may feel a strong connection with parents or brothers and sisters, or events may have led to less affiliation. With organisations, affiliation may be formal but not intense. Assessment of people's affiliations can often help social workers' understanding of the nuances of people's connections and relationships. Many Chinese people value 'filial piety', a duty of respect and care to parents that is appreciated in Confucian thought, and this is often a factor in working with clients of Asian heritage.

Affirmation

in social work is expressing the worth of another person, being explicit about their achievements, attributes and commitment. Being affirming can maintain clients' motivation and commitment to working on issues that are important to them and is endorsed in several practice theories. In **crisis intervention**, for example, affirming achievements is seen as stabilising clients' progress. **Motivational interviewing** uses affirmation as a communication skill to support clients' motivation to achieve change in their lives. Clients may gain affirmation from **participation** in decisions and processes that affect them. An affirmation model of **disability** (Goodley, 2017) focuses on ways in which societies often devalue disabled people, requiring compensatory affirmation of their personal worth and social contribution.

African-centred practice involves drawing on African discourse and

philosophies to 'recover' helpful cultural traditions and social worldviews and connect them with social work practice both in African communities and with African peoples in other societies. This is similar to **Indigenist** practice in countries settled by colonisers. The historical experience and legacy of **slavery** is particularly important for African peoples, both in the countries where slaves originated, in territories where they were enslaved and in the attitudes of peoples who operated or participated in the historical slave trade, or benefited from it economically. This historical experience may also be relevant to the experiences of people involved in and victimised by modern slavery and people trafficking.

Graham (2002: 21–42) shows how **Enlightenment** thought rationalised ethnic and racial hierarchies as part of the contours of Western knowledge which are still incorporated into social work thought. Kreitzer (2012) argues that patterns of social work education and practice reflect colonial and Western models of research and thinking, and **post-colonial** continuing influences. African social work education has not had the opportunities or resources to develop African traditions and incorporate them powerfully into social work.

Graham (2002: 66–8) identifies three main **liberation** traditions.

- Redressing the cultural, political and social position of African peoples, wherever they are, as it is still affected by colonialism, racism, slavery and their consequences.
- Understanding and working on the constraints affecting present African societies, wherever they are, as a consequence of post-colonial cultural and economic oppressions.
- The potential of African knowledge and philosophy in contributing to wider knowledge and thinking, displacing the centrality of Western philosophy and research methods, including within social work. Kreitzer's (2012) work is an example of this movement taking place in social work.

African cultural elements relevant to social work are as follows:

- All things, both natural and human, are interconnected.
- Human beings are by nature **spiritual**.
- Connections are made between collective and individual identities and collective and inclusive family structures.

- Body, mind and spirit are one.
- Interpersonal relationships are always to be valued (Graham, 2002: 69).

These ideas are not absent from Western social work, particularly in its **humanistic** traditions or from other cultural sources, such as the Chinese sources of **body–mind–spirit practice** and **mindfulness**. Examples from contemporary African social work literature integrate many of these ideas into practices that all social workers can draw on.

Further Reading

Gray, M. (Ed.) (2017). *The Routledge handbook of social work and social development in Africa*. Abingdon: Routledge.

Ageing
is the process by which human bodies change as they grow older. It affects practice with older people, their carers and families.

Biological theories of ageing fall broadly into two groups:

- Programmed theories propose that various biological mechanisms, such as hormones or expression of genetic factors, set a timetable for physical longevity, continuing the phases of physical development in childhood. Many theories argue that senescence brings evolutionary advantages.
- Damage and error theories propose that the stresses and strains of life or accumulating biological errors reduce the capacity of physical bodies to sustain themselves (Jin, 2010).

Important social theories of ageing are as follows:

- Disengagement theory (Cumming & Henry, 1961) sees later life as a progressive disengagement from social relationships, preparing for the ultimate disengagement of advancing disease and death. Against this view, disengagement is not a universal process; people's preferences for social engagement vary throughout their lives (Rose, 1964). Older people and the people around them often do not see disengagement as desirable, and many continue to seek personal development and positive **activity** in social **networks** in later life. It may also be argued that capitalist, **neoliberal** thinking disengages, by detaching people from active involvement in the economy and social policy provision, such as retirement pensions. This might benefit neoliberal economies by managing or reducing costs of employment; for example, cheaper younger people can be employed rather than more expensive experienced older workers, or of social welfare provision for older people.
- Activity, continuity and successful ageing theory (Havighurst, 1961; Rowe & Kahn, 1987; Baltes & Baltes, 1990; Atchley, 1999; Lupien & Wan, 2004) underlie many

contemporary developments in services for older people. Activity theories propose that older people benefit from maintaining and enhancing their mental, physical and social activity. Continuity theories propose that older people benefit from continuing social links and networks and activities important to them in earlier stages of life. Successful ageing theories are informed by **life course** ideas, and suggest that individual biographies and **social movements** have **intersections** with social structures, so that as social change takes place it affects how older people are able to pursue or are pushed away from past experiences (Elder, Johnson, & Crosnoe, 2003). Activity theory is criticised for imposing middle-class aspirations and family lifestyles on all older people (Katz, 2000). There is also little evidence to say what kinds of activity are useful, and pushing unremitting activity may be undesirable compared with a reflective, spiritual approach to later life. Activity theory is also problematic if it does not incorporate older people's needs and limitations (Versey, 2016).

- **Attachment** and **strengths** ideas have been proposed as useful perspectives to inform practice (Blood & Guthrie, 2018). Developing **support** and other **networks** among family and friends is an important strategy where these are absent (Katz, Holland, Peace & Taylor, 2011), with formal services being required where older people are childless and have limited existing networks (Deindl & Brandt, 2017).
- Transition theories focus on helping older people's responses to changes in social structures, particularly of the economy and the state. Robertson (2014) emphasises changes such as retirement from full-time work, downshifting from a family home to a smaller property, relationship breakdowns, becoming a long-term carer, bereavement, long-term health conditions, starting to use care services and preparing for the end of life.

One important theorisation of transitions in older age groups is the proposal that there are four 'ages' in the life cycle (Laslett, 1996), the third 'young–old' phase being a period of active ageing, with the fourth age 'old–old' phase being where people begin to experience greater health and social problems. The critique of this idea is that only economically secure, middle-class people benefit from an active lifestyle in the third age, and the idea of a fourth age pushes problems into a later stage, which emphasises a negative view of **dependency** and lack of control.

- Social determinants of health issues particularly affect older people. This refers to worldwide and British research (World Health Organization, 2008; Marmot Review, 2010) suggesting that there is a social gradient of health inequalities in which richer people who are more in control of their life and work are healthier for longer than poorer people. The poorer you are, the more likely it is that you will suffer from more serious health problems in later life.
- **Critical** theories of social work with older people (Ray, Bernard & Phillips, 2009) focus on how neoliberal economic thinking devalues older people's reduced

participation in the labour market and alternatives such as artistic, creative and interpersonal achievement. Similarly, **feminist** theory emphasises how policy on ageing accentuates gender differences, for example seeing men's retirement from the workforce as problematic, rather than valuing opportunities for reintegration into community and family life and valuing the contribution of women.

Ageism, prejudice against particular age groups in society, affects all groups in society, but particularly older people. Ageism, for example, may devalue the social contribution and maturity of young people, focus on difficulty in adjustment to change in the middle years, as well as devaluing older people. Older people may be excluded from **participation** in social relations or families by changes in family structure, or separation from younger generations because they are physically slow and disruptive to younger people, or because of poverty arising from poor pensions or other social entitlements. They may also lose rights of **citizenship**, becoming 'de-citizened' by social **exclusion** (Payne, 2017) or by being placed in care environments or separated housing.

Ayalon and Tesch-Römer (2018) identify several sources of ageism. One view focuses on group, organisational and social structures, for example in labour markets, where middle-aged or older people are thought to be too set in their ways to be employable or to be potentially challenging when subordinate to younger managers. People internalise negative stereotypes of ageing, looking at older people mainly according to perceptions of the physical and social effects of ageing. For example, physical slowing down in old age feeds an incompetence stereotype; emphasising positive social roles such as grandparenting generates a warmth perception. Increased focus on economic achievement and development, geographical mobility, secularisation and **individualism** reduces family links and supports that might value older people's participation in church, community, family and society. Instead, such trends enhance the value given to younger people's knowledge and skills.

Evolutionary assumptions also feed ageism. Younger people are seen as important because they are 'the future', while older people no longer represent an evolutionary 'survival of the fittest' but a burden of dependence. Advances in technology and medicine have led older people to survive longer, placing a burden of **dependency**, frailty and disability on wider society. Their life experience is devalued by rapid technological change. Intergroup conflict also provides theoretical explanations of ageism, with older people seen as a group thwarting economic and social progress by retaining control of resources such as housing or political power (Willetts, 2010). Older people remind younger people of their mortality and vulnerability, stimulating them to unconscious fears about their own mortality (Greenberg, Solomon & Pyszczynski, 1997). Separating and distinguishing themselves from older people allows them to preserve equanimity against fears of ageing. All this may lead to age segregation, where older people are cut off from involvement in education organisations or community and family life.

Intersectionality theory suggests that ageism is a lens through which other **discrimination** **A** and **oppression** may be seen and that older people are a minority group that connects with the experience of other minority groups. Ageism also operates through people's personal reactions to ageing and older people. Social **identity** theory proposes that people maintain a positive self-identity by valuing characteristics of youthfulness and distinguishing them from assumed negative characteristics of old age. The life course and active ageing ideas accept these unhelpful stereotypes. They do this by emphasising that ageing contrasts with youthfulness and promoting positive lifestyles that mimic youthful stereotypes rather than acknowledging the reality of physical and social difficulties in ageing. Because these ideas underlie common social and healthcare approaches in practice with older people, social work risks reproducing unhelpful stereotypes of ageing in its practice.

Social work responses to ageism require **anti-discriminatory** thinking and practice to respond to attitudes about and perceptions of ageing in ourselves, carers, colleagues, and families and others around clients, as well as in agencies and their policies.

Further Reading

Scharf, T. & Keating, N. C. (2012). *From exclusion to inclusion in old age: A global challenge.* Bristol: Policy Press.

Agency has two meanings in social work theory, as follows:

- An organisation providing and responsible for social work services. These are usually called 'agencies', drawing attention to their aims to have an impact on the world. The theoretical issue is the extent to which social work aims influence agencies' practice or policy thinking based on wider cultural, political and social objectives, or whether such culturally-derived views influence social work, perhaps inappropriately.
- The capacity of individuals and social groups to have an impact in the world. This meaning of agency refers to one of the great **discourses** of sociology: to what extent are our social relations developed through human agency or by social **structures**? Or by **cultural** influences (Archer, 1996)? And this issue relates to one of the great issues in philosophy: to what extent are actions the product of human free will or **determined** by the natural and social environment?

The mandate, objectives, organisational processes and structures of the agency affect the social work carried out on its behalf. Thus, agencies always influence social work actions and objectives. **Functional** social work theory elaborates how 'agency function' gives social work processes form and purpose.

Most social work agencies are governmental organisations, often based in local government. The relationship of local with regional and national policy therefore arises. They necessarily implement government policy, but the agency is continuous from before and beyond the present government. Administrative systems and legal requirements affecting practice often persist over time. There may, therefore, be continuities of policy and practice, or disjuncture. Lack of political and policy interest in or support for social work may inhibit practice changes. Profit-making or social enterprise agencies may reflect business rather than social purposes. Social work in not-for-profit or 'third sector' organisations may compromise social work with the requirements of fundraising or the elites who establish and finance charities.

These characteristic features of its organisation, including the relationship of social work to the state, fuel debate about social work's **professionalisation**. Toren (1969) contests functional theory in arguing that social work cannot be a profession while agency responsibilities control its practice.

The second concept of agency refers to people's capacity to control or influence their activities. Individual agency, called in psychology **self-efficacy**, may be hidden, since socialised norms and structures of belief may constrain or direct people's agency (Pettit, 2020). **Bourdieu**'s (1980) concepts of habitus and field suggest that habits and norms may prevail in deciding what we do or they may be so influential that we are effectively automata. Butler (1990: 142–9) suggests that important aspects of our identity lead to **performativity**, the social requirement to take part in repeated ritual acts constrained by norms and discourses – an example is where women in families are expected to carry out caring acts and men household repairs. Here considering agency is not about people having the power to act; rather it requires us to explore how culture and discourse set whether it is socially possible to act. There may also be collective agency, for example, civic or political agency (Pettit, 2020). Oosterom's (2020: 170) research talks about '**coping** agency' and '**citizen** agency', which condition how people react to the difficult stresses of violence or negotiate with the authorities. A woman subject to violence from an intimate partner, for example, often finds ways of trying to prevent, or manage the consequences of, the violence in her home for the sake of children or to 'keep up appearances', or negotiates escape with police, lawyers and refuges who are supposed to mediate violent situations.

Aggression is inappropriately forceful attitudes and behaviour, in which people react in an angry, dominating way towards others. In social work, aggressive behaviour is often raised as a concern in clients' behaviour towards, for example, family members and intimate partners. Part of the concern about aggression as a behaviour derives from social work's historic connection with **psychodynamic** theory, since **Freud**, the founder of **psychoanalysis**, saw aggression as an important human disposition to seek mastery and control that led to disintegration and was a barrier to civilisation (Frosh, 1987: 50). This idea connects aggression to others with a need to maintain psychological control of the **self**, and social workers often find that people who are uncertain about themselves and their own social position respond by being aggressive towards others. Bandura, Ross and Ross' (1961) research on aggression shows that young people learn aggressive behaviour from parents and other models in their social environment, and ideas such as this influenced social workers to help parents reduce aggression as part of child rearing.

There is also concern about 'microaggressions', acting, organising the social environment or talking in ways that covertly or deniably express devaluing thoughts about another person because they are part of a marginalised social group, for example, ethnic or religious minorities (where the term originated), women or disabled people (Spencer, 2017). An example is telling a joke about transgender people but denying the insult by saying 'it's just a joke' (a microassault). Another example is telling the parents of a successful African professional 'how proud you must be', thus being overtly complimentary but also expressing the assumption that professional achievement in an African is unusual (a microinsult). A further example is where women employees have the same number of WCs in the office toilets as men, who have more urinals, thus communicating a devaluation of one group's needs within an apparently neutral environment (a microinvalidation) (Torino, Rivera, Capodilupo, Nadal & Wing Sue, 2019: 4). It is often useful to call out microaggressions by identifying the reality of the attitudes expressed and the inappropriateness of the behaviour.

Aggression management is a series of primarily **cognitive behavioural** procedures, often undertaken in groups, to help people regulate aggressive behaviour that has become habitual or problematic.

Alienation is a process in which a person loses identification with something appropriately or formerly important to them, becoming separated from it. There are two areas of social work theory where it is important.

- **Existential** and **humanistic** ideas recognise that people may become cut off from wider aspects of their life, ideas, people and social relations that are important to them. Social workers would explore how and why it has happened, that what is important is nevertheless now lost to them, and would then try to understand and help people with the emotional consequences of that loss.
- **Critical** and **Marxist theory** see capitalism as alienating workers from the means of production. In a capitalist system, they lose control of the production process that they are part of, they do not own the machinery and tools that they use and they may not see the final product and its customers. Capitalism alienates them, cuts them off, from the process that they are involved in, from the product of their labour and from other workers with whom they compete for work. Since satisfying work is a crucial part of being human, they are also alienated from aspects of their own humanity. Critical social work values cooperatives and involvement in work processes, giving control of work and humanity back to workers. If this is not possible in their employment, other opportunities for participation and sharing responsibility through community and family may benefit them.

Alliance has several important meanings in different aspects of social work, as follows:

- In general, alliance means working together with a client or worker with a positive commitment to collaborating with their family, community or agency, cooperating in defining and carrying out objectives and coordinating your activities to achieve shared objectives.
- Therapeutic alliance is a concept borrowed from **counselling** and psychotherapy. It means creating a sense of alliance with clients and the people around them to identify and work towards shared objectives.
- In **anti-oppressive, critical, feminist, macro** and **social development** practice, building alliances and coalitions with activists and organisations, and representing clients and social groups, is an important practice strategy. It involves not just cooperation, but a commitment to the political and social objectives of the organisations that practitioners are in alliance with.

Altruism is acting for the benefit of others without thought for our own interests, the opposite of **egoism**. Arguments for **professionalisation** often claim that professionals, as opposed to employees, are disinterested in their actions and decisions. But professional altruism is questionable because professionals are paid and may also gain personal or other gratification from helping others. Volunteering, working for a charity or in the public interest might therefore be seen as more altruistic rather than being a paid professional. This view, however, devalues professional education and skill.

Non-altruistic benefits also arise from professionalisation (Saks, 1995: 17–34). An example is where a social worker takes an authoritative decision, like taking a child into public care. This may benefit the child, and sometimes the parent, and the public interest in ensuring the safety of vulnerable people. This is possibly a just or neutral decision, but is it altruistic? And if the public interest is in doubt, for example where parental rights are counterposed with children's needs, is the decision in the public interest partly motivated by fears of public opprobrium if the professional gets the decision wrong? That is not personal gratification, but a decision made with avoiding public criticism or disapproval in mind cannot be said to be altruistic, because it is not wholly without thought for the practitioner's interests.

Is altruism merely the internalisation of social expectations, for example women being expected to exhibit **caring** behaviour in a family? If caring is supposed to be part of their psychological make up, and women have internalised those social expectations (Dalley, 1988), this is not altruism. Similarly, is it altruism for social workers to provide for clients' legal and social rights, or pursue social justice, or some other kind of duty? (Banks, 2012).

Is altruism informed by reason or by emotion? If it comes from reason, it is not altruistic just to be effective in achieving a personal and social end. And it is not an altruistic act to do something to benefit society because the altruistic actor benefits from the improvement of society, and so is not disinterested. Alternatively, should an altruistic act be outside emotional influence? An altruistic act is done because of the interests of the other person, but not because you care about that person, or you are horrified by their distress. If you acted because of your emotions, there would be no certainty that a professional with a different emotional reaction would provide a consistent service. Banks and Gallagher (2009: 66) distinguish between feelings, which are more immediate and more raw, and **affect**, which includes an element of cognition or rational thought. They argue that emotions always contribute to motivation and therefore to actions, that they permit us to respond sensitively to the situation and allow us to appraise our actions bearing in mind this emotion–rational balance, rather than simply reacting. Social workers are not altruistic because the social mandate of **caring** professions means that they are expected to have compassion, to act with care and concern and perhaps in accordance with policy (Hugman, 2005: 48–66). Caring, according to the **ethics of care** view, is about attending to both emotional and rational requirements of the situation, and a professional assumption of altruism may not be an appropriate requirement.

Ambiguity arises where there is more than one interpretation of behaviour or events. **Technical rational** views of social work seek to reduce ambiguity in explanations and representations of understanding, while seeing social work as an **art**, or **humanistically**, accepts that much human behaviour is ambiguous and that in practice the ambiguity allows complexity of the environment of human living, of society and in the impact of social structures on humanity to be expressed and worked with. Focusing on ambiguity in practice often allows opportunities for change to be explored.

Ambivalence is having contradictory, mixed or uncertain feelings about another person or course of action. It often means that you are unable to make decisions or act decisively because it takes time to work out the contradictions. This can lead to slowness in reacting and to constantly changing your mind. When you are ambivalent, the feeling of uncertainty influences your behaviour and your cognition, how you think about it (van Harreveld, Nohlen & Schneider, 2015). Ambivalence is a factor in many psychological and sociological theories.

Psychological ambivalence may be caused by complexity of knowledge about the issue, or having insufficient knowledge or understanding. One social work approach to it, therefore, is to work through the issue with clients to help them gain knowledge of the issue that is causing them difficulty. This may involve researching their understanding. The issue may be more about their **insight** into their feelings and thoughts, so an insight-based approach of working through the detail of attitudes and thinking may help people to arrive at a clearer position. An important element of **motivational interviewing** is the acknowledgement that ambivalence is commonplace, and certainly people are usually ambivalent about making important **changes** in their lives, because there are usually gains and losses. Another approach to ambivalence may be a decision-making approach, looking at the pluses and minuses of a course of action.

In sociology, **discourse** and **postmodern** analyses of social relations say that social processes are inevitably ambivalent since there is a continuing interactive process within them which affects human behaviour and organisational reactions to it. Organisations and social relations are expressions of iterative processes, in which cycles of action and reaction inevitably lead to constant shifts to which we all constantly adjust. **Bauman** (2000a) characterises this as 'liquid' **modernity**, where constantly changing reactions are expressed in the way in which collective structures operate in relation to human beings. He argues that while modernity is often seen as seeking ordered and understandable social relations, it also has a dual or ambivalent nature, with new knowledge and understanding constantly overthrowing traditional forms of culture and economy. Both elements are characteristic of contemporary societies.

Anti-discriminatory practice (ADP) is where social workers,

in providing their services, tackle prejudiced treatment of people because of unjust **discrimination** against groups in society. ADP focuses on how people and services devalue others, while **anti-oppressive practice** focuses on the impact of social power or social privilege. 'Institutionalised discrimination' occurs when services incorporate, possibly hidden, attitudes, assumptions, conventions, expectations and social structures that mean they are organised in ways that discriminate against devalued groups in society.

Discrimination is not in itself inappropriate; it means the capacity to draw distinctions between people or things with clarity and discernment. But ADP is used where distinctions arise because of prejudice against devalued categories of people. **Anti-racism** was the forerunner of ADP, which developed as practitioners became aware that similar processes affected many social groups, who could not achieve **equality** and **social justice** because societies did not accept and value cultural, religious and social **diversity** (Thompson, 2016: 11–17). ADP values social justice, equality and diversity in social work thinking and practice, in the way their agencies operate and in society more broadly. By social workers and their teams influencing how people are treated in practice, social work aimed over time to have a broad anti-discriminatory impact.

Thompson's (2016: 35–9) personal, cultural, structural (PCS) analysis thoerises levels of discrimination:

- The personal or psychological level of discrimination in ourselves or others.
- The cultural level, shared assumptions, patterns of thinking and any taken-for-granted consensus.

- The structural level, social divisions and power relations cemented into the way organisations and procedures incorporate law and social expectations into how they do things.

This analysis is concentric: you start from the personal, which incorporates the cultural, which is determined by social structures. The critique is that interactions between these aspects of discrimination operate in more complex ways than 'levels'.

Areas where discrimination is likely to be an issue for social work are **ageing** and ageism, **disability** (some people talk about disablism), **gender** and sexism, **ethnicity** and racism, sexuality (some people refer to heterosexism), belief or faith and **religion**. Some people are affected by discrimination in more than one, and perhaps many, of these. It is important to recognise that discrimination is not cumulative; if you are affected by more discriminations, it does not necessarily increase the impact. And one factor does not trump another; for example, ethnicity is not more important than gender or disability. Instead the interaction of various factors is **intersectional**, with the impact varying according to the circumstances and history of the interaction.

Further Reading

Thompson, N. (2016). *Anti-discriminatory practice* (6th ed.). London: Palgrave.

Anti-oppressive practice (AOP) is a practice theory responding
to the needs of groups affected by **oppression**, cruel, restrictive and unjust treatment by social groups exercising power improperly because of their sense of **privilege** over the **other**. The crucial distinction between anti-oppressive and **anti-discriminatory** practice is that oppression is concerned with unjust treatment by groups claiming or perceiving their privilege, that they are in some way more important or valuable than others, whereas discrimination is about people who make distinctions devaluing others without necessarily abusing power or thinking of their privilege. Mullaly's approach to AOP particularly empha- sises analysis and understanding of privilege (Mullaly & West, 2018; Mullaly & Dupré, 2019).

Baines (2017a) and Morgaine and Capous-Desyllas (2015) see the main aims of AOP as **social change** that achieves **social justice**, through a political **process** alongside helping individuals in a **caring** process. In doing so, it builds allies and works with wider **social movements** and causes, developing theory and practice based on struggles by oppressed and marginalised people. This therefore requires **participation** by clients in the social work process. Morgaine and Capous-Desyllas (2015: 15–20) emphasise the importance of individual and group social **identities** in creating the location for oppression, and therefore see important aspects of AOP as creating self-awareness and **dialogue** as approaches to liberation, although merely acknowledging devalued identities is tokenistic. To Baines (2017a), oppression is created in both micro- and macro-level social relations, in everyday experience of many oppressions and crucially in the experience of **resistance** to them. AOP is a heterodox theory, one that does not conform to a single accepted approach, and therefore takes in many elements without prioritising one. It requires self-**reflexive** practice, and social analysis of and commitment to a wide range of social justice perspectives. Social change and social justice practices are informed by **eco**, **empowerment**, **feminist**, **Marxist** and **structural** social work theory (Morgaine and Capous-Desyllas, 2015; Baines, 2017a). To Baines (2017a), it also draws on **postmodern** analyses that require us to examine multiple **voices** and oppressions. Her analysis includes the importance of the political context for social work (Baines, 2017b), including the importance of social work's relationship with the state: is it part of the state or in tension with its demands? This is the issue raised by the contradictory position in **radical practice theory**. Using AOP also requires a concern with tackling **inequalities**, dominant contemporary political ideologies that are inimical to social justice, pre-eminent among which at present she identifies as **neoliberalism**, and a clarity about the social justice objective in working on social change.

Further Reading

Baines, D. (Ed.) (2017). *Doing anti-oppressive practice: Social justice social work* (3rd ed.). Halifax: Fernwood.

Anti-psychiatry was a social movement active in the 1960s and '70s associated with the psychiatrist R. D. Laing and collaborators. It questioned the **medicalisation** of **mental health** issues, arguing instead that behaviour seen as symptoms of mental illness constituted reasonable reactions by people trying to assert their **identity**, their **self**, within destructive patterns of relationships in social structures, particularly in the dynamics of some **family** relationships. Laing's (1965, 1971) early work focused on the development of self in the context of society in psychotic patients; Collier (1977: 2) argues that the key concept here is 'ontological insecurity' – people insecure about their **being** think about the world differently from those who are secure in their **identity**. Experimental work in clinic and residential settings led to publications that explored the sources of symptoms of schizophrenia in young people in their family relationships which create that sense of insecurity (Cooper, 1970; Laing & Esterson, 1970; Esterson, 1972).

These ideas influenced social workers seeking social explanations and possibility of social interventions in mental illness. Many of the ideas were seen, however, as criticising parents for their children's illnesses and for breaking up families. Some of the ideas of the anti-psychiatry movement persist, such as in critiques of diagnostic certainty in psychiatry, for example of the **manualisation** of diagnostic criteria in psychiatric handbooks such as the *Diagnostic and Statistical Manual of Mental Disorders* (**DSM**) of the American Psychiatric Association and in the **recovery** movement of mental health patients, which contests **medical models** of **diagnosis** and treatment.

Anti-racist practice is combating **discrimination** against people and

groups in society who are devalued because of their **ethnicity**. This is one of the most significant forms of discrimination in many societies, deriving from historical attitudes to people who are seen as **other** rather than as valuable human beings, because of their ethnicity. It may be especially significant when this is connected to colonial hierarchies (for example, the racist person thinks of someone of different ethnicity as from a culturally or economically inferior former colony) or **slavery** (for example, the racist person thinks of someone of different ethnicity as socially inferior because their people were historically slaves). This may become connected to inferior social status because immigrants to former colonial countries or migrants within countries often find themselves employed in low-status jobs or housed in devalued areas or properties, and the culture and education of their home country is devalued.

Social workers meet racism in their own thinking, the thinking of colleagues, the policy and structure of their **agency**, the policy and practice of agencies they work with and the attitudes and behaviour of clients and other people in their community. Strategies for dealing with this include the following (Bartoli, 2013; Thompson, 2016: 103–6):

- Avoid taken-for-granted racism, always bearing in mind structural factors that may affect your organisation and your practice. Examples are ideas about assimilation, that people of different culture, ethnicity and faith should adopt the behavioural and cultural expectations of the majority, and multiculturalism, that all cultural expression should be treated as contributions to a valuable cultural diversity and social **pluralism** without valuing black and minority ethnic identities.
- Acknowledge and compensate for the people's difficulties that come from accumulated disadvantages in education, health, housing, poverty and social relationships.
- Challenge actions, attitudes, behaviour, language and social situations that express discrimination.
- Think about and be prepared to step in when situations arise in which people from minority ethnic groups may be affected by backlash against them, for example, where other people experiencing difficulties, unemployment or poverty may be resentful of migrant neighbours or where global or political conflict is raising issues that may increase racism.
- Work on improving your competence in dealing with and understanding the needs and experiences of a minority ethnic group, but without expecting them to educate or inform you.
- Encourage people to share experiences and ways of responding to racism.
- In hearing about people's experiences, be prepared to give them cues that enable them to talk about communication, interactions and relationships.
- Empower people of different ethnicity to gain control of actions and decisions affecting their lives.

- Encourage, expect and support managers and organisations in raising and dealing with ethnicity and racism issues.
- 'Permeate' anti-racism by raising issues about it frequently and regularly, as part of everyday experiences in groups, meetings, procedures and training.
- Be aware of situations in which people from minority ethnic groups may be isolated in a predominantly white organisation or situation, picking up the responsibility for responding to racism, rather than expecting them to do so.
- Using **critical race theory** ideas, take opportunities to think through, perhaps with colleagues, experiences of whiteness and privilege that come out of your work, and accept and enable clients who have experiences that raise these issues, but who may not have the confidence or language to express them to you.

Further Reading

Bartoli, A. (Ed.) (2013). *Anti-racism in social work practice*. St Albans: Critical Publishing.

Art is a theorisation of a way of understanding social work practice, seeing it at least partially as an artistic endeavour, in which subjective understanding is a valid element of humanity. The view contests **technical rational** ideas such as **evidence-based practice** that claim that social work knowledge and intervention rely on rational understanding and responses to the social. Bowers' (1949: 417) well-known definition refers to social work as an art and a science, seeing practice as requiring at least some artistry, while knowledge should be from science. Boehm (1961: 150) argued that it was wrong to create a dichotomy between art and science, that an artistic component was required in the practice of scientific social work and that art in practice is capable of being studied and understood scientifically and provided for in social work education and practice. He connects art with intellectual endeavour, having a high quality of response in understanding the world in a unified way combining specialist knowledge with a general interest in forming realistic, believable ideas about it. Art seeks in every situation its originality, the surprises that it offers, and it tolerates and rejoices in difference and dissent, so that it welcomes conflict, tension and polarity. England (1986: 85–100) argued that art incorporates intuitive and subjective understanding, for example of **ambiguity**, into practice in ways that rational understanding in the social sciences cannot achieve. Social work in this view involves the self of participants in situations of fluid reality, which may be understood and communicated but not finally pinned down in rational understanding.

Using art in practice involves work on understanding similarities between processes of creating art and doing social work, and using artistic materials such as literature, painting, poetry as part of intervention processes; this helps communication by providing a wider range of media. This has contemporary import as we consider the use of blogs, emojis, social media, vlogs and other information technology as forms of communication. Techniques of artistic or literary criticism can help critical thinking in social work.

Further Reading

England, H. (1986). *Social work as art: Making sense for good practice.* London: Allen and Unwin.

Assessment is a process in all social work practice and is also frequently seen as a function or role of social work when it is part of wider social care services. Assessment is the contemporary development of the idea of **diagnosis**, describing the process of understanding the nature of the issues to be dealt with in social work interventions, but 'assessment' carries more complex implications. Many social work services, particularly where they are public services, use social workers to determine eligibility or **need** for service provision, and in **case** or **care management** in adult social care services, this is an important legal function. Alongside this, there may be requirements to undertake financial assessments where services are charged for. Assessment of this kind is often an initial assessment, undertaken before intervention or service provision and then only periodically reviewed, whereas practice assessments are usually taken to be a continuous part of the **process** of social work intervention.

These elements of assessment for services may interfere with the practice uses of assessment because they may be used to ration services, or plan service provision in ways that are distant from clients' and carers' wishes. As a result, practitioners might be acting on behalf of the managers of the service rather than in the clients' interests. Social workers may deal with this, for example, by explicitly separating assessment of need from assessment as part of interventions or service provision, and may be helped in this because other providers of services also carry out additional assessments as they engage with clients. The **ethics of care** view argues that assessment for care cannot separate formal definitions of care from the people involved in the process, which must inevitably explore the interpersonal consequences of the intended caring process, and therefore must include both caregivers' and receivers' parts in that process (Tronto, 1993: 137–55).

Assessment may be theorised in different ways, and Milner, Myers and O'Byrne (2015) use the analogy of different types of map of the terrain of the client's life, connecting these with social work practice theories, as follows:

- Assessment of a wide range of elements and networks to place the client in relevant social contexts; **systems theory**; a satellite map.
- Assessment of complex interactions in the human life and thinking of the client and people around them; **psychodynamic theory**; a map of the ocean.
- Assessment of specific elements of behaviour relevant to the issues in the client's life; **CBT**; an ordnance survey map (a detailed map of a specific area).
- Assessment of agreed issues to be dealt with in the intervention; **task-centred practice**; a handy tourist map.

- Assessment of areas to be explored in order to achieve a goal; **solution** or **strengths practice**; an explorer's map (of unknown territory).
- Assessment of belief and issues in the client's life; **macro** and **spirituality** practice issues; a map of the universe.

Attachment theory is a practice theory emanating from the work of John Bowlby, a psychoanalyst and psychiatrist. It seeks to repair disturbances in people's behaviour that arise because their attachment relationships with important **caring** figures in their lives have been disrupted. Attachment relationships are 'affectional' bonds (and therefore involve intense emotion) between people in which one relies on the other for a sense of **security** (Prior & Glaser, 2006: 56–70). It developed from the **psychoanalytic** focus on the importance of the mother in childhood development, and it has been a significant part of practice in UK childcare services (Howe, 2005; Shemmings & Shemmings, 2011, 2014, 2019) and more widely (Bettmann & Friedman, 2013). It has also been a significant development in clinical psychology, counselling and social work practice with adults (Bennett & Nelson, 2010; Howe, 2011; Mikulincer & Shaver, 2016; Cassidy & Shaver, 2018).

Social work has had a long history of involvement with Bowlby and his ideas, and it has more recently been strongly integrated into social work in child and adolescent **mental health** services and in child **safeguarding**. Critiques of attachment ideas note that it is easy to use it as a deficit model, looking primarily at assumptions about parents' or caregivers' failings; this is also true of working with adults by looking back at past 'failed' attachments. Use of neuroscience ideas, connecting physiological factors with psychological issues concerning emotions, may mean that people come to see change as difficult or impossible. It also means that difficulties with attachment may sometimes be seen as irreparable, whereas difficulties in attachment can be repaired, relationships skills can be improved or people may develop alternative attachment figures. There has also been criticism of an over-concentration on attachment, rather than exploring other types of bond that might be developed, for example affectional bonds, friendship bonds, and bonds with other family members (Prior & Glaser, 2006). Particularly as children get older, they have other opportunities for personal development, with peer relationships becoming more important than caregiver attachments. For adults, sexual pair bonds may provide important attachment experiences. Many compensatory experiences are possible (White, Gibson, Wastell & Walsh, 2020).

The attachment model of behaviour with children is as follows:

- People learn as infants to seek proximity to carers who have become attachment figures.
- Attachment figures provide a **secure base**, which becomes a **safe haven**, within which children feel safe to explore new experiences.
- If children become separated from attachment figures, and this leads to distress, separation protest and proximity-seeking behaviour, they attempt to find the carer or remain close to them.

- How carers behave in their relationships with children leads to well-established patterns of attachment behaviour in children.
- Patterns of attachment behaviour persist unless they are amended, and this can affect adult behaviour and how adults regulate their **affect** and **emotions**.

This model is developed in adult practice, but is broadly similar, as follows:

- Faced with a threat, people's attachment systems generate proximity-seeking behaviour with an external or internalised attachment figure.
- If an attachment figure is available, people feel relief and security; if not, they experience rising insecurity and distress.
- If proximity seeking is possible, people become active in seeking support, and are very vigilant in avoiding threats and seeking **support**. If attachment support is not available, people distance themselves from threats and from attachment (Mikulincer & Shaver, 2016: 27–41).

The adult attachment interview, a lengthy questionnaire, was the original assessment tool for adult assessment, but there is a shortened version. Other assessment techniques include 'story stem' **(narrative)** techniques, where vignettes of situations that raise attachment issues provide the basis for exploring attachment issues in adults' lives.

With both adults and children, there are similar patterns of attachment behaviour. Most people have an established pattern that is organised or secure. A small proportion of children and adults have not experienced consistent attachment, particularly in childhood, and so their attachment pattern is disorganised or insecure because they cannot trust an attachment figure to help them feel safe.

The main approach to attachment practice with children is to explore the attachment relationships and behaviour patterns of a child. Most practice is concerned with two ways of repairing attachment relationships between parents or other caregivers and children who are presenting behaviour difficulties:

- Attunement – caregivers' capacity to be sensitive to a child's reactions and needs. This is difficult to do, and while it is useful to improve people's capacity to respond to others' reactions, it is also helpful to improve their recovery in situations where they get it wrong.
- Mentalisation – people's capacity to reflect on their own and others' behaviour by having a mental picture of their own state of mind, which they get from being able to picture others' views of themselves. People have to be able to see that others may see them differently from how they see themselves, so that they can work out how others' reactions reflect perceptions of themselves.

Techniques for working on these issues might involve enhancing parents' and children's relationship skills, improving low capacity in mentalising, using guided tasks to give people practice in working on their relationships or using 'story stems' (starting people off with the beginning of a story about what might go wrong in relationships) to help people reflect on options to respond to relationship issues (Shemmings & Shemmings, 2014).

Attachment work with adults is focused on the regulation of affect or emotions, both psychologically and using **neuroscience** ideas, since emotions are related to both physio-logical and psychological changes in people (Schore & Schore, 2011).

Further Reading

Howe, D. (2011). *Attachment across the lifecourse: A brief introduction*. Basingstoke: Palgrave Macmillan.

Authenticity is sometimes used as a synonym for genuineness in counselling. It means that the practitioner is real and true in representing their attitudes, ideas and personality. It is sometimes related to the idea of 'self-disclosure', being prepared to communicate personal experiences and feelings to clients, to help them feel that you are engaging with the client as a human being, not just as a professional.

Authentisation was a process, now associated with **colonisation** and **post-colonial** thinking, in which social work intervention ideas and theory, having been adapted for use in non-Western countries and cultures through **indigenisation**, were accepted as part of a local model of practice culturally relevant in that non-Western society (Walton & el Nasr, 1988). Ragab (2017), referring particularly to Islam, argues that authentisation was conceived as adapting inherently sound models of practice requiring only minor cultural adjustments. Contemporary theorisation suggests that a significant reformulation of social work was required to encompass core social and **spiritual** values in many non-Western countries. For many countries, the Islamisation of knowledge was required alongside changes in social work more widely to be inclusive of movements to include spirituality within social work. Western science requires sifting for congruence to the Islamic worldview.

Authority is influence or **power** exercised by right and given by law, an organisational or political mandate, or personal or professional status.

It has been an important issue in social work, since practitioners are part of governmentality (Garrett, 2018a: 167–88), the formal and informal social processes through which behaviour and relationships are managed in societies. Also, social workers enforce the law, carry out official **assessments**, and are often part of large **institutions**, such as hospitals, law courts and schools, which exert discipline over the public and their clients. Using authority in these ways is in tension with ideas that social work is a professional activity carried out **non-directively** for **altruistic** reasons for the benefit of **self-determining** clients.

The contemporary emphasis is on power rather than authority, but power is exercised to avoid **risk** or improve safety, and authority is still relevant. For example, in child protection situations, the **solution-** and **strengths**-based **signs of safety** approach to risk management explicitly enjoins the use of 'nuanced' authority. This involves clearly explaining the reasons for authoritative interventions, connections with the court or agency requirements and not taking emotional or aggressive reactions personally (Turnell & Murphy, 2020: 32).

Discourse about this issue is political and there are two sources of criticism of social work's authority from Right and Left political positions. The Right critique, a **liberal** and **neoliberal** perspective, sees social work as representing the 'nanny state', interfering on behalf of the state in people's entitlement to freedom to act as they wish within the law. The Left critique, a **Marxist** or **socialist** perspective, sees social work's authority as given by the state using claims of altruism to interfere oppressively in people's lives on behalf of dominant class, gender or other social interests.

Social work may become authoritarian by using moral or political pressure. For example, it was criticised for moral authoritarianism in the debate about **social role valorisation** (a form of **normalisation**), because training intellectually disabled people to pass as non-deviant was not done for the benefit of the clients, but to avoid others' bullying or hostility towards them (Dalley, 1992). More recent sociological analysis demonstrates how it is that many social processes represent authoritative interventions in people's lives. **Bourdieu** (1991), for example, shows how actions gain authority by the way in which they are used in rituals that demonstrate appropriate behaviour. For example, the professional authority of the social worker is demonstrated in simple ways: you have to make an appointment to see them, they manage the interview, they visit your house at their convenience in a car. It is also demonstrated in more complex rituals: the social worker writes the report, makes the application and can gain access to decision-makers not available to a client.

Autonomy

Autonomy is the idea that people have the capacity and right of **self-direction**, what they think and do not being controlled or decided by other people or other forces. Of course, there are such forces, but an autonomous individual can apply their mind to consideration of them and decide for themselves whether to accept or reject their influence. Doyal and Gough's (1991) influential account of social **need** argues that having autonomy to make informed choices about what to do and how to do it is an essential attribute of being human. But it is not an individual autonomy, since how we make our choices comes from social expectations and the social structures that condition our choices. This idea contests the assumptions of 'public choice' theory, a **liberal** and **neoliberal** idea that services such as social work should be organised so that people are **free** to make choices about their options in a market, rather than having their decision constrained by public expenditure on a more limited range of provision.

B

Balance is an issue in several social work contexts. One concern is equity. Examples representing different interests are in **advocacy**, 'the middle way' in **Buddhism**, **equilibrium** in **crisis intervention**, **fairness**, or harmony in Chinese philosophy. Similarly, balance may be an issue in understanding contested theory, for example between **action** and **reflection**. Some practice aims to achieve balance between two behaviours that are considered inappropriately extreme, in some psychological practice theories, such as **cognitive behavioural therapy,** or the more sociological, such as **critical** practice. A critique of concern with balance is that seeking balance **excludes** people or social groups at extremes and may be too concerned with order and structure, rather than creativity, flexibility and innovation.

Bauman, Zygmunt (1925–2017) was a British sociologist of Polish heritage. Committed to a sociology that sided with poor and dispossessed peoples, he argued for a moral commitment to community and solidarity, seeing **modernity** as a totalising order favouring rational economic and intellectual **progress**. Rapid economic and social change through **globalisation** shifts 'solid modernity' towards fluidity and polarises divisions between insecure and **oppressed** groups and social values that prize economic and social success only through consumption. In a 'liquid' modernity, anxiety about losing economic **security** leads to **cultural** and social distance, and **social exclusion** and denigration of **dependence** on state social provision. Social work is a creation of modernity, controlled and managed in liquid modernity through increasing **neoliberal**, **managerial** mechanisms such as **marketisation**, modernisation and **proceduralisation** to achieve **individualised** social **inclusion** rather than **human rights** through social solidarity (Smith, 2011).

Further Reading

Bauman, Z. (2000). *Liquid modernity*. Cambridge: Polity.

Beck, Ulrich (1944–2015) was a German sociologist who coined the term 'risk society' and, working with various colleagues, explored how **globalisation**, **individualisation** and **modernisation** were universalising risks, so that all social classes were widely affected by economic and environmental insecurity. The sense of precariousness led to risk-averse social norms, and to government and social processes excessively concerned with risk analysis and security, leading in turn to attempts at greater control and surveillance.

Being is an important concept in philosophy, and existential and humanist practice theory, exploring human existence: we are human **beings**, psychology and social work depend on and follow from existence. May (1983) distinguishes between grasping another person's being and knowing specific things about them. A social work assessment gives you information about a person, but to know their being you must have the kind of relationship in which you encounter them fully. 'I am', their internal self, sums up how their thinking, feeling and doing interact and are expressed in human relationships, in language and interactions with the world. **Existential** practice proposes that knowing a client's **self** in this way is a precondition to helping; mere information misleads you. Ideas such as this contest **evidence-based** and **technical rational** ideas about understanding people.

Bereavement is the psychological and social process of adapting to loss, in particular the death of a loved one, and is an important aspect of social work in end-of-life and palliative care, more so than for other professions in this area of provision. Bereavement is a normal response to loss, a natural corollary of affiliation and attachment (Parkes & Prigerson, 2010[1972]).

Stage or **task** theories of bereavement (Glick, Parkes & Weiss, 1974; Bowlby, 1988; Worden, 2010) suggest that people move through a period of adverse psychological reaction, rejecting the reality of the loss. They then move towards acceptance of the loss and restructuring their life towards adjustment. The critique of such theories is that they assume that people must move through an adjustment process, and that the pattern of progress is consistent, while evidence suggests that some people do not 'move on' in this way.

Sociological theories of bereavement therefore focus on other processes that may affect people. Klass, Silverman & Nickman (1996) developed a 'continuing bonds' theory, suggesting that people integrate the deceased person into a healthy ongoing life, redefining themselves with a new **identity**. This includes the past relationship by forming a bond with a new internal **representation** of the deceased person, avoiding idealising them and evolving a new **equilibrium**. The **dual process** model (Stroebe & Schut, 1999) proposes that people shift between focusing on their loss and the **emotions** around it, and on restoration to a new life. **Meaning** reconstruction (Neimeyer, 2001a, 2001b) is a **constructionist** theory proposing that dealing with grief is a unique process in which people reorganise their identity to attach meaning to their new personal situation and social relations.

Grief may become complicated if the reaction is delayed, exceptionally profound or prolonged, and this may require specialised psychotherapeutic or psychiatric help for depression (Stroebe, Schut & van den Bout, 2013).

Further Reading

Currer, C. (2007). *Loss and social work*. London: Learning Matters.

Biestek, Felix P. (1912–1994), was an American Jesuit priest and social work academic, whose work on **self-determination** as an important value in social work and his theorisation of the social work **relationship** as part of **helping** were influential in the mid-twentieth century.

The **biopsychosocial model** of social work includes biological, psychological and social issues (sometimes '**spiritual**' is added) as relevant factors in practice, particularly assessment.

Black perspectives are views of the experience of discrimination and racism expressed by Black people themselves. Ahmad's (1990) account focuses on the **identity** and solidarity experienced by black people, **empowerment** in resisting **institutionalised** norms, cooperation in finding both personal and **community** resources for **social change**, and use of legal and procedural **advocacy** forwarding the interests of black people.

The **body** is an important concept in many aspects of social work, as follows (partly from Cameron & McDermott, 2007):

- The body is a biological physical entity, which **represents** an internal person and the **emotions** and psychology embodying the social relationships of that person to outside observers. **Diagnostic, psychosocial** practice and **traditional social work** focus on the **person-in-situation**, later the person-in-environment; this is the body and its physical and social relationships. People's **identity** is associated with their body, their emotional and psychological states being recognised, for example in assessment, by their body's representation of them. For instance, social workers carrying out assessments might evaluate tension by how the body is held. **Bourdieu** (2003: 93–4, cited by Garrett, 2018a: 126–7) considers that how the body moves or speaks, writes someone's 'habitus', including social class, into their body. Thus, the **social** is always embodied and social workers evaluate **embodiment** to understand people's identities and relationships. Body consciousness, an awareness of non-verbal forms of communication by the holding and positioning of people's bodies, is an important skill to develop (Morgaine & Capous-Desyllas, 2015).
- Bodies are associated with **places**, and where the body is placed – for example the sick person in the bedroom, the client in a residential institution, the family in its living room – expresses something about them and their social relationships.
- The placement of the body is important to a relationship, for example, the fact that a social worker visits a client, or needs to be visited in their office or a clinic, or to

meet in a personal office or a neutral interview room. Where they sit expresses attitudes and relationships, for example close to a client or separated from a client by a desk.

B

- People's bodies may be felt to be vulnerable, for example, to abuse where there are concerns about **safeguarding**, or because of disability or illness. As a consequence, social work becomes concerned for the body and not just with the mind or social relations, yet social work discourses, for example in social work education, often fail to address the body and physicality, rather than the mind and the **social**. Twigg (2000) suggests that **neoliberal** thinking and **new public management** discourses emerge from economics, accountancy and organisation, and are consequently distant both from concerns about the person and social relations, and also from caring for bodies and physical vulnerabilities.
- Social work interventions may have implications for people's bodies. For example, social workers may move children's bodies in public care from the care of their parents into foster or residential care, and the bodies of mentally ill people from their home compulsorily or otherwise to a hospital or clinic for treatment.
- **Care** includes care for the body, for example in services providing bathing for disabled or older people. Puig de la Bellacasa (2017) argues that the embodied presence of a caregiver is perceived as an important aspect of **care**.

Body–mind–spirit work is an interpersonal social work practice which adapts

concepts from Chinese medicine emphasising a **holistic** model of intervention in human problems (Lee, Ng, Leung & Chan, 2009). It promotes a sense of harmonious, **holistic** wellness seeking **balance**, between mind, spirit and body, and personal growth and **transformation**. This moves beyond cognitive management of personal problems, emphasising bodily movement to nurture **spiritual** and mental balance, and tranquillity. Its founders have undertaken research, mainly in health settings, to provide empirical support to its overall approach.

Boundary is a concept in two distinct areas of social work theory:

- In **systems** theory, a system is defined by its boundary, which separates one part of a system from another. More energy interchange takes place within the boundary than across it. Boundaries may be relatively impermeable, or permit transfers across them. You identify the boundary by observation, seeing where energy flows are most active. Energy flows across the boundary indicate linkages with other systems (Anderson & Carter, 1999: 28–31).
- Boundary is also relevant in counselling and practice **ethics**. To achieve mutual trust, practitioners maintain a boundary in their professional **relationships** with clients, distinguishing between actions that have professional objectives and their personal interests.

Bourdieu, Pierre (1930–2002) is a French philosopher and sociologist, a major late twentieth-century thinker, whose ideas have begun to be significant in twenty-first-century social work (Garrett, 2013, 2018a: 28–32; Thorpe, 2018). Like many sociologists in this period, he has been concerned with **language** and **discourse** about **social reproduction**, how **culture** and **power** have been established and maintained from one generation to the next. His ideas bridge **structural** theories that claim social structures determine social relations and **action** or **constructionist** views that focus on the formation of social relations through cultural influences and human preferences (Lawler, 2013: 109–10). Another important area of his work was how people and interest groups responded to the politics of **neoliberalism** (Rogowski, 2013: 149–50). He also contributed ideas about **reflexivity**. Bourdieu's concepts influential in social work are as follows:

- **Capital**, including cultural, economic, social and symbolic capital. These refer to resources that individuals, families, social groups, communities and interest groups build up. Capital gives them **strengths** to operate in the world in relation to other individuals or organisations. We are familiar with economic capital, financial resources. Cultural capital is resources of knowledge and understanding. **Social capital** is human links and social **networks** that we have connections with. **Symbolic** capital is our ability to use ideas that exist within the world in which we operate, and we do this by our use of **language**; how effective our language is affects the influence we can build. The more capital of all kinds that we have, the more power we have in our relations with other people and within the discourses in society.

  These ideas theorise a range of assets that strengths practice aims to develop. They also explain how we can strengthen our practice by building up cultural capital (our professional understanding), social capital (links with other professions and agencies) and symbolic capital (our capacity to explain and be accountable for our practice and demonstrate our success).

- **Field** refers to the social **spaces** in which we operate, which are structured by forces that create them and which generate power within them. They are 'networks of objective relations between positions' (Bourdieu & Wacquant, 1992: 97), so we can identify and research these relationships and the positions people occupy in relation to others. The social work field, for example, is structured by the social sciences, by the practices that social workers carry out when they do social work, by the **agencies** and their legal and social responsibilities, and by political and social policy forces; other factors may also be relevant. Fields **intersect** with each other, so when we are working with a **disabled** client, we intersect with medical and healthcare professional fields, and the field of collectives and interests of disabled people and their caregivers.

These and other interests interact with and shape social work conceptions of what we are doing, as our views shape their fields. Child **safeguarding**, for example, involves different professional fields, with practice conceptions in conflict or in tension. This involves media, children, parents and an interested public all with forces upon them in their fields making an impact on the safeguarding field, and through this on the social work field (Parrott with Maguinness, 2017: 78–96).

The social work field builds power as social science, practice methods and agencies gain influence in other fields. If local government social care services and clients' carers value social workers, this builds the social work field's influence in intersections with other fields.

- **Habitus** is the dispositions, ways of seeing and reacting to the world, that we acquire through our childhood and life experience such as social work education. More than attitudes, habitus is patterns of actions that are observable and can be researched. Habitus allows people to know likely responses to issues that they experience. Habitus forms tendencies towards action in the fields in which we operate, and the habitus of individuals and groups operating within a field form, to some extent, the nature of that field.

    Social workers' habitus derives from their social commitment and their approach to issues. These influence the ways they typically respond to interactions within their field. That typical response will come to be known and understood by others in the field and influence their own reactions forming their own habitus.

- 'Symbolic power' and 'symbolic violence' provide an account of how the concepts and language used in a society, in relationships and in social interactions achieve dominance for some social groups over others. A group or individual that uses the available language or that creates language to exert power over others can influence habitus and field. An example is discriminatory concepts in social discourse, such as racist insults or abuse about disabilities. This forms symbolic violence; a verbal assault is committed, sometimes a 'microaggression' (see **Aggression**). Symbolic violence occurs in cultural and academic discourses, for example in how ideas become available and develop. **Solution** and **strengths** practice used ideas available in positive psychology to contest **problem-solving** as a conceptualisation of social work. Ideas can have symbolic power within a field and influence the habitus of people within it.

One of the important aspects of Bourdieu's thinking is the way in which the language that generates symbolic power and violence is 'authorised', given **authority** by the social conditions in which it is used and by rituals that create boundaries of behaviour or distinctions between what is considered appropriate and inappropriate behaviour in a field

(Bourdieu, 1991). A positive example is the way in which social workers' experience and training in dealing with emotional conflict in relationships gives them confidence and techniques to help other people in ways that are not typical of everyone. A negative example is the way that a group of young people living on a housing estate might build up a pattern of abusing a resident with intellectual disabilities. Doing this is using symbolic violence; it seems nothing, injury does not occur, but it asserts abusive domination of the group's conception of the resident's humanity.

Further Readings

Parrott, L., with Maguinness, N. (2017). Bourdieu and social work. In L. Parrott with N. Maguinness, *Social work in context: Theory and concepts* (pp. 78–96). London: Sage.

Thorpe, C. (2018). Pierre Bourdieu: Symbolic violence and self-exclusion. In C. Thorpe, *Social theory for social work: Ideas and applications* (pp. 107–23). Abingdon: Routledge.

Broker is identified in **functional role analyses** of social work as a role of social work where practitioners assist clients to negotiate arrangements for appropriate help. It is used in the 'travel agent' form of **case management**, where practitioners work alongside clients in negotiating a package of services from different sources to meet their needs, rather than directly planning and organising the package.

Buddhism is one of the principal world **religions**. It has been influential in forming social work ideas in India and Asia, and is increasingly prominent in social work thinking elsewhere. It emerged as one of the challenges to Indian Vedic ideals in ancient times, and its influence extended throughout south-east Asia. Intersecting with Chinese Daoism ideas, it formed an ideology of Zen **Buddhism** in Japan (Brandon, 1990[1976]). It proposes that sorrow and unhappiness due to selfishness and greed may be overcome by a 'middle way' that seeks interpersonal and social harmony and opposes the uncontrolled satisfaction of human desire, resisting evil, respecting and avoiding injury to others, self-control and maintaining focus through **activity** such as meditation in which one seeks understanding of existence both within oneself and also of humanity in general (partly from Desai, 2002: 109; Sakamoto, 2012). Buddhism also influences **mindfulness** practice.

Bureaucracy is a conceptualisation of **authority** and **power** relations within organisations. It is important in social work because government organisations, where in many countries social work is placed, are often regarded as bureaucracies. Social workers

are often therefore **bureau-professionals** or need to understand and deal with important aspects of bureaucracy and its problematic features, such as inflexibility, obstruction of change and slowness in decision-making and reaction, devaluing its useful characteristics such as stability and clarity.

Weber's (Gerth & Mills, 1948: Ch. 8) influential account sees bureaucracy as a system of jurisdiction in which rules set by law or managerial mandate govern organisations, with responsibilities distributed in a stable way according to levels of graded authority, as duties of officials in the organisation. Authority to give commands and sanctions to require compliance is distributed according to the rank of the officials. Management and responsibility are developed through specialised training and are documented in written (or increasingly by computerised) records, in social work **case records**. **New public management** claims that professional management skills are required in order to combat bureaucratic inflexibilities, by separating professional skills and decision-making from administrative responsibilities in social work agencies. Consequently, leadership is vested in managers rather than social work professions.

One of the answers to bureaucratic inflexibility is bureau-professions, in which professional **discretion** is permitted for decisions within the competence of the profession and this is combined with the systematic features of bureaucratic authority. Sennett (2003: Chs 6–7) argues that critics of bureaucratisation regard a monolithic centralised state as the only model of bureaucratic organisation, devaluing the usefulness of professional discretion and public service. More flexible and localised elements of government permit greater respect for social work clients. One of the objectives of de**institutionalisation** policies was to achieve greater flexibility and **respect** in the **community** basis of a reformed **welfare state**.

Further Reading

Gerth, H. H. & Mills, C. W. (Eds.) (1948). *From Max Weber: Essays in sociology*. London: Routledge and Kegan Paul.

Business has become an issue in social work as **globalisation** and **neoliberal** thinking and **new public management** have led to developments that bring business ideas and language into social care and social work services organisations. Two important aspects of this are the increasing involvement of private sector organisations in providing social care and social work, and the impact of private sector management theory and practice contesting the policy-oriented public administration model of management common in public sector organisations (Harris, 2003).

C

Capacity-building is an objective in **community** or **macro** work, and sometimes in family, group and interpersonal social work, connected to ideas of **self-efficacy** and **resilience**. It seeks to increase or demonstrate the capacity of individuals to achieve their objectives. A community worker builds tasks to enable community members to develop improved or new skills as part of group activities. A criticism of capacity-building is that it devalues existing confidence and skills in a community or individual.

Capital, in accounting and economics, is an accumulation of assets or wealth that can be used for starting a business or organisation. As a metaphor, it refers also to non-financial resources needed to start and support an activity, organisation and social structure. In **Marxist** sociology, the accumulation and use of capital in developing manufacturing is seen as the basis for the Western social class system of capitalist social domination. **Bourdieu** explored capital to conceptualise different kinds of resources, and the power that derives from possessing them, in social relations, in particular **social capital**.

Care and **caring** are theorisations of the nature of social work and its activities, for example describing it as a 'caring profession'. These ideas contest **helping** as a theorisation of social work's nature. An important development from the 1990s is the **feminist** conception of the **ethics of care**.

Care is a universal characteristic of human life and human societies; **humanism** and **humanistic social work** practice see caring for each other as essential to humanity (Payne, 2011). Developing the capacity to care is potentially universally available, building on people's **intersubjective** experience in relationships between parents and children (Hollway, 2006), but caring has been undertaken mainly by women, ethnic minority workers and slaves, servants and working-class people, who are badly paid, poorly educated, inadequately supported. So, it is valued in principle but marginalised in reality (Tronto, 1993: 111–17). Consequently, policy thinking treats the nature and social organisation of care as a residual issue (Lynch, Kalaitzake & Crean, 2020), ignoring professional literature on caring. Analysis of UK public perceptions of care activities suggests that personal and physical help may for most people only be provided by a spouse, a female relative or a paid care worker. Other kinds of help might be provided by men or by neighbours (Parker & Lawton, 1994).

Since the **Enlightenment**, virtuous citizens have had a moral responsibility for caring for others and for important political principles (McBeath & Webb, 1997). Medical and social care are valued as the collective expression of that responsibility. The provision may be seen as **altruistic**, benefiting people personally, without benefiting the carer. Images of care locate it as individualised, private and concerned with personal relationships, for example as mothers caring for children, or health and social care workers caring for disabled, older and sick people.

But health and social care also has general and public benefit, preventing the spread of disease and social stress arising from care needs interfering with the economy and social life. Care is, therefore, both actually and potentially political. A central aspect of these services is intense personal care of the **body**, and nursing the body, bathing the body, injecting medicine into or carrying out surgery on the body (Fine, 2007: 171–98), and in the case of social work, **safeguarding** and **security** of the body and its mental health and social relationships. Touch as part of care and avoiding touch as part of security are therefore important issues.

Care is not only interpersonal, as between a mother and child (Tronto, 1993: 103). People may care for ideas, for populations, for animals and for non-human and non-living aspects of the world, such as the environment (Puig de la Bellacasa, 2017); this is increasingly important for social work **eco** practice. Thus, Fisher and Tronto's (1991: 40) widely cited definition of care is '… a species activity that includes everything that we do to maintain, continue and repair our "world" so that we can live in it as well as possible…'. 'World' here includes our bodies, our selves and our environment, and part of caring is our attempt to weave all these things into a 'complex, life-sustaining web'. Care must therefore inevitably be social as well as concerning the body. Its availability raises issues of **social justice**, since care may be less available to some groups than others because of their patterns of relationships (Barnes, 2012).

At one time, psychological research assumed that young people developed ideas about social concern (including caring) and **justice** by working out conceptions rationally about what social relations are effective and worthwhile. Gilligan's (1993[1982]) famous analysis suggests that this reflects a male **gendered** view of human development. Women's development involves incorporating relationships with others into their conception of their **self**. Thus, women's caring derives from a moral reaction invoking relationships that are important to them. This is, moreover, a cultural and social judgement, since Finch (1989; Finch & Mason, 1993) sees obligations as complex reactions to social obligations and cultural expectations. Gilligan's analysis forms the source of the ethics of care view of caring.

Tronto (1993: 105–8) identifies an integrated process of four phases of caring:

- 'Caring about' is recognising that caring is necessary.
- 'Taking care of' is taking up responsibility for caring and deciding how to respond to the need.

- 'Caregiving' involves the direct work of meeting needs for care. This usually involves contact between carer and the object of care, but increasingly care is provided by technological means. Social work may therefore need to offer interpersonal help so that care through Internet link or television screen is acceptable (Puig de la Bellacasa, 2017).
- 'Care-receiving' involves responses by care-receivers and people around them to caregiving. Such responses affect the extent to which care needs are met and the quality of the caring experience, for example whether caregivers are respected and care-receivers can preserve their dignity.

Care management refers to systems for organising practice, as follows:

- In healthcare and day or residential care, it is a system for coordinating the care provided by different employees, services and specialists. It usually involves appointing a **case manager**, keyworker or 'primary nurse' for each client or patient. In a hospital ward, for example, a primary nurse would be named as the point of contact for a patient, and, when on duty, do most of the physical caring for that patient, preparing a nursing plan and keeping in touch with specialists, tests and treatments. A case manager or keyworker in any setting would be named as the focus for coordination and planning for clients', patients' or residents' care, coordinating action and planning, and liaising with colleagues, external agencies and services. If they are part of the team of care staff in the day or residential setting, they would also lead care and support for that attender or resident.
- Care management is also a UK renaming of American **case management** processes. The NHS and Community Care Act 1990 used it to coordinate the provision of social care services to adults in a 'quasi-market' (see **Marketisation**). It was also sometimes extended to refer to keyworker responsibilities in children's social care. Later, through the **personalisation** policy agenda, care management became an element of **self-directed care**.
- Assertive care management, or assertive community treatment, is a psychiatric practice in which a multiprofessional team of psychiatrists, psychiatric nurses and sometimes psychologists and social workers reach out to people with serious mental illnesses living in the community, not allowing them to avoid or lose contact with services, and therefore improving their social functioning and preventing crises, emergencies and hospitalisation (Marx, Test & Stein, 1973; Dixon, 2000). Evidence suggests that continuing contact and low caseloads are necessary if this is to be effective (Simpson, Miller & Bowers, 2003). Attempts to adapt the UK 'care programme approach' (CPA) to provide such a service for severely mentally ill people, including a '**crisis** plan' did not allocate sufficient resources to achieve this (Marshall, 1996; Farrelly et al., 2014). The CPA was not well integrated into other care management arrangements and did not adequately engage with carers and service users (Carpenter et al., 2004).

Case is a theorisation of how **social work** service to an individual, family or community is formed. It conceives of a social work service as a **process**, a sequence of connected actions with one or more people. Social work takes on the whole of their needs, personal characteristics, relationships and their social situation and it does so for the whole period of an agency's or its practitioners' involvement with the case. Criticisms of the theorisation of case attend to the risk of categorisation and dehumanisation. Instead of putting a person or group of people at the centre of our thinking, we risk seeing them as a category of **problem**, 'a single parent family case', for example, rather than a parent troubled by the pressures of providing for a family's emotional and practical needs alone. This problem may be exacerbated by an agency's administrative need to categorise its work for public accountability and, with official agencies, the need to comply with legislation defining services according to categories of need. Such categorisation also contributes to some of the problems of specialisation.

The source of the theorisation of case in social work comes from its earliest days. The aim of charity organisation societies' practices in the period leading up to the development of social work was to avoid treating each application for financial or other assistance as a separate request for help. All the circumstances that were relevant and all the people involved would be considered together, and help given would be connected up, so that it met the identified needs in a coordinated way. Each applicant for service became part of a case, information was collected about all their circumstances and help was brought together over a period until their needs were met. Information was coordinated into a **case record**.

Working with cases, rather than responding to single applications for help, individuals and specific helping acts, means that social work can build a pattern of helping activity covering multiple areas of a client's life and relationships and do so over a period. Each helping act, each meeting of a need, each individual involved is treated as part of a whole, taking into account the range of relevant factors and people influencing the situation, and building on the interactions of the problems, helping actions and persons and their relationships. Thus, formulating social work as 'case'-based is more **holistic** than dealing with separated episodes of service. More broadly, you can describe different sorts of 'case', and this allows ideas about the service to be generalised and researched as categories of helping actions.

Case management is a formulation of social work practice created in the USA from the 1960s onwards. It systematised a social work role in coordination in the absence of integration of services. Increasingly, although it develops from a social work model of practice, it is used by a range of health and social care professions (Frankel, Gelman & Pastor, 2019). Frankel et al. (2019: 5–6) distinguish case management from 'managed care', the American system for financing coordinated provision. The UK derivative of case management, **care management**, has increasingly used the terms **personalisation** and

self-directed care focused on 'cash for care' or 'direct payments', while the underlying case management processes are still present.

Five successive processes are included in conceptualisations of case management:

- Identifying all potential clients within the service criteria. This aimed to decide priorities from a position of full knowledge of the population. From the point of view of the service provider agencies, it also enabled them to assess the level of service needed.
- **Assessment.**
- Goal setting, service planning and resource identification.
- Implementing the care plan.
- Monitoring and evaluating service delivery.

This model of service reflects the **traditional social work** model of study–diagnosis–treatment and a more modern formulation of it as assessment–intervention–evaluation. Three types of case management were as follows:

- Social care entrepreneurship, where case managers tried to be creative entrepreneurs, interweaving state, private, third sector and informal care services into a coordinated package. This helps retain agency control of assessment and planning, while encouraging creative options, and best describes the approach taken in the UK.
- Brokerage, adapted from Canadian practice (Brandon, 1989), where **brokers** work with clients and families, helping them negotiate among options. This places clients and families in the lead to implement their own vision of a good service and worked well where participants' engagement was crucial to implementing the plan successfully.
- A multidisciplinary team model (Pilling, 1992) where the team takes joint responsibility for assessment and planning, often delegating involvement with clients to keyworkers. This had the advantage of drawing all the agencies into early cooperation with the assessment and plan (Beardshaw & Towell, 1990: 18).

Further Reading

Frankel, A. J., Gelman, S. R. & Pastor, D. K. (2019). *Case management: An introduction to concepts and skills* (4th ed.). New York: Oxford University Press.

The **case record** is a document, now often computerised, that records information about clients and their families and social networks relevant to the case and the actions, assessments, decisions, interventions and reviews of planning and thinking of social workers involved with them. Case recording is integrated in social work **professionalisation** through its use in **accountability**, education and supervision. Although it is sometimes seen as an administrative procedure integral to social work in a **bureaucracy**, the creation of case records is part of early theorisation of social work as based on **cases**. Collecting comprehensive information from disparate sources to give a **holistic** picture of the circumstances of people who applied for relief was essential to the nineteenth-century charity organisation movement. The aim was 'scientific charity' and 'realistic description and systematic record-keeping became the flesh and blood of casework practice in the early twentieth century as these techniques spread to diverse social work and reform organisations' (Tice, 1998: 38). Over the twentieth century, records became a complex process of communication and interpretation of meaning involving a range of potential authors, including carers, clients, managers and practitioners all with conflicting interests (Askeland and Payne, 1999). Records' representations of social work were affected by the intended purposes of the writer, and agency uses for evaluating employees' work. Garfinkel (1967), in a classic ethnomethodological study, for example, found that professional records were often written to demonstrate compliance with agency requirements, rather than to provide accurate information. Opie (1993) showed that records were shaped by organisational and political discourses.

Computerisation of records started in the 1970s and is now universal, and this led to greater structuring of information, but also to greater concern for the system technology and 'informationalisation' of records rather than their use for professional purposes (Harlow & Webb, 2002). This led, however, to a top-down process of design, and a more practitioner-focused process of design is likely to lead to records more suited to practice purposes (Wastell & White, 2014).

Client access to records was made available from the 1980s, and there was talk of open records (Doel & Lawson, 1986; Payne, 1989) and openness about the contents of reports and official documents, but practice did not develop to help clients interpret the content they had access to (Morgenshtern & Yu, 2020). Records have also become important as resources for clients' understanding of their life histories (Humphreys, McCarthy, Dowling, Kertsez & Tropea, 2014; MacNeil, Duff, Dotiwalla & Zuchniak, 2018).

Casework, or social casework, was the major form of **social work** practice and theorisation of the social work process for much of the twentieth century, and remains important in understanding social work practice. The concept emerged from social work practice in the early twentieth century, for example Richmond's (1965[1917]) early text refers throughout to social casework. Her later text (Richmond, 1922) sought to define social casework by examining cases in agencies of the time, and defined social casework holistically as all the work involved in the case.

Bowers' (1949: 417) definition, in a thesis researching definitions of social casework from 1915 to 1947 in the USA, sees the practice as an **art** that uses scientifically derived knowledge:

Social casework is an art in which knowledge of the science of human relation skills in relationships are used to mobilise capacities in the individual and resources in the community appropriate for better adjustment between the client and all or any part of his [sic] total environment.

Change is an important theorisation of the aims of social work and its interventions. Three forms of change are important as social work aims:

- Behaviour change refers to change in the attitudes, behaviour and emotions of individual clients, or occasionally groups or collectives.
- Environmental change refers to a client's social environment, to the physical places and social networks relevant to individuals, groups or communities that the social work is intervening with. An example is **ecological systems theory** or the **life model** of practice. During the twenty-first century, however, growing concern about the ecological sustainability of the physical environment has led to **eco** practice concerned with helping people live sustainably and respond to ecological **disasters**.
- **Social change** refers to changes in social organisation and structures, carried out through **macro** practice or community work, or through social **activism**.

The traditional view is that targets, processes and outcomes of change processes are definable. **Postmodern** thinking contests this by proposing that society and its relations are characterised by **ambiguity**, that social relations shift and diversify. While social work, therefore, may be a part of such processes, it is doubtful that we can specify an intervention sufficiently well to claim change. In this conception of social work, we participate in **discourses**, **processes** and **relationships** aiming to shift their direction and power in people's lives in ways that help them achieve their interpersonal and personal choices within the social movements that we all participate in. **Chaos theory** also contests the traditional view of social work change.

Chaos theory is a kind of systems theory, using some ideas transferred from physical science, devised by René Thom, the originator of 'catastrophe theory' and others (Hudson, 2010: 29–30). Complex events may be understood using simple mathematical equations. This tells us that what seems to be chaotic arises from small-scale changes, often repeated. Although changes happen on a consistent basis, every time they are repeated, the outcomes change, and so the next cycle of events varies again. An example is the weather: in some countries it is constantly changing, but there are consistent patterns. Weather forecasting has got better, in part by using chaos theory to look for consistencies in the changes. The message for the social worker is 'look for patterns and the factors that create them'.

In social work, chaos theory deals with social systems, such as families or friendship groups, that seem at first sight to be hard to understand but are:

- Complex, so there are several elements that interact.
- Dynamic, so the elements and the parts that they play in the system are constantly changing.
- Nonlinear, so there are several different factors that may explain changes, but no one sequence of changes occurs, and different elements are involved so it is hard to see why changes and sequences happen.

C

'Chaotic' systems are, therefore, between the two extremes of being totally random and being always patterned. Patterns may be apparent, but they never repeat themselves exactly. Systems theory tells us that patterns are created by feedback. Negative feedback loops are control mechanisms, like a thermostat or a trip switch in an electrical fuse box. A family example is when people in the home see the signs of a violent father getting angry, they all react in their various typical ways to avoid upsetting him further. Each event that causes the anger is different, it may happen at different times and people may not always be aware or see the signs, but if you were present for a period and observant, you would be able to see the pattern. Positive feedback loops are events that amplify themselves. Another family example: if a teenage boy is unselfconfident and becomes easily depressed, family members often take the trouble to compliment him on things that he does successfully, and this helps to keep him away from low mood. As a result, he will do the successful things more often, and they will work at building him up. But external events, perhaps at school, can have too much of an impact, and even quite a lot of effort does not counteract his low mood. And family members may not always be consistent, and miss opportunities to help him, so the pattern of reactions varies.

Chaos theory tells us that, as in this example, events move in constantly varying cycles, and how the cycle goes each time depends on its starting point, the event that sets it off cycling. It also tells us that the cycle will go off on its sequence, and over time a succession of sequences will fall into a fairly stable pattern. This is an 'attractor': as a sequence starts up that people recognise, they are pulled in by their perceptions of what's going on in the network, to perform their role, cooling down the father or psyching up the teenager. But there will come a point, a chaos threshold, at which there is too much anger or low mood and the usual cycle does not complete itself. This may lead to 'bifurcation' of the system, in which, following these examples, the violent father goes out drinking with his friends and does not contribute to the family, and the teenager focuses on his computer screen and cuts off from the family. This can have effects on other people, and their families.

At present, chaos theory is not applied to social work in any comprehensive theory of practice, but social workers often use its ideas to help when in confusing situations. For example, you can have a strong impact with an intervention at a threshold point rather than at another time. Also, restoring broken-down cycles re-establishes them as a **supportive** mechanism. Chaos theory may also help with **assessment**, by identifying events from outside the system that have stopped a cycle working, to change the course of a disruption or to encourage input that will disrupt a cycle that is having unfortunate effects.

In this way, chaos theory clarifies some of the aspects of general systems theory that have been problematic: it is hard to decide where in a system to intervene. These ideas also help with **cognitive behavioural therapy** or **solution** approaches, by identifying reinforcing factors or possible targets of change.

Further Reading

Hudson, C. G. (2010). *Complex systems and human behavior.* Chicago, IL: Lyceum.

Children are an important client group in social work, and how **childhood** is theorised is, therefore, an important issue. Ariès (1996[1962]) suggests that before the Enlightenment there was little separate conception in Western culture of childhood as a separate social identity. In the eighteenth century, debate about education, particularly Rousseau's treatise and reaction to it, led to a reconception of childhood and a reconsideration of adult responsibilities towards children. Themes in debate about childhood include the following (partly from Heywood, 2001; Gabriel, 2017):

- 'Depravity', from the Augustinian tradition in Christianity that human beings were born into 'original sin', with children needing to be led towards purity: this conception contests 'innocence', the assumption that children had not yet been perverted by the evils of the world, in particular by sexuality. There are, consequently, different views of the purpose of education and child development, and either view is sometimes hidden behind attitudes to children.
- 'Nature', including accepting and educating children to take the class and social position of their birth, and 'nurture', that adults have responsibility for development and education. Among the issues here is that children move through stages of neurological and physical development and this limits educational, psychological and social development.
- 'Dependence' and 'independence' are ideas that children depend on their parents, needing help to progress towards independence, and in the meantime require a special degree of **safeguarding**. Some cultures, unlike Western ideas, lean more towards continuing interdependence within a community, family or tribe. Since **dependence** has become accepted, there is a stronger emphasis on the social importance of child development, particularly in early life.
- Age groups, the Western assumption that human development is a series of **stages** rather than a trajectory of development followed in later life with decline, or that life has phases of forwards and backwards movement.
- Parent–child relationships, considering the role of parents in the life of their children, and how the positions of mothers and fathers may vary. Some cultures emphasise the father's authority in family life, and there is discourse about the

caring role of mothers and managing the relationship of family and parenting and work roles.

- Marxist commentary on **social reproduction** sees the role of the family in reproducing social class and inequalities during childhood.
- The role of governments in supporting education and health through interventions in the labour market and provision of services. There has been a discourse about 'investment', as well as concern about 'management' of child behaviour and difficulties, including a discourse of governmentality and **surveillance**, and childhood and parenting.
- The development of conceptions of children's **rights**, both in general human rights discourses and in particular rights to personal development, participation in decisions about their lives and self-expression.

Social work is engaged in many of these discourses and is part of the relations between the state, in advocacy, management, safeguarding and supporting children in many different contexts.

Further Reading

Gabriel, N. (2017). *The sociology of early childhood: Critical perspectives.* London: Sage.

Christianity

Christianity is one of the major world **religions** and an important source of social work theorisation. Christian organisations are important providers of social care and social work services both to adherents and to the community in general. An important theoretical issue is a tension between **critical** practice and Christianity, because of the institutional power of Christian churches allied to capital and conservative politics in many Western countries. Alongside this, there is a critique that critical, **Marxist** and **radical** social work ignores **spirituality** as an issue (Warkentin & Sawatsky, 2018).

Citizen advocacy See Advocacy.

Citizenship

Citizenship is a status and **identity** denoting an individual's connection with a country and also a **process** by which people attain **affiliations** with a country. It provides a structure of social order, connecting a population with the right to control a territory and with the economic, political and social life that creates **power** relations within that territory. In citizenship processes, people may be **subjects**, acting to become citizens or to withdraw from citizenship, or **objects**, in that citizenship is given to or taken from them (Lister, 1998). This may be done intentionally, by naturalising a migrant as a citizen, or removing citizenship when deporting an offender to another country. Losing 'social citizenship' comes about by social exclusion or marginalisation, for example by injustices in treatment by the policy or criminal justice system, or inequalities leading to poverty, or inability to participate in democracy or social life. For example, failing to tackle income insecurity for older people migrating to Canada prevented them from settling and building satisfactory social lives (Alternative Planning Group, 2008).

Social work citizenship practice theorises ways of using people's **rights** to **participate** in social structures and relations to strengthen individual, group and community capacities (Beresford & Croft, 1993), and **resilience** and has been important in work with young people, especially when leaving care, migrants and older people.

Three areas of citizenship are as follows:

- Civil rights to legal protection of their freedom and equality.
- Political rights to vote, stand for election and participate in political processes.
- Social rights to welfare and participation in social relations with others (Marshall & Bottomore, 1992[1949]).

Social work theorisation of citizenship practice focuses on rights associated with social citizenship. The critique is that this sectional interest fails to place it in the context of legal and political rights as the prerequisite for social rights. Van Ewijk (2009), however, argues that contemporary changes in the state require 'active citizenship'. Social work should explore clients' rights and responsibilities, include self-responsibility, considering how far human and social rights are met by states that increasingly impose conditionality on social welfare provision and social responsibility for family, neighbours and the community. Practice should develop social education of young people in **family** and **community** structures, respond where **social care** and individual **help** are required, and provide support within attractive, safe and secure communities. Smith (2005), concerned with contemporary crises of ecological sustainability, argues for a 'green citizenship' which goes beyond ecologically sound lifestyles, towards using **social development** structures connected to social provision in the **welfare state**.

Citizenship practice with the emphasis on social rights has been pursued in working with older people. Marshall and Tibbs (2006) emphasised social rights to participate in and contribute to society using creativity, lifetime experience and strengths. This analysis contests a purely biopsychosocial approach as inadequate.

My own accounts of citizenship practice with older people (Payne, 2012, 2017) argue that citizenship practice requires integration of older people within their family and community, integration of social care services with other provision for older people and, to combat **ageism**, integration of older people in age-friendly communities, mainstreaming older people as part of wider lifestyles. Services should work at 'citizening' for older people, ensuring their participation and social rights, and avoid 'de-citizening' by taking away participation and rights. 'Re-citizening' is needed where de-citizening has removed opportunities and social rights.

Codes of ethics are documents that offer comprehensive statements of **ethics**, moral principles that regulate an activity or profession. They are usually created by professional bodies, reflecting established professional opinion at the time of publication about appropriate action, behaviour and self-management in carrying out professional duties. They thus form concise and concrete conceptualisations of social work **values**.

The 'global statement of ethical principles' (International Federation of Social Workers, 2014b), guiding the contents of national professional codes, indicates relevant social work issues. These are: confidentiality, **dignity**, **human rights**, privacy, professional integrity, **self-determination**, **rights to participation**, **social justice**, treating people as whole persons (**holism**), and use of information in technology and social media.

In a trait view of **professionalisation**, which seeks to establish markers by which we may judge whether an occupational group is a profession, the enforcement of a code of ethics is sometimes seen as a characteristic of a profession. It became an important objective for national organisations of social workers as part of the professionalisation 'project' within social work in the mid- to late twentieth century.

Like definitions of social work, codes of ethics may provide an authoritative source for social workers to claim justification for their actions in cases of dispute with employers or public controversy, promote education and debate on ethical practice, and provide guidance on ethical practice for practitioners and clients (Watson, 1985).

Criticism of the use of codes of ethics includes the following:

- Social work's ethical principles may conflict with social workers' responsibilities where they are managers of services, or where they have responsibilities for law enforcement, for example taking **children** into public care, or participating in the compulsory admission to hospital of **mentally ill** people.
- Codes of ethics used for professional **accountability** according to general ethical standards, may conflict with codes of practice from employers or regulators concerned with wider public accountability.
- Codes express principles and values and are often not detailed enough to be used as guidance in practice and management situations.
- There are, moreover, questions about whether **principle-based ethics** are appropriate or useful accounts of professional values, so codes consisting of principles may not be a useful element of practice.
- Because codes of ethics are considered an important marker of professional status, they may be created merely for this purpose and not actively used by practitioners to improve their thinking or practice.
- Codes may only be useful for training or socialisation of practitioners into social work early in their career, rather than being used to inform practice as ethical issues arise.

Cognitive behavioural therapy (CBT) is a practice theory

drawn from clinical psychology practice and psychological research. The knowledge base includes research and theoretical analysis on learning theory, social learning theory, cognitive theory, behavioural psychology and cognitive behavioural theory. Most writing now treats CBT as a unified theoretical perspective and practice method (Scott, 1989; Cigno & Bourn, 1998; Corcoran, 2006; Ronen & Freeman, 2007; Sheldon, 2011). It is, moreover, a multiprofessional practice, dominated by clinical psychology practitioners and a research base in psychology. In contemporary social work, CBT is primarily practised in intellectual disability and mental health clinical settings, in which social workers play some part, and training and professional supervision in CBT for clients' needs in that setting helps them to adopt it as a model of practice.

Critiques of CBT fall into six main points:

- It is **individualistic** in its research and theoretical base, and neglects **the social** in general and **social change** social work objectives in particular.
- The practice focus on behaviour **change** may lead to 'blaming the victim' and adapting behaviour to social norms rather than looking for change in a client's social environment. Maintenance of the status quo rather than behaviour change may be more appropriate for some clients, for example people experiencing intellectual or physical disabilities or ageing.
- Behaviour change may not be what a client needs or wishes, not fit the agency's mandate.
- CBT is a **technical rational** intervention, applying standardised techniques, rather than creative interaction in relationships, even though a **relationship** is valued for carrying out assessments and for working with the client.
- **Ethical** concerns question the element of manipulation of people's behaviour and thinking, to which they cannot give full informed consent. While clients may consent to a programme of treatment for having a problem behaviour removed (this is essential for the techniques to work), they will not be aware of and therefore able to consent fully to all the implications for them and their social relations of the proposed actions and changes in their behaviour or thinking processes entailed.
- Its research base is limited to Western cultures and is weak on specific needs of Black, Asian and minority ethnic groups (Gonzalez-Prendes & Cassady, 2019). This may mean that it is not applicable, or has not been adapted to, the needs of minority groups and it does not pick up or may be inimical to Indigenous philosophies.

As an amalgamation of sometimes conflicting cognitive and learning ideas, the contemporary form of CBT used is strongly cognitive, so a lot of the focus is on how thinking, cognition, intervenes between events that provide the stimuli for actions. Practitioners bear in mind the mantra: antecedents (the things that happen that stimulate a reaction) > behaviour (the reaction) > consequences. Behaviour modification changes the antecedents, so the behaviour and social consequences change. Cognitive practice inserts thinking and perception processes into the antecedents; changing these processes again alters the behaviour and its consequences. In addition to anxiety and depression, CBT has been shown to be effective with eating and sleep disorders, various kinds of **trauma** in life, and substance misuse and addiction.

Colonialism

Colonialism occurs when one country gains administrative and political control over another area or country, holding it using military power, to facilitate economic exploitation, often including settlement by citizens of the colonising country. Colonial societies assume the coloniser's superiority in culture, economic, administrative and government systems over the traditional social structures and relations of the colonised territory. Colonialism was characteristic of **globalisation** in the eighteenth and nineteenth centuries, carried out by European countries to secure human and natural resources from territories in other continents. It included a substantial involvement in **slavery**. Provision of social welfare services in colonies was minimal, and often reflected the colonial power's approach to social provision and social work practice. Domination by Soviet Russia over territories in Eastern Europe and Asia, Japan during the twentieth century in Asia and the Pacific, the USA over the Pacific area and South America, and the Han Chinese over minority ethnic groups within China might also be regarded in many respects as colonialism.

Post-colonialism describes the continuation of domination by cultural and economic processes after the withdrawal of administrative and military control. This is accompanied by attitudes of cultural superiority over former colonies in former colonial powers. **Decolonisation** may be achieved by removing vestiges of colonial culture and power within former colonies and changing colonial attitudes in former colonial powers towards cultural and social structures, and also by reducing and eventually removing the social consequences of slavery in both former colonies and former colonial powers. This may also lead to the recognition of **Indigenous** cultures and traditions in territories where colonial settlement took place (Tamburro, 2013).

Commodification

Commodification is the degree to which individuals depend on an economic market to satisfy their needs. The concept became important because of Esping-Anderson's (1990) studies of different kinds of **welfare state**. One of his measures of different types of welfare states is the extent to which states encourage or permit commodification. A highly commodified society would rely on markets to provide social welfare and social work services.

The critique of commodifying social welfare is that most users of such services are in poverty and cannot pay a market rate for the costs of services that they need. Commodified welfare states, therefore, are part of **neoliberal** economic policy, establishing **quasi-markets** to provide some degree of public choice between **marketised** services. This means that what was previously a coordinated, unified public service becomes wastefully fragmented.

Commonalities is a feminist practice concept, claiming that all women share

life experience of the oppressed position of women in patriarchal societies, particularly of oppressive behaviour by men and discrimination by male-dominated organisations and social structures. Focusing on commonalities assists social workers in **empathising** with and understanding women clients and groups, particularly oppressions. Also, **groupwork** involving women and **community work** with women's groups are facilitated by that shared life experience. The critique of the idea of commonalities being useful is that it refers mainly to middle-class women with a feminist commitment. Women with this background have less shared experience, for example with black and working-class women in poverty, where oppressions are often of both men and women and are concerned with lack of resources.

Community is a broad social concept referring to the experience of connected-

ness among groups or populations of people. A community can refer to people connected to each other in various ways, and underlies a variety of practices concerned with stimulating collective provision. A community may be connected in various ways:

- By interaction, for example in a care home.
- By shared interests, for example people recovering from mental illness.
- By shared identification with a locality or place, such as a neighbourhood (Willmott with Thomas, 1984).

Community development is a theorisation of an aspect of com-

munity work that concentrates on starting, improving and expanding organisations in a locality or concerned with a particular social interest. The aim is to strengthen **resilience** with a sturdier social infrastructure and make greater **support** available to people facing particular difficulties. From the 1940s, community development was used by **colonial** powers, particularly France and the UK, as a strategy for improving social welfare provision in Asian and African colonies. Experience of this practice influenced approaches to community work in the UK, emphasising citizens' **participation** in developing local organisations, contesting **social action** approaches to community work derived from civil rights community practice from the USA. Community development continues as **social development**, the main form of social intervention in many African and Asian countries.

Community social work (CSW) involves locating a general social

work service in neighbourhoods within a local government area, including domiciliary social care and local links to other social care provision. The aim is for social workers, even if they are outsiders, to develop fuller involvement in and understanding of the culture and interests of the local **community**. Also, social workers build networks among local organisations that can provide information about individuals and resources in the community that could support social care and social work provision. CSW emerged within the UK's newly developing local government social services departments (SSDs; social work departments, SWDs, with different responsibilities in Scotland are similar). These agencies brought together a range of social work practice and social care provision for the first time in the 1970s. One of the characteristics of this organisational development was to create 'area teams' of social work practitioners and other staff located in the geographical areas that they served, and CSW was a way of structuring and theorising their work, including the new element of domiciliary care which had been transferred from local government health departments.

Reports began to emerge of different modes of practice and structures (Hadley & McGrath, 1980). A professional interest group associated with Roger Hadley coordinated this, stimulating evaluation research (Hadley & McGrath, 1984). The main focus was to develop social work practice at a neighbourhood level, which would encourage a reduction in state bureaucracy and local responsiveness in service provision (Hadley & Hatch, 1981).

When the government supported a committee of inquiry into the roles and tasks of social workers (Barclay Report, 1982), it included Hadley among its members and recommended adoption of CSW, although there was a strong dissenting voice in a minority report by Robert Pinker, who saw it as a distraction from the main care responsibilities of SSDs. A number of SSDs adopted CSW as the main mode of organising area teams, with some positive outcomes (Hadley & Young, 1990). An independent consumer-oriented study, however, found that CSW did not engage with service users effectively (Beresford & Croft, 1986). The model died out as SSDs were reorganised in the 1990s according to client-group specialisations, perhaps vindicating Pinker's views.

Community work is one of the classic forms (or modalities) of social work, alongside **casework** and **groupwork**. Practitioners focus on **networks** and organisations in their locality to build and sustain a good social infrastructure, both in general and also to provide resources to assist people in difficulty. While attentiveness to organisations rather than individuals or groups is the defining characteristic of community work, it can seem concerned with structures rather than the personal and is among the reasons **structural** practice adopts it as a **social change** aspect of social work. The interest in 'community' within social work refers, however, to communities of people, rather than primarily to the structures, since the focus of community work is engaging people in the organisations that form the infrastructure of relations within their locality and using community resources to assist clients.

Professional contributions in early analyses include organisational and policy analysis and development, community problem-solving by helping community members and organisations identify problems and work towards solutions, being a change agent on behalf of government or the community itself, and managing social conflict (Kramer & Specht, 1969, 1975, 1983).

Popple (2015) analyses contemporary community work models, as follows:

- Community care, building self-help, social networks and voluntary services for groups served by social workers.
- Community organisation, coordinating welfare services.
- Community development, helping groups build confidence and skills in serving their locality or special interest groups.
- Community education, promoting local and special interest education initiatives, with an emphasis on equality and participation.
- Community action, class-based, conflict-focused direct action.
- Community economic development, promoting local business initiatives and **social entrepreneurship**.
- Feminist community work, focusing on women's health and wellbeing.
- Ethnic minority and anti-racist community work, developing and supporting groups pursuing the interests of minority ethnic groups.
- Environmentalism, enabling groups that support eco and green issues.

Further Reading

Popple, K. (2015). *Analysing community work: Theory and practice* (2nd ed.). Maidenhead: Open University Press.

Complex adaptive systems is a form of systems theory, which

focuses on how systems (which can include individual human beings or social groups and social institutions) continually change to adapt to the pressures on them. These ideas are a primary focus of contemporary systems theory in management and the natural sciences, but this is not yet strongly developed in social work.

Consciousness-raising (the feminist term) and conscientisation

(the **radical** term, derived from Freire, 1972) is a collective process in which practitioners facilitate dialogue or groupwork with people who share similar experiences or concerns. Building on this, there is collective identification of the consequences of how power and privilege have created oppression. The process of exploration and sharing of experience allows people to see that their experience is not **individualised** and has been **privatised**: the oppression is not of the individual, and the troubles it causes are not their private affair. The consciousness gained through exploration of experience allows people to gain the capacity to be critical of the processes by which they are oppressed. Because the experience is shared, moreover, the effects are a matter of public concern, for policy and political action to be planned and taken. This permits a **praxis** to be developed in which action directly derived from the experience and the shared dialogue are both individually and jointly taken forward.

C

Contracts are formal agreements in law, but the word is used more widely to refer to formalised reciprocal agreements between individuals and organisations. In law, an important element of the **reciprocity** is that when one contractor provides goods or services, the other responds with 'consideration', a money payment or other contribution. In charity and social provision by the state, this element of consideration is often absent. In social work, contracts are sometimes used to formalise agreements between clients and social workers that seek to clarify aims, objectives and actions of practice.

Task-centred practice was an important site of debate about using contracting in this way. More recently, the use of contracts with clients is part of 'contractualism' (Solvang & Juritzen, 2020). This is a form of conditionality extended from social security and social welfare policy more widely into social work. It provides for social work services to be offered conditional upon clients' compliance with requirements set by the agency. Such a policy raises the same ethical issues as contracts that are part of practice theories, that clients are dependent on services and not free to exit from the agreement without sanctions. They may feel in some measure forced to comply, in order to receive services, or to avoid authoritative actions, such as removal of children. Analysis using **Foucault**'s concept of governmentality suggests that this is a form of covert policing of behaviour and social relations and is inimical to the **empowerment** objectives of social work practice.

Constructionism and **constructivism** are ideas from social psychology and sociology that had an important impact on social work during the 1990s and early twenty-first century as part of the influence at that time of **postmodern** thought. Four different theoretical concepts are relevant:

- Personal construct theory is George Kelly's (1955) psychological theory, which proposes that individuals manage their behaviour not according to concrete evidence that anyone could perceive, but by 'constructs' or pictures in their mind of people and events that they are part of.
- Constructivism analyses how views of the world reflect perceptions being processed in different ways and research explores how patterns of perception and thinking about reality affect people's behaviour. Increasingly, connections are made with **neuroscience** (Franklin, 1998).

- Social construction theory in sociology (Berger & Luckman, 1971[1966]) underlies constructionist theory in social work. This analyses how knowledge is legitimated and maintained by social structures within societies through patterns of social relationships. Whereas Kelly's personal construct theory sees individuals as creating their own mental constructions of the world, Berger and Luckman see social constructions as **intersubjective**, created as collective constructions agreed among people through social processes.

- Social construction theory in social psychology is represented by Gergen's (1994, 1999; Gergen & Gergen, 2003) analysis. Gergen (1994) starts from **epistemology** in social psychology. Knowledge is not valid in itself, but depends on the social processes that create and use it in any historical and social context. To understand these processes, we must examine how language operates within cultural patterns of various social groups in social life. It is not that there is no reality, it is that there are realities that depend on how social groups examine and process the evidence of what lies outside ourselves. Describing a social situation, for example, is **performative** because it does not just say what we have seen and experienced, it is pushing someone to accept or at least understand how we have experienced it.

To Gergen, taking a social construction position in a social interaction, language use shifts from communicating to persuading the listener of what we say. These views of social relationships are helpful to social workers because they suggest how in relationships we can work in a cooperative, participative way to achieve personal and social change, rather than, as in **cognitive behaviour therapy**, trying to overcome and replace a behaviour or, as in psychodynamic **relational** or **systems** practice, redirect problematic towards acceptable **adaptive** behaviour. Many therapeutic interactions aim to change social constructions in individuals, relationships, groups and communities (McNamee & Gergen, 1992).

Construction ideas in social psychology research these social processes, for example by understanding communication patterns through researching speech and social practices (Hall, Juhila, Matarese & van Nijnatten, 2014). In another example, Hall, Juhila, Parton and Pösö (2003) describe studies looking at how interactions generate perceptions of carers not coping, clients as 'bad' rather than encountering difficulties, or couples as being successful in parenting.

- Social construction of social **problems** refers to the process by which problems come to be defined as a result of social processes when interest groups assert grievances and make claims about a social condition, seeking to have it regarded as problematic by government or other authorities (Spector & Kitsuse, 2017[1977]). Understanding the processes helps to explain how this occurs. Four stages are:

  o Defining the problem and representing it as problematic.
  o Achieving official recognition of the problem.

- o Showing how present procedures for dealing with the problem are unsatisfactory.
- o Establishing new procedures as improvements.

How competing interests interact, the availability of resources and the legitimacy of the groups involved are factors in the problem-claiming process. There are also social processes around maintaining the issue as problematic. An application of these ideas is **moral panics**, which explore how issues are selected and become inflated by cultural and media processes into serious social problems.

Further Reading

Franklin, C. & Nurius, P. S. (Eds.) (1998). *Constructivism in practice*. Milwaukee, WI: Families International.

Context is the idea that physical and social settings interact with behaviour and social relations that occur within them. Social work always deals with the interaction of the personal and the **social**, in concepts such as the **person-in-situation**, or -in-environment. Contextual understanding of the historical time and place where actions and events take place is therefore required in all social work assessment, evaluation and intervention.

Coping is a continuing effort to manage demands that you feel are exceeding your capacity, particularly when there may be a potentially harmful outcome. Harm in this case might include behaviours, such as alcohol or drug misuse; thinking processes, such as panicky rather than thoughtful reactions; emotional reactions, such as anger or fear; and physiological responses (Gutiérrez, 1994). An essential feature of coping is that you feel for quite a time the pressure of only just being able to do the things that you have to do. Some people feel it is demeaning to be 'only' just coping, as opposed to managing well. In response, social workers may **affirm** the efforts made, results achieved and **strengths** revealed. It may also help to emphasise that perfection in dealing with every life event is not possible, and people do not expect it of you; coping is enough.

Research into coping finds that helpful internal resources include feeling that you have choices, feeling in control, finding **meaning** in the experience, being accurate in how you appraise situations and being able to use your problem-solving skills. Helpful external factors include having good social **networks** of **support**, getting involved in communal efforts to cope, having contact with others in a similar position, being able to express feelings such as anger or anxiety safely and having access to financial or other material resources (Gutiérrez, 1994: 207).

Crisis practice, because of its focus on a disturbance in social functioning or thinking, emphasises assessment and identification of – and intervention to improve – 'coping mechanisms' and 'coping skills'. This involves identifying precisely how people managed difficulties prior to the crisis, how this was affected by the crisis and what new mechanisms and skills they could use. **Solution** practice questions on coping propose identifying interim strategies to manage events as people move towards a more sustainable solution: 'What keeps you going?', 'What helps you manage?'

Criticism of using the idea of coping in social work suggests that it leads to too strong a focus on internal resources, and Gutiérrez (1994) suggests that an **empowerment** response focuses on building social capabilities and social **capital**.

Co-production refers to packages of **social care** services devised, planned and implemented by clients, their families, and supporters and practitioners working together, and by extension managing and planning service provision or social work education with involvement or leadership by clients. The idea conceptualises a stronger sense of client control, equality and, to go further, leadership forming a contemporary approach to client **participation** in social work; it connects to the traditional ethical value of **self-determination**, with the more contemporary term **self-direction** now often preferred.

The **core conditions** of relationships in **counselling** or **helping** are part of Carl Rogers' conception of **person-centred practice** (Thorne, 1992). They are that clients should perceive that the practitioner behaves as follows:

- They treat clients and the people around them with unconditional positive regard; that is, they regard them as people of worth who they can work successfully with, and maintain that view of them whatever the attitude, behaviour and emotions of the client.
- They behave with authenticity, congruence and genuineness: they are and behave consistently in accordance with their beliefs and their self.
- They display **empathy** with the clients' experience and troubles.

Counselling is a practice using psychological techniques to facilitate people's decision-making, insight into and understanding of concerns in their lives and personal planning to overcome them. In many countries it is now an intervention and profession separate from social work, but in the mid-twentieth century, and still in many countries, social workers provide counselling services and contribute counselling skills to helping services. Counselling differs from social work in its concentration on helping a focal client **non-directively** to manage issues of psychological concern to them, and is often

clinic- or office-based. In contrast, social work incorporates **the social**, takes **action** and works with **agencies, community** and **family** members involved, often makes practical arrangements, and organises and provides social care services and visits to observe and intervene in home, school, work and other community settings affecting the client.

c

Counselling in social work can be theorised as implementing a psychotherapeutic element which has been present in social work thinking at least since the adoption of **psychodynamic** ideas from the 1930s and dominant in many formulations and reviews of social work theory (Payne, 2021[1990]). Alternatively, counselling can be seen as a set of skills that are implemented within social work or social care service responsibilities, for example in changing behaviour in children or parents, or enabling people to manage mental illnesses (Riggall, 2012).

An important account of counselling in relation to social work is Paul **Halmos'** (1965) study of social change. He claims that the influence of medicine and religion reduced, in favour of professions responding to an increased social concern to achieve psychological and social self-actualisation.

Further Reading

Riggall, S. (2012). *Using counselling skills in social work.* London: Sage.

Crisis is relevant in two aspects of social work, as follows:

- In **critical** and **Marxist** theory, it refers to social disruption that arises from contradictions in the social structure caused by class inequalities. Examples might include the 'fiscal crisis of the **welfare state**' when tax receipts are considered no longer capable of sustaining social provision due to the demands for capitalising economic production.
- In **crisis intervention** theory, it is the state of disequilibrium and stress that arises when disruptions in people's **coping** abilities prevent them from managing events in their lives.

Crisis intervention (CI) is a practice theory used particularly in mental health services, and in crisis, **disaster** and emergency services, such as rape crisis work. It was developed as a model of preventive mental health intervention, and its most common usage is to prevent admission to psychiatric treatment in mental health emergencies, helping to keep people in their community setting. Although the theory provides a terminology and model to analyse and manage many disruptions in people's lives, this is a less common use of the theory. Although it has this specialised source, CI can also help practitioners respond to continuing clients, for example troubled families with children

in care, when there is a difficult phase in their lives. Comparing it with task-centred practice, CI focuses more on stabilising a distressed reaction when trouble strikes, whereas task-centred practice focuses more on rational planning and activity.

Five models of CI (James & Gilliland, 2017: 19–20) are as follows:

- The **equilibrium model** sees crisis as causing psychological disequilibrium in people. The aim is to return them to a **steady state** in which they can cope with issues in their life.
- The **cognitive model** (Roberts, 2005) sees people as thinking in a faulty way about events around the crisis.
- The **psychosocial transition model** uses Erikson's (1965) **stage** theory that people experience as a crisis the psychological and social changes as they move from one stage of life to the next.
- The developmental–ecological model also uses Erikson's (1965) developmental stages and connects them with **ecological systems** theory. Assessment and intervention focus on the social environment in which people are facing a change in their life situation.
- The contextual–ecological model similarly uses ecological systems theory to emphasise the context in which people struggle with crises. Practitioners work with clients to examine layers of meaning that emerge from the events that caused the crisis. Particular focuses are the closeness or distance of relationships affected, the timing of events and special occasions such as anniversaries.

CI's account of how crises occur is the most distinctive element of the theory. In Caplan's (1965; Parad, 1965) original formulation, a crisis arises at the end of a process in which a 'hazardous event' causes difficulties for a client in managing events in their lives using their usual **coping** skills, raising the level of tension in their life. Thus, crises do not occur unless circumstances put clients in a position to be at risk of their occurring. A later 'precipitating event' leads to a sharp increase in tension and disorganisation in managing life, and eventually immobilises clients from acting to deal with events. This is the state of active **crisis**, in which there may be considerable distress and casting around for solutions. Active crisis lasts for a few weeks until a way is found to take on active life again. During this period of both danger and opportunity, clients are open to help to achieve improved social functioning, but may only resume coping at their former level of functioning. Alternatively, the aftermath of active crisis may mean that their capacity to function decreases.

The approach draws on **ego-oriented** practice based on psychodynamic theory. This set of ideas focuses on how people manage external realities in their lives, and on the psychological consequences of those attempts to management. Its **psychodynamic** origins are evident in the focus on emotions. A distinctive early part of intervention is about enabling clients to express emotional reactions.

Roberts' (Yeager & Roberts, 2015: 21) seven-stage CI model is a well-established formulation of the process of intervention. It starts with assessing the crisis, and especially exploring 'lethality', the risk of suicide. Then practitioners work rapidly to establish a relationship, identify the major problems and crisis precipitants, moving on to listen actively to and validate feelings expressed. The next phases are about resolving the issues that led to the crisis, generating and exploring alternative options for action, creating an action plan, moving to resolve the crisis and then establishing a follow-up plan. A critique of this model, and Roberts' cognitive view of crisis, is that, like many psychological and mental health-oriented models of interpersonal practice, it focuses too much on helping the individual, rather than looking to resources in the family and community supports. Although **emotions** are a distinctive element of CI, the assumption is that expressing these in the early stages resolves them, and it moves rapidly on to an emphasis on rational planning and cognition.

An important development of CI was research on **support networks**. It became obvious that people's coping capacity in recovering from crises was enhanced by support from friends, neighbours and relatives.

Further Reading

James, R. K. & Gilliland, B. E. (2017). *Crisis intervention strategies* (8th ed.). Boston, MA: Cengage.

Critical incident analysis is an approach to critical reflection,

reflexivity or supervision, originally a technique created in teacher education by Tripp (2012[1993]). It involves identifying a specific incident in a practitioner's work and analysing it for learning purposes. The aim is to avoid getting stuck in repetitive analyses of similar events, what Tripp (1994: 69) calls 'lock-step' thinking. The **process** is to record a specific event, typical in your biography, so exposing it for detailed analysis, in particular focusing on the **values** expressed in your actions. You select events that, in your perception, went well or badly, where you lacked confidence or enjoyed the work, where you felt under pressure, had difficulties in your relationship with the client, felt lacking in knowledge or unsupported (Davies & Kinloch, 2000: 140). Part of the process is verifying the accuracy of your account and looking for alternative ways of thinking about it, thus disrupting and reshaping your conventional thinking.

Critical practice theory is the over-arching contemporary approach

to practice that aims to achieve or give priority to **social change**. It applies critiques of capitalist and (currently) **neoliberal** economic and political thinking to the position of people in social groups experiencing **oppression** and **poverty**. Advocates of critical practice distinguish it from other aspects of criticality, such as **critical thinking** and **critical reflection**. It incorporates them, but they are insufficient.

The original source of critical practice in social work is **Marxist** and **radical** practice theory, whose critical politics focus on class-based social oppression as the source of other oppressions. An important strand is **structural** social work practice, and concerns about **inequalities** and **social injustice** baked into many important social **structures** affecting the education, health and social assistance for people in poverty. Structures might include issues such as attitudes to parenting or offending, or gendered discourses in childcare issues (Robb, Montgomery & Thomson, 2019). Critical analysis of social work in childcare and child protection services, for example, starts from listening to the voice and experience of the child to guide its direction. This is particularly so where the child is from an **Indigenous** background (Esquao & Strega, 2015) or otherwise of devalued identity.

Critical social work practice more broadly has shifted from being informed only by class-based critiques towards identity politics and issues-based social movements. While not rejecting class-based analysis, this critical practice uses **postmodern** critiques to contest the **determinist** aspect of radical practice and positivist social work education, research and practice. Contemporary critical practice incorporates **feminist** gender-based critiques and movements for **anti-oppressive** practice, **decolonisation** and **social justice**. It also takes up identity concerns relevant to social work client groups around the political economy of **ageing**, sexuality and social models of **disability**. **Eco practice** concerned with environmental sustainability, in view of looming environmental **disasters**, is also an increasingly important location for critical action. Elements of **advocacy, empowerment** and **macro** practice, when they are used in pursuit of critical political objectives, are valued practice techniques.

Critical practice theory uses a structural analysis of how oppressive cultural, economic, political and social ideologies are implemented within important social structures informing or providing for cultural life, education, employment, family, healthcare, housing, leisure and social provision. For example, international economic and political **discourse** currently emphasises neoliberal thinking on reducing the costs and role of the state in social welfare, and this affects how problems that arise for people are defined and how services respond or fail to respond to them. Social work services therefore start from a policy of minimising service provision, and this leads social work often to advocate or fight for a response to a person or group of people, or into assessing and prioritising needs to meet the requirements of a restrictive service. Critical practitioners take up three responses to these issues:

- Look for opportunities to meet people's **human rights** and **social justice** and reduce inequalities.
- Focus on social models of disability, health and relationships and promote **participative** and **citizenship** approaches to benefit clients and the people around them.
- Practice in **dialogic**, equal relationships with clients and colleagues and build cooperation to achieve social improvements.

For example, critical practice strategy in childcare involves balancing social justice for children and parents, and correcting power imbalances that arise by not listening to the child's, the parents' and the community's voices (Esquao & Strega, 2015).

An important critical practice strategy is **disruption**. This is not a hostile or aggressive attitude, but seeks to disconnect oppression and inappropriate use of power from clients' lives. Three disruptive practices involve:

- Changing adverse impacts of organisations and policy on people's capacity to develop and survive by advocacy, **dialogical** practice, **family support**, self-help, **peer support**.
- Challenge adverse impacts on people's social identities, for example by enabling gay and lesbian parenting to be acceptable to local agencies such as schools.
- Helping people become aware of and combat political and social policies that lead to barriers or demands upon them, such as inappropriately restrictive safety concerns affecting the lives of disabled and older people.

The initial critique of radical practice was that an **activist** stance and broad political and social aims meant that social work ignored the immediate needs of clients in favour of broad social objectives and structural change. Also, it might create hostility towards clients and within client groups who are already stigmatised by social attitudes. This is contested with the more practical bent of contemporary critical practice, and the recognition given to clients' **voice** and **participation**. Many practice strategies with a critical emphasis are possible, and activism compatible with social workers being officials is also increasingly theorised, for example by Fenton (2019).

Critical race theory is a theory about **anti-racist** practice and **racism**, mainly in use in education in the USA deriving from legal studies and the American civil rights movement. It emphasises identifying and using formal, legal and procedural processes to challenge racism in organisations you are dealing with. Its analysis focuses on building **Black perspectives** and understanding and contesting white privilege. Colour-blind approaches are also unacceptable, because they do not recognise the importance of valuing black culture and experience. In this view, **cultural competence** or sensitivity approaches do not go far enough to challenge the structural sources of racism.

Further Reading

Delgado, R. & Stefancic, J. (2017). *Critical race theory: An introduction* (3rd ed.). New York: New York University Press.

Critical realism is a view of knowledge which accepts **postmodern** scepticism about reality. This argues that what we define as reality is filtered through cultural, historical and social influences on interpretations of our perceptions. Nevertheless, there

are phenomena that exist beyond our perceptions (Houston, 2001; Morén & Blom, 2003). Research should avoid assuming that there is universal knowledge that informs every cultural context and historical period. Instead, it should explore the **ambiguities** and complexities of constantly changing and diverse interpretations of reality. Kazi's (2003) account takes up Pawson and Tilley's (1997) formulation of critical realist research in which similar actions in different places are investigated, and this clarifies the range of factors and outcomes involved. Kazi proposes a cycle of constant reassessment of findings in different contexts, to identify the value of different practices relevant in a range of service contexts:

- Changes in outcomes vary as different contexts lead to different practices.
- Changes in models of intervention occur as exigencies in service provision require shifts in practice.
- Changes in the context of clients occur as social relations vary.
- Changes in the social mechanisms that affect clients' lives.

Critical reflection is a process for learning in professional practice by examining aspects of the practice through reflection, contemplating actions and events in a renewed perspective. The management theorist Argyris and management educator Schön (Argyris & Schön, 1974; Schön, 1983, 1987) developed reflection from earlier ideas from the **pragmatist** philosopher, **Dewey**. They argued that professional practitioners cannot use **technical rational** thinking. Instead, they identify when new situations occur and adapt their thinking to them, trying out practical experiments to see what works. Successful practice allows them to create new guidelines for action in the future. The reflection process operates in a cycle:

- Identify new experience, describe and/or record it.
- Reflection explores the experience, understanding better the event, actions taken and possible options.
- **Action** is renewed in different ways, or accepted practice reaffirmed.

Reflection is possible at different stages of practice.

- Reflection-for-action arises when we approach a new situation and plan to adapt our usual approach.
- Reflection-in-action is when we identify a new situation as it is happening, and reflect on new options as we go along.
- Reflection-on-action takes place after the experience phase is complete. This is often done in supervision.

Reflexivity is a possible element in reflection. It involves rotating your perception of the event to see it from the point of view of other participants, for example clients, carers, colleagues, other agencies and professionals and managers. You adapt your future actions by including these alternative perspectives in your approach.

'Critical reflection' (White, Fook & Gardner, 2006) adds critical perspectives to this process, drawing from practice theory that is critical of the economic and social order and oppression, and sceptical of taken-for-granted practice approaches. This theoretically critical scepticism enables you to contest organisational and professional liturgies, avoiding the need to think along the lines of religious adherence to repetitive professional thought (White, 2006). Fook and Gardner (2007) propose a training model, for groups of staff and whole agencies, that develops critical reflection in groups. This contests both the managerial models of a large bureaucratic organisation where **new public management** incorporates **neoliberal** thinking, and also the tramline thinking sometimes found in small agencies. The group process allows critical thinking to emerge and create a **praxis** as **consciousness-raising** achieves in **feminist** and **Freirean** approaches to oppression. Fiona Gardner (2014) argues that this facilitates **holistic** practice that responds to a range of issues that affect clients and their families, as well as their starting point and agency requirements. It also enables staff groups to develop practice ideas that can contest the organisational, political and social assumptions incorporated into agency policy and management.

Further Reading

Mantell, A. & Scragg, T. (Eds.) (2019). *Reflective practice in social work* (5th ed.). London: Sage.

Critical thinking is guiding thinking processes using systematic procedures based on ideas of logic and rhetoric. It includes identifying the focus and premises of statements, arguments and the evidence supporting or contesting them, analysing the logic of arguments and statements and of the validity of conclusions drawn. Critical thinking may also involve considering an argument's rhetorical features, that is, attempts to persuade, and evaluation of **ambiguity**, probability and uncertainty (Bowell, Cowan & Kemp, 2020).

In social work, critical thinking is less concerned with formal argument, and more with thinking about persons and situations appropriately. Social workers avoid hidden and untested assumptions, ideological pre-sets. They view situations from different points of view, looking for contradictions and ambiguities in the situations. This involves open-minded, reasoned consideration of arguments, evidence and information, evaluating them in their social contexts. It also affects the way practitioners conduct practice relationships, maintaining the equality, openness and participative approach and structures that call forth honesty and trust in the participants. Some writers connect critical thinking with **evidence-based practice**, for example Gambrill (2019), others with critical social theory that interrogates how macro social structures form social **inequalities** (Healy, 2014: 185–91).

Cultural competence is expressing – in practice, and in managing, organising and providing services – respect for and understanding of the cultural **identity** and heritage of clients and their communities. Achieving cultural competence aims to make social workers' practice and agencies' service provision congruent with the cultural distinctiveness of clients' and communities' needs and wishes (National Association of Social Workers, 2015). Starting from concern about **discrimination** against minority ethnic populations, particularly their **spiritual** preferences and needs, cultural competence extends to people with **disabilities** (Cole & Burke, 2012; Dupré, 2012), people in **poverty** (Jack & Gill, 2013) and other minorities such as LGTBQ+ people (Fish, 2012). Contemporary practice focuses on a continuing journey (Saunders, Haskins & Vasquez, 2015) for each agency and social worker to adopt, through critical reflection, education and developing experience and training, competence in working with relevant minorities of all kinds. Listening and responding to clients' experience is also important (Jack & Gill, 2013). It is useful to acknowledge **ambiguities**, **intersections** among experiences of oppression and uncertainties in the expression of cultural difference (Garran & Rozas, 2013).

Critique of the idea of cultural competence is concerned about the emphasis on **culture**. Other aspects of ethnicity, such as spirituality, or social experiences, particularly of discrimination or oppression, may be more important. Further critique concentrates on the concept of competence, which seems to deny the complex attitudes that practitioners and managers may have; 'cultural humility' is a useful attitude to develop. Exploring interpersonal and agency competence also fails to examine and work with the structural sources of discrimination and oppression (Nylund, 2006). Simply building knowledge about diverse minorities does not develop competence in relating to or respecting minority groups, particularly if these are diverse (Johnson & Munch, 2009). Neither does it remove the possibility that we will see and respond to them as **other** (Ben-Ari & Strier, 2010). It may also be better to work with clients to understand what is important to them than to use generalised understandings of minority culture. Hollinsworth (2013) argues for exploring their biography, which would focus not only on culture, but on life experiences and the effects of oppression and trauma.

Cultural imperialism arises when present or former imperial powers increase the impact of their domination of colonies or former colonies by using cultural and linguistic influences on the **Indigenous** and traditional cultures. This also occurs when dominant ethnic groups maintain cultural influences in territories where Indigenous groups also exist. Midgley (1981) drew together commentary from many Asian and African countries that transfer of international social work knowledge and practice raises this issue.

Culture is a shared view of behaviour and **values** that are characteristic of an ethnic or social group, expressed in its aesthetic, artistic and intellectual achievements. The culture of a society is the way in which it transfers to others and in particular across generations, its understanding of its behaviours and values and their expression. The culture of an ethnic group is part of its **ethnicity**, but is expressed in diverse ways.

D

Decolonisation aims to exclude and remove from contemporary social actions, knowledge, structures and understanding the consequences of the colonisation of countries primarily in Africa, Asia, the Middle East and South America by economic and military domination by external nations, primarily in Europe, and in particular the racist consequences of **slavery** and the slave trade. Complete decolonisation may require changes to assumptions about and narratives of colonisation and slavery, which may devalue the faith, family structures, languages, traditions and values of colonised or enslaved peoples. Social structures created by colonisation continue and influence both colonised and colonising nations. For example, economic ties may continue colonial economic and trade exploitation. Also, education, government and social systems, including social welfare, may reflect colonial customs. For example, social work may be centred on adoption, so that Western intercountry adoption is facilitated, or on urban youth offending, so that urbanisation can continue to support Western economic interests. The populations of colonial powers may assume that the culture, identity and traditions of the **other** continue to be less valuable than their own. Such **colonial** attitudes may continue, even though the other's country has become independent and nominally the equal of the colonial power, and even if it is accepted that all faiths and secularism are acceptable beliefs.

Achieving a more complex degree of decolonisation may, therefore, require considerable ideological, intellectual and organisational change in former colonies and countries influenced by economic, political and social ties. Less obvious assumptions such as how knowledge or research is done, or what is considered **caring, just** or **supportive**, may continue to reflect colonial intellectual traditions. For example, social work academics in former colonial countries may only be valued and achieve promotion if they use Western research methods, such as random controlled trials of social work procedures, and their work may be correspondingly devalued if they focus on exploring the use of traditional faiths and thought. Colonial attitudes and economic, political and social structures also continue in former colonial powers, also requiring decolonisation. For example, migration from former colonies to low-paid undervalued work in subordinate positions may be accepted and encouraged to maintain advanced health and social care services in former colonial countries.

One element of decolonisation is to reconsider **indigenisation** and **authentisation** processes. These were ways of adopting Western social work practice and theory, presenting it in ways that connected with local interests, needs and traditions. Even though these practices allow social workers in former colonies to make use of non-Indigenous concepts, their adapted form may sustain colonial thinking and power structures. For example, concepts of confidentiality and **self-determination** may cut social work off from community, family or tribal decision-making structures. An aspect of decolonising processes is to explore and restore traditions of faith, social organisation and thinking. This is an important element of **Indigenist** theory; see **African-centred practice** and **Tongan social work.**

Further Reading

Hetherington, T., Gray, M. & Yellow Bird, M. (Eds.) (2013). *Decolonizing social work.* Farnham: Ashgate.

Deconstruction, in **postmodern**, and particularly post-**structural**, thought

involves taking apart how we express conceptions and words in order to understand their constituents, and the development, formation and structures of our thinking. It is particularly concerned to disclose hidden **power** relationships. A valued concept in **critical, feminist** and **radical** practices, it comes from cultural and literary studies, implying a careful analysis of the thinking disclosed by language use.

Dependence or dependency arises in social work thinking in various

ways:

- Avoiding dependence on public services was an important objective of **liberal** thinking in nineteenth-century Poor Law policies, and intermittently continues to be a motivating factor in funding and organising social welfare provision. People therefore often experience dependency as **stigmatising** and, if they receive social work or other help, may need help to work out how they want to deal with their own dependency and others' views of them.
- Wright (1983: 404–13), writing about disability, wrote of the glorification of independence, and of both dependence and interdependence as universal needs.
- Dependency is one of the three 'basic-assumption' behaviours of Bion's (1961) group theory, in which group members achieve psychological security in the group by informally accepting the authority and power of a leader figure.

Determinism and determinants reflect an age-old philosophical

debate about the extent to which human action is decided or determined by what has happened previously or by social structures which set the assumptions of people in society. Social workers need to reflect on this issue, both in daily specifics and in professional generalities. Was a client's action determined by social structures such as family, school, work, social expectations? Or was the client free to make a decision and run with it? Is social work created by the expectations of a **neoliberal** economic and political system?

Or are social workers free to make decisions according to their own judgement of what will be helpful? Does the system say what would be helpful, or can clients or social workers say what would be helpful?

Development is a complex and contested concept implying that, with effort, things grow, improve and **progress** over time. The belief that this is natural, and that development should be encouraged, is characteristic of Western political philosophies and social thought (Midgley, 1984). Particularly in the USA, the **progressive** era, around the turn of the twentieth century, influenced the acceptance of the desirability of development into social work thinking (Reisch, 1998).

In social work, three main usages are important:

- In **child** development, the expectation that with education and socialisation, children will improve their intellectual capacity and social skills, often through a series of stages, in a progression towards adulthood.
- In administration, management and organisation of agencies or parts of them, the wish that activities to meet the organisation's objectives can increase, improve their achievements and be renewed, for example through development projects or in **team** development.
- In economic and social development, that policies that economies, social relations and structures, and rural and urban areas can, with effort, be helped to increase in activity and size, in interconnectedness, and support increases of value to their populations. Development policy and studies are important constituents of international economic development, for example in policies such as the **Millennium Development Goals** and campaigns such as 'Make Poverty History'. The social work practice of **social development** in part contests, but is also integral to, such policies. Economic and social development of this kind may contribute to **post-colonial** social relations and structures, but may also help to stimulate initiatives that lead to **decolonisation**.

Dewey, John (1859–1952) was a Chicago-based American philosopher of **pragmatism** and an educationalist with influence on social work ideas during the **progressive**-era formative period of American professional social work. Later he influenced the Chicago-based social work academics Charlotte Towle and Helen Harris Perlman, the social psychologist George Herbert Mead and the educationalist Donald **Schön**, whose ideas on **reflective practice** were influential on professional education for social work and supervision. Education, in Dewey's pragmatist view, was better achieved if people were able to explore ideas using practical experience. Thus, Towle sees field or practice education as a crucial element of social work training and Perlman's practice theory emphasises joint exploration of problems by social workers and their clients.

Diagnosis in social work, now usually called **assessment**, involves exploring and

understanding clients and their circumstances so that interventions may be planned and undertaken. Important from the 1920s, for example in Mary **Richmond**'s (1965[1917]: 114) 'Social diagnosis', diagnosis is an example of **medicalisation** in social work thinking. It was a key plank of **diagnostic theory**, a leading practice theory of social work during this period. A development of the idea is the concept of differential diagnosis. This follows medical thinking in believing that it was possible and useful to distinguish in detail between differences in clients' circumstances and problems and the effects of them, so that interventions or treatments could be adapted to specific diagnoses. Diagnosis was important until the 1960s, when social work's centre of emphasis shifted from medical care to a wider range of government agencies. These used the broader idea of social work **assessment** to decide on eligibility for services, or for evaluating criminality, deviance or moral worth.

Diagnostic practice theory was influential from the 1930s to '50s,

particularly in the USA, and the basis of **traditional social work**. Its distinguishing tenet was the value of making a full **diagnosis** of the complex factors in a client's psychological functioning, that led to a request or referral for social work help. There were elements of concern for professional status in adopting this well-understood medical terminology since it gave a sense that there was a professional clarity and solidity about social workers' understanding of the problems being tackled. Developments of it were **ego-oriented** practice theory, Hollis' **psychosocial** practice, and Perlman's theory of **problem-solving** practice. As these declined in influence during the 1960s and '70s, further developments of psychodynamic theory led to the current iteration of **relational practice** theory, which incorporates many elements of diagnostic theory.

Dialectic is a philosophical conceptualisation of processes in resolving conflicts

between contradictory or opposing ideas. Classically this is done by understanding a 'thesis', an argument for one point of view, an 'antithesis', the contradictory argument, and arriving at a 'synthesis', which brings together your understanding of both. In **Marxist** theory, dialectics are conflicts between opposing social forces, revealing contradictions that help our understanding of social realities. This idea informs the 'contradictory' position in Marxist social work, that social work raises consciousness about the contradictions and injustices in society by its position of helping people in poverty, while at the same time acting in the interests of capitalism and the state. The Marxist view contests the philosopher Hegel's belief that you could resolve inconsistencies by theoretical analysis; Marxists argue that your ideas must respond to the realities that you experience in the world, and this leads you to act on your understanding – this is a connection with the idea of **praxis**. 'Dialectical materialism' refers to the process of testing out your ideas on the real, that is, material world as part of a process leading to consciousness of inequality and injustice.

In social work, a dialectic can also be a mental process in which you review opposing views or understandings of the world in your thoughts, setting them against one another to understand them better.

Dialogue and **dialogical practice** are important in social work in various ways:

- In general, dialogue refers to the practice skills concerned with equal interactions between social workers and clients, listening to and responding to each other. It contests a more governing or controlling form of interaction, but it is not necessarily **non-directive**, since a dialogue has the characteristics or objectives adopted by the parties to it. Dialogue is considered in **existential** and **humanistic** thought as characteristic of humanity and central to human interaction, involving openness and attentiveness in meeting with and being present for others (Garavan, 2013).
- Dialogue is an essential practice in **Freire**'s (1972) radical education through **conscientisation**. Practitioners engage groups of people to explore the social origins of issues that face them. In Freire's radical education approach, you use dialogue to draw out subjugated perceptions of **oppression**.
- Dialogic approaches are a crucial element in the relationships between practitioner and client in **feminist** practice, in particular because of its implication of democratic equality in the relationship.

Difference refers to an aspect of something that clarifies that it is not the same as another thing. It is important in social work theory in various ways:

- To avoid confusion, people identify and describe differences to distinguish between things or issues of concern. Social work often involves dealing with complex and perhaps hidden aspects of social life, such as individual characteristics, personality or relationships. Observing, describing and accounting for differences, for example between what people say and what the practitioner observes, therefore, is an important professional skill.
- Differences of characteristics between different social groups, for example in their behaviour, culture, physical characteristics and social class, lead to social divisions, discrimination and oppression of excluded or subordinate groups by others. This is an important aspect of **anti-discrimination**, **diversity** and **anti-oppressive** theory.
- **Rawls**' (1999) 'difference principle' is important in his theory of **social justice**. It proposes that where there are social inequalities, the least advantaged members of society should have the greatest benefits from social arrangements, so the rich should not be able to gain advantage without providing for the poorest.
- Derrida's (1982[1968]) complex discussion of **différance** and **différence** is important for understanding how we assess difference. All words contain

elements, sometimes well-hidden, of different interpretations, representations or understandings of them, so representations of ideas in language always convey complex connections with related or even opposite ideas. Derrida draws attention to how we may not be able to describe and account for differences that we are aware of, but this nevertheless affects our behaviour and social relationships.

Also, Derrida shows how the Latin source of the word 'difference' includes the concept 'defer'. Because differences in human and social aspects of life are sometimes emerging, insubstantial or still to be found, this sometimes leads us to defer to others' thinking about differences that may be apparent to us. Consequently, people may avoid focusing on difference which should be made clear. An example is where a social worker avoids acknowledging discrimination or racism because this means discussing difference when it may be unacceptable to others, for instance where powerful people see talking about these issues as 'politically correct' or 'woke'.

Dignity is an increasingly desired practice value in social work, and more broadly in everyday life. It involves people having worth as human beings. Dignity is partly a way in which we treat people as having value to us as persons, and partly about the characteristics of their person and the social structures around them that allow them to possess dignity. These two aspects of treating people with dignity are connected. If we follow the principle of '**respect for persons**', we assume their dignity. Where they do not have dignity, it may be because they are devalued in some way by their circumstances and the social structures that influence the expression of their being as people and their position in society. Someone in **poverty**, for example, who has to scrabble to survive and bring up their children in **security**, is not experiencing dignity because of their social position. Simply having a social worker treating them with dignity is not a genuine offer of dignity, so we cannot express dignity in our professional work unless we also seek to change the way poverty in society creates a lack of dignity.

Disability describes both effects on individuals and also social categories. It refers, first, to the physical and personal consequences of **bodily** and health impairments and, second, to the social disbenefits of such impairments, and the social divisions and **inequalities** that result. It therefore raises issues about how these impairments interact with society and its assumptions and ideas. Discourse about impairments is strongly influenced by healthcare and medical concepts, and is therefore affected by concerns about **medicalisation** and a **medical model** of disability.

Theoretical models of professional knowledge and practice in disability include the following (partly from Macdonald & Deacon, 2019):

- A biomedical or medical model emphasising biological and medical understanding of loss or abnormality of people's anatomical, intellectual, psychological or physiological function or structure. In social work, this is often extended, particularly in the USA, to refer to a '**biopsychosocial**' model of practice.

- A social model, which sees disability as arising from economic and social barriers that exclude disabled people from equal **participation** in society. This perspective, as presented originally by Oliver in his (1983) social work text, derived from **Marxist** historical materialism. It led to the development of 'disability studies', part of a wider disability rights movement in the USA and UK (Rothman, 2018), which particularly influenced the professional fields of education and social work.

- A social relational model, associated with Shakespeare (2006), which, while valuing the social model, emphasises the **transformation** in disabled people's lives caused by the experience of disability and impairment, for example physical limitations and pain.

- A citizenship or civil rights model, referred to by Goodley (2017: 13) as a 'minority model' which contests the **individualism** of views of disability as an individual loss, and may lead to people with disabilities being excluded from receiving citizenship or rights in society. People who become disabled may thus become 'de-citizened' (Payne, 2017) by progressively losing some of their rights to participation and opportunity.

- An **affirmation** model, associated with **cultural** studies and post-**structuralism**, shows how medicalised concepts of disability form a basis for social and cultural distinctions (Goodley, 2017; Macdonald & Deacon, 2019: 443).

Disability is a worldwide issue, and in many countries continues to lead to stigma for both disabled people themselves and also their families. Countries where **social development** is the pre-eminent social work practice often develop community-based rehabilitation (CBR). This aims to address **poverty** alleviation and **participation** structures, while providing services by relying on local resources where there are limited resources for service provision. Higashida (2019: ix) suggests that community-based rehabilitation may reflect a **medicalised** prioritisation of rehabilitation, but that the World Health Organization (2003) usage of the term connects it with addressing **empowerment** of disabled people and disability-related **inequalities** and **poverty** through community-based inclusive **social development** as well.

The **disabled living movement** was a campaign aiming at **normalisation** in the lives of disabled people. In particular, it sought to ensure that people with disabilities should be able to live in **ordinary housing** (Bayliss, 1987) adapted to enable them to be active participants in non-disabled communities and as far as possible without specialised care (Morris, 1993). This applied to physical disability ideas from the movement for de**institutionalisation** that started in the closure of large psychiatric hospitals. A similar movement for **ordinary living** for people with intellectual disabilities (Towell, 1988) was similarly influential in the 1980s.

Disadvantage is an unfavourable position in comparison with another per-
son. Viewed collectively, it is unfavourable circumstances experienced by a social group, reducing their opportunities for personal and social development, and self-actualisation. At one time, seeing a group or individual as disadvantaged was considered an acceptable, destigmatising and neutral way of understanding the position of people affected by social **inequality** and **poverty**. In contemporary social work thinking, **oppression** and **priv-ilege** conceptualise social barriers to achievement and a satisfactory social life; thinking about disadvantage tends to **individualise** and **privatise** understanding, and devalues social analysis of the difficulties that communities and people experience.

Disasters are wide-scale natural and human events such as fire, floods, extreme weather events and conflicts, disease (including pandemics), major accidents, terrorism and war. Responses to disasters often fall to the responsibility of emergency services, but increasingly, awareness of post-traumatic stress disorder and other psychological consequences of experiencing disasters have led to a broader social response that often includes both social work and planning for expected disasters (Mathbor, 2007), as well as psychological and social responses immediately and in the long term to disaster management (Javadian, 2007).

Discourse is how people explore and express, in social relationships, their under-standing of the interactions and structures that affect how they think and act. The idea comes from cultural studies and linguistics (Flowerdew & Richardson, 2018), extended by **post-modernist** writers, particularly **Foucault** (1972), to wider social practices. A social work discourse, for example, is about the nature of social work, and in language it is expressed in discussions between social workers and others ('Am I doing social work here, or coun-selling?'), in the social work literature ('This writer says social work is mainly about helping, but others say it aims for social change') and in actions by social workers with clients and non-social worker colleagues. This is not in language but in what the person chooses to do or not to do, how they choose to do it and how other people understand and react to what they do. But it is interpreted in language in which they would express their understanding.

Discourse analysis explores ways in which people argue for and express their understanding of the world in their language and actions. Fairclough and Fairclough (2018) see contemporary discourse analysis as **critical** in that it seeks to explore '**dialectical** reasoning', how differences and disagreements about influence and power in **social change** are played out. This takes place in **action** and language that offers critique, explanation and action of the social so that the world might be changed for the better. Discourse analysis, in this understanding of it, therefore connects with social work's objectives. As we take part in discourse by what we say and do in the world through our social work, we can analyse and understand better struggles around **hegemony** and **ideology** in the aims and methods of practice. For example, a contemporary issue in social work theory is **decolonisation**. To understand it better, we can look at how Western white people talk and think about people in black and minority ethnic groups in their personal and professional lives and understand better how they reflect the history of colonialism in their lives. Also, we can see how literature and theory about social work have contributed to a devaluation of African, Asian and black ideas and knowledge. Both of these analyses of discourse refer both to hegemony and ideology in social work and to how it is expressed in our communication and practices as we go about social work.

Discretion is having the freedom to make decisions using the information available to you without having to abide by managerial expectations or regulatory controls. Some views of **professionalisation** in social work regard having the power to use discretion in helping decisions about clients as a mark of social work's acceptance as a profession.

Discrimination See **Anti-discriminatory practice, Anti-oppressive practice, Oppression** and **Privilege**.

Disruption is an aspect of critical practice, which proposes that practitioners should intervene to disrupt taken-for-granted social assumptions about appropriate behaviour or social relations. The aim is to free people to explore alternative and perhaps more helpful options in their lives.

Diversity is being composed of many different elements. In management, political and social work discourse, it refers to diversity, mainly of ethnicity and gender, in the populations served. It superseded ideas of **cultural competence** and **multiculturalism** to refer to populations with differences of ethnicity, being more neutral than those terms' emphases on **culture**. Its use has extended to other differences of concern. Referring to diversity assumes that people should be aware of, promote and value the range of different characteristics in any given population, treating people with differing characteristics equally. A mark of diversity in organisations, services and workforces is that they reflect the diversity in the population they serve.

Dread is an existentialist concept also called 'existential crisis' or, the German translation, 'angst'. Seen by the existentialist philosopher Kierkegaard as connected with the Christian experience of 'original sin', it expresses something of the feeling of overbearing struggle of doing anything useful with our lives. It arises as people become aware of the difficulties of **being** and struggling with existence in the world. Social workers often find that people with anxiety or depression struggle with fears about the unknown consequences of difficulties in the future.

DSM is the *Diagnostic and Statistical Manual of Mental Disorders* published periodically by the American Psychiatric Association. It is an authoritative listing of mental disorders, symptoms by which they may be diagnosed and appropriate treatments. There is a critique of this and similar publications by other countries' psychiatric bodies, since they lead to authoritative **labelling** of people with conditions on the basis of difficult-to-define symptoms (Wakefield, 2013).

Dual process theory (Stroebe & Schut, 1999) is a **social construction**

theory of **bereavement**, which contests **stage** and **task** theories, particularly those of Kübler-Ross, Parkes and Worden. It proposes that bereaved people shift between looking backwards at their losses and forwards in planning for the future. Both processes are a necessary part of bereavement. This idea reflects the **ambiguity** and lack of control that people often feel in bereavement, but allows realistically for flexibility in thinking about bereavement processes. The social worker would help clients to understand that they should not feel guilt about forgetting their loss during those phases when they are working for their future and should accept that their loss will be a continuing part of that future.

Eclecticism, in social work theory, involves combining two or more theories to inform practice. Criticisms of this common practice are that it can be hard to have a firm grasp of several practice theories to select from and combine them without missing or transgressing important aspects of them. Another difficulty is that some ideas are theoretically inconsistent, so combining them can violate important principles. Some practices are inconsistent with the administrative and legal responsibilities or the managerial style of particular agencies. A common approach is to agree with colleagues an informed selection of techniques relevant to the agency and its aims (Epstein & Brown, 2002; Payne, 2021[1990]: Ch. 2).

Eco, ecocentric, ecological, ecosocial and green social work

are critical practice perspectives developing in the twenty-first century. They emerge from political and public concern about the sustainability of the natural environment and its flora and fauna, **holistically** proposing that because the quality of human life is inextricably linked with the environment, the issue is relevant to social work objectives. Eco practice is distinct from **ecological** (or **eco**) **systems theory**, which focuses on the social rather than the natural environment.

The critique of these concerns is that they are not yet a priority for clients of social care services in Western countries. Increasingly, however, environmental issues are raised for families in poverty and people affected by ageing, childcare problems, disability and mental illness since they are affected by poor environment in their health, housing and daily lives. Responding to environmental issues can be motivating for clients as part of social work on child protection or adult social care provision. Reflecting policy development on environmental sustainability, social work is adapting generalised policy actions to be relevant for communities, families and individuals that they work with, where ordinary policies fail to make provision for environmental sustainability.

Eco practice principles connect with other practices. For example, ideas of integration and connectedness chime with **feminist** thinking, community and local relationships with **critical**, **macro**, **radical** and **Marxist** practice, maintaining **diversity** with **anti-oppressive** and related practices; and looking for possibilities and doing more of what has been beneficial in the past connects with **motivational interviewing**, **solution** and **strengths practice**. Eco practice aims to promote a greater connection with sustainability in the natural environment.

One focus of the practice seeks issues of local importance for communities, families and individuals and adds eco concerns, such as better food together with food security, gardens and nature in leisure activities, health, pollution, sustainable housing, transport and water resources. Thinking about eco issues increasingly makes connections between the non-human, the personal and the environmental. Puig de la Bellacasa (2017), for example, argues that conceptions of **caring** require action caring for the environmental implications of social change. Ife's (2012) account of **human rights** practice states that collective rights include a good environment.

Ecological systems, or **eco systems theory** are two formulations of a **systems theory** that includes elements of ecological thinking, primarily in its use of the idea of helping clients to make an **adaptation** that enables them to fit with the social environment in which they live, for example their family system or culture. Ecological systems theory is primarily an American development, associated with Gitterman and **Germain**'s '**life model**' of practice; eco systems theory is associated with Carol Meyer (1983); but both originated in the same period, that is, the late 1970s and early 1980s. Both are usually treated, for example in Wakefield's (1996) extended critique, as iterations of the same set of ideas. They are not part of the **eco** practice of the early twenty-first century since they do not address sustainable development and the natural environment.

Ego, in the **structural** aspect of **psychoanalysis**, is the structure within the mind that manages relationships with aspects of reality outside the person. These aspects include people, practical problems and social structures. They are external to the mind, and called 'objects' of mental activity; the ego, thus, manages 'object relations'. Social workers concentrate on improving how clients work on practical tasks, on relationships with important people in their lives and on social environments in which they operate, such as schools or workplaces.

Ego has a broader meaning in ordinary conversation – we say things like 'He has a big ego' or 'She is very egotistical'. This usage derives from egotistical or egoistical behaviour. There is a difference between these two concepts, but everyday talk does not always recognise it. 'Egotistical' people are self-important, thinking that they, their abilities and their needs are more important than other people around them. 'Egoistical' people believe that **individualism** is a natural human state that people inevitably pursue their own interests. We have, therefore, to take this into account when we deal with people. Egoism informs **liberal** and **neoliberal** thinking.

Ego psychology is an aspect of psychodynamic theory that came to pro-minence in the 1950s, as social work working on people's management of reality rather than the psychoanalytic focus on unconscious behaviour. It influenced **crisis intervention**, since ego psychology was the source of its emphasis on immediate realities and emotional reactions to difficult events in clients' lives.

Ego-oriented practice included **support** for people to manage difficulties in their lives, mobilising **strengths** (Bandler, B., 1963: 33), rather than exploring internal psychology. Similarly, the social environment was not a static external factor in people's lives, so clients should be helped to change within the context of their family, and cultural and social factors should be reformed (Stein, 1963). Helping a client's ego's strengths grow by developing competence in dealing with external problems, and reducing the effect of psychological barriers to using those strengths, is part of that process (Garrett, 1958; Bandler, L., 1963). 'Object relations' are also important, creating friendly and loving bonds with others and integrating important relationships and outside realities into the structure of a person's thinking. This builds an integrated and coherent **self**, used to manage and deal with the outside world (Goldstein, 1984: 125–230).

E

Emancipation is a change in organisation or practice that removes barriers, decreases oppression and increases both individual and organisational freedom in ways that are relevant to the issue of concern. Emancipatory, **transformational** change is often an objective of **critical**, **radical** and **structural practice**.

Embodiment is the process by which social **identities** are **represented** in people's bodies, for example **ethnicity** or **gender** identity are usually identifiable in a bodily physical manifestation; but sometimes not, as in what may be the ambiguous embodiment in a trans person. Embodiment is a conception or perception that the person has of themselves and that other people may have of someone's body. See **Body**.

Emergence is a characteristic of social relations and structures in **postmodern** thinking. It contests the idea that knowledge about the **social** can be established with certainty through observation and research. Instead, emergence proposes that understanding emerges over time from exploring complex interrelationships. The idea of emergence suggests that some social actions, events and experiences are often **ambiguous**, having emergent properties, and contain the seeds of a change or movement that we only gradually become aware of.

Emotion is a strong feeling, a mental reaction that is conscious, so we are or become aware of it. It is associated with physical changes, including chemical and neurological variations in our bodies. Some emotions, such as anger, desire, fear, happiness, hatred, love or misery, are well-established in everyday discourse and psychological research. Emotions are reactions to internal mood and external events. They are both felt and expressed in behaviour. Other people can sometimes identify emotions in our behaviour, or may interpret behaviour as representing an emotion, and may see them as reactions to changes in mood or to recent events. For example, a period of depression may be seen as resulting from internal propensities or chemical changes, or as reacting to change or loss in relationships that are important to us. In psychology, **affect** conceptualises a person's emotional state or the pattern of their emotional reactions.

Rational behaviour and emotion are sometimes contrasted; some traditions, including **humanism**, regard rational thinking as a valuable characteristic of humanity. By implication, they regard behaviour driven by emotion as inferior to cognition (Barbalet, 2001: 23–5; Wetherall, 2012: 38–9). Ekman's (1992) research on facial recognition across different cultures proposes that there are 'basic' emotions, others being more culturally developed. Wetherall (2012: 40–4) suggests that there is little evidence of biological reactions generating recognisable emotional responses and that culture is an important source of emotional behaviour. So both emotional and rational behaviour are characteristic of human beings, and social workers assess both elements. Barbalet (2001) suggests that affect and emotions often develop as a result of social structures. For example, class and other social inequalities may breed resentment and vengeful feelings, and structures that seek to provide social order and conformity generate anger and shame. **Anti-oppressive** and **critical** practice help clients explore powerful affect and emotions that act as barriers to change.

Contemporary accounts of affect and emotions (for example, Wetherall, 2012) focus on discourse in which emotional behaviour is represented by people and understood by others in a joint process of making **meaning**. Sequences of emotional expression account for others' behaviour, positioning them for example as caring or responsive, as part of a **narrative** of the relationship. In this way, emotions solidify and confirm the **habitus** and emotional **capital** that people experience and may have available to them in a relationship, reflecting for instance expectations of the **ethnicity** or social class of the people involved.

Further Reading

Wetherall, M. (2012). *Affect and emotion: A new social science understanding.* London: Sage.

Emotional intelligence is the idea that the ability to observe, assess, evaluate, and then react appropriately to other people's emotions and responses in social interactions can be measured (Goleman, 1996). Social intelligence, the ability to understand social structures and long-term relationships, may be equally important (Goleman, 2007). Emotional intelligence is an interaction between self-awareness and self-management (intrapersonal intelligence) and awareness of others and capacity to manage relationships with others (interpersonal intelligence) (Morrison, 2007).

Emotional intelligence involves practitioners moving from observing and monitoring their own and clients' behaviour towards managing the expression of emotions in people's environments (Howe, 2008). 'Attending to' people through the connectedness required in caring relationships is part of intuitive human awareness of and responsiveness to other people. It is also part of the development of the human **self** and **self-actualisation** that is important in **humanistic** practice. Human beings seek and want to experience psychological and social attachments that achieve such awareness and responsiveness.

Social work ideas that call on emotional and social intelligence in this way include the following:

- **Affiliation** and **attachment**, encouraging people to experience and build connections with other people.
- **Caring**, enabling people to observe and review their connectedness in social interactions and relationships.
- **Mindfulness**, building a constant awareness of our impact on others and their reactions to use.
- **Narrative** practice, building understanding of people's interpretations of their life and experience.

Further Readings

Goleman, D. (1996) *Emotional intelligence: Why it matters more than IQ.* London: Bloomsbury.

Howe, D. (2008). *The emotionally intelligent social worker.* Basingstoke: Palgrave Macmillan.

Emotional labour conceptualises how cultural and organisational expectations affect how people manage the expression of their emotions in social relations (Hochschild, 2012[1983]). Practice should take account, in assessment and intervention, of the reality, experienced by many **carers**, that dealing with emotional reactions to any social situation is hard work and exhausting .

Empathy is being able to appreciate and experience the emotions and reactions that people are expressing, and demonstrating that to them as they are communicating with you. Expressing empathy is one of the three **core conditions** of achieving effective helping relationships. There are two elements of it:

- A cognitive awareness of what people are communicating about their internal states, such as feelings, intentions, perceptions and thoughts.
- Expressing in your behaviour and language that you are experiencing something of their internal state (Hoffman, 2000).

Empathy requires a response in you that picks up the mood and nature of their state. Your behaviour has to be appropriate to the state that you perceive, and to be engaged.

In this way, people can feel and see you interacting with their state of being. Empathy is not sympathy; you express how you are experiencing their reactions, not your regret about them. It is particularly important to express empathy with strong emotions and reactions, and when clients are being open about their assumptions and values.

Empiricism is a view in epistemology that knowledge comes only from human experience and evidence derived from the senses applied in observation and experimentation, together with reflection and rational deduction from that evidence. This is the basis for scientific research, and views such as evidence-based practice in social work and other professions. Empiricism is contested by rationalism, which argues that knowledge can be developed by analysis and thought based on ideas.

Empowerment is a social work practice objective and strategy. In the international social work organisation's global definition of social work (International Federation of Social Workers, 2014a), it is connected with liberation as one of the three main objectives of social work. Critical and positive psychology practice theories emphasise its importance.

Despite this status as a practice objective, however, empowerment is not clearly theorised as a practice. Several writers (for example McBeath & Webb, 1991; Dominelli, 2012b) note that empowerment can be interpreted as a critical response to structural inequalities or alternatively as a neoliberal appeal to enhance social competence; both elements are present in social work. Teater (2014), for example, focuses on psychological strengths and uses Greene and Lee's (2011) account of combined narrative and solution practices to put forward a strengths and solution account. Turner (2017) includes an updating of Lee's formulation drawing mainly on inequalities affecting minority ethnic groups (Lee & Hudson, 2017). My own accounts (Payne, 2020 on practice; Payne, 2021 [1990] on theory) treat it, respectively, as part of anti-oppressive and part of social justice and advocacy practices.

Three approaches to its practice may therefore be identified, as follows:

- Empowerment as a form of critical practice with black groups, the original source of empowerment practice. By extension, this approach could be used with other minority groups, but generally anti-oppressive and anti-discriminatory practice is the preferred lens for this.
- Empowerment as a critical sociological and philosophical analysis of power relations adversely affecting the social groups with which social workers often practise.
- Empowerment as a positive element of anti-oppressive or critical practice, aiming for behavioural and social competence and removing barriers in clients' lives. It is one of the ways in which these perspectives can present positive forward-looking options for practice; other options include advocacy and social justice.

An important early source of empowerment ideas in social work is black power movements in oppressed minority ethnic communities in the USA. The founding text is Solomon's (1976) 'black empowerment' and an authoritative account from this source is Lee's (2001) work. Solomon's (1976: 16) account focuses on 'valued social roles' that individuals and social groups cannot perform effectively because they experience 'negative evaluations' (1976: 19) which have caused them to devalue themselves so that they are not in control of emotions, knowledge, skills or material resources that they need in order to achieve their goals. This is an **identity**-based interpretation before identity became an explicit discourse in social work. Lee's (2001: 49) analysis explores a frame of reference, a 'multifocal vision', which provides a 'lens' through which people can explore their present experiences.

E

Sociological and philosophical analyses of **power** relations have influenced social work from discourses within **feminist** analyses of patriarchal power, critical theory concerns about inequalities, oppression and social exclusion affecting many social groups, and the **postmodern** analysis of power as widely implicated in social relations, for example, **Foucault's** analysis of governmentality and surveillance. Such discourses reveal how the use and impacts of power are often hidden. These analyses also contest some aspects of the **Marxist** and **radical** practice theory which focus on social groups in society that hold a great deal of social power because of their economic power. Postmodern views of power suggest that not all power is exercised oppressively by dominant groups and that many kinds of influence are available to less obviously powerful groups. One of the arguments for **activism** and advocacy is that disclosure of oppressive and unjust uses of power often limits or restrains injustice. This approach to empowerment suggests that making people aware of opportunities to take up unused power that they might have, and of unjust uses of power by institutions and in social relations, can be effective means of empowerment.

The third use of empowerment is within advocacy, anti-oppressive, critical and structural perspectives. These approaches to empowerment emphasise, first, being clear when we are dealing with excluded or oppressed groups and picking up the impact on society of their exclusion. Second, they look at the sociological understanding of power to identify the mechanisms by which it is used oppressively, ways in which this might be combated, and ways in which alternative power may be used. Third, they look for practical ways of giving people positive experiences of using their power and resisting oppression.

Empowerment practice, therefore, aims to help people overcome barriers in themselves and their social relations that obstruct them in achieving important goals. In psychological theories it is partly associated with **self-efficacy**, aiming to facilitate clients' skills and **strengths** in achieving their goals.

Further Reading

Lee, J. A. B. (2001). *The empowerment approach to social work practice: Building the beloved community* (2nd ed.). New York: Columbia University Press.

The **Enlightenment** was a period of eighteenth-century philosophical and scientific ferment in many different countries which established the importance of human rationality as the basis of a scientific method of developing knowledge. It led to a rejection of **authority** of monarchies and religion as the basis for knowledge and understanding. Enlightenment thinking underlies **empiricist, individualist, liberal** and **neoliberal** economic thinking and scientific method and **evidence-based** views in **epistemology**. These social principles are seen as an important element of the success of European and Western culture in economic development and industrialisation.

Entrepreneurship is the idea that energetic forward-looking risk-taking is useful in creating, establishing and advancing a business, and by extension any innovative organisational activity. **Liberal** thinking suggests that such a style is not associated with **bureaucratic** management styles, which emphasise consistency and stability.

The contemporary development of **social entrepreneurship** or 'social enterprise' is creating businesses that incorporate and recycle surpluses to support social objectives. By establishing a business rather than a charity or public service, the entrepreneur rejects externally set objectives, making the organisation autonomous from political structures and often developing a participatory ethos with the organisation providing service to a population (Ashton, 2010). Varied models of management can be applied both in small-scale development and in management of Western health and social care systems (Oham & Macdonald, 2016). Participation from clients and of professionals is also possible. An example of the latter is the inclusion of social enterprises as one model of governance in a UK experiment to set up 'social work practices' like family doctors' general practices to provide elements of local government social care provision, including child safeguarding (Le Grand, 2007).

Epistemology is the study of the nature of knowledge, its limits and how we get it and represent it in analysis and explanation. **Feminist** and **postmodernist** thinking have raised the profile of epistemological issues in social work. **Critical** theory, drawing on the work of **Bourdieu** and **Foucault** particularly, also raises issues about how power is understood.

Equality is where everyone has the same legal rights and status and is held in the same regard, being **respected** as having the same worth as other people. If there were equality in a society, **discrimination** would be absent, and people would be treated equally in official and social relationships, including in elections. People who are equally valued would be free to pursue their interests, only limited by the interests of others, with conflicts of interest being resolved by laws that would give everyone equal standing. Equality is enforced within legal jurisdictions, which may be local, national or international, but it is also enforced in society generally by people's attitudes and behaviour expressed in relationships.

Social work, therefore, is concerned with equality in two ways. Because it is part of public services, its practice represents constitutional or legal requirements for equality. Its agreed professional **values** also include equality. Practice, consequently, requires social workers to engage in productive relationships with clients and the people around them, and this is only possible if clients are seen and treated by social workers as equal in rights, status and worth with all other human beings. Evidence suggests that equality is emotionally and personally more satisfying for everyone in their relationships, and leads to better social relations generally (Wilkinson & Pickett, 2010).

Two approaches to securing equality are equality of opportunity and of outcome. Equality of opportunity acknowledges that the human attributes of individuals vary so that people cannot achieve equality in every aspect of human life. Everyone, in this view, should have 'equal opportunities' to achieve the best that they can in those areas that they choose to pursue. Equality of outcome criticises the equal opportunities position because opportunities are restricted by economic disadvantages and social stratification in society, which gives advantages to people because they were born into richer and more valued families in society. Evaluating equality in this view looks at population groups, rather than individual fairness. **Rawls**' theory of justice, in its '**difference** principle', argues that where inequality exists, people with disadvantages should be treated more favourably.

Concern about inequality arises for social work both in personal relations and in social requirement. In personal relationships, social work values require clients and the people around them to be treated with equality as part of professional practice. For this reason, equal **dialogic relationships** and between practitioners and clients are important. Social equality is also an objective, for two reasons. First, equality in professional relationships is not possible if the groups that social workers serve are unequal within social structures. Second, social work values seek a better society, so equality is a necessary objective anyway.

Inequality of any kind therefore is an important area of understanding for social work, in its education, knowledge, professional development and research. Social work concern centres on health and **poverty** because of its historical involvement in these areas. They are connected, because good health is socially determined internationally (World Health Organization, 2008) and in the UK (Marmot Review, 2010). Inequalities, however, are **intersectional** and aspects of inequality connect in complex ways. 'Poverty alleviation' is an international policy objective, influential in **social development** practice. Access to care and services is generally important in tackling inequality, and particular kinds of inequality are relevant to some social work responsibilities. For example, **affective** inequality means that many people are not able to express and receive love, care, achieve personal development and **self-actualisation** objectives, or achieve recognition of mental illness and stress in their lives (Lynch, Baker & Lyons, 2009). Another example is technological inequality, where some families do not have equal access to Internet or other technical resources, disabled people do not have access to technology to help them, and older people are not facilitated to have access to and use technological improvements.

Further Reading

Bagilhole, B. (2009). *Understanding equal opportunities and diversity: The social differentiations and intersections of inequality.* Bristol: Policy Press.

Equilibrium is an element in thinking about social work in several different areas of practice:

- In general, concern about equilibrium follows from a conservative assumption that successful societies and social relations require a **balanced** adjustment among different forces. This view is characteristic of social work theories aiming for social cohesion, seeing social work as concerned with creating and maintaining social order in society.
- **Crisis intervention** theory originated with a conception that crises in people's lives derived from upsets in a steady state in which people were able to cope with adverse and difficult events.
- Continuing bonds theory (Klass et al., 1996) about **bereavement** focuses on people finding a new equilibrium in their lives, and this is implicitly true of other bereavement theories that see people as readjusting to a new life after the disruption caused by the death of an important person in their lives.

Ethics is the study of moral ideas that regulate behaviour or an area of activity; social work ethics are, therefore, moral ideas that regulate social work activities or the social work profession. Being articulate about ethics empowers practitioners to work with clients and the people around them with respect, treating them with justice (Bowles, Collingridge, Curry & Valentine, 2006). Moral ideas are often formalised into sets of generalised 'principles' relevant to many circumstances. **Principles-based** or 'deontological' ethics is a significant ethical system in social work, alongside the **ethics of care,** relationship-based ethics and **virtue ethics** (Banks, 2012). While, therefore, principle-based ethics is not the only way of making moral decisions in social work, rejecting them also questions the value of **codes of ethics**, which usually state ethical principles. Because they are generalised, ethical principles do not deal with specific circumstances. Instead, as we come across a situation, the ideas contained in principles are applied to the detail.

Ethics are linked to but distinguishable from values. Values are attributions of worth, enduring beliefs that ways of behaving or particular end-states are more worthwhile, or preferable, to potential alternatives (Yelaja, 1982: 6–7). They are 'emotionally charged conceptions of what is desirable' (Reamer, 2018: 15). Value systems are sets of values that are connected with or represent a social or theoretical commitment, for example to a faith, or to socialist ideas (Beckett, Maynard & Jordan, 2017: 5). Values are more **holistic** and take account of a broad range of issues, whereas ethics are more specific statements of moral judgements.

Bauman (2000b, cited by Bowles et al., 2006: 20–22) and Hugman (2005: 105–24), argue that having clear moral positions helps social work practice. It enables social work to identify the importance of human interdependence in societies and the existence of social responsibility for other humans. They argue that this is important in the context of the influence of **liberal** thinking, which justifies social provision only by referring to any economic benefits it may have, and **postmodern** relativism, which argues that agreement to ethical positions is the constantly variable product of **social construction** rather than having moral validity.

Further Reading

Banks, S. (2012). *Ethics and values in social work* (4th ed.). London: Red Globe.

The **ethics of care** position is a feminist view of caring which has been influential in contemporary social work, and develops debates on **care**. The starting point is Gilligan's work (1993[1982]) showing that women and men have different modes of reasoning about moral questions, including the nature of caring (Rhodes, 1985). Davies (1985) applied Gilligan's idea to social work, picking up **gender** issues. She argued that female voices, both generally and in social work, have been suppressed in favour of a male perspective, picking up the gender issues and the approach to understanding and knowledge.

These ideas have subsequently been developed. Among important writers, Tronto (1993: Ch. 1) is significant in shifting the debate onwards from gendered interpersonal relations. Caring about both people and things goes beyond moral thinking into the political decisions we make about what is important and beyond the private into public issues. The same is true of the focus on moral points of view; this is Gilligan's point. What is moral, considered good, is not a matter for distant considerations of duties and rights, but a matter of what concerns us, what we pay attention to. These are all universal issues, not just a matter of different gendered attitudes. Tronto (1993: Ch. 4) goes on to define caring as something that human beings do to '… maintain, continue and repair our world so that we can live in it as well as possible' (1993: 103, quoting Fisher & Tronto, 1991). This applies both to interpersonal caring and care for the environment and politics, the way the world makes important decisions.

In Tronto's view, caring is defined culturally and is a central part of how any society establishes what is moral; yet it is marginalised in moral and political philosophy, which concentrates on issues of principle such as duty, freedom and justice. We must, therefore, pay attention to the cultural importance of care. An ethics of care contains four elements:

- Attentiveness – we have to pay attention to the world and make an effort to identify and know about matters that might require our care; allowing ourselves to remain ignorant is not an option.
- Responsibility – looking beyond formally defined duties, we have to become aware of the consequences if we do not trouble ourselves to care.
- Competence – we have to provide good care, as soon as, by paying attention, we realise that we have responsibility. This is integral to the responsibility of a professional to say, 'I am not competent to provide that service'. For example, the inexperienced surgeon does not agree to carry out major innovative surgery; teachers do not agree to teach subjects they know nothing about; the new social worker does not agree to make the decision in a complex child-safeguarding case. They share the responsibility and make it clear when they cannot act because it is beyond their present ability.
- Responsiveness – accepting interdependence and the duty to become involved, rather than demanding total autonomy of vulnerable people.

Looking at how this ethic of care might be implemented, Tronto (1993: 137–55) questions several issues relevant to social workers, including rejecting **othering** of people involved in care situations. In **assessing** needs, these four elements of care ethics require attention to the particulars of the care process, including the people involved in it. Comparing this situation with formal statements of criteria in a detached way will not achieve a caring assessment according to this view of care ethics. Sevenhuijsen (1998: 55–68), applying feminist ideas to caring **processes**, emphasises the importance of moral subjectivity, not separating thinking from feeling, evaluating what feels right, and therefore the importance of narrativity and context, the particular story and context that has created this need for care.

More recent accounts of the ethics of care draw attention to a wide range of social issues, such as **interdependence, intersectionality** and **reciprocity**, in the way people in different contexts think about care, and are supported or constrained in their practice by policy and cultural assumptions (Barnes, Brannelly, Ward & Ward, 2015).

Further Reading

Barnes, M., Brannelly, T., Ward, L. & Ward, N. (Eds.) (2015). *Ethics of care: Critical advances in international perspective*. Bristol: Policy Press.

Ethnic group and ethnicity are terms referring to groups of people who share common distinctive features, such as culture, language or religion. There is no clear distinction from '**race**' in everyday talk, but race more strongly includes biological and physical characteristics based on an ethnic group's genetic heritage.

Evidence-based practice (EBP) is a social movement present in
the politics of social work theory arguing for an **empiricist** approach to knowledge.

Exchange is important in a number of aspects of social work, as follows:

- In **ecological systems theory**, including Gitterman and **Germain's life model**,
  the focus of practice is to assist **adaptation** of people and environments to
  facilitate exchanges between people and their social environment.
- In **caring** relationships, people may seek to achieve **balance** in care given and
  received over **time**.
- **Reciprocity** in social relations is an important social objective.

Exclusion is a process that cuts certain social groups off from economic, polit-
ical and social engagement with mainstream society because of poverty, uncertain and
irregular employment and income, and insecure or insufficient social welfare benefits and
services, allied to discrimination, poor education and poor living conditions. The concept
comes from French social policy in the 1980s, which has a long-standing concern with
social cohesion, partly due to the influence of the Roman Catholic church and the rights
of **citizenship**. In turn, the concept influenced European Union policy. Levitas (1998)
identified three elements of exclusion policy:

- A redistribution view that social forces leading to poverty can only be eliminated by
  redistributing wealth through progressive taxation, and effective social benefits and
  welfare services.
- A moral **underclass** view that some neighbourhoods house a residuum of the
  population detached from mainstream social institutions and adopting
  anti-social behaviour and values, which requires intervention to manage their
  behaviour.
- A social integrationist view that entrance to the labour market to achieve stable
  paid work would facilitate reintegration within the social mainstream.

Accounts of social work practice with social exclusion (Barry & Hallett, 1998; Batsleer &
Humphries, 2000; Percy-Smith, 2000; Pierson, 2002) start from being clear about what
kind of thinking about social exclusion informs the practice that agencies implement.
Interventions include the following:

- Maximising income and **welfare rights**.
- Strengthening clients' and families' social networks, to develop social **capital**.
- Build partnerships with agencies, particularly in education, housing and healthcare,
  that have similar concerns, developing their capacity to be culturally and socially
  competent.

- Promote participation by clients and communities to strengthen clients' and communities' integration.
- Work in neighbourhoods on improving the environment and living conditions.
- Focus on the needs of children within socially excluded families and of young people implicated in the criminal justice system and drug abuse.
- Focus on groups excluded by discrimination and stigmatisation because of excluded identities, migrants, or people with devalued sexual identities.
- Strengthen people's citizenship, re-citizening (Payne, 2017) people where they have lost engagement with decision-making systems.

Further Reading

Pierson, J. (2002). *Tackling social exclusion*. London: Routledge.

Existentialism

Existentialism is a twentieth-century philosophy concerned with the cultural, psychological and social consequences of human existence. It has influenced psychologies, psychotherapies such as Frankl's logotherapy, and social work, and also connects with **humanistic** social work (Payne, 2011; 2020: Ch. 13). The concern of existentialist thought is the **being** aspect of the 'human being'. This is important to social work because existentialism says that our thinking and acting in interpersonal encounters is what constitutes us as a human being. We need to think, therefore, about humanity and talk about things such as **human rights**, as part of the humanistic aspects of social work. Existentialism asks us to think also about what it means to 'be'. By meeting and beginning to interact with another human being, we are confirming to them that they exist and by reacting to us they are confirming that we exist. Existence, therefore, emerges from and progresses through our human interactions. Our existence is always dynamic, changing, developing in our life as human beings with other human beings. We discover ourselves through being in existence with others (May, 1983: 48–53). Existential practice involves helping people develop self-awareness through experiencing life openly and realistically in dialogues with a practitioner, so that people may direct their future actions (Krill, 2014).

Krill's later formulation proposes (2017: 171–3) five organising concepts:

- Disillusionment. To help a client's 'unique personhood' (2017: 172) emerge, practitioners help people move away from the defences that prevent them dealing with the realities of the world as it affects them.
- Freedom of choice. This involves helping clients make choices to act on things that are available to them and worthwhile to them.

- **Meaning** in suffering. Practitioners should not eliminate or discredit feelings of fear, anxiety or guilt, as for example **CBT** would, but accept that realistic fears identify the directions they should move in.
- Necessity in dialogue. Becoming **authentic** in their responses to their environment and people around them means that clients have to express their concerns and needs through dialogue with the social worker and others.
- Commitment. By affirming the authentic worldview that clients come to express in their dialogues with the social worker, they can build up commitment to deciding on changes in their lives.

The changes that practitioners work on include: provoking a desire for and preparedness to change, sustaining people who need stronger affirmation to make changes, working on changing a specific behaviour, environmental or relationship change, and helping people to decide on and implement a change in direction in their lives.

Griffiths (2017) identifies a range of historical lines of thought within social work that may contribute to an existential practice, and suggests there are many insights that help towards opening up alternative ways of thinking and acting in social work practice. These can help people find creative ways of using their lived experience to deal with the complex interactions of change and control in the social factors affecting their lives. Social workers need to take the responsibility of being present through their interactions around the fear of trauma and the need for security.

Further Reading

Griffiths, M. (2017). *The challenge of existential social work practice.* London: Palgrave.

Fairness is just, impartial, reasonable treatment of individuals without bias, discrimination or favouritism; it is connected with **justice** which is about the fairness of **systems** or **structures**. There are two main ways of achieving fairness: a process view, which emphasises being fair in how we do things, and an outcome view, which emphasises achieving fair outcomes.

Process fairness is often implemented by **procedures**. These demonstrate that you have gone through the process of looking at the required aspects of the situation, but procedures do not necessarily cover everything that people want included. Procedural fairness proposes that unless people can see that you have acted fairly in making a decision, they will not think it fair, even if they are happy with the outcome. Sometimes people will balance procedures and outcomes and expect to see both present in the actions that social workers take (Weale, 1980).

Outcome fairness is concerned with identifying and balancing benefits and disbenefits of various courses of action for the people concerned. A difficulty arises where one group or person benefits from while another is disadvantaged by a social worker's actions. Practitioners would work to identify such situations, and achieve outcomes that confer mutual benefits or avoid disbenefits, negotiate an outcome agreeable to everyone involved, or empower people to work through the issues to find what they consider a fair outcome. Sometimes, process fairness is a way of gaining acceptance of outcomes that do not benefit a certain group or individual.

The **family** involves kinship, households and living arrangements, together with economic relationships. Lifestyle, domestic life or domesticity, 'home', intimacy and privacy, and care and child development responsibilities are part of it (Morgan, 1996). In most societies, family is important to social order, stability and governmentality, the way that society manages and **surveils** social relations. Many religions see families as a base maintaining **religious** and **spiritual** discipline and influence. **Marxist** theory regards the family as an important site of **social reproduction**, in capitalist societies socialising children into industrialised work roles. **Feminist** theory argues that economic oppression also leads to **oppression** of women in **caring** and domestic roles.

Family relationships are pursued in diverse ways. The traditional solidarity required by economic and social pressures became less important as disposable income rose and urbanisation dispersed pressures towards social conformity. Welfare states reduced the rigours of the **market**, so family members pursued a wider range of choices. Pressures grew for women to have a life and **identity** separate from or in addition to family roles. More frequent divorce and multicultural experiences of family living led to 'conjugal succession and elective family relationships' (Beck & Beck-Gernsheim, 2001: 96–7). If life became a process of **individualisation**, everyone conceiving and producing their own identities, families could develop diverse 'family practices', rather than fitting their identities into a standardised social structure (Morgan, 2011).

Social work interacted with changes in family life. Major social work agencies developed **family social work**, and interventions in families interact with social work ideas. In the early twentieth century, families were often seen as a cause or site of neglect or violence towards children and as a cause of child and youth offending. This was mostly the working-class family, but there was also wider concern about divorce and family break-up. In many such situations, the target family was seen as deviant from an idealised model of living, failing in caring and other social roles or producing social dislocation and problems. Families in working-class areas during the 1930s' economic depression were sometimes **labelled** as **problem families** because of poverty and unemployment. In a century in which widespread armed conflict and war also disrupted families, and events such as the Holocaust and racist movements scarred the social order and created troubles for family life, there were also attempts to shore up family life.

In the 1960s, UK social work, building on the success of local government children's departments established in 1948, began to see the whole family as the ideal location for tackling many social problems. Policy documents, reports and studies, for example the Seebohm Report (1968), proposed bringing together local government social work agencies to tackle the new problem of juvenile delinquency, rediscovered family **poverty** and child neglect. Social services departments (SSDs) were set up to coordinate social work through engaging with the whole family and its problems. Studies of family work in SSDs, however, found a focus on child behaviour problems. Family crises, such as financial problems, often involved **advocacy** with families' creditors and official agencies, but hopes for behaviour or attitude change 'in these grossly disturbed and deprived families' (Goldberg & Warburton, 1979: 107) were unrealistic. Instead, these families formed a residual group of SSDs' responsibilities. But despite the original intention that social work in SSDs would focus on the family and its needs, this did not work out, and after its high water mark in the 1970s, family social work in the UK receded into individualised practice.

Family group conferencing (FGC) is an international movement

based on Maori tradition from Aotearoa New Zealand. A family participates in conferences to decide with professionals planning for children, often where they are in public care. This practice (Crow & Marsh, 1998; Burford & Hudson (2017[2000]) draws on an **Indigenous** model using traditional community and family ideas, and therefore an example of Indigenist practice (Hart, 2019), as well as being an example of client and carer **participation**. Burford & Hudson (2017[2000]) make links to **ecological systems** practice, **person-in-environment** thinking, and **community social work**. FGC can be criticised as prioritising family participation over children's rights.

The success of family group conferencing has led to the transfer of the idea to adult services restorative youth justice (Wachtel, 2017[2000]), and policing (McCold & Wachtel, 2012), from a social work context. A similar practice of family conferences in healthcare is not theoretically connected in the social work literature with the research on family group conferencing, since the relationships between patients, patients' relatives and professionals is different.

Family social work refers both to agencies and to social work practice whose main objective is to help people within the context of their families, particularly in their care responsibilities in general and especially for children.

Families became the 'central focus' (Hartman, 1981) of social work in nineteenth-century practice. English Poor Law's lesser eligibility policies broke up families by separating husbands, wives and children as a disincentive for **dependence** on state services; this policy was exported to British colonies and the USA. Isolating children in this way, adversely affecting close personal relationships and problematic for child development, was part of the critique of Poor Law policies. More important for social work practice theory, charity organisation societies wanted to supplant alms-giving to individuals, to see individuals as part of a family that took responsibility for its members, like the Poor Law avoiding dependence, but this time on charity (W. Jordan, 1975).

In the USA, these concerns led to a substantial development of 'family agencies' in many cities, and family social work was an important locus of the development of social work. Mary **Richmond** (1965[1917]: 158) saw the 'family group' as crucial to social work assessment and practice:

> The good results of individual treatment crumble away often because the case worker has remained ignorant of his [sic] client's family history ... Early contacts with members of the Family Group are on a somewhat different plane from those with other sources of information, because the need of their co-operation in treatment is usually greater, and further contacts are more likely to follow. The family has a history of its own apart from the histories of those who compose it.

Mass unemployment in the 1930s led to an emphasis on family work in the UK to support impoverished people, but led to some families being seen as **problem families**. Wartime experience in the 1940s as children were evacuated from the cities demonstrated that supporting families also helped children (W. Jordan, 1975: 37–8). When local government children's departments were established in 1948, social work provision was separated from financial help for people in poverty. The initial focus was on regulating foster care and residential care for orphans. Post-war re-domestication of women after menfolk came back from the war, however, was a phenomenon of the Western world (Iacovetta, 1998) and increased ideological focus on family life. Agencies in north America and Europe saw family work as a preventive measure, avoiding the need for receiving children into public care.

Family support implements, in services and practice, in children's homes and the community, **activities** reinforcing social **networks**, so that early intervention prevents admission to public care, promoting and protecting children's health, wellbeing and rights within their families.

Theoretical constructs informing family support are as follows (Canavan, Pinkerton & Dolan, 2016):

- Social ecology, seeing the **family** as the microsystem, exploring outwards in wider systems, including community and school.
- **Resilience**, processes by which the family navigates and negotiates within systems surrounding the family.
- Social **support**, finding assistance from networks of outside individuals and agencies, building closeness and **reciprocity** in family and community networks.
- Social **capital** drawn from social support networks.

Frost, Abbott and Race (2015) argue that family support services produce a non-stigmatising service integrated within wide-ranging community provision for children. Sawyer and Burton (2016) also emphasise the importance of integrating services through joint protocols and strategies to promote shared working cultures and policy, client **participation**, staff training and skill development, and on tackling **race**, and **culture** issues, **stigma**. This also makes it easier to reach and involve fathers.

Family therapy is a multiprofessional form of specialised practice working with all or most members of families together as a group, addressing concerns about the family collectively and seeing issues affecting individuals as the product of family interaction, organisation and structure. It involves clinical psychologists, psychiatrists and sometimes social workers, usually in a clinic setting. There are three main forms:

- 'Structural family therapy' identifies and helps family members to alter patterns that form structures in their family relationships. For example, it may be difficult for parents to set boundaries for children.
- 'Strategic family therapy' helps people change or manage their identities as members of the family and everyday strategies for communicating with other family members. For example, people may get into repetitive patterns of behaviour, such as children ganging up to devalue their parents' attitudes.

- 'Systemic family therapy' explores the social rules about relationships within the family. For example, there may be conflict about roles in disciplining the children (Walker, 2015).

Feminist practice theory is a perspective on social work deriving

from feminist thought. Waves of feminist campaigns reflect different focuses on women's oppression (Wendt, 2019):

- The first wave (late nineteenth to early twentieth century) focused on women's political and legal **equality** in Western societies.
- The second wave (1960s onwards) concentrated on how barriers in the private sphere, such as family **caring** and oppressive interpersonal relationships with men, obstructed equal opportunities in work, in political influence and in the public sphere.
- The third wave (1990s onwards) shifted to how cultural values and **power** relations devalued women's experiences, and personal and social identities. Campaigners sought to generate a more complex and **intersectional** understanding of women's positions, for example black and disabled women's perspectives. During this phase of developing feminist thought, interaction with **postmodern** thinking formed social work's feminist practice analysis (Sands & Nuccio, 1992).
  A backlash also occurred against feminist campaigning, leading to claims of 'post-feminism', that feminism had achieved its aims, and created disadvantages for women, for example in denigrating women who chose private caring rather than public and work roles.
- A fourth wave identified issues about the representation of women and their concerns, asserting women's bodily **autonomy** and campaigning against misogyny, sexism and violence against women.

Critiques of feminism claim that it reflects Western middle-class and professional concerns, rather than the interests of women in **poverty** and those in resource-poor countries, where cultural, economic and political demands on women present different **oppressions**. Some arguments claim that feminism regards men as problems, heightening hostility and social barriers. Featherstone (2001) argued that feminist social work theory at that time failed to engage with debate about mothering and fathering and the negotiation of intimate relationships with men. Many men, however, adopt a 'pro-feminist' position, supporting the justice of women's campaigns. In social work and other helping professions, there are also concerns that a focus on feminist practice restricts work with women to specialised settings, such as agencies concerned with domestic violence, and fails to engage with mainstream settings. Against such views, there is pro-feminist practice by men concerned with women's oppression (Pease, 2001; Burrell & Flood, 2019), work on men's difficulties in relation to women, and mainstream practice focused on equality and **social justice** for women in many issues that social workers deal with.

Perspectives on feminist practice draw on various feminist positions, as follows:

- Liberal feminism, emphasising equal rights in **family** responsibilities and work.
- **Radical**, lesbian and cultural feminism, challenging **patriarchy** as giving power to men.
- **Marxist** or socialist feminism, exploring inequality generated by the class structure and its intersection with other **inequalities** and oppressions, together with women's role in **social reproduction**.
- **Black perspectives** and multiracial and cultural oppression, connecting with campaigns against other injustices.
- Postmodern, including 'queer' theory, concerning complex social relations and constructions of gender, and challenging surveillance in men's interests.
- Transnational and **post-colonial** concerns, challenging cultural legacies, child abduction, domestic slavery, female genital mutilation, people trafficking and similar transnational injustices (Saulnier, 1996).

The importance and value of these divisions are debated, but all these ideas contribute to actions helping women, and challenging how relationships with women and institutions exclude, **include** and respond to women.

Feminist practice (Wendt & Moulding, 2016; Butler-Morkoro & Grant, 2018) emphasises a **dialogic** style of interaction, in which practitioners promote equalised relationships. A review of studies of feminist practice effectiveness (Gorey, Daly, Richter, Gleason & McCallum, 2003) suggests that the source of its value lies in this mutuality of client–practitioner relationships in working on social issues facing clients, avoiding a behaviour-**change** perspective. Practice aims at opening alternatives to clients, raising clients' **consciousness** of gendered assumptions that limit their options and countering oppression of women. In interventions, feminist practice builds on women's **strengths** in three main areas:

- Issues about caring, focusing on mothering and fathering, equal caring roles with disabled or older relatives, reducing conflict in caring arrangements.
- Issues about relationships, particularly equality, intimacy and sharing, maintaining family ties, flexibility in family roles and relationships, building self-esteem and self-expression and resolving conflicts and violence.
- Issues about identity, valuing gender and sexuality, opening up new experiences and dialogue about identities, working on experiences of microaggressions.

Further Reading

Butler-Mokoro, S. & Grant, L. (Eds.) (2018). *Feminist perspective on social work practice: The intersecting lives of women in the 21st century.* New York: Oxford University Press.

Field is an important concept in social work, as follows:

- Lewin's (2010[1958]) field theory, one of the earliest sources of social psychology, influences **milieu** therapy, seeing human behaviour as the product of tensions and pressures interacting within the social environment. It explores identifying forces that act upon people as they operate within the limitations of social fields.
- **Bourdieu** conceptualises 'field' as social spaces in which we operate, forming consistencies in relationships between our position and that of others.
- **Fields** of practice ideas picture social work as a territory divided into fields of practice; practice methods or objectives vary according to the field's requirements. Defining fields of practice links with ideas about social work **specialisation** (Bartlett, 1961, 1970).

Fordism, from Henry Ford's name (the American motor car manufacturer), refers to the economic and social consequences of industrial manufacturing, with complex tasks divided into actions carried out in sequence on a production line. The resulting routine repetitive tasks cut costs and increase the speed of production of complex products like motor cars, by using less-skilled workers rather than traditional craftsmen. This increases the employer's power, and the power of capitalist elites, because unskilled workers can be easily replaced, thus displacing the power of representatives of workers' interests, such as trade unions.

This 'flexibilisation' allows capital and employers greater socio-economic control of labour resources, so that workers' tasks can be readily changed to fit the requirements of production. An industrial economy results, with low-paid workers having little influence on their work and life opportunities. In 'post-Fordist' and 'post-industrial' society, even these workers are displaced by robots, so that low-skilled, low-paid industrial work becomes less available, unemployment more commonplace and employment less secure. 'Massification' is the process by which industrialised societies see individuals as part of an undifferentiated herd who can be treated as a mass. The concept is similar to the eighteenth and nineteenth century concern about the existence of a volatile 'mob' of urban working people hostile to capitalist economic interests. In the late twentieth century, the idea claims that mass media misdirected people to favour the interests of capitalist elites and towards trivial entertainment rather than creative personal **self-actualisation. Freire** (1974[1967]: 32–5), the Brazilian radical educationalist and community worker, saw education as a countervailing process, and social work's **individualisation** of urban people offers another alternative social structure opposing massification.

Pinch (1994) argues that this process has increasingly affected service activities, including social work and similar professional activities. **McDonaldisation**, breaking complex discretionary tasks down into routinised **procedures**, is a tendency of contemporary practice theory associated with **neoliberal** economic thinking and **managerialist** approaches to administration in large organisations. This industrialises social work, **deprofessionalising** it so that its knowledge and skills are less valued, poorly rewarded and less influential.

Foucault, Michel (1926–1984), a French sociologist, is extremely influential in social work (Chambon, Irving & Epstein, 1999; Garrett, 2013: 167–88; Powell, 2013: 46–62; Hodgson & Watts, 2017: 52–62). He developed original conceptions of **power** relations in society based on work on **mental health**, and **institutionalisation** in mental health services and prisons, and the history of **sexuality** – areas of interest to social work, although he rarely addressed social work as such. One comment he made is as follows:

> … [S]ocial work is inscribed within a larger social function that has been taking on new dimensions for centuries, the function of surveillance-and-correction: to surveil individuals and redress them, in the two meanings of the word, alternatively as punishment and as pedagogy (cited in Chambon, 1999).

His work influenced **epistemology** and social theories of knowledge. Important concepts are as follows:

- 'Discipline' describes how people's behaviour is guided by applications of power, including formal punishments, like those applied by teachers in schools, or by the courts. Informal restraints in social relationships have the same effect, for example friends' and parents' expectations about behaviour. Disciplines such as these inform social work's practice knowledge about using power to manage deviance. Social work is one of the ways by which discipline is brought about, through facilitating learning and personal development. All its techniques are part of this. For example, **cognitive behavioural therapy, systems** or **relational** practice help people understand how the world works, so that they can comply with its demands. And helping people experience and understand how to influence their world through techniques such as **critical** and **feminist** or **macro** practice also disciplines their engagement with society.
- 'Governmentality' refers to the range of actions, knowledge, practices and understandings that manage and control how people behave in social institutions and relationships. It is how people know what should be done and for what purposes in society, drawing on social influences, interests and relationships. People are managed by law and regulation, but also by **self-direction** using knowledge from parents, school and institutions such as social work. Self-direction helps people gain power by learning how society finds it best to maintain control over their lives.

- **Surveillance** is an aspect of 'bio-power', that is, 'technologies' devised in societies to manage populations through control of people's **bodies**. Examples are managing health behaviour through health improvement ideas, leisure facilities, motivating stable lives through commitment to places linked to their social relationships in communities and families, and disciplining deviance from valued lifestyles. A specific example is how infection control mechanisms in the 2020 coronavirus pandemic included 'lockdowns', periods when people were required to stay at home and prevented from leisure and social contacts. Surveillance of populations, using electronic mechanisms such as security cameras in public transport, traffic cameras, automatic number plate recognition and automatic facial recognition software, is used to manage everyday movements of bodies. Human interactions such as home visits by social workers enable authorities to exercise power and allow people whose lives need management to be surveilled. Awareness of surveillance also contributes to discipline through self-management.

Foucault's work also refers to **normalisation** as the process through which ideas and rules about appropriate social behaviour and organisation are formulated and transferred in the social expectations that are present, and that we perceive, in social relations.

Foundationalism and 'essentialism' are ways of thinking about ideas and the world that assume that our knowledge and understanding is built up from our perceptions about the reality of the world. What we perceive and sense, to the foundationalist, provides a foundation on which we build all our understanding and arguments. Talking about the 'foundations' of a subject assumes that there is a starting point for building a logical superstructure of understanding.

All things, including ideas, have a set of natural characteristics which define them and make them what they are, an essence. An example is defining social work assuming that it has similar characteristics everywhere. This leads on to a view that categories of people also have an essence, a defining set of characteristics by which we understand what they are; for example that women and men or homosexual and heterosexual people are different in characteristic ways. These positions contest **interpretivist** and **postmodern** views that knowledge and understanding are **contextual**: it depends on the social assumptions that come from historical development of and the social relations within a particular situation. They are, moreover, **objectivist** and universalist, assuming that we can clarify the definition of something by neutral analysis and observation, so that we can identify it whenever we see it, and that this understanding holds true anywhere.

Frame analysis and framing theorise how people organise their perceptions and understandings of the world around them, and lead to the important practice concept of **reframing**, changing people's analysis of the issues that face them.

Influential sources of these ideas are the American sociologist, **Erving Goffman**, **family therapy** and Jacques Lacan.

Fraser, Nancy is a **feminist** philosopher whose **identity** politics position argues (Fraser, 2000) that **recognition** of oppressed social groups contributes to social justice but fails to assert fair 'redistribution' of resources. Her theory of **justice** (Fraser, 2008) proposes that **globalisation** requires supranational mechanisms for **equality** and justice.

F

Freedom, and its connected term, liberty, underlies social work values such as **self-determination** and **participation**, and is sometimes contrasted with the idea of **determinism**. It also influences the importance of **human rights** in social work thinking and connects with issues of **power** and practice theory on **empowerment**. Many human actions assume that human beings are in nature free to make decisions and take **actions** based on those decisions, but in a social animal such freedom is constrained by the needs of the **community** (Haines, 1966). These matters are significant to social work practice because their interventions may be seen by clients as constraining or interfering with their freedom. Since clients may already be affected by **disadvantage**, distress or **oppression**, social work may be an attack on their already restricted freedom, cloaked in positive professional values such as **caring** or **helping**.

Freedom has three elements (MacCallum, 1967):

- An agent – someone or something that is acting in a situation.
- A constraint – someone or something that is constraining the agent's action.
- An objective – what the agent wants to achieve.

The source and the area of constraint contributes to understanding how someone's freedom is limited (Berlin, 1969). We can think of freedom in various ways, as follows:

- The absence of constraints on freedom to act.
- The availability of choices to allow us to decide.
- The ability and resources to act effectively.
- The status of possessing social rights to act freely.
- Self-determination and free will, the opportunity to establish our social position so that we can express our choices in our actions, 'to be the author of our own actions'.
- To be able to meet our desires, to do what we want to do.
- Self-mastery, the personal intellectual and social capacity to take up our choice among the options available (Gray, 1991).

These points are elements in people's freedom to act without constraint. To pursue social work ideals and manage appropriately the exercise of professional **authority**, influence and **power**, social work practice and theory need to include constraints on freedom.

Freire, Paulo

Freire, Paulo (1921–1997) was a Brazilian educator, whose ideas about creating social change through a critical pedagogy (Freire, 1970, 1972), produced during a time of political ferment in South America, were internationally influential. He argued that the 'banking model' of education, in which teachers put knowledge into the receptacle of a student's brain, needed to be replaced, particularly for oppressed people. Instead, a **dialogical** pedagogy would raise **consciousness** of class and other oppression and enable people to explore and gain collective control of alternative ways of living their lives. The educator worked as a 'problem-poser' to help groups identify issues that were hidden from them and identify their importance to them in their personal experience.

Freire's approach includes connection to personal experience through **praxis**. This is a process of becoming informed by critical dialogue about experience that has strengthened your consciousness of oppression. People become able to construct actions that implement understanding derived from that experience. Interpreted into social work practice, this enables practice interventions to use theory to incorporate consciousness from critically analysed experience. Rather than relying on theory alone, practitioners inform interventions using the understanding gained from their critical pedagogy. Shor (1993) identifies four qualities of Freirean practice:

- **Power** awareness: understanding that people create history by people organising to take up power available to them.
- **Critical** literacy: building skills in analysing events and experiences, going beneath routine and surface understandings.
- Resocialisation: recognising and challenging social assumptions generated in everyday discourse, particularly where it is produced in popular culture and the mass media.
- Self-education: seeking opportunities to explore and research **transformational** possibilities, for example those that avoid or reduce unequal distribution of power.

Leonard (1993) argues that bringing together both **Gramsci**'s critique of cultural hegemony as a basis for oppression and Freire's approach to practical critical analysis allows practitioners to develop both methods and understanding that can inform a critical practice.

Further Reading

McClaren, P. & Leonard, P. (Eds.) (1993). *Paulo Freire: A critical encounter.* London: Routledge.

Freud, Sigmund

Freud, Sigmund (1856–1939) was a Viennese neurologist and psychiatrist, who, around the turn of the twentieth century, created **psychoanalysis**, a treatment for mental illness and a system of cultural thought. Its wide influence in Western psychiatry and culture continues today, through developments by his followers and critics. It had a strong impact on American social work from the 1920s until the 1960s, and later in other countries (Yelloly, 1980).

Functional analysis of social work **roles** or **tasks** was an important area of

study in the 1970s that influenced conceptions of social work specialisation (Briggs, 1973). Widely cited US studies (Barker & Briggs, 1968; Teare & McPheeters, 1970) differentiated roles in 'intra-professional' teams in social work services that could be undertaken by non- or para-professionals (what would now be called 'social care workers' in the UK), where qualified social workers, in short supply at the time, were not available or required. The model distinguished three aspects of role or task differentiation, as follows:

- Domains of living (like the contemporary concept 'activities of daily living') where clients experienced difficulties.
- Status of clients' functioning (from wellbeing, through stress, **problems**, **crisis** to **disability**).
- Obstacles to clients' functioning (personal or environmental deficiencies, rigid law or regulation, catastrophes).

Teams, including qualified social workers and paraprofessionals, were allocated tasks according to complexity (Barker & Briggs, 1969; Brieland, Briggs & Leuenberger, 1973); teams were seen as **small groups** and a connection was made with interprofessional practice (Kane, 1975: Ch. 3). The British Association of Social Workers (1976), pursuing a **professionalisation** agenda, used this work to differentiate tasks within social work practice, designating some as requiring professional qualification. Interest developed in the use of **teamwork** to respond to increasing workloads in the reorganised UK social services (Lonsdale, Webb & Briggs, 1980). A similar concept in healthcare of 'skill mix' is also connected with interest in developing inter- or multiprofessional teamwork, although there is no evidence that such management arrangements are more effective than other ways of organising teams, for example in professional groups (Needleman, 2017).

Functional practice in social work was a psychodynamic practice theory

prominent from the 1930s to the 1960s. Its theoretical position is unconnected with **functionalism** in sociological theory. It was created by Jessie Taft and Virginia P. Robinson, influenced by the psychoanalytic ideas of Otto **Rank**. Rank stressed the role of an inborn 'will' towards 'individuation', achieving a personal **identity**, a **self**. Rank's position is one of the sources of self theory in **psychoanalysis** and more widely. Functional practice methods focused on the meaning of clients' difficulties in the here-and-now as part of their struggle towards self-identity, rather than (as in the **diagnostic** theory of practice) seeking to diagnose, differentiate and 'treat' behavioural problems; it was therefore less **psychologised**.

The **agency** function held both worker and client in a shared reality, which differed from the reality in another setting. Agency function, not the practitioner, sets the focus of **activity**, through resources given for its purposes by its community and management. Clients also do not set the purpose, because they come or are sent to the agency because of it. Smalley (1967: 22) argues that agency function is, therefore, a defining feature of the process that is enacted as practitioner and client work together, imposing limits of action and timing on what is to be done. In this way, functional casework is an important source of planning and thinking about timescales within the service, and favours agency rather than clients' and workers' definitions of practice aims.

During the period of its importance, functional theory contested the pre-eminence of **diagnostic** casework, in a tension thought at the time to be unresolvable. Functional social work claimed first that social workers were not healthcare or psychiatric adjuncts, and second, that social casework had a distinctive contribution to make in its areas of service, as follows:

- Providing **help**, not healing or treatment.
- Because of its process, using a relationship to provide the help.
- Because of its accountability to wider social policy through providing interventions that fulfilled agency function, hence the name of this theory (Timms, 1983: 78–82).

Further Reading

Smalley, R. E. (1967). *Theory for social work practice*. New York: Columbia University Press.

Functionalism is a theoretical position in sociology; see **Structural-functionalism**.

Gandhi, Mohandas Karamchand (Mahatma [venerable] Gandhi)

(1869–1948) was an Indian lawyer and politician, some of whose political thinking has been developed to form a **Gandhian** social work in Indian practice and social development. Its view of peaceful resistance is inspirational as an aspect of **activism** more widely. His ideas aroused interest for his ideological position. Active work by his supporters aimed to achieve social reconstruction prioritising provision for lower caste 'dalit' or untouchable people and other oppressed Indian populations, including women. It is thus a theorisation about working to remove social class divisions. Desai (2002: 138–9) judges that social and political movements supporting Gandhi were unattractive to the **professionalising** Indian social work education during the 1960s, which sought to achieve a less activist role at that time, but Gandhian social work still has adherents.

Gender is identity connected to the cultural and social norms of male or female sexuality, rather than the biological differences.

General systems theory was an early development of **systems** theory,

first influential from the 1940s to '70s in social work. It provides the basic concepts of systems ideas, which inform the practice theory. Derivations from it include in particular **ecological systems** theory and the **life model** practice theory, and general terminology such as **macro** practice.

Generalist and generic practice have related but separate meanings.

Generalist practice is an American term referring to practice using more than one of the practice 'modality', in particular the traditional practice specialisms of casework, groupwork and community work, to address a wide range of clients' difficulties and social environments. Generic practice makes essentialist or **foundationalist** claims that there is a shared set of social work practices that, together with broad knowledge and understanding about human behaviour and social situations, form a transferable core of principles and skills capable of being used in any specialised form of social work. A single practitioner works with people at different stages of life in different settings with different forms of practice. The main critique is that this requires too much knowledge about the issues facing each clients, and that specialisation in particular problems or populations is more effective, and better understood by clients and professional colleagues.

A generalist practitioner has the capacity to shift from one modality to another, or use more than one, working with individual clients, in groups and developing community resources. The critique of doing this is that modalities have different timescales and objectives, and agencies may reject valid professional practice activities in a particular situation. An example is where public or agency policy focuses on child **safeguarding** rather than **family support** in the community.

Generic practice has implications for **social work** education, claiming that a generic core can be applied in any setting or form of practice. This permits specialised knowledge and understanding, for example about specific client groups or fields or forms of practice, to be added at a later stage to practitioners who are competent in the generic principles and skills. Generic social work education practice was controversial in the USA from the 1940s to '70s. This had a worldwide impact on the understanding of social work and was an issue in debate about the **professionalisation** of social work.

These issues arose during the first part of the twentieth century, where US social work education in major urban centres developed Master's-level education on **casework** practice in major family charities. Smaller towns and rural areas often centred on more collective and public service approaches to social work, especially in the major economic depression of the 1930s, and in areas where there were substantial black populations. In the early 1950s, American social work education coalesced round a generic Master's-level education. US development of international social work to support Western democratising policies in the Cold War transferred this to become a global gold standard (Askeland & Payne, 2017: Ch. 1).

One of those influences was on the British social services department developments in the 1970s, providing a broad official social work. The aim was to create a system similar to 'general practice' in primary healthcare. Social workers would assess new clients, providing basic care and services, and refer complex problems on or be supported by specialised advisers. Not every generic social worker was well-suited to serve all client groups, and trying this led to a loss of confidence by clients, families and professionals in education and healthcare, in social workers' expertise and understanding.

Generic practice theory emphasises understanding **agency** and practice objectives, social concepts such as the **family** or **power**, building good interpersonal skills and knowledge of practice theory. Increasingly, however, detailed understanding of the issues facing particular client groups is more valued. Some issues were also policy priorities in agencies. In the period of the Blair and Brown Labour governments of 1997–2010, implementing policy priorities led to an emphasis on specialised jobs being created to meet specific policy objectives, even though their practice largely implemented generic skills (Jordan with Jordan, 2000).

Germain, Carel Bailey (1916–1995) was an American social work
academic, influential in creating the **life model** of social work practice with Alex
Gitterman. Her accounts of the history of social work theory (Germain, 1970) and of
concepts of time (Germain, 1976) and place (Germain, 1978) in social work, written as
building blocks to the life model, were also influential.

Giddens, Anthony is an important sociological theorist based at the
University of Cambridge, UK. His contribution to social work theory is through his
extensive theoretical commentary on contemporary affairs, including **globalisation,**
modernism and **postmodernism** (1990). In the later twentieth and early twenty-first
century, he was a prominent exponent of 'third-way' politics, seeking a **progressive**
alternative politics to conservatism and socialism (Giddens, 1998, 2000).

G

Gilligan, Carol is an American **feminist** educationalist and psychologist, whose
book *In a different voice* (Gilligan, 1993[1982]) is an important source of the **ethics of**
care values perspective.

Globalisation is a historical process connecting economic, political and cultural
trends that reduce the strength of national boundaries and national **identity**. Four
features of late twentieth-century globalisation are as follows:

- Deregulated global markets in services such as banking, insurance and transport,
  and in consumer goods.
- New global actors, such as multinational corporations integrating production and
  marketing, and attempts at global regulation by groupings of national governments.
- New rules and norms regulating global activities such as human rights conventions,
  environment conventions and multilateral trade agreements.
- New communication tools such as the Internet and email linking many people
  simultaneously, cellular (mobile) phones, fast cheap air transport and computer-
  aided design.

Economic accounts of globalisation focus on capitalism and **neoliberal** economic policy. In contemporary economies, capitalism or 'late' or 'advanced' capitalism, **business**
organisations have become increasingly efficient at accumulating capital to finance more
complex and extensive activities, particularly through transnational organisations.

Political and social structures mirror this process. Nation states are less in control of
their economies, and transnational companies often have larger economies than states.
Nations cannot manage their economies to protect local producers or social welfare.

Developed nations get richer, while less-developed nations are less able to compete and lose employment.

Important cultural changes arise from migration and travel. Migrants usually form somewhat separate communities in the new country, retaining cultural and social traditions. This then leads to **diversity** as social traditions from different cultures make many countries more heterogeneous. Globalised consumer opportunities and trends create a more homogenised generalised culture, and national cultures may lose some of their identity. On the other hand, a global economy makes a wide range of cultural possibilities available to more people, and local cultures may have opportunities to have influence elsewhere. As the nation state's political power declines, localisation, ethnicity and culture may become more important than nationality in defining and defending people's social identities, and globalisation may make cultural links across national borders more important than national identities. Consumerisation creates identities connected to fashion and trends in the mass and social media.

Economic, cultural and political changes of this kind emphasise constantly changing economic development. This makes it hard to maintain stability in social identities and relationships, and in providing social welfare. While some social groups gain economically, others lose out, but cultural change demands constant adherence to consumerised lifestyles and there are fewer resources and less commitment to providing social welfare and social work.

Further Reading

Stiglitz, J. (2002). *Globalization and its discontents*. New York: Norton.

Goffman, Erving (1922–1982) was an American sociologist of Canadian heritage,
whose work was influential in social work because of his early research on **total institutions**, based on work in large psychiatric hospitals previously called 'asylums' (Goffman, 1968[1961]), and **stigma** (Goffman, 1968[1963]). Both of these studies affected how social workers perceived the importance of **deinstitutionalisation** policies in the 1960s and people's reactions to **stigmatisation** because they experienced personal and social problems. This was not just a process of **labelling**, but involved complex social relationships in which social workers played a part. Studies of everyday life and how people **framed** their views of social interactions (Goffman, 1974), and adapted how **performances** managed the impressions that others have of them (Goffman, 1968), created a dramaturgical **role** theory and underlies many of the ideas later developed in **social construction** theory.

Goldstein, Howard (1922–2000) was an American social worker and
academic. His use of systems ideas as a unifying approach to social work practice

(Goldstein, 1973) contributed to the significant impact of systems theory on social work in the 1970s. He subsequently contributed to **cognitive** theory with **humanistic** elements balancing the rational and subjective elements of behaviour change (Goldstein, 1981, 1984) before its incorporation into **cognitive behavioural** practice.

Gramsci, Antonio (1891–1937) was a prominent Italian **Marxist** philosopher and revolutionary, whose major works were notebooks written during his imprisonment by Mussolini's Fascist regime. His crucial contribution to social work theory, in particular **community work**, was cultural **hegemony**, the idea, subsequently taken forward by **Habermas** and other Frankfurt School theorists, that capitalist classes influenced cultural ideas to maintain the dominance of oppressive economic and social understandings of society.

G

Group care conceives of residential care, particularly of children, as consisting of looking after people in human **groups**. These groups may represent an ideal of community or social responsibility for childcare, but are sometimes seen as, perhaps inadequate, substitutes for family care. Communal living and utopian models of care were influential in the 1960s. These sometimes proposed that group care enabled socialisation of children into socially appropriate attitudes, behaviours and values. Examples include idealisation in the 1960s of Soviet boarding schools and Israeli *kibbutzim* where children are cared for collectively, partly to secure commitment to the society's social ideologies (Wolins, 1969[1965]). The direction of **therapeutic community** developments for work with behavioural disorders and adults with mental illness derive partly from such concerns in this period. During the later twentieth century, ideas of group care sought to professionalise and improve the therapeutic quality of residential care by emphasising groupwork as an important professional skill in institutional settings (Ainsworth & Fulcher, 1981). Similar ideas and objectives are represented in **social pedagogy**, and in efforts to introduce it in the UK.

Groups and **small groups** are often the setting of social work practice, particularly in **groupwork**, and they are also the basis of thinking about **teamwork**. A group may be of any size, but the concept implies connections between the members.

Groupwork is a form of social work in which the practitioner aims to achieve social work aims through interaction with a small number (usually between 3 and 15) of clients or other target service users, such as carers or relatives. The practice emerged from the settlement movement and informal education, particularly of young people (Reid, 1981). Aims in groupwork history include rescue (often leading to groupwork in community, educational and residential care settings), mutual aid, social action, leadership development and **liberation** objectives (McCaughan, 1978). Groupwork was important in ideas on **community** organisations as **networks** and groups, propounded by Mary **Parker Follett**,

Grace Longwell Coyle and Ada **Sheffield** in the 1920s. Coyle (1939a), for example, argued that groupwork could help casework practitioners understand the importance of non-family groups in people's lives, for instance for young people in school and leisure settings, and emphasised people's collective lives (1939b: 567) and also that educational groupwork should raise clients' consciousness of needs for social action. Parker Follett (1998[1918]) saw collective process in local groups as developing collective will. This brings a unity in social processes, which is always in tension with the **individualism** of **liberal** thinking.

With the impact of psychotherapeutic thinking on social work, groupwork developed enabling, personal development and psychotherapeutic aims (Shapiro, 1991). In the UK, Bion's (1961) psychodynamic work was influential. It explored hidden social needs for **dependency**, managing **authority** and **power** within group relationships that impelled non-task-related behaviour.

Papell and Rothman's (1966) analysis of groupwork objectives is as follows:

- Remedial groups help individuals with problems change unwanted patterns of behaviour. All behaviour-change groupwork is remedial.
- **Reciprocal** groups involve group members in **co-production** in self-help and mutual support.
- Social goals groups develop community, family and personal education activities.

Much contemporary groupwork is pragmatic to meet agency aims (Trevithick, 2012; Lindsay & Orton, 2014), and is interagency or interprofessional in its organisation, personnel and setting, requiring careful planning.

Psychotherapeutic theories used in groupwork (Crawford, Price & Price, 2016) include **cognitive behavioural** (Bieling, McCabe & Anthony, 2006), **empowerment** (Staub-Bernasconi, 1992; Lee, 1997), **feminist** (Butler & Wintram, 1991; Turner & Maschi, 2015), **humanistic** (Glassman, 2009), **psychodynamic** (Tosone, 2009) and **solution** (Sharry, 2007) ideas. **Self-directed groupwork** is a model of groupwork practice that focuses on empowerment and social change objectives (Mullender, Ward & Fleming, 2013).

Among the issues in many groupwork settings are **affiliation**, associative and interactive processes, how people become attached to a group, build connections with each other and interact to achieve what they want from the group (Douglas, 1993). Other theoretical models are concerned with the process of the development of the group itself, rather than the members of it (Bernstein, 1965, 1970; Douglas, 1979: Ch. 6).

Further Reading

Crawford, K., Price, M. & Price, B. (2016). *Groupwork practice for social workers.* London: Sage.

H

Habermas, Jürgen is a German philosopher and public intellectual, a contemporary representative of the tradition of the Frankfurt School of **critical** theory, which has developed Marxist thinking. Habermas' interest for social work lies in three areas;

- 'Communicative action' explores problems of **modernity** in providing for empowerment and liberation, the second 'Global Definition of Social Work' (International Federation of Social Workers, 2014a) objective. While the **Enlightenment** allowed for **freedom** from **authoritative** control by the use of reason, this led to stultifying **bureaucratic** rationalisation and **commodification**, particularly in state organisations like those where social workers often practise. Official organisations were cut off from the communities they served, damaging bureau-professions such as social work. Habermas uses **systems** ideas to distinguish an over-rational 'system world', comprising bureaucratic institutions in capitalist and state organisations, and the 'lifeworld', comprising the domestic, family and community sphere and organisations where human communication and interpersonal values dominate. The system world is increasingly invading the lifeworld. Social work clearly operates in the lifeworld using human communication as its most important tool, but by often being part of the state or large organisations, its aims have been subverted, first by excessive rationalisation and then by a **neoliberal** emphasis on economic rationalisation rather than human relationships.

  Houston (2013) discusses communicative action in this process. The human way of organising things is through people reaching a consensual reasoned understanding about their aims and actions. This requires cooperative, open and participative people working together through communication. Doing this, they identify where 'disorders of discourse' mean failure to agree on a way forward. This contrasts with 'strategic action', commonplace in business and management circles, where people work for their own ends, and communication is focused on achieving selfish outcomes.

  Critiques of these ideas suggest that it is impracticable for bureaucratic and neoliberal influences to be countered by different forms of communication. Garrett (2018a: 153–66), for example, suggests that transparent communication and effective discourse are not enough to overcome oppressive misuse of power in social relationships. **Feminists** also argue that ideas about the lifeworld contain patriarchal assumptions that the domestic sphere, family and women should be the response to economic and structural issues. Many social workers find, however, that the life and system worlds ideas clarify issues that they experience in their work and in political and social conflicts.

- Habermas treats **discourse** as a form of social analysis within social communication. Communicative activity includes norms of argument and discussion, but discourse arises when we question taken-for-granted assumptions about how we choose our agenda for discussion and the arguments that we make. Unless this is possible, public debate becomes twisted. Gray and Lovat (2008), looking at moral and **religious** discourse, suggest that Habermas' idea of 'emancipatory knowing' helps social work free up understanding by exploring where ideas come from, in different moral and political discourses, and what they mean in practice. For social work, this connects with why it is useful to **disrupt** the distorted assumptions by which people operate (Blaug, 1995). In practice, we look for ways to get people to think again about what seems possible, and positive practices such as solution and strengths practices aim to do this.
- Habermas' account of contemporary political economy sees **globalisation** and **neoliberal thinking** as distortions in discourse and moral reasoning leading to disruption of the lifeworld.

Habitus is a concept developed by **Bourdieu**, and refers to people's usual ways of seeing and reacting to the world in patterns of behaviour. For example, people often have patterns of **emotional** reaction to situations and others who know their emotional habitus have expectations about how they will usually react to a situation that generates emotions. They may react to the habitus, trying to forestall expected reactions that they want to avoid or stimulate reactions that may be useful to them. Social workers may therefore find it useful to explore and understand habitus in people that they are involved with, to understand what others expect in social relations and how they respond to that. Cultural expectations may also influence people's emotional habitus, and social workers can also learn about a group's culture and history by understanding habitus.

Halmos, Paul was a British social scientist, who argued (Halmos, 1965) that helping professions, which he termed '**counsellors**', were displacing political and spiritual solutions to human problems. Later, Halmos (1970) extended this to propose that the need for care, education and helping professions has become never-ending in advanced industrial societies. He also (Halmos, 1978) argued that helping practice in social work could not be displaced by political and social action; both needed to be held in balance.

Hegemony is the idea that cultural ideas can dominate people's thinking, thus regulating their actions in social relations and governing the policies of institutions, as powerfully as or more so than coercion. It is an important aspect of the ideas of **Gramsci** and **Habermas** and shows how cultural ideas exercise social control in society.

Helping, one of the main theorisations of the identity of social work, sees social work as a 'helping profession', contesting **care** and **caring** as a theorisation of social work's nature. These ideas propose that social work may be understood as an institutionalised, organised extension of natural, even instinctive, human behaviour. Theorisations of helping emphasise the importance of addressing people's reality in the help offered, and the value of openness and interpersonal engagement by clients and practitioners in a helping **process**.

Keith-Lucas' (1972) classic account of helping derives from **functional** practice, which identified helping as one of the distinctive features of social casework, as opposed to a **medicalised** view of cure, diagnosis and treatment (Taft, 1962[1937]: 312). In this view, help is something tangible or intangible given by one person to another or one group to another, in such a way that the other can make use of it to increase their choices in improving self-fulfilment in their experience of life. Most people do not want to be helped, and helping includes recognising that it must be given in such a way that the helper facilitates the choice to use it actively and willingly, even by being demanding or insistent. Helping, therefore, contains the following factors:

- A connection with the reality of the situation that the helped person faces.
- Empathy that the situation must be faced.
- Support in facing and dealing with the situation.

Empathy opens the door, **support** allows the person being helped to take the required actions. Helpers may gain satisfaction from giving the help and its outcomes but should not be preoccupied by its difficulties; they need not be perfect or self-abnegating, but they should be satisfied by helping without needing a defined outcome.

Jordan's (1979) account of helping places it in the context of helping in the services of large **bureaucratic** public agencies, emphasising access to services that mitigate **inequalities** and **oppression**. Social workers provide help because of their life experiences of helping and being helped. Empathy, using experience of reverses in practitioners' lives, allows practitioners to **affirm** and respond to clients' experiences of oppression. We experience the truth of their reality, and they experience the truth of our commitment to helping and engagement with them.

Shakespeare (2000), focusing on disability from his own experience, identifies four unhelpful aspects of help:

- Polarisation, creating a stronger distinction between the problem you are helping with and the situation where your client does not have a problem, like discrepancy in **motivational interviewing**. This suggests that social work help should not exaggerate or affirm the problems but should emphasise the opportunities; challenge should be **normalised** because we all face challenges.

- Burden, seeing problems as a burden on others or on society, creating **dependence**. Rather, social work help should value the positives of needing and using **helping** to build relationships and networks among people.
- **Voice**, lacking the opportunity for clients to speak for themselves to define the issues that they face and the help that they need.
- Infantilisation, seeing someone who needs help as infants needing care for everything, instead of identifying their specific needs for help and building on their **strengths**.

Many accounts of helping deriving from psychology focus on using interpersonal skills. An example is Carkhuff's model of helping, recently re-formulated by Carkhuff with Benoit (2019). The helper develops an interpersonal process between helper and 'helpee'. A pre-helping phase is the social work engagement process, to create **alliance**, attending to the helpee to involve them in the process. Then there are three phases of helping:

- Responding to what the helpee says, to facilitate exploring the issues, akin to the social work assessment process.
- **Personalising** the issues to facilitate understanding of how they are affecting the helpee, developing their **meaning** and the relevance of potential goals of their actions. All this is again part of social work assessment.
- Building on the understanding achieved, the helper works at initiating action with the client; this is a process of developing a programme of actions, identifying steps to take and monitoring what has been done.

This account of the helping process is a formulation, from the point of view of helping, of the conventional psychological models of behaviour **change** that we find in **cognitive behavioural**, **solution** and **task-centred** practice. Like such models, used in clinical psychology and **counselling** it treats helping as a **technical rational** process, used primarily with individuals, although it can be adapted to families and groups.

Holism, connects **respect** for persons with seeing the world as interconnected, only understood with reference to the whole. A longstanding ideal, this view contests **individualism**. Applying holism in social work leads us to think of Donne's (1624) meditation: 'No man [sic] is an island entire of itself.' From social work's beginning, theorising clients as a **case** documented in a **case record** was about the whole situation, not individuals and particular events or problems. This idea is particularly characteristic of **eco** practice, where human life is entwined with the natural environment. An important practice tradition of the person-in-situation or person-in-environment typical of ecological systems practice and its forerunners – diagnostic and psychosocial practice and Richmond's view of social **casework** – emphasises practice that brings together psychological and social aspects of issues facing social work clients. Holism is also important in various aspects of assessment, critical reflection and social justice, and in many **Indigenous** traditions incorporated into social work across the world.

Imbrogno and Canda (1988) review social work's holistic thinking in social work. **Systems** theory sees everything as part of a wider whole. System levels are interdependent, homologous in structure, seeking correspondence between structures. **Humanistic** and **spiritual** practices argue for a phenomenological, non-dichotomous understanding of people and the world, and much Eastern thinking along with Western **postmodernism** is concerned with desirability, emergence and possibility contesting the exactitude sought by **evidence-based** ideas' concern with causality, objectivity and logical dichotomy. Dichotomous thinking is also contested by **feminist** thinking: not 'either–or' but 'and–also'. Chinese thinking observes constant flow and change, natural and constant, and in Ying/Yang opposites there are also connectedness, the complementary and mutually inclusive.

H

Hope is an expectation that something positive will happen, although balanced in action by rational assessment of reality. Many interpersonal practices propose helping people to feel hope, including **existentialism**'s emphasis on **dread**, the **life** and **relational** models of practice. Social workers offer hope in **relationship** with clients, particularly where clients seek **recovery** from mental illness, depression and anxiety. Both **motivational interviewing** and **strengths** practices hold hope as important to their objectives.

Human rights are rights, moral or legal entitlements, possessed by everyone because they are human beings. Not all rights are human rights, since belief, faith or moral thinking may confer entitlements, and categories of human beings gain rights from efficient management or policy; human beings may confer entitlements on animals or other non-humans. Because human rights are an entirely human creation, a **discourse** constantly in debate, they are expressed in codes or laws. Complying with and promoting human rights is a requirement of many social work codes of ethics and of the Global Definition of Social Work created by the international associations concerned with social work (International Federation of Social Workers, 2014a). If agencies and states accept this, human rights codes will form a direction for or restrain social work practice.

Ife's (2012) account of human rights social work recognises human rights as a product of **Enlightenment** thinking, and therefore of **individualised** Western culture, which is not necessarily consonant with alternative political philosophies and spiritual ideas. In particular, an Asian critique seeks adherence to collective rights. He suggests that human rights must apply to all humanity, be widely accepted across cultures, be realisable without being in limited supply and not contradictory to other rights. This last point suggests that there is no right to use arms or hold others in **slavery**.

He identifies three generations of human rights:

- Civil and political rights, such as rights to self-expression and the vote.
- Economic, social and cultural rights, for example to work, achieve healthcare, education, personal development.
- Collective rights responding to the Asian critique, to economic development, or a good environment.

Ife raises a range of issues concerned with practice, including engagement in local discourses about rights, and methods such as **praxis**.

Further Reading

Ife, J. (2012). *Human rights and social work: Towards rights-based practice* (3rd ed.). Port Melbourne: Cambridge.

Humanistic practice interprets for social work a tradition of psychological and therapeutic theory. A personal helping practice, humanistic work attends primarily to clients' beliefs, feelings and responses about their life and the world, rather than to their relationships, unlike **relational** practice. It focuses on the most intimate or troubled relationships that people need to think through. **Existential** and **person-centred** practice are important humanistic practices. Drawing on person-centred practice, humanistic practitioners would use the **core conditions** of practitioner behaviour in effective therapeutic relationships to facilitate the relationship and enable clients to use the practitioner's help.

Humanistic psychotherapies, including social work, help people to make the most of their experience of being an **object**, with the world's impacts affecting them. They use these experiences to have greater impact on the world as a **subject** with human **agency** and **self-efficacy**. With this external impact, they make progress as part of the group of people around them, moving cooperatively towards **self-actualisation**. This empowers people as human beings to gain more control in their social relations.

Two important sources of these approaches are as follows:

- Humanism is a philosophy or system of spiritual thought emphasising the capacity of human beings to use rational thought to manage their lives and the natural world. It therefore values all human beings and all human knowledge and understanding, including art, human creativity of all kinds and science. Secular humanism rejects the idea of a supernatural being or god being able to intervene in that human rationality, while religious humanists emphasise human responsibility to use divinely given humanity to accept personal responsibility for their environment and human life. Human beings are social by nature, and find meaning in relationships, seeking self-actualisation by developing their capacities to benefit society through humanitarian action. Humanity's social nature is expressed through accepting democratic collective responsibility for cultivating the progress of human civilisation and society. Such values have informed social work throughout its existence. Contributions to social work using this perspective are **Goldstein's** (1981, 1984) integration of cognitive psychology and humanistic psychologies focusing on **artistic** and creative activity, and my later formulation (Payne, 2011).

- Phenomenology, derived from Husserl, suggests that experience enables our understanding of things outside ourselves; it is important to pay attention to all the aspects of our experience of the world. All knowledge and understanding, therefore, comes from the appearance of things, how we perceive and process those perceptions, although the reality of what we perceive contributes to that appearance. Shared knowledge comes from how we examine, describe and explain our observations of the world.

H

Consistent with humanist values, humanistic social work practice seeks self-efficacy so that people's self-actualised capacity can contribute to the shared responsibility for collectively managing human institutions and social relations. Valuing all human beings implies working to achieve equality and social inclusion for everyone. This includes both affective and social equality, the freedom to engage with their feelings and social relationships, including equal involvement in **discourse** with others, **dialogue** on equal terms with others and building individual and shared **narratives** of their lives and relationships. Practitioners explore complexity and seek flexibility in people's lives, promote caring, mutuality, artistic achievement and creativity, and help them develop self, identity and spirituality in their lives.

Further Reading

Payne, M. (2011). *Humanistic social work: Core principles in practice*. Basingstoke: Palgrave Macmillan.

Humanitarianism is distinct from humanism. It is a belief in the importance of being concerned about and securing human wellbeing through social action or social reform.

I

Identity is the collection of characteristics that allow us to distinguish a person or thing from others, particularly if they are similar. In all nature, there is **diversity** which provides a range of human and natural resources. Except for manufactured artefacts, completely identical people or things do not exist. The social sciences, including social work, are concerned, therefore, with features:

- that distinguish a person from other people, their personal identity.
- that a person uses to define the nature of their humanity, their **self-identity**.
- that distinguish social groups from other groups, their social identity.

Identity cannot be a totalising reality of a group or individual, but we cannot reject the importance of the group or person's internal concept of their **self** (Craib, 1998). People have differing experiences of individuals, and social **contexts** in which identities are created and experienced by others are complex. But **psychoanalysis** tells us that self-identity is not complete, because the **insight** into un**conscious** knowledge and understanding is always a possibility.

Postmodern thinking questions the stability of identity. It is an **individualist** concept, in which the similarities define stable distinctions in social relations. Bauman (2000a: 83) claims: 'Identities seem fixed and solid only when seen, in a flash, from outside. Whatever solidity they may have when contemplated from the inside of one's own biographical experience appears fragile, vulnerable and constantly torn apart...' In this view, people's identity constantly dissolves and reconstitutes itself through our life experience. An identity, a personality or a self is therefore reconstructed by events and experiences. This makes social work worthwhile, since it suggests that individual **change** is possible, and that individual changes will also make impacts on the social. **Goffman's** (1968) ideas on how people present themselves in **performances** require understanding of the social context in which behaviour takes place, if we are to perceive the surface presentation alongside other more hidden aspects of identity. Underlying the surface presentation, however, is a more stable identity which creates and stimulates the performance. The concept of role also suggests that elements of social context assist people in maintaining identities because the social expectations of their roles form a stabilising influence.

Social work's professional identity recognises it is not a collectively or individually self-constructed identity, but is concerned with social workers' enactments of the profession and negotiated **boundaries** with other occupational groups. Part of this is **performance** in inter-professional settings, in shared work environments and terrain (Webb, 2017).

Identity politics refers to social movements that challenge dominant ideas about a devalued characteristic, asserting and theorising the distinctiveness and value of that identity to achieve political and social inclusion. It emerged from **race** and later **gender** identities, but class, nationality and sexuality are also important (Alcoff & Mendieta, 2003). People become involved in identity politics because they experience devaluation in aspects of their identity that is important to them. Indigenous and minority ethnic groups, or women or commitment to ideas such as environmental sustainability can generate and sustain important identities. One example in 2020 is how the Black Lives Matter movement to contest police brutality towards black people in many countries developed towards a broader interpretation of the importance of black lives in many spheres of social experience.

An **ideology** is a coherent system of beliefs and ideals that influences individual and institutional behaviour. The idealistic and systematic character of many ideologies leads some, particularly conservative, political and social thought to complain of an inability to interrogate parts of the whole and their implications. In social work, this criticism is sometimes made of **Marxist** and **psychanalytic** theory, because objections are framed as representing, respectively, class interests or psychological resistance.

Impartiality is the principle that people should act and make decisions in matters of concern without favouring one person or one aspect of the issue over other people or aspects. Impartiality in making social work decisions may be considered an **ethical** responsibility or a duty that derives from the legal duties of a practitioner's employing **agency**.

In social work, impartiality is an aspect of **respect for persons** because if we are on one side or the other in a disagreement or dispute, or if we act for our own benefit, or follow our agency's policy, we are treating someone as a convenience, and thus disrespectfully. This is because we would be pursuing our own or others' interests, rather than looking at the decisions or actions that clients, as rational human beings, want to take.

Inclusion See **Exclusion**.

Indigenist theory is social policy and social work knowledge and understandings drawing the traditions of **Indigenous** peoples. These are people who, as individuals, self-identify, and are accepted, as part of a community with historical continuity with pre-colonial and pre-settler societies. Such communities have a strong link to identified territories and their natural resources and have distinctive social, economic or political systems, and distinct language, cultures and beliefs. Because they form non-dominant groups in their society, they maintain and reproduce their distinctiveness within their ancient environment and social systems (Hart, 2019, drawing on United Nations, 2007).

Indigenist theory is an example of **decolonisation** in social work theory, seeking to bring forward ideas from cultural minorities within countries or territories where settlers forming dominant or majority populations have cultures that devalue traditional cultures and social systems. Indigenous groups often share cultural characteristics such as spiritual philosophies, living in the natural environment, valuing collective and community relations, family life, egalitarianism and respect for other individuals in the community. Important influences on social work theory have developed in **African-centred practice, family group conferencing** from Aotearoa New Zealand, faith-based ideas from Asia and North America, and theory from **Tongan** and other Pacific and South Asian cultures.

Historically, in the 1970s, 'Indigenous' workers were people employed in social work agencies in the USA, as part of projects to employ staff from local communities with a different class or ethnic identity from staff with social work qualifications (Loewenberg, 1968).

Individualisation is an ethical and practice principle in social work. Its use in social work connects with philosophical debate about 'individualism' and from it the concern to promote 'individuality'.

Individualism proposes that it is characteristic of human beings that they are separate from each other. This view emerged in the **Enlightenment**, and contests a strain of thinking, typical of many **religious** beliefs, that humanity forms a connected and continuous body, part of nature. These ideas are linked with **holism**, a perspective that sees human beings as complete entities living as part of their world, and underlie **humanistic** practice, and some views of **relational** practice and **traditional social work**. Some religious and social beliefs go further to connect humanity to the whole of creation, the environment in which we live, and thus underlie some conceptions of **eco** practice. The idea of individualism connects with **liberal** thinking and Western ideas of **freedom** and **self-determination**.

Elements of individualism from many different traditions include the following (Lukes, 1973):

- Human dignity, autonomy and self-direction are valued.
- Privacy, the idea that people should be left alone to act and think without **surveillance**, underlies **normalisation** ideas and concerns about **institutionalisation** arguing for people in care to pursue an independent environment that they value, rather than be subsumed into a de-individualised collective regime.
- **Self-actualisation**, the idea that the ultimate human achievement is to work for the development of their human capacities.
- The abstract individual, the idea that human beings have their own interests, needs and wants, which emerge from their personal **identity**, contrasts with social relations being created by human collectives to meet their interests. Consequently, societies cannot create the human beings that are part of them because the humans are individuals, able to respond to and modify social relations.

- Because society consists of abstract individuals, rational and independently thinking their own thoughts, human beings have individuality in many areas of functioning because their individual **agency** creates the collective structures.

These ideas about individuals are central to ideas of **equality, freedom** and other **human rights**, because they depend on individual humans being independently worthy of respect. To argue that it follows that individual action and behaviour is the only source of society, and of psychology and economic systems, however, is wrong because it limits our understanding of human beings to what we can observe and classify within our current modes of thinking. Social work, alongside the social sciences, realises that individuals contain intentions and purposes to engage in activities and self-actualising tendencies that together constitute capacities that create social structures and their possibilities for the future (Lukes, 1973: 146–57). This is the argument underlying positive psychologies and **solution** and **strengths** practice.

This conception of individualisation also emerges from the **postmodern** sociology of **Beck** and Beck-Gernsheim (2001). They argue that the Enlightenment view of the individual is that people are born individuals and develop mastery of the world around them through human understanding; the economic system comprises individuals operating in markets pursuing their own interests. **Neoliberal** economic and social policy demands this form of individualism. But postmodern social relations see individualisation not as something that is done for someone, but as a process that people pursue throughout their lives, always 'becoming' through creating and recreating changing identities in a 'liquid' society (Bauman, 2000a) in which patterns of social relations are also constantly changing, with new patterns **emerging**. Individuals create new reciprocal **systems** and non-linear institutions, flexible and creative new institutions and relationships.

We can see examples of this in new **caring, family** and **gender** relations, a rejection of outdated **ageism, racism** and other forms of discrimination. If social relations are truly inclusive, they must also be creative because they engage new possibilities. Social work's ethical and practice principles of individualisation thus take the position that taking on human rights and respect for people necessarily implies an inclusiveness of individuals, so that those individuals can create a society that enables the **self-actualisation** that ideas of individualism require.

Inequality See **Equality**.

Insight is an issue in social work in different ways:

- The intuitive understanding concerns the value of forming a full understanding of a person or situation, both the hidden and the obvious, and their ramifications before acting.

- **Psychodynamic** theory develops the intuitive understanding of insight in its theory of the un**conscious**. It proposes that many drivers of our behaviour are hidden from us in our unconscious thinking. Behavioural or social difficulties demonstrate hidden thinking that has been repressed because it is damaging or upsetting to us. Repressed thinking is not available to us, and much of the treatment of traditional psychoanalysis consists of helping us to achieve insight into it, with our new awareness enabling us to behave more rationally. Many clinical psychology theories, and CBT in particular, contest these ideas, suggesting that mere insight does not help us to change, but because behaviour has been learned an active focus on present behaviour allows us to relearn specific behaviour or to find solutions to behaviour problems.
- In **critical, feminist, Marxist** and **radical** theory, the idea of **critical consciousness** and the practices of **conscientisation** and **consciousness-raising** also imply that insight into hidden social processes will enable people to become aware of and resist social injustices. This idea may be criticised, as with psychodynamic insight, because insight into social injustice does not necessarily enable people to take action to avoid or resist it, although it may be necessary to take such action. The critical theory responses to this are two-fold. First, conscientisation can only be achieved through collective **dialogic** work; it is not individual insight, but a group or societal understanding mutually achieved and therefore supported. Second, it involves **praxis**, the idea that intellectual insight is inseparable from practical action, which must also be collective, taken in the light of the insight. Thus, to critical theory, insight can only be collective and necessarily leads to action.

Institutionalisation has two main meanings in social work:

- The idea refers to how attitudes, the interests of particular groups and ways of thinking and working became part of general assumptions about how the world works in important decision-making processes and social structures. In this way, ideas or social conventions become institutionalised by becoming the widely accepted way of thinking or acting. This has been a particular concern with institutional **racism**.
- The effects of living for long periods in residential care institutions, particularly if they are **total institutions** (Goffman, 1968[1961]), establish undesirable sets of behaviours, called 'institutionalisation', 'institutionalised behaviour' and 'institutional neurosis' (Barton, 1959), including apathy, lack of motivation and repetitive behaviours. Institutionalisation in this sense became an issue in social work when large psychiatric hospitals and other institutions were being closed in many countries in the late twentieth century; the process continues across the world.

The two ideas are connected by the human tendency to accept, as true and unchanging, actions and behaviour that come from an established social structure, instead of questioning the humanity, justice and value of the accepted ways of organising and thinking about our social arrangements.

An example of institutionalisation of sets of assumptions is the idea that commitment to our **families** is important in maintaining a strong social order, and so is often supported by national legal and tax systems. In these ways, it is institutionalised both in everyday social relations and also in the decision-making structures of societies.

Social structures and social relations change over time, and therefore some sets of assumptions and social structures may become outdated in how they have institutionalised particular ideas. To continue the family example, the form of families has changed in the late twentieth century, so that a wider range of family structures, such as single-parent families or families headed by gay and lesbian partners, is more commonplace, and marriage has become less common in some societies as a way of forming nuclear families. Assumptions baked into formal structures, or shared assumptions in some groups, may, therefore, no longer apply, and the formal basis for social relations structures becomes outdated.

Institutionalisation becomes controversial if some groups in society are **excluded** or **oppressed** by widely shared assumptions. The example of racism refer to prejudiced discrimination against people in minority ethnic groups. Institutional racism is included in unthinking degradations hidden in conventional behaviours, concepts, judgements, language, law, mechanisms, procedures, sensitivities and insensitivities, and formulas of everyday life. This includes actions and decisions taken by social workers. The message for social workers is never to accept or act on commonplaces in legal and procedural expectations until you have thought how they may discriminate against the interests of minority groups.

Interdependence conceptualises the idea that dependence works both ways; people depend on each other financially and psychologically, even though observed at any particular time, one group or person brings more apparent resources to the relationship. The concept contests **dependency** as a political and social concern. Interdependence is often an important value in **eco** and **humanistic** practice and **Indigenous** cultures.

Interpretivist theories of knowledge, such as **constructionism** and pheno-menology, propose that understanding always involves an interpretation of observations and perceptions of reality, contesting **empiricist** ideas that knowledge may only be based on organised human observation of an external reality.

Intersectionality explores how oppression in one aspect of an identity interacts with other aspects of oppression affecting that person or group, forming a complex matrix of factors in the experience of **oppression**. This arises because **power** and **privilege** converge in particular locations within social structures of economic, political and social influence, so that several sources of subjugation act together.

Crenshaw (1995) describes the importance of mapping the intersections of different sources of oppression in work with women from minority ethnic groups subjected to domestic violence. They were often affected by poverty or underemployment, and therefore by their social class identity, but there were many other layers of their lives that affected the impact of violence, which was different in every situation. No one form of oppression always dominates, so class is not always more important than race or gender more than age. Neither is the process additive, so that the more oppressions people experience the more they suffer. It is always important to look at the broad context of the life experience of people experiencing oppression, and explore the dynamism of the interactions as shifting circumstances affect the pattern of oppression (Murphy, Hunt, Zajicek, Norris & Hamilton, 2009: 9–13). For example, at a time of high unemployment, class may be an important factor; later where housing is poor or unavailable, exploitation by property owners may have a greater impact, and where migrants are insecure in their **citizenship** status, fear of action by immigration authorities may limit their options.

Inequalities in access to resources and support, inclusion or exclusion in decision-making, marginalisation or invisibility of a particular factor are common intersections in a matrix of oppression. In some social locations intersecting factors are separated in the reaction of agencies, for example where agencies are specialised so do not respond to all the visible aspects of the oppression. For example, a woman who is trafficked for prostitution may end up in the legal system **labelled** as criminal, while childcare responsibilities, health problems, immigration, citizenship and violence towards her are not dealt with. Hollingsworth (2019) identifies another aspect of location, that people experiencing severe difficulties will often orientate themselves towards options that seem practicable rather than look for a resolution that deals with all the oppressions that they are experiencing.

Intersubjectivity is a postmodern concept originated by the philosopher Husserl. It refers to the interaction of the ideas and minds of two or more people to form a shared discourse, which may include disagreement, about a topic of concern. The idea recognises that understandings of the world are subjective, emerging from the perception and interpretation of realities by people's minds. Any such understanding is also influenced by interactions with others' perceptions and interpretations. In acting or responding to events, therefore, human beings inevitably incorporate into their own thinking understanding from shared conceptions of reality. All their understanding is, therefore, the result of intersubjective relationships.

Intervention is the contemporary theorisation of the main process of social work, preferred since the 1970s to 'treatment', avoiding that term's **medicalised** implications. One of the implications of intervention is the feeling that it is a **disruption** or interference in the client's life. Practitioners cross boundaries in a community or family when intervening with a member, and an intervention invariably is an intrusion. Some of the ideas about communication and **respect** in practice ethics and theories are about smoothing that intrusion. The positive about that is that you shake things up, moving away from the status quo and therefore beginning a process of **change**; the negative is that people can perceive it as an invasion of private affairs or family life. Explicitness about intrusion in the social work **relationship**, client preferences, and **time** limits can help to reduce the sense of intrusion.

Mishra (1981: 3–4) argued that traditions of social reform have been concerned with defining and intervening in social problems, rather than understanding the social issues that might underlie them. Bailey (1980: 105) similarly argues, referring to sociology, that the social sciences developed from 'interventionism', a wish to use knowledge to intervene in 'practical affairs in society'. These criticisms of the social sciences are also true of social work.

'In vivo' (in everyday life) work is a cognitive behavioural technique widely used in clinical psychology practice, and therefore in **psychologised** social work practice. It is activities carried out by clients in between discussion sessions with the practitioner. It is sometimes called 'homework', but some practitioners do not like the reference to schooldays in childhood implied by that term; others use the more neutral terms 'activities' or 'exercises', with their implication of rehearsing behaviour.

Islam is one of the major world religions, with many adherents, and like other religions, there are alternative views represented in different communities; also, not all Muslims are equally devout. It originated in the Middle East and is a significant or state religion in many countries. Conflict between Islam and other religions is connected to political conflicts involving different national interests. Because the dominant practice of social work derives from Christianity, another world religion, which is also significant in political conflict, questions are raised about whether social work as understood in Western countries can be practised in Islamic countries and with Islamic populations in other countries. Islam is regarded by adherents as a complete way of life, uniquely comprehensive compared with other religions or systems of thought (Barise, 2005; Hodge, 2005). Consequently, secularisation is not an acceptable approach to helping. Practice by non-Muslims therefore needs to recognise the cultural and faith context of any helping, but practice according to most practice theory carried out respectfully of this context is acceptable. Islamic formulations of social work, similarly with **Indigenous** and other cultural and faith constructions of social work, are developing.

A concern around Islam is conflict between political blocs connected to Islam and other faiths, giving rise to Islamophobia and possible discrimination arising from it, and political and social radicalisation associated with extreme Islamic activism. This leads to concerns about social stability in some countries affected.

Further Reading

Ashencaen Crabtree, S., Hussain, F. & Spalek, B. (2017). *Islam and social work: Culturally sensitive practice in a diverse world* (2nd ed.). Bristol: Policy Press.

J

Judgement, and professional judgement in the exercise of **discretion**, are important aspects of the role of any professional occupation, including social work. Moral systems and codes of practice, however, make provision for making judgements in a professional context, and many people would accept that being able to do so is an important element of professional work. Banks (2012) refers to the ideas of 'considered' and 'good' judgement, the former thought-through and therefore with a high consistency and validity, and the latter reflecting accumulated experience and reflection.

'Non-judgementalism' – not making moral evaluations of clients' behaviour – in relationships is an important part of effective **relationships** in social work interventions, according to Biestek (1961). Social workers' personal preference and many practice theories suggest avoiding explicit criticism of clients' judgements, or behaviour that gives the appearance that such judgements are being made. On the other hand, critics such as **Wootton** (1959) have argued that where it is relevant to the social worker's role and required of officials and professionals by social expectations, exercising moral judgement is necessary and avoiding it is false. There are also arguments that moral judgements are an implicit requirement of social work agency responsibilities, even though this is concealed in some professional rhetoric (Payne, 1999).

Important aspects of professional judgement include:

*   Managing uncertainty.
*   Creating and adopting analytical, empirical and statistical models to inform actions and decisions.
*   Establishing and using decision-making processes.
*   Handling a range of opinion and values.
*   Identifying and evaluating economic, ethical, legal, organisational, professional and social contexts (extended from Dowie & Elstein, 1988).

Justice See **Fairness** and **Social justice**.

L

Labelling is a sociological theory connected with **symbolic interactionism**. It is concerned with the processes by which people are classified and stereotyped with a 'deviant' **identity**. Becker (2018[1963]) on young offenders and Scheff (1999[1984]) on mental illness demonstrated how professional definitions of offending behaviour and mental ill-health were accepted and adopted as stereotypes in powerful social institutions such as hospitals and the court system. There was also an impact of the **self-identity** of people affected. These ideas influenced social work because they showed how social workers' reports and **case records** created and perpetuated labels, devaluing and disadvantaging the people they wanted to help.

Language issues and the **linguistic turn** are movements in thinking in the late twentieth and early twenty-first centuries, building on **semiotics**. These affected social work in several ways:

- Social work is a talking practice, and using language to explain and persuade is an important skill.
- Language is part of colonial and post-colonial oppression, and therefore an important way in which devalued and oppressed social groups express their culture and Indigenous traditions. An example is the importance of the Welsh language in Welsh national identity.
- Use of language created oppression and racism, and using language appropriately was part of challenging these sources of difficulty for many groups and individuals that social workers worked with.
- In contemporary social science thinking, for example in the work of **Bourdieu**, Derrida and **Foucault**, language is the medium of communicative action, deconstruction, discourse, interaction, intersubjectivity, symbolic exchanges through which the social construction of reality takes place and social structures and social relations are established.
- Business language is evidence of the invasion of social work by **neoliberal** economic imperatives (Harris, 2003).
- Alongside the linguistic turn, the **narrative** turn develops language as part of narratives to help explore and intervene with important experiences in people's lives.

Liberal ideas are of two kinds, a political philosophy and a description of social attitudes. Social liberalism accepts that people should be free to choose to adopt a life-style and social relations, for example sexual relations outside of marriage, or gay and lesbian lifestyles, provided they do not cause damage to others. It is sceptical of claims that social disorder ensues from such freedom.

Liberal philosophy developed from the **Enlightenment**, which shifted ideas of government from relying on sources of authority such as churches and monarchs. The American and French revolutions are part of this movement towards democratic ideals. The liberal approach is **individualistic**, with individuals being self-reliant, liberated to pursue their own economic and other interests using their personal human reasoning and knowledge.

Liberal thinking influenced economic and social thought throughout the nineteenth into the twentieth century. There were three phases (O'Brien & Penna, 1998: 21–44). Liberal thinking displaced the English aristocracy's influence with industrial and commercial interests in the 1830s, leading to an era of industrial and economic **development** and **colonial** exploitation. Public and private interests were divided and government was disconnected from collective responsibility for any elements of the economic system. Its role became to support individual economic endeavour and to exclude responsibility for the poor, the sick and for working people, through the new Poor Law in 1832. Economic development through capitalism and industrialisation expanded industrialists' economic and political control derived from ownership of property. People had the incentive to work to avoid **poverty**, which was unmitigated by **support**, except at extremes of destitution.

During the second phase, reaction against this extreme individualism came with state action being seen as a necessary evil to respond to the complexities of modern industrialised and urbanised societies. For example, the state took on policing the poor, removing the burden of crime and mental illness from local responsibility with locally managed municipalities implementing national systems of social provision.

In the third phase, in the early twentieth century, the state developed social provision to manage increasing industrial and social conflict.

Liberalism became discredited during the economic depression of the 1930s and the period when welfare states were developing after the Second World War (1939–45). The liberal philosophy of reducing government action was displaced by a social democratic approach with social provision supporting the stability of the economic market through **welfare state** policies of comprehensive social welfare provision and full employment. Liberalism was renewed with different emphases as **neoliberal** thought. This came about after economic change in the 1970s led to a 'fiscal crisis of the state', in which it was argued that industrial and commercial activity could no longer sustain comprehensive tax-supported social welfare provision.

Liberation means freeing people or helping people to free themselves. The idea refers to political freedom from oppression for individuals and social groups, and this continues to be part of social work interpretations of liberation. Within the Global Definition of Social Work (International Federation of Social Workers, 2014a), however, the 'empowerment and liberation of people' is presented as one of three broad objectives of practice rather than as a 'principle'. It therefore also incorporates into social work practice humanistic ideals of liberation from constraints in psychological and social processes, for example mental ill-health, stress and damaging social relationships.

Liberation theology is an important Latin American Roman Catholic social movement, which influenced the **reconceptualisation movement** in Latin American social work. This had an international impact as an example of a **social change** model of reaction to poverty and oppression (Gutiérrez, 1973).

Life course theories propose that all people typically follow a similar process of progressing through **stages** during their life, such as birth, child development and socialisation, adolescence, adulthood, middle age and then **ageing** which leads to a decline in human faculties and death. The advantage of this is its inclusion of both human and social factors in looking at human behaviour, biological, psychological, social and **spiritual** aspects interacting in human experience, a **biopsychosocial** plus spiritual perspective. It also allows for people to have a continuous personal **identity**. Criticism of a life course perspective raises several doubts, as follows:

- Life course ideas assume a pre-ordained progression, starting with birth and ending with death, one stage developing from the foregoing stage towards the next. But people start anew, abandoning areas of development, or change direction.
- The life course link between biological development and psychological and social development assumes that sexual choices, social competence or wisdom goes alongside physical change. These factors are, however, different areas of people's development, where they make different decisions at different stages.
- Life course models assume the primacy of child development and value particular models of the family; they often devalue later life. In the cycle, children are born in a nuclear family, are supported through developmental stages to independence, when they marry and start the cycle again. But what does that mean for older people's life choices? And what about those societies where it is more common to live in a multigenerational family, or with parenting in an extended family or tribe?
- **Social construction** and **postmodern** views of **identity** argue that we continually reconstruct ourselves within our social relationships as they also change and that the assumption of continual **development** is false.
- Stages in the life course are not always clear: When does the child become adolescent? What are the implications of middle age emerging from adulthood? And Erikson's (1965) work on life stages, adopted in **crisis intervention**, suggests that transition may be difficult.
- The model may lead to the assumption that there are particular life **tasks** to be completed in each stage and people may be devalued or discriminated against as social failures or 'underdeveloped' if they do not, for example, marry and have children.

- Life courses may vary in different cultures and some stages are social constructions: for example, adolescence became more important in Western societies with the construction of the idea of a 'teenager' in the 1950s; the idea may not be relevant in other societies.
- World events may disrupt the life course for individuals or for large populations. Examples are disasters, political or regime change or wars, and their social consequences, such as lack of marriage opportunities in European countries after the 1914–18 war, changes in national boundaries or enforced migration.
- People travel through their lives in different orders: education, for example, may be picked up at any time; people may marry early, late or not at all; people's commitment to or interest in spirituality may vary during the lifetime.

The **life model** is an **ecological systems** practice theory (Gitterman & Germain, 2008). Social work aims to release '… potential for growth and satisfying social functioning … while increasing the responsiveness of their environments to people's needs, rights and aspirations' (2008: 71).

This is a re-statement of the traditional theorisation of social work as being about a **person-in-situation**, an individual in interaction with the social situation in which they live, in a direct line from **traditional social work**. Ecological systems theory's impact in the USA changed this to the **person-in-environment**; Karls and O'Keefe's (1994) handbook classifies clients' issues according to various personal and environmental problems.

The life model uses conservative ecological systems terms, with adaptedness and fit replacing the idea of a steady state, using feedback loops in **coping**. Other conservative ecological systems terminology (1994: 59) includes habitat, defined as the 'place where an organism is found', and niche, the 'position occupied by a species in a … community'. Again, people are assumed to be in a defined and definable **place** and an **object** determined by it, rather than a **subject** with personal **agency**.

Other important concepts refer to exploitative and coercive **power**, both analyses of power about, respectively, the withholding and abuse of power by dominant groups rather than a postmodern view of power as widely distributed in society. **Time** is divided into historical, individual and social time, contexts of **social change** affecting, respectively, different groups, the individual and the social transitions, all influencing clients as objects rather than subjects; in ecological systems theory, people are done to rather than doing.

Life model practice is a **stage** theory, describing four phases. The preparatory phase is about practitioners collecting information and **reflecting** on it, its cultural meanings and its relevance and impact on the situation that is presented. As with other systems theories, the life model permits eclectic use of other theories, and it can be hard to identify specifically its main thrust. This seems to lie in the importance of seeing people within their **life course**, shifting it to help people to be adaptive.

McDonaldisation is Ritzer's (1996) sociological theory proposing that **neo-liberal** economics apply rigid **Fordist** organisational principles to services to break them up into small elements of unskilled work. Producing a beefburger for the fast food restaurant chain McDonald's becomes not a skilled cooking operation, but a process of assembling standardised elements, with both ingredients and work processes defined and applied internationally. The costs of the service are reduced, the organisation's management simplified. **Surveillance** of the operations and personnel maintains quality, through information technology, target-setting, control of production and close supervision of outcomes.

Dustin's (2007) consumer research sees this process in **care management** in the UK adult social care services, where social workers and other professionals construct 'packages of care' from standardised elements. Services are, therefore, **commodified** and clients either receive elements of service selected mostly from private sector suppliers or, in **self-directed** care, receive funding to buy services through 'direct payments' in a cash-for-care system.

The critique of this argument is that in social care, as opposed to commercial services, clients dislike the dehumanisation of the processes of assessment and prefer help to use services in a flexible way. McDonaldisation leads to reduced choice and reduced personal **help**, for example with emotional and psychological difficulties. It may also lead to public agencies withdrawing from responsibility for working towards the overall benefit of the community. They may avoid taking responsibility for failures of coordination and changing needs because continuing service is replaced by episodic engagement with clients, the contrary process to social work's original conception of the **case**. In this way, social work is **deprofessionalised**, devaluing a service committed to human social cohesion and solidarity. Opportunities for clients and their families and communities to benefit from creativity, discretion and flexibility in the construction of services to fit their needs is lost.

Further Reading

Dustin, D. (2007). *The McDonaldization of social work.* Aldershot: Ashgate.

Macro practice is a practice for investigating and resolving larger scale **social problems** by intervening with organisations and social institutions. It engages individuals and communities in the interventions, using collective activity and social action. The concept draws on **systems** terminology, emphasising the scale of the social problems tackled and the organisations, in comparison with the micro (individualised) and meso or mezzo (small scale social groups and families) level of more therapeutic interventions. Macro practice is a redesignation in the USA of what elsewhere is called **community work** and **social development**. Mayo (2009) suggests that, while this is often supported as a natural role of professionals directly concerned with social issues, and directly relevant to social work's wider roles in society, a conflict perspective of it is often rejected. Nevertheless, community work has survived, despite setbacks, because it is a necessary response to important issues. Ferguson (2019), with a **radical** perspective, similarly sees macro practice as an implementation of **social action** social work, which has been devalued and undermined as a professional responsibility in contemporary societies. He suggests that resistance by agencies and political leaders to the involvement of social work practitioners in macro approaches arises from **neoliberal** policies seeking to restrain social action.

Maintenance is an issue in several social work theories:

- Psychological theories concerned with behaviour **change** such as **CBT**, **motivational interviewing** and the **transtheoretical theory of change** usually include procedures designed to maintain the change after intervention is completed.
- Hollis' (1964) **psychosocial** theory includes procedures for sustainment, a form of **support** which entails maintaining the relationship with clients despite their anxiety about **dependence** in seeking **help** and about making changes in their lives.
- Davies' (1985: 28–46) maintenance theory of social work suggested that much social work provision is concerned with maintaining the status quo in clients' lives, preventing deterioration in their social situation, rather than working on psychological or social **change**. Providing general **care** in **family support**, foster care and long-term care, for example with older people, is an undervalued aspect of social work. This politically conservative position contests overemphasis on both psychotherapeutic and social change views of social work.

Managerialism See New public management.

Manualisation is a method of presenting practice theories in a manual of treatment, in which practitioners follow set sequences of **procedures**. This may be helpful for newly qualified practitioners or those taking up a new post or working with a new theory of practice. It may help both clients and practitioners follow a complex set of processes and give both self-confidence that they are following a well-established process. Manualisation also helps to provide accountability because fidelity to the manual can be self-monitored and also evaluated by teams or managers.

The critique of manualisation is that it may limit creativity and development among practitioners and be inflexible in dealing with complex and unusual problems presented by clients. It may encourage not listening to clients' accounts of the issues that they face, with practitioners shifting into a standard process, rather than responding to the personal concerns presented by clients.

Market forces refer to economic factors, mainly supply and demand, that affect the behaviour of consumers and traders in an economy. The 'market' is a nostalgic metaphor calling on images of a traditional environment of small stalls where goods and services are bought and sold between consumers free to choose between multiple traders free to negotiate a sale. The model assumes that prices fall and quality improves, because buyers will choose the best product or service for the lowest price available. Markets are, however, usually imperfect: perhaps consumers do not have the knowledge to choose rationally, or traders agree prices beforehand or merge to form monopolies so that there is little choice. Or poverty inhibits consumers from choosing the best quality, and financial incentives pressurise traders to increase prices and reduce quality. Markets are usually 'regulated' to avoid such problems, that is, they are managed by administrative and legal procedures both to prevent consumers being exploited and to prevent traders from competing unfairly.

Some market regulation is by the state, acting on behalf of consumers and traders in the electorate. One way of doing this is by requiring information to be provided, such as accurate labels on food. A social care example, in UK residential care, is a regulator, the Care Quality Commission (CQC) at the time of writing, that inspects care homes regularly, and publishes reports which the care home must make available to potential residents and their relatives so that they can compare homes and make an informed decision. Some activities are not susceptible to this sort of approach, where complex, **discretionary** actions are involved. An alternative regulatory mechanism is **professionalisation**, but this is criticised because professions have a 'producer' interest in provision; because expenditure on improvements is to their financial and ideological advantage.

Marketisation is an element of **neoliberal** thinking, in which services provided in the public sector of the economy are moved towards competing in a market system of provision, without necessarily **privatising** them by shifting them into private companies. Marketisation might include 'market testing', to see whether outcomes and service costs are equivalent to those in a private company; setting up **quasi-markets** in the public sector; **social entrepreneurship**, in which not-for-profit companies returning surpluses for social purposes provide the services, or not-for-profit, charitable or third sector organisations.

Marx, Karl (1818–1883) was a political philosopher whose ideas continue to have a profound effect on thinking in economics, politics and social affairs generally, and in social work. His influence is particularly strong in **critical**, **radical** and **structural** social work practice and theory, and in discourse between these and alternative perspectives on social work. This discourse is important because it centres on debate about social work's political role in relation to **activism, poverty, social action** and social class.

The underlying theory of Marxist thought is historical **materialism**, which is the study of how goods are produced through history (using and producing physical materials, hence the use of the term 'materialism') in different societies. It is a conflict theory that contests **structural-functional** and similar social theories for their assumption that societies function to contribute to social stability. Marxism, to the contrary, sees social order as imposed on working-class people by elites in society in pursuit of their own interests. Marx was writing at the time that nation states were solidifying their boundaries and significance in international relations, and conceives of the state as an instrument of domination of working-class people by capitalism.

The importance of conflict between different social interests is an important element of social work theory drawn from Marxist thought. Marxist sociology became influential on social work during the 1970s, as social sciences increased in significance in Western universities. It introduced into social work questioning about whether the purposes of social work are always benign to minority and working-class interests. This led to critiques of **professionalisation** in social work professional organisations, and of the role of social work as part of the state, which Marxism sees as in part a mechanism for dominating the working class.

Marxist social work is based on **Marx**'s sociology, and is a major contributor to **radical** social work practice theory. Rojek (1986) distinguishes three alternative Marxist positions:

- The progressive position sees social work as a positive agent of social change. It connects the knowledge and understanding of educated middle-class professionals through services that mitigate capitalist domination of the working classes. By promoting **collective** and **community** action it assists in **consciousness-raising** about inequality and injustice in society, which also contributes to social change. This position is commonplace in the 1970s radical movements that were epitomised by the work of Bailey and Brake (1975; Brake and Bailey, 1980) in the UK and Galper (1980) in the USA.
- The reproductive position sees social workers, particularly in their work within the state, as agents of capitalist domination of the working classes. It particularly focuses on enabling **social reproduction**, through helping families to function in their caring roles for children and **disabled** and older people. This enables the capitalist system to reproduce its domination of working-class interests across the generations.
- The contradictory position sees social work as part of both capitalist class control and processes that potentially undermine capitalism. Their helping role mitigates the impact of capitalist domination and enables working-class communities to function

better. They gain consciousness of other contradictions in capitalism and skills in resistance and moving towards social change and social justice. This position is characteristic of the radical practice ideas of Corrigan and Leonard (1978) and of contemporary radical theory associated with Lavalette (2011) and colleagues.

Radical social work, sometimes with an explicit Marxist position, developed as part of the critique of **traditional social work** in the 1970s. It was associated with the increase in the size and reach of social work services in **welfare state** provision, and increased **bureaucratisation** and emphasis on service management characteristic of this period. One of the critiques of it was its emphasis on political and **social action** and on collective and **community work**, which was in tension with the main **social cohesion** roles of state social services and the primarily **individualistic** practice and need for psychological understanding that arose from it. Attempts by Leonard (1984) in generating a Marxist interpretation of psychological human understanding balanced this tendency, and the construction of a radical casework by Fook (1993) demonstrated that theoretical progress could be made. The growth of the fiscal crisis of the welfare state during the 1980s and the associated prominence of **neoliberal** critiques of welfare provision led to interest in radical theory receding, and Marxist theory seemed to be overthrown with the collapse of the communist regimes associated with the Soviet Union.

In the twenty-first century, however, radical ideas were picked up again by critical theory's incorporation of feminist and postmodern theory into the mix, and gained a resurgence in contemporary radical social work and action with a radical reaction to globalisation and neoliberal politics, and interpretation of twenty-first century economic and environmental crises (Lavalette & Ferguson, 2007; Ferguson & Woodward, 2009; Lavalette, 2011; Ferguson, Ioakimidis & Lavalette, 2018).

Materialism is relevant in three ways to social work:

- It is a philosophical system claiming that since physical matter is the basis for everything that exists, it must also be the basis for everything else, such as mental states, including mental illness, and social relations. This views the psychological and social issues that concern social workers as created by and secondary to the material and physical. For example, materialism sees emotions and thinking as produced by chemical and other physical changes in the brain and body, and this gives credence to research and practice using **neuroscience**. Such a position also supports **technical rational** practice theories such as **cognitive behavioural therapy**, **task-centred** practice and **empiricist** approaches to knowledge, such as **evidence-based practice**. It would contradict **interpretivist** and **social construction** approaches to knowledge, practice and research such as **humanistic, mindfulness** and **narrative** practice and qualitative research methods such as appreciative inquiry and participative action research.

- Materialism refers to a personal and social attitude that values the accumulation of property and goods, in contrast to attitudes that give priority to personal and spiritual growth. **Existential** and **humanistic** values in social work, as well as often religious values, endorse personal psychological **liberation**, which, for example in the Global Definition of Social Work (International Federation of Social Workers, 2014a), is an important social work objective. Such views contend that materialism is not an ultimately satisfying human motivation, but many political and policy positions endorse materialism to motivate people to work in **neoliberal** economic systems. This issue raises tensions between social work values and many economic and political policies.
- The historical materialism of **Marx** investigates how goods are produced in societies, and this system of thought underlies **critical**, **radical** and **structural** social work theory. It may be criticised because it focuses attention on the political consequences of economic structures, and gives inadequate attention to meeting human needs and developing personal **identity** and psychological functioning.

Meaning is an important concept in social work, as follows:

- A meaning is something of significance to a person, who may not fully understand its importance or how to express it. Even if someone does understand the meaning of something, they may not be able to communicate or explain it fully. Or its meaning may be communicated but its implications may not be understood by another person. During assessment particularly, but throughout social work, the meaning given to an event may affect decisions about intervention. Social workers may realise that an experience or issue is important to a client, but it may take time and effort for both client and worker to understand the nature of and reason for its significance.
- Meaning-making is an important aspect of **narrative** practice, where **deconstruction** of narratives about life events enables people to make connections between different aspects of their lives and organise how they understand what has happened to them (McTighe, 2018).
- Wetherall's (2012) account of **affect** and **emotion** proposes that understanding meanings of emotional expression is collectively or jointly socially constructed.
- Meaning-making about life experiences is an important aspect of people's **spirituality**; beliefs or religious faith may enable people to appreciate the significance of experiences in decision-making about their future, planning future directions and socialisation.
- Searching for the meaning of life or experiences within it is the focus of Viktor Frankl's (2011[1948]) logotherapy, developed shortly after his experience of concentration camps in the Second World War. Many people struggle to grasp the impact of difficult experiences on their lives, and meaning-making may help them to do so.

- Finding meaning in a situation has been found helpful in **coping** with stressful situations (Gutiérrez, 1994: 206–7).
- Meaning-making, or meaning reconstruction (Niemeyer, 2001), is an important aspect of Niemeyer's (2001, 2005; Neimeyer & Anderson, 2002) **constructionist** practice theories on bereavement. These propose that when someone dies, someone close to them may review the relationship, sharing experiences with others, and reconstruct their meaning in their lives. In this way, they reconsider the deceased person's contribution in their life course.

The **medical model** refers to an approach said to be characteristic of the way medical practice responds to illness and its treatment, and is claimed to be different from social work approaches. Critique of the medical model refers to inadequacies in a specialised, technological medical care system focused on particular conditions or parts of the body, rather than looking **holistically** at the whole person (Kane, 1982: 315). It also emphasises the medical process of diagnosing a disability or illness in a patient, then prescribing a regimen of care or medication to treat the illness. This cures or manages it so that the patient returns as far as possible to independent self-management of the condition within their normal mode of living.

One criticism of the medical model is that it assumes a normal state of the body and that disability or illness is a deviation from that normality. Thus, a disabled or sick person is always abnormal, even deviant, always 'other', and blame or criticism may be attached to a patient because of a risky or unhealthy lifestyle. Another problem of the medical model is that it is a **technical rational** model relying on professional experts (Weick, 1983: 467) to define the problem, the treatment and perhaps the patient's human or social identity, as opposed to the social work preference for a collaborative process of exploring difficulties, opportunities and strengths. The directive style of questioning necessary to narrow down from a range of possibilities to a diagnosis uses a linear model of explanation and makes it difficult for the doctor to move to an open-ended style of exploration to understand relationship or social issues. **Ambiguity** or uncertainty may prevent progress to a diagnosis and subvert treatment. In some areas, particularly psychiatry, the diagnosis may be disadvantageous or even feared, **labelling** or **stigmatising** a patient as less than human.

Alternative models are present in medical care. Weick (1986), for example, explores a 'health model' that promotes healthy living, and there are preventive, public health or epidemiological models that provide other alternatives.

Medicalisation is describing or thinking of a condition or problem as though it were a medical condition. Often, but not necessarily, this means dealing with it using a **medical model** of care or treatment. See also **Psychologisation**.

M

One aspect of medicalisation is the adaptation of medical terminology for social work processes, for example **diagnosis** and treatment. Recent debate about medicalisation raises concern that **neuroscience** and **biopsychosocial** ideas overemphasise biological sources of behaviour, devaluing human skill and understanding, and social science knowledge.

Mental health refers to a health condition, an aspect of health service provision and a social work specialty, although its connection with physical health is complex and controversial. The health condition concerns people's emotional and psychological wellbeing revealed in their social relations. A mental illness is a disturbance in mental functioning that has adverse effects on people's relationships and capacity to carry out their responsibilities in their social environment. Health services provide treatment for mental illness using psychotropic (mind-altering) drugs, psychotherapy, and in-patient, out-patient and day and home care. Social care provision and social work are elements of those services, so mental health becomes a specialised element of social care and social work, although most non-specialist social workers come across mental health issues to some extent in their work.

Mental health is both like and unlike physical health. It is unlike because it may involve behaviour that is strange and frightening, and therefore is socially disapproved as deviant and stigmatised. Both mental and physical ill-health involve interaction with healthcare systems and medical treatment, and this provides a location for social work engagement with troubled people.

It also influences social work theorisation. In some countries, notably the USA, social work is a significant mental health profession. This has consequences for social work theory because the US continues to have a dominant position in the academic and professional development of social work. The US mental health emphasis generates a strong interest in psychological theorisation and mental health service provision, leading to **medicalisation** and **psychologisation**. Countries where **social development** methods are a priority or where social work is engaged in broad public social provision with a lesser mental health emphasis, seek and sometimes sustain a different theoretical balance.

Milieu therapy is a mental health treatment relying on the life **space** (Lewin, 1951), a **communal** setting within which mental healthcare is provided. There is no single theorisation, but Smith and Spitzmueller's (2016) study indicates some of the elements, which connect with ideas about **therapeutic communities**:

- The whole environment in an institution such as a clinic, day centre, hospital ward, or residential care home, including the patient group, contributes to the impact of the practitioners working in the setting.

- The milieu or setting is an active part of that impact, for example allowing privacy, or having a calming effect because of the style of the building or its natural surroundings.
- The milieu provides a space in which modelling and rehearsal of **actions** can be practised; **in vivo** work can occur immediately after new behaviours are demonstrated and reinforced.
- The milieu offers an ethos of **democracy** and **participation, freedom** within the **boundaries** set by the institution.

Millennium Development Goals (MDGs) were eight targets

set by a United Nations summit conference in 2000 to influence global economic and social developments to be achieved by 2015.

- Eradicate extreme poverty and hunger.
- Achieve universal primary education.
- Promote gender equality and empower women.
- Reduce child mortality.
- Improve maternal health.
- Combat HIV/AIDS, malaria and other diseases.
- Ensure environmental sustainability.
- Develop a global partnership for development.

Many successes were achieved, and these aims connected with policy interests in social work. The international social work organisations, through their institutional connections with UN agencies, participated in these activities, creating a shared global agenda of their own. Four policy priorities were identified: promoting social and economic equalities, promoting dignity and worth of peoples, working towards environmental sustainability, and strengthening human relationships (Truell & Jones, n.d.). This represented a shift in the priorities of international social work organisations towards a policy-informed agenda from a previous agenda which largely focused on increasing the influence and spread of the social work profession (Askeland & Payne, 2017: Ch. 1). A further series of 17 'Sustainable Development Goals' set a connected series of objectives for 2030 (United Nations, 2020), covering a wider range of social objectives with a stronger emphasis on environmental sustainability. These influenced a further development of the international social work associations' Global Agenda in 2020.

Mindfulness is a form of psychotherapy and a self-improvement technique,

based originally on **Buddhist** thought, which has been adapted to social work. It has been used in social work as an intervention, mainly in therapeutic settings concerned with people's reactions to stress, during important changes in their lives or stressful events, such as bereavement or recovery from mental illness. Wong (2019) cites studies of successful groupwork by social workers with older adults, homeless young people, interpersonal violence survivors, vulnerable children, people with addictions and caregivers. It is also used in practitioners' self-care, cultivation of therapeutic relationships and building self-awareness and critical reflection (Wong, 2019: 259).

The approach has been used in brief **groupwork** programmes based on Kabat-Zinn's (1990) mindfulness-based stress reduction (MBSR). Another well-used technique is **acceptance** and commitment therapy (ACT) (Boone, 2014). The aim with ACT is to improve people's flexibility in dealing with their lives. You do this by encouraging people to stop avoiding difficult things or avoiding 'fusion', where past failures fuse with present events and cause people to think that they can't achieve something that they want to. Moving on from this, you get them to think about 'workability', to look for things they can try out in practice and avoid being immobilised by worrying about doing it perfectly. Instead, people can achieve some parts of it, then have another go to improve.

Hick (2009: 5) identifies three elements of mindfulness:

- Intention, purposefully committing yourself to a process of mindfulness.
- Attention, turning your mind attentively to concentrate on the impact of your thoughts on your body.
- Attitude, being mindful in particular ways that bring the benefits of the techniques.

The techniques involve a series of exercises to strengthen people's ability to manage emotions, thoughts and relationships, building capacity to pay attention to important aspects of body, environment, mind and spirit. The process is to develop a curiosity about important factors in life, observing and describing them in detail. What is your mind saying to you about your environment? How is that affecting you? Avoid evaluating your thoughts – they're not right or wrong, bad or good; you take some time and thought before reacting to them.

The criticism of mindfulness, as with all meditation and other 'thinking it through' psychotherapies, is that they can seem mystical and vague. But the techniques are practical and have the effect of slowing things down and achieving focus. They emphasise rational cognition, and so have connections with **cognitive behavioural therapy**.

Further Reading

Boone, M. S. (2014). *Mindfulness and acceptance in social work: Evidence-based interventions and emerging applications*. Oakland, CA: Context.

Modality is an American term referring to a form of social work, such as clinical practice, community work, groupwork, macro practice or social development.

Modernity is the system of social life that emerged in the **Enlightenment** which favoured social order and stability in social structures, such as the state and statutory organisations, based on rational planning and organisation, on **progress** in universalised human knowledge and understanding applied to the management of natural resources through industrialisation and science. Social work is modernist in the sense that it harnesses the social sciences to achieve individual and social development.

Giddens (1990: 53) suggests that modernity lifted social life out of fixed and inflexible traditional local relations, developing systematic knowledge about social life that enabled larger structures and wider planning. Among the social processes that allowed this to happen is an increasing importance of expertise and **cultural** and **symbolic** ideas that involve creating trust in societies to generate security in spite of greater flexibility and insecurity in life. Initially this took place in nation states, but later in increasingly globalised structures, which allowed the rolling **social reproduction** of increasingly complex social relations and structures. Social work can be seen as part of that increasing social complexity, facilitating it and participating in the management of it to maintain trust in spite of complexity.

Further Reading

Giddens, A. (1990). *The consequences of modernity*. Cambridge: Polity.

M

Moral panics are social issues that come to be defined as a threat to established moral and social values by stereotyped presentation in mass or social media (Cohen, 2002[1973]). Three processes take place in the mass and social media at an early stage of this process: the presentation of the issue is exaggerated or distorted, dire consequences of failure to act are predicted and the issue is symbolised by an single idea. Moral **entrepreneurs** take the lead in demonising the issue. The authorities are sensitised to the issue, and the high public profile of this issue generates unconsidered reactions. These processes are an extreme example of the claim-making process by which **social problems** are identified in social **discourse**. There are two main approaches to these issues: Cohen's (2002[1973]) processual view claiming moral panics emerge from media distortion and public reaction, and Goode and Ben-Yehuda's (2009[1994]) analysis, which explores an excessively volatile and disproportionate social construction by contending interests (Critcher, 2016).

Social workers are involved in these processes either because they raise the initial concern by early awareness of a new issue coming forward, or because they are pressed by the panic to overreact in providing help or care, or because they are part of the established services that judge that the issue is being exaggerated. Reactions, particularly in a **neoliberal** social environment, may be unreasonably punitive or damage human rights and make it difficult to make balanced professional decisions that respect clients' free will and self-determination.

Further Reading

Cree, V. E., Clapton, G. & Smith, M. (Eds.) (2016). *Revisiting moral panics*. Bristol: Policy Press.

Motivational interviewing (MI) is a practice theory, based on the

transtheoretical model of change (TTM). It is designed to assist in working with people who are difficult to engage in helping interventions, and this has made it of great interest to social workers working in child safeguarding, criminal justice and mental health services. Originally created by Miller and Rollnick (2013) for use in alcohol and drug treatment services during the early 1980s, elements of it have been adopted in a wide range of clinical psychology, counselling and social work services. The approach is **manualised**, with mnemonics for sequences of interventions. This concentration on the mechanics of practice is sometimes seen as atheoretical, but the use of TTM, with its emphasis on psychological change, its focus on communication skills, and awareness of shifts in patterns of talk reflects aspects of **postmodern social construction** ideas which demonstrate a distinctive theoretical position. As presented by the originators, MI mainly focuses on a clinic or care setting, but Corcoran's (2016) and Hohman's (2016) social work interpretations cover broader implementations.

The techniques highlight communication skills as a way of handling and maintaining clients' motivation to work on issues that they face. The underlying theory assumes that practice is about behavioural and lifestyle **change**, leading on to the stable **maintenance** of the person's successful change. Research support for the theory, like that of many behaviour change approaches, shows achievement of positive changes but in this case with a client group where success may be more difficult. In the original alcohol and drug misuse settings, however, there may be a reaction effect: introduced into a typically confrontative style of treatment in substance abuse treatment settings, MI's more involving style may have produced most of the benefit (Miller & Rollnick, 2013: 381).

An important strategy is to develop discrepancy. This is the difference between the situation now and how the client would like it to be. Talk through the disadvantages of now and the positives of the possible future. If the talk is of problems, what would it be like if they were solved? If the talk is of sunlit uplands, what are the clouds obscuring the sun now?

Further Reading

Hohman, M. (2016). *Motivational interviewing in social work practice*. New York: Guildford.

Multicultural practice is an anti-discriminatory and anti-racist

approach to practice mainly concerned to promote **cultural competence** in social work and **diversity** of social provision as a response to **racism**. It values multiculturalism and incorporates groups different from the dominant population into a nation or community by valuing their cultural contribution to the whole and emphasising the value of diversity and **pluralism** (Rex, 1997). Multiculturalism encourages participation in the dominant culture and minority ethnic groups maintaining ethnic and religious traditions. For example, residential care homes would celebrate relevant religious festivals. The criticism of this approach is that it encourages 'orientalism', seeing minority groups as exotic but as **'other'** without respecting their faith and traditions as a comprehensive way of life; see also **Islam**.

Multidisciplinary, multiprofessional practice and teamwork recognises that social work is part of a range of disciplines, practices

and professions providing services in connected and overlapping organisations, sharing similar values and theoretical sources. Organisational, professional and structural initiatives to coordinate and integrate services within this variety have led to theorisation of ways of linking them:

- Agency links focus on the clarifying administrative and legal responsibilities of agencies.
- Discipline links focus on understanding distinctive and shared knowledge and techniques.
- Professional links focus on establishing distinctive roles of different professional groups.
- The prefixes 'inter-' and 'multi-' are used interchangeably and refer to bringing staff groups together and to interweaving work.
- Teamwork refers to cooperative practices and sometimes also to cooperative interpersonal relations.

Two different approaches exist. **Group** development approaches attempt to improve interpersonal relations among a group of team members. Knowledge-management approaches focus on the flow of information and resources among practitioners with different agency, disciplinary and professional backgrounds and roles (Opie, 2003). Whether group development occurs naturally with interaction or whether enhancement of relationships requires active management is contested in the literature (Payne, 2006b). Research suggests that identifying and sharing team members' preferences for contact with colleagues, the type of work they do and the kind of organisation involved is crucial. In particular, approaches relevant in residential care settings where all team members work together may be different from those required in field organisations where members' practice is carried out mainly alone away from a work setting (Miller, Freeman & Ross, 2001).

N

Narrative practice theory is a social construction theory of the 1990s, reflecting a narrative and **linguistic turn** in cultural and literary studies, and the social sciences. The originators, Australians White and Epston (1990), have connections with social work. Parton and O'Byrne's (2000) 'constructive' practice adapted narrative and related ideas as a constructionist model of practice; Greene and Lee (2011) interweaved it with **solution** practice. Narrative practice has a record of practical theorisation of people's 'telling their story'. Other advantages are that it is intuitive to clients and the people around them and emphasises listening fully and respectfully to their perspective.

The critique of narrative practice is its focus on individual experience, unhelpful if clients' experiences come from social and structural issues in society. Narrative practice may lead to a sense of responsibility for things experienced that were out of the client's control. The idea of externalisation, a key innovation, may help clients appreciate how they were blaming themselves for things outside their control. Positive psychology, **solution** and **strengths** practice criticise its backward-looking concern with clients' past experiences and problems, rather than concentrating on goals. On the other hand, narrative methods involve learning from the past, to reconstruct understanding for the future. The other main critique of narrative practice is similar to critiques of **insight** in **psychodynamic** practice and **consciousness-raising**. Understanding does not necessarily lead to change, and rethinking a narrative is not robust in dealing with abusive or offending or other damaging behaviour that must be actively confronted. Narrative theory's methods of change often seem insubstantial to people who need or want to make significant differences to their lives.

Narrative practice emphasises psychological adjustment to personal and practical difficulties, after distressing or **traumatic** events. It may also help with reminiscence work (Haight, 1995; Gibson, 2018) with people with lost memories, and life review (Haber, 2006) of important experiences. Examples are children leaving care or who have been adopted looking back on their birth families or journey through care, people who are divorced or **bereaved** looking back on their lost relationships, or people with long-term medical conditions, dementia, **mental illness** or physical **disabilities**.

Narrative practice aims to **deconstruct** the story of the experiences that led to the problem. People have many stories, each with many potential plot lines, and these can offer another direction for our lives. Exploring past experiences sometimes reveals things that were successful and worthwhile, and these can be picked up and tried again, or reconstructed to fit new circumstances. Other things that did not work out can be identified and avoided in future.

The narrative method asks clients to tell the story of the issues that bring them to the agency, using 'experience-near' descriptions and exploring how the narrator gives coherence to the events (Béres, 2014: 33). Intervention aims at 're-authoring' or 're-storying' the events (2014: 67). 'Externalising' the problem enables clients and those around them to perceive it as outside themselves. Together, client and practitioner think how the event might be differently understood, 're-membering' by identifying potential new participants in the story, new skills and new initiatives to be taken. People create a new **identity** for themselves and identify **self-efficacy** in the experiences they review. This is done using **language**, picking up how clients describe the problem or the events leading to the problem. This is an example of how narrative practice theory is part of a linguistic turn in social science theory. Their language is used metaphorically to describe the problem as external to, and not the responsibility of, the client, so the experience of numerous debt problems is a cascade, problems at school are because of the bully-boys, compulsive behaviour is the straitjacket.

Further Reading

Béres, L. (2014). *The narrative practitioner.* Basingstoke: Palgrave Macmillan.

A **need** is something desired that is experienced as important because without it there would be significant harms. A need, therefore, is not absolute, although recognising a need implies a pressure to meet it. Needs are a **discourse** between different political positions and views about what is important and how to evaluate it (O'Brien & Penna, 1998: 124–8). Policies and systems of administration define the criteria and objectives that establish and define need that will be met by a service; the extent to which need is recognised. Social work is often responsible for assessing collective, family or individual need, comparing it with organisational and policy criteria and objectives.

Different types of need interact, influencing each other. One of the reasons for introducing care (case) management into UK adult social care, requiring assessments of need by social workers, was research that showed that assertive demand by a client or carers influenced decisions about whether a service was provided. The experimental study of case management showed that assessment by social workers according to established criteria reduced the impact of such pressures on rational resource allocation (Davies & Challis, 1986).

Doyal and Gough (1991) argue that some universal basic needs are required in order to **participate** in social life. These are physical health and **autonomy** to make decisions about their lives. The **agency** to make priority decisions about needs is inevitably affected by social assumptions and expectations, so the autonomy is not wholly individual. In Doyal and Gough's account, a range of intermediate needs contribute to physical health and autonomy, which include the physiological needs, things like housing to keep us safe, non-hazardous work and physical environments, economic and physical security, education, safe birth control and childrearing, appropriate healthcare and security in childhood. Doyal and Gough also argue that particular groups, for example minority **ethnic** groups or women, have particular needs that arise from their **oppression**. Many of the issues that social workers grapple with are included in the intermediate and special needs that Doyal and Gough describe. Social work, therefore, contributes to meeting basic needs by ensuring that many contributory factors are dealt with in society. This is another aspect of the argument that needs are interlocking; for example, the doctor and healthcare are not more important than social workers and social care because, while physical health is a more basic universal need, social factors contribute to meeting that basic need.

Another useful account of needs is Fraser's (1989: 163) account of 'thick' and 'thin' needs. Her example is homeless people. It is easy to agree that they need shelter, a thin account of need. If we think about specific individuals, however, we need a thicker, more complex account of need. What kind of shelter should we offer: a bed in a hostel, a tenancy in a private apartment or public sector housing? What kind of help do they need in order to make use of the shelter, such as furniture grants or help with cooking and caring for themselves in the new setting? Social workers are often concerned with helping agencies and people to make decisions on these more complex issues, and therefore with collecting, evaluating and presenting this information in ways in which both agencies and clients can make decisions about needs.

Dean (2020) suggests that an aspect of need is whether the decisions we make about it contribute to a flourishing, worthwhile society, as well as meeting individual or group needs. Thus, a social worker contributes to a better society through their **assessments**, thick high-quality social information about individuals to the agencies that meet people's needs on behalf of society.

Further Reading

Dean, H. (2020). *Understanding human need* (2nd ed.). Bristol: Policy Press.

Neoliberalism has two elements: it is a set of ideas and a political campaign by a group of capitalists and economists dissatisfied by political consensus during the period after the Second World War. Neoliberalism picked up part of the failed nineteenth-century **liberal** economics, but there is one important difference. Liberalism rejects the value of the state in favour of the market, while neoliberalism uses the power of the state to enforce and extend **marketisation** into every area of social life, including social provision such as social care and social work.

Garrett (2018a: 78–9) identifies six facets of neoliberalism affecting social work:

- The erasure of the post-Second World War political settlement in which damaging aspects of liberal economic and political thinking were balanced by social constraints and welfare provision.
- Remaking the state's activity to support and develop the economy rather than balancing economic with social welfare elements. Social workers became the facilitators and managers of private sector services.
- Redistribution of resources from the poor to the rich.
- 'Precarity' – increasingly precarious lifestyles creating new forms of social discipline of people in poverty, for example in social work, managing disability services to encourage employment or using safeguarding to pressurise the behaviour and living conditions of poor people.
- The 'new punitiveness', with social welfare increasingly conditional, delayed and delegated to charity, and immigration centres, prisons and surveillance measures to manage behaviour, rather than helping people.
- 'Failing forward' by stimulating constant neoliberalisation with repetitive crises such as economic crashes, and initiatives such as Brexit, waves of illness or immigration to struggle with.

Neoliberalism also has practical effects that communities as collectives and social workers as helpers of individuals, groups and communities have to deal with. Rani's (2001) study of the marine food-processing industry in India showed that its high profits led to exploitation of women workers and their consequent poor health.

Networks are systems of connections or links between groups, people and things. Various aspects of networks may be described mathematically, for example how many links a group or person has in any particular field, or the frequency or strength of contacts between people. These characteristics of networks allow social workers to think about connections between people without focusing on relationships in the psychological sense. It allows social work to explore and theorise the nature of social relations without focusing on personality, and particularly gives rise to ideas of **social capital** as a way of thinking about the value of links in general. These aspects of network arise in various aspects of social work theory:

- In **African-centred** and many other **Indigenous** practices.
- In working with **ageing** and in **bereavement** work, to build support and reduce loneliness.
- In **assessment** and engagement, to ensure that clients' family and community networks are explored.
- In **attachment** practice, to find alternative attachment figures.
- **Eco** practice, particularly Dominelli's (2012a) green theory.

- **Ecological systems** theory, and other aspects of **systems** practice, particularly Meyer's (1983) eco systems theory.
- When dealing with **exclusion** to help strengthen clients' social **capital**.
- In **Bourdieu's** concept of 'field', defined as 'networks of objective relations'.
- In all kinds of **community** and **groupwork** practices, where building networks develops community connections and interpersonal links.
- As an aspect of **family group conferencing, family support** and **signs of safety** practice to enhance children's support and safeguarding through community and family links.
- In building **resilience, support** and 'support networks' in many situations.

Neuroscience is the science of the brain and nervous system, which consist of neurons. Neurons fire chemicals called neurotransmitters, such as serotonin, across gaps in the system and help the brain process information; changes in the chemicals affect behaviour and perceptions (Applegate & Shapiro, 2005: Ch. 1). Neuroscience has become increasingly relevant to the study of causations of the ways in which human behaviour is expressed, and this has begun to influence social work explanations. It is attractive to **empiricist** views of social work knowledge and supporters of **evidence-based** practice, because of its basis in empirical medical research. Over-enthusiasm for its application in social work is criticised because it **medicalises** understanding of behaviours that are partly constructed by social relations (Carey, 2019). Most neuroscience practice that involves social workers arises in interprofessional practice involving medical and psychology professionals, in particular where medication is used.

The main areas of concern that involve social work are around **affect** regulation, for example how people manage powerful emotions such as anxiety, anger and depression, attachment issues, brain functioning, memory problems and the development of mental health in children (Applegate & Shapiro, 2005; Farmer, 2009). MacFadden (2017) argues that the capacity to explain and work with emotion in a scientific way is potentially an important contribution of neuroscience to social work.

New public management (NPM), a policy of **managerialism**, is a global trend that emerged in the 1980s (Cheung, 2002) following a claimed 'fiscal crisis of the state' (Pollitt, 2002) over the claimed costs of **welfare state** comprehensive social provision. It is an aspect of **neoliberal** thinking, which gives priority to the **technical rational** management of finance, priorities, resources and services through expertise in economic and general management, rather than by specialised managers with a primary expertise in professional service provision (Newman, 2002). Although justified by an appeal to clients' interests through consumerism, it sees these interests as personal, privatised rather than a collective public responsibility for **citizens**. It also rejects the complexity of interpersonal issues underlying **social problems**.

Non-directiveness is a counselling practice, part of Rogers' **person-centred** practice and **Biestek**'s account of social work relationships, which proposes that practitioners should enable the exploration of options and facilitate clients' decisions about their objectives and intended outcomes. The concept claims that the client is thus **liberated** from constraint and empowered to make their own decisions. The critique of this analysis is that it assumes constraint and direction come only from the professional authority of the practitioner in the social work process. It does not actively facilitate exploration and elimination of other constraints on the client's objectives from social pressures or **structural** barriers, and it does not help clients deal with **ambiguity**, or lack of energy or **motivation**.

Normalisation, also called **social role valorisation (SRV)**, is a strategy for managing social care services, and especially residential care. The idea emerged during the 1960s and 1970s in Nordic countries at a time when services for people with intellectual disabilities were shifting away from **institutionalised** towards community provision. It proposes that services should be **rights**-based, giving clients and residents a way of life that is as near as possible to that experienced by 'normal' people, that is, people without the disability or difficulty which led to their being in care. Service users were to have equal social rights and quality of life, but segregation into institutions was not rejected (Emerson, 1992: 3).

The concept of normalisation was developed in North America by Wolfensberger (1983). He sought to emphasise the social objective of integration of people with intellectual disabilities into social relationships seen as culturally normal in the community, recognising and seeking to dispel the negative social attitudes of people towards engagement with people with intellectual disabilities. Wolfensberger's (1983) 'social role valorisation' tries to clarify the meaning of 'normal' in this context. It proposes that services should seek to enable people in care to pursue social roles in ways that everyone would value, avoiding care that brings clients and residents disbenefits. To achieve this, a change in social attitudes towards intellectually disabled people is required, but it would also require educating people with disabilities to avoid behaviours likely to excite stigma in others and 'pass as normal'.

Goffman's work on **stigma** and presenting oneself in a **performance** suggests that many people do this, and **labelling** theory explores social processes by which this happens. Debate about SRV raised a question of whether it promoted 'moral **authoritarianism**' and a conservative assumption that 'dominant' views about people with learning disabilities were part of a uniformly hostile culture. This is because it trained people to avoid social deviance not for their own benefit, since the deviance is an externally imposed perception, but in order to lessen others' hostility (Dalley, 1992: 103), when seeking to change cultural views would lead to a shift in cultural views about intellectual disability. Aborectur sanimporecea nos

O

The **object**, referring to people, conceptualises them as being inactive in social relationships, manoeuvred or oppressed, having things done to them, rather than being in control of their destiny. People are rarely only objects, so it can be helpful to think about in what circumstances or ways or to what extent they are being objects. We can also think about the balance between being an object or a **subject**, or circumstances where or ways in which they have more control or reasons why they may be more pushed around than pushing. People value understanding the possibilities for control. Social workers may therefore find it useful to explore people's feeling that they are objects, and how they see behaviour that you see as treating them as though they are objects.

Object relations is the **psychodynamic** theory concerned with how people influence and respond to people, situations or things outside themselves. Because they are external, they are not in the control of the mind, and relations are managed, according to the theory, by the **ego**. An image of the object is internalised, and so the response to and behaviour concerning the object may be in response to the internalised object rather than the characteristics of the external object. Thus, difficult or irrational behaviour may result from a client's misperception of or misunderstanding about the object, whether it is a thing, a situation or a person. Although 'object relations' is a psychodynamic concept, it sometimes helps us to think how patterns of dealing with externalities grow up in someone's mind and mislead them into following the pattern, rather than responding to new situations. People say things like: 'I always try to have things organised when I'm dealing with…' officials, or conflict situations or someone who is usually argumentative. It is often better to think through whether this particular official we are presented with is not being bureaucratic, or what is often conflictual is this time not so, or when our argumentative son is being helpful at this moment.

Oppression See **Anti-oppressive practice**.

The **ordinary housing** (Bayliss, 1987) or **ordinary living** (Towell, 1988) **movements** encouraged **normalisation** for intellectually and physically disabled people in the UK during the phase of de**institutionalisation** from large institutions in the 1980s. An important feature of these trends was the theorisation of housing environments as an important element in the process of **normalisation** and the emphasis on **place** in the process of caring for and helping within social care services and social work.

The **other**, **othering** and **otherness** refer to processes in which a social group thinks about or treats another social group as though they are different, threatening and of less value in important ways compared with themselves. This process separates the 'other' group from the first group's perceptions of the mainstream, and contributes to creating inequality between groups. The concept has been important in **post-colonial** theory, originating in work by Spivak (1985). Her account of a historical document is about processes of making the other aware of the power of the group in defining them, defining the other as inferior and dangerous and implying that the powerful group has a monopoly of knowledge and understanding.

Krumer-Nevo and Sidi (2012) argue that this process can be countered in three ways:

- Narrative, so that broader and subjugated aspects of identity and the history of relationships between the groups may be expressed and identified.
- Dialogue, which can allow alternative interpretations to be explored in an interpersonal way, making differences less significant to the people involved.
- Reflexivity, which allows both groups to see each other's points of view.

P

Parker Follett, Mary (1868–1933) is now best-known as a founder of management theory, but she started out as a social worker in community organisations, and became part of a US movement to develop community centres in local schools. With Grace Longwell Coyle and Ada Eliot **Sheffield**, she became an important member of the Inquiry, a social reform organisation, which promoted democratic group organisations. She argued that organisations should be seen as **networks** of groups rather than as hierarchies.

Participation and **client participation** constitute a strategy of encouraging clients to contribute to service and social work decisions and interventions affecting them and the people around them. This may extend to participation in service management, social work education and research.

While the social work profession demonstrates commitment to facilitating client participation in pursuit of **social justice**, **power** asymmetries and **exclusionary** mechanisms in campaigning and political processes make it difficult to empower people to participate in campaigning on complex social issues such as poverty. Boone, Roets and Roose (2019) distinguish between **affirmative** and **transformational** approaches to participation in anti-poverty campaigns they researched. Clients may gain affirmation from participation in social change, being helped to improve self-confidence and social skills, but may not experience transformational effects in their social relationships, for example participation may not achieve greater social mobility for poor people.

Pathologisation is viewing behaviour, a human condition or a social situation as abnormal, often medically or psychiatrically so, and therefore undesirable. As a concept, where the abnormality is considered to be a medical or psychological deviation from the norm, it is connected to **medicalisation** and **psychologisation**. Part of the criticism of pathologisation is that by treating conditions as undesirable, there is a hidden and unjustified assumption that any deviation from the norm is undesirable. Another problem with pathologisation is the potential for **stigma** associated with a 'problem' condition, or as a **social problem** rather than taking broader views of clients' lives, potential strengths and relationships.

Patriarchy refers to social structures or societies that systematically permit domination by men and exclusion of women from power, originally referring to descent through the male line and the domination of families and households by males. In social work, concern about patriarchy is a characteristic of radical **feminist** theory.

Peer advocacy See **Advocacy**.

Peer support is an approach to **recovery** from **mental health problems**, in which people with lived experience of mental illness act as mentors to **support** newly recovering patients.

Performance raises two concerns for social work, as follows:

- **Constructionist** and many other ideas identify aspects of human and social behaviour that are performances, in which people **represent** themselves in particular ways, either positively to show characteristics that people value, or to show characteristics that are useful in the particular social situation but that might not be represented in other circumstances. Behaviour is, in that sense, never **holistic**; instead it is adapted to the situation. For example, social workers might often present themselves as experiencing an emotion as part of their relationship with a client to show the client how their behaviour affects other people, expressing anger about a racist comment, and frustration about **ambivalence**. To be **authentic** or genuine in their relationship they will have to express part of what they feel, but they may also experience other more complex reactions, which they do not fully represent to the other person.
- 'Performativity' is a characteristic of language explored by Austin (1962). He distinguishes between 'constative' and 'performative' language. Constative language describes aspects of the world that can be verified by observation, for example 'the room is cold'. Performative language takes action in the world, for example instructions like 'please leave the room'. Judith Butler (1990) takes up this idea, suggesting that cultural expectations in many societies anticipate heteronormative behaviour, so we represent ourselves as heterosexual in everyday interactions with people. It is a political act to do so, since we are performing the power that in this society reinforces compliance from everyone with heterosexual norms. A **deconstructive** act would be to represent ourselves as ambivalent or gay, and in doing so, we are acting politically again, because we are problematising the norm, saying that it is a problem to make this assumption.

P

Person-centred practice, originally called 'client-centred', is a counselling theory which influenced social work from the 1960s onwards, created by Carl Rogers. It is a **humanistic** practice theory, drawing on phenomenology. Critiques of its ideas as a social work theory derive from its counselling and psychotherapeutic base, primarily about helping people to explore and understand their own mental processes, rather than

to identify precise improvements in their behaviours or social environment. It does not inform social work tasks such as deciding to admit children to public care or organising practical provision such as packages of services for adults. Nevertheless, the approach has been found robust for the interpersonal helping elements of the social work process, particularly in its formulation of the **core conditions** of helping relationships. Although these are derived from a good deal of empirical research, and are clearly helpful as part of any **relational** form of practice, it is not clear that they are sufficient to be found helpful in all situations (Munro, 1998: 75–87).

The main aim of practice is to describe, explore and understand the personal experiences of clients, using 'experience-near' language from clients' descriptions of what happened (McLeod, 2013: 165–88). This phenomenological idea contests the psychoanalytic emphasis on **insight** into past experience and relationships; person-centred practice works in detail through clients' current 'here-and-now' experiences, rather than the 'there-and-then'.

People behave as they do in order to achieve **self-actualisation**; all other needs contribute to this goal (Rowe, 2017: 39). Practice seeks to understand, through accurate **empathy**, a client's internal **self-concept**, internal perceptions of self and its relations with others, and the values attached to those perceptions. Clients experience incongruence if their experiences in life do not support their self-concept. Incongruence leads to anxiety and achieving congruence leads a client to be open to all experience without defensiveness and an increase in a sense of wellbeing.

With clients, practitioners demonstrate the three core conditions of therapeutic relationships. First, they value clients' personal worth, having respect for their person, and therefore treat them with unconditional positive regard. Second, as a result of this, they demonstrate congruence and genuineness in their relationship with the client; that is, their self-image is consistent with the external perceptions of their behaviour. Third, they demonstrate **empathic** understanding of the client's internal **frame** of reference; thus, their own congruence allows them to perceive and respond to clients' incongruence, and help to release them from their anxieties (Rowe, 2017: 41). Helpful ways of doing this include helping clients to review important aspects of their being, personal **identity** and relationships, reconcile conflicts between different aspects of or priorities within their feelings, and consider uncertainties or **ambiguities** into a **holistic** understanding of themselves and their relationships. Practitioners try to reunite the forgotten or excluded oppositions and conflicts into a full picture of their lives (Payne, 2020: Ch. 7).

Further Reading

Rowe, W. S. (2017). Client-centered theory and the person-centered approach: Values-based, evidence-supported. In F. J. Turner (Ed.), *Social work treatment: Interlocking theoretical approaches* (6th ed.) (pp. 34–53). New York: Oxford University Press.

Person-in-situation or updated to the **person-in-environment** (Karls & O'Keefe, 1994) is a theorisation of social work's **holistic** concern for the interaction of both the psychological and the **social** in clients' lives, both treated equally, neither coming first in consideration or intervention.

Personalisation in social work refers to adapting services and practice to the specific needs and wishes of a particular client, particularly in the context of **self-directed** packages of services provided through direct payment, the British implementation of cash-for-care policies (Gardner, A., 2014). As an IT term, personalisation describes adding personal touches to routine mail-merged communications, and the social work usage may similarly imply surface humanisation of routine service provision. But in policy developments in the UK during the early twenty-first century, personalisation has become the generalised theorisation of a more participative model of **care management** characterised by greater co-production and inclusivity of clients, their carers and the range of service providers, and health and social care practitioners.

Personalisation is also part of Carkhuff's (Carkhuff with Benoit, 2019) formulation of **helping** processes. Having explored with the client the issues of concern, a helper personalises these, thinking about the **meaning** to the client of the issues they face, the personal impact of them and the personal relevance of potential goals they might want to achieve. This aims to facilitate understanding of how they are affecting the client.

Further Reading

Gardner, A. (Ed.) (2014). *Personalisation in social work* (2nd ed.). London: Sage.

P

Pessimism is an issue relevant to practice doubts about **critical** theory, identified by Leonard (1993, 2004). Seeking transformation of what seems like an all-powerful social system dominated by **neoliberal** thinking may lead to pessimism that nothing can be achieved. This leads to adverse comments about critical theory, for example Rojek et al.'s (1988) point that critical and **radical** theory seems to accumulate criticisms of society without offering a way of dealing with the problems. Leonard (1993) argues that understanding of mechanisms of cultural **hegemony** through **Gramsci's** ideas and critical theory from the Frankfurt School, and interventions such as **Freire's** **consciousness-raising**, offer both understanding and possibilities for action that make the social system seem less monolithically immovable. By bringing together the awareness of oppression gained through Freire's critical pedagogy, with the aim of solidarity in the struggle to build resistance to oppression and implement transformation, practitioners can achieve a viable **praxis**.

Place signifies the importance of the psychological and emotional connection to particular locations and their **meaning** in the social context of people's lives (Kemp, 2010). Also relevant is how people use and feel commitments to space, such as home, school or work, and in **residential care**. **Bourdieu**'s concept of **field** and Lewin's field theory focus on place as an issue, with **power** being expressed in the location of place and space, becoming significant in how powerful social forces **govern** and **oppress** populations.

Pluralism views positively a situation in which a number of different groups or opinions co-exist. In political philosophy and science, pluralism often refers to plurality of **authority** or **power**, arguing that it is desirable that influence and power are spread among different groups, for example between local and central government, or between public, private and voluntary bodies.

'Post' ideas in sociology refer to changes in cultural and social assumptions following the 1980s, until which period 'modernity' was the main frame of social debate. The main critical analysis is of **postmodernism**, which is primarily concerned with epistemology and knowledge, but there are several other 'post' ideas that supplement postmodernist critique, which are noted in the following entries (Boyne & Rattansi, 1990; Rose, 1991; Hall, Held, & McGrew, 1992; Bertens, 1995; Sim, 1998).

Post-colonialism refers to the replacement of the domination of colonies using military and political control with economic and cultural domination by transnational companies and the cultural artefacts of Western countries, associated with a phase of **globalisation** in the later twentieth century, continuing into the twenty-first. Examples are transnationally distributed products of computer hardware and software such as Apple, Facebook and Google, of industrialised food production such as McDonald's (see **McDonaldisation**), and of telephone companies or television streaming companies such as Netflix. These replace culturally relevant and locally produced products and ideas expressed in local languages. World languages, such as English, and products using them, such as academic journals, books and streamed music and video production, replace local languages and oral traditions. Consequently, supporting documentation in social work education and in helping processes is not available for local use and this has led to **Indigenist** campaigns and theoretical developments to produce more relevant practice theory. **Decolonisation** policy and practice need to address post-colonial tendencies as well as vestiges of colonial influence.

Postmodernism is a trend of the 1990s and early twenty-first century which contested ideas of **modernity**. It proposed that the modernist emphasis on **technical rational** knowledge to create social **progress** through designing and manufacturing goods and creating knowledge and understanding about the world through science has been displaced. In its place, postmodernism proposes that knowledge is provisional and arises and is applied only in specific historical and social contexts. As history leads to **social change**, knowledge and understanding, particularly of psychology and society, also changes. The result is a rise in uncertainty, a rejection of the idea that there is a stable social order and established social structure and an increase in people's experience of insecurity and **risk**. Modernist elements of society react to this uncertainty by increasing mechanisms of 'governmentality' and '**surveillance**' (ideas developed by **Foucault**). Social work is, arguably, modernist because it assumes that society, social relations and social structures can be understood by rational means, and **interventions** prescribed through that understanding can maintain existing social order and structures, or at least contribute to better social arrangements. Postmodernism suggests that such understanding is at best temporary and unstable, and prescriptions for social **change** cannot be agreed or comprehensively secured. Thus, social work and its professional ideas are always struggling with complexity and insecurity, alongside its clients.

Poverty arises where an individual, family or community does not have enough resources to meet their needs. Its nature and definition is highly contested. Absolute poverty is where the resources of an individual, or some other unit such as a family, is not enough to meet their basic or minimal **needs**, as defined in some authoritative way, but the problem of definition remains because of contested understanding of need. Relative poverty is defined by comparing an individual or group with others in the same position. This also is contested, because some political positions in rich countries reject comparisons with others in the same country, since levels of poverty in many countries where the level of economic development is less are significantly worse than most of the poorest in Europe, the UK or the USA.

P

Poverty has been at the centre of social work discourse since its outset, since early social work was largely concerned with material aid for the poorest in nineteenth-century societies, and early social work debate was concerned with whether aid should be dispensed according to the extent to which recipients of aid were morally deserving because they tried to avoid **dependence** on charitable and state assistance and were active in helping themselves and their families. Social work's concern with active intervention was becoming distinct in this period from efforts at social reform and social research, which were the main responses to poverty.

Welfare state protections against poverty during the twentieth century developed alongside the more individual practice of social work, although social workers were often **activists** and **advocates** for **social change** to defeat poverty.

The contemporary period of **neoliberal** thinking and the consequent withdrawal of state commitment to responding to poverty alongside the devaluation of social welfare responses in many countries means that campaigning against poverty and for good social work provision are again connected issues. It is closely related to attempts to respond to wider aspects of **inequality**. Poverty alleviation using **social development** strategies is an important aspect of the **Millennium Development Goals** for responding to poverty worldwide.

Further Reading

Cummins, I. (2018). *Poverty, inequality and social work: The impact of neoliberalism and austerity politics on welfare provision.* Bristol: Policy Press.

Power is an important concept in political philosophy. It is 'polysemic', having multiple and diverse meanings depending on the situations in which it arises; and it is always contested, so that an agreed account of power is impossible. There are a variety of forms of influence such as 'coercion', where person or organisation A uses physical force to get person or organisation B to comply; 'influence', where A changes B's mind without using threats; '**authority**', where B complies because A's demands are accepted as legitimate; 'force', where A removes B's choice; and 'manipulation', a type of force where B complies with A's wishes without realising what is going on (Lukes, 2005[1974]: 21–2, citing Bachrach & Baratz, 1970).

Power has become an important issue in social work, developing from the concern in the 1950s and '60s with authority in the context of agency and professional influence over clients when social work was seen as a **non-directive** therapeutic activity with **self-determining** clients. An **empowerment** practice developed, responding to ideas of **exclusion**, and relying on **Black perspectives**. This led to a concern for understanding power relations.

In the context of political philosophy, power is involved with processes that take place when groups in society resolve conflicts in interest between them. In an influential analysis, Lukes (2005[1974]) discussed three dimensions of power, as follows:

- A one-dimensional **pluralist** view goes back to Weber's (1978[1910–14]) view that power is about individuals realising their preferences. This view focuses on behaviour, capacity and outcome. It starts from the capacity of A to get B to do something that B would not otherwise do. This view assumes that there are plural points of view, that conflict exists between the subjective interests of the people or organisations that hold them which leads them to have preferences for one action or policy rather than another. The conflict and the interests are revealed when decisions have to be made, the plural interests take part in a process to resolve the conflict and the outcome of that process discloses the power of one of the participants.

- A two-dimensional view identifies problems with the pluralist view, which requires there to be decisions and interests represented in the decision-making process. This dimension focuses both on decisions and also on situations where decisions are not made because people are excluded from the decision-making process so that their interests are not represented. Who controls the agenda and how issues are kept out of the political process are thus considered important aspects of power. This is a dimension that social work is concerned with since clients are often excluded from decision-making processes and **advocacy** is a recognised social work role. Social work aims to include people through client **participation** and similar processes.

- A three-dimensional view argues that the one- and two-dimensional views are too behaviourist: they only consider observable differences in, and conflicts over, known interests. But powerful people or organisations also shape attitudes and culture so that issues never arise in the first place, so people and organisations do not become aware of their interests, and perhaps those interests are never defined. Nevertheless, unexpressed or unknown interests may be identified from analysis. Social work could engage in a more complex process of analysing interests and bringing them to notice. Lukes notes that this requires a value system or ethical position that this is considered possible, appropriate or necessary.

Taking a three-dimensional view of power therefore, does not answer all the questions about power. Even if a group were aware of the exercise of exclusionary power, for example, they might still accept the power of the other. Social work has been familiar with this issue, with suggestions that **insight** into both **critical** and **psychodynamic** theory, and **consciousness-raising** in critical and **feminist** theory do not necessarily lead to action, but may inform **praxis** where collective action develops from better understanding of experience. And it suggests that social work's value system demands active analysis and exploitation of human and other **rights** on behalf of client groups' interests and is necessary to an **empowerment** methodology.

P

Pragmatism is an American philosophical tradition, influential around the turn

of the twentieth century, as social work began to form its professional identity in the USA. It is a development, originally by Peirce (Atkin, 2016), of Kantian philosophy (Thayer, 1970). Its main position is to say that you cannot understand a theoretical concept until you can see the outcome of taking action to apply it in the real world. This is important for social work's view of practice–theory links. Pragmatism says that a social work theory must be formed in such a way that you can act upon its ideas in the real world and can experience the results of that action. Critics say that this view influenced American social work's theory development, because it only values theory that can be practically applied and has concrete results, whereas theoretical discourse and wider understandings could usefully be applied in social work. This critique claims that a consequence of the early influence of pragmatism is the emphasis in Anglophone practice theory of seeking explicit prescriptions for action, a **technical rational** approach to practice ideas, and demanding **empiricist** theory, such as **evidence-based practice**.

Further Reading

Atkin, A. (2016). *Peirce*. Abingdon: Routledge.

Praxis is a Marxist concept, picked up in **Freire**'s pedagogy and practice theory based on it, and is commonly used in community work and macro practice. It suggests that practice is **dialogical**, in that it incorporates ideas gained from experience which influences how we think about the practice. Ronnby's (1992) account of 'praxiology' is a holistic conceptualisation proposing that human **action** and experience create both the practice and the thoughts and ideas about the practice, which are all part of the same system of ideas. In a later formulation (Ronnby, 2013), he constitutes praxis with **reflexive** and **critical reflection** interacting with both new experience and dialogue about new knowledge.

Principle-based ethics is an approach to ethical practice in which statements of norms of action are expressed as principles derived by rational argument from general values such as **autonomy**, beneficence, **respect** for persons and **social justice**. Deontological principles, that is, those based on duty, are often called Kantian, after the philosopher Immanuel Kant. Another form of principle-based ethics is utilitarianism. According to these ideas, actions are evaluated by the extent to which they are effective or useful in meeting the interests of the people receiving the service. Because principle-based ethics requires establishing agreement on concise and concrete statements of moral principles, it underlies the construction of codes of professional ethics. Criticism of principle-based ethics argues that they place too much emphasis on a rational, **self-determining** human decision-maker. In social work, they focus too much on individual behaviour and responsibility rather than social and structural sources of action. They also fail to consider whether agencies facilitate ethical behaviour, making and enforcing ethical judgements, and allowing for disagreement and dissent about ethics.

Further Reading

Banks, S. (2012). *Ethics and values in social work* (4th ed.). London: Red Globe.

Privatisation is an issue for social work in two ways:

- Social work in many countries is substantially financed by the state and until the 1980s it was usually also provided by state organisations. Privatisation refers to transferring social care and social work services to non-state actors. Van Ewijk (2009) identifies three aspects of this meaning of privatisation: privatisation from the state to the market, to civil society and to the community. In addition, there have been recent experiments with **social entrepreneurship** to form a stable model of finance, without dependence on state funding. All these require **marketisation**, since shifting services from the state to civil society and community require a market or **quasi-market** system.

- The other concern with privatisation is a critique of **individualisation** in social work. Because it is a professionalised intervention, social work allows widespread problems with social origins to be dealt with in interpersonal interventions, subject to professional rules of confidentiality. As a result, oppressive social causes are not addressed, and each iteration of the problem is dealt with as though its causes were personal rather than social. This attaches blame to the person suffering the problem, rather than to social institutions that also contribute to the causes, and assumes that resolution of the problem is a personal responsibility, rather than one that might fall to the collective or the state.

Privilege is a striking element of the **anti-oppressive** and structural practice theories of Bob Mullaly, and his co-authors, Marilyn Dupré and Janice West (2019 and 2018 respectively). It refers to advantages and rights given to people because of their membership of an identifiable social group and is the flip side of **oppression**. When people within a social group are oppressed, others gain unjustifiable privilege, and when people gain privileges it inevitably leads to others being oppressed by the absence of access to those privileges. While all oppressions have concomitant privileges, Mullaly emphasises 'white supremacy' social movements, particularly in the USA, as persistent expressions of longstanding **racism**.

P

Problem is a theorisation of an important way of understanding what issues social workers focus on in practice. A problem is a matter of difficulty where there is no certain outcome and that is obstructing further action or decision. The social work concept assumes that some problems are so difficult to resolve that getting movement towards an outcome requires help outside the ordinary social relations of the people involved. While the idea of problem refers to a single matter, problems come with a history, in patterns and in relationships, but social work focuses on the problem as a way of getting to the obstructions to **action** and decision, for example in **problem-solving** practice. Doing that will allow the social worker to help people tackle the obstructive history, pattern and **relationship** issues. The idea of seeking help from a professional with a problem is intuitive because of experience in healthcare. The **medical model** says that people with health 'problems' go to a doctor, who will diagnose an illness and carry out or prescribe treatment. Problem-solving, then, emulates in social work this respected professional approach.

The critique of 'problem' as the basis for focus in practice is that it starts from a negative, a difficulty. Independent adults are, moreover, assumed to be able to solve their own problems, while an illness is accepted as requiring expert attention. People may risk being **labelled** as **dependent**. If they are referred for help, they may resist it, therefore, and – an added difficulty – people, including other agencies, may see them as 'the' problem or the problem comes to define them, and becomes **stigmatising**. Alternatives to 'problem' as a conception of the focus of social work are concepts seen as positive, such as **solution**, **strengths** or **task**, but the difficulty with these is that they are less intuitive and being positive they seem therapeutic rather than practical. It seems a bit effete to getting help with identifying your strengths. Arguably, the difficulty here is attitudes to being **helped**, which bear strongly on the stigma of **dependence**, rather than the concept of problem itself.

Disagreement between clients and practitioners about the definition or nature of the problem to be tackled through social work intervention presents ethical issues. This is because **non-directiveness**, non-judgmentalism and client **self-determination** implies acceptance of their moral judgements and their definition of the problem (Leighton, Stalley & Watson, 1982: 27–34). Professional **judgement**, however, sometimes reinforced by **agency** and legal responsibilities, may require the use of **authority**, influence or **power** to change a client's view of the problem. Such changes may be disliked or resisted by clients, or practitioners may take a more positive view than clients.

Problematisation is analysing an issue so as to appreciate the difficulties it presents for understanding and for social and social work intervention. It is often an objective of **critical** and **postmodern** thinking to problematise taken-for-granted social assumptions.

Problem or **troubled families** is a theorisation of conceptions that small numbers of families in working-class areas form an 'underclass' which generates most childcare problems, criminality, destitution, poverty and worklessness. Starkey (2000) shows, for example, that 'feckless mothers' were **stigmatised** as part of 'problem families' in the early history of a UK family agency, Family Service Units, with associations with 'eugenics', the belief that social problems could be dealt with by genetic purity (Starkey, 2000). In the 1960s, UK legislation provided for work with families to prevent children being taken into public care, and legislation (Children and Young Persons Act 1969) tying offending behaviour to deprivation was not implemented by an incoming Conservative government, although the family service recommended by the Seebohm report (1968) was developed in local authority social services departments, and a policy linking deprivation and offending was implemented in Scotland. The political imperative to see families as problematic continues. In the 1970s, a Conservative government introduced a programme seeking to reverse a 'cycle of deprivation' in which family problems were transmitted from one generation to the next. Tony Blair, the Labour Prime Minister, made a speech in 2006 referring to families with a 'multiplicity of lifestyle problems' (Blair, 2006). The English Conservative-led government in 2011 introduced a 'troubled families' programme, seeing families who were troubled and caused trouble for agencies as requiring intensive intervention to resolve childcare, health and unemployment problems (Hayden & Jenkins, 2014). While help with childcare problems was achieved, help with more structural problems such as unemployment was more difficult.

In many countries where the discourse of social concern is influenced by religion, the priority given to family engagement in social work often reflects the religious priority given to maintaining the family structures as the basis for social order and continuing religious commitment through family involvement. An important example is the subsidiarity policy of the Roman Catholic Church, which also influenced European Union social policy.

Another justification of the importance given to focusing on family in social work is growing awareness of child abuse from the 1970s onwards. Criticism of childcare social work (Reder, Duncan & Gray, 1993) led to a shift from **family support** to a service primarily concerned with 'governmentality' and **surveillance** of families (Parton, 2005) through a **proceduralised** child safeguarding service (Parton, 1985, 2014).

Problem-solving theory pictures helping practice in clinical psychology, counselling, psychotherapy and social work as assistance in solving problems in people's lives.

In social work, Perlman formulated problem-solving in the 1950s as a **process** in which caseworker and client explored four 'P's of the casework situation: the person, the problem, the **place** and the process. The account of practice focuses strongly on the 'beginning phase' in which **diagnosis** is the thinking on which later interventions were founded; Perlman argued that this phase, as a foundation of future work, was more important than elaborating interventions.

P

Criticism of Perlman's practice theory argues that its focus on the four 'P's concentrates on factors concerning individuals and their 'place' (their social environment and **relationships**) as the main source of their problems. This fails to give enough importance to external social factors, such as social **inequality** and **oppression**. These, rather than the person and their immediate social environment, may generate the people's problems, and be a barrier to resolving them through an interpersonal process. The emphasis on problems has been criticised, particularly by positive psychologies in the late twentieth century, as starting from negative assumptions about a client.

Despite this, problem-solving is an intuitive formulation of social work action, akin to the 'symptoms' that patients bring to their doctors for diagnosis, and to the conditions that people may identify as **social problems** disordering society. The Global Definition of Social Work created by the international social work organisations at the beginning of the twenty-first century included 'problem-solving' as one of the three main objectives of social work. Because of the critique of problem-solving as the basis for social work, this was displaced by a focus on the objective of 'social cohesion' in a later redrafting (International Federation of Social Workers, 2014a).

Proceduralisation is the development, by policy-makers and managers of social workers, of increasingly detailed procedures for social workers to follow in their practice. It is part of **bureaucratisation** and may develop from the increasing distrust of professional discretion (Banks, 2004: 149–94). It contests and devalues **professionalisation** and the use of **discretion** and professional **judgement**. It is often a product of '**new public management**', in its turn an element of **neoliberal** thinking.

Process is a theorisation of how social work practice is undertaken as a whole, a series of actions, and the factors affecting them that go towards making or achieving something. Contacts between a practitioner and people being helped form in this way a well-established cycle of practice. The process is an accepted way of doing things that structures connections that those involved can understand between actions and events that take place at different times leading to identifiable outcomes.

Important sources of process ideas in social work are as follows:

- **Psychodynamic** ideas in **social casework**, which saw social work as a 'living event' (Hamilton, 1951: 3–4). Process emerged from **functional** theory in social work. In a classic paper, Taft (1962[1937]) argued that **agency** function structured the process of casework intervention, so that the actions taken by practitioners were informed by the legal and social mandate given by the agency for the work to be done. Hofstein (1964: 15), another functional theorist, defined process in the functional view as a 'recurrent patterning of a sequence of changes over time and in a particular direction'. Process ties together work with service users to indirect work with the agencies and people around them (Irvine, 1956; Smalley, 1967: 16–17), achieving unity of purpose between different aspects of the work.
- Groupwork explored 'group process'. For example, Mary **Parker Follett** (1998[1918]: 24), argued that being part of a group created a 'group idea ... better than any one of our ideas alone ... produced by ... the interpenetration of us all'.
- Feminist and critical theory, emphasising integrity and integration between the personal and the political for collective action.

Process describes social work **generically**, rather than referring to the content such as child or adult safeguarding, disability or family conflict. Aims and content of social work can only be understood fully by including how it works and what it works on. It must involve the connectedness that comes from **caring**, the engagement with **complexity** inspired by **systems** ideas, communication and **contextual** thinking all undertaken within a **time** sequence (Payne, 2009). Sheppard's (Sheppard, Newstead, di Caccavo & Ryan, 2000; Sheppard & Ryan, 2003) research on assessment shows that process is an important understanding of thinking in practice.

Professionalisation is the social process by which occupational groups attain

professional status. Professionalisation and **deprofessionalisation** have been significant issues in social work since the early twentieth century. Professions are occupational groups that represent the institutionalisation of altruism, benefiting individuals, the community, social stability and wellbeing, as opposed to art, craft and profit-making work. 'Trait' theories of professions propose that an occupational group is a profession if it incorporates specific characteristics such as complying with a code of ethics, acting in service users' interests, high-level education with specialised knowledge and having self-regulation. 'Professionalisation' theories propose that as societies become more complex, occupations accumulate these requirements for being a profession because more specialised knowledge and skill is more valued in society. The critique of these views is that, although professions claim altruism, they gain advantages in control of their work, freedom of action, higher incomes and social status. Marxists also argue that they gain social influence by acting on behalf of the state and dominant economic interests, which sometimes disadvantages users despite the profession's ideals. Feminists argue that professionalisation reproduces in the workplace relationship hierarchies in society that devalue women's domestic labour and exclude women from important social roles. In traditional professions, such as the church, the law and medicine, women are excluded from power and placed in subordinate professions such as nursing, social work and teaching.

As social work became a source of employment mainly for middle-class women in the early twentieth century, it sought to professionalise, mimicking the medical profession. An important conference speech by Flexner (2001[1915]) used a traits view to argue that social work did not display the 'six key elements' of a profession, including a systematic body of theory and knowledge, a professional culture and authority coming from, for example, a professional association, a code of ethics and a mandate from society to practise. A professionalisation project emerged among American social workers, followed by others, aiming to achieve these markers of professionalism. When a unified professional association was formed in the USA in 1955, an influential paper by Greenwood (1957) argued almost half a century on that social work had still not achieved professional status. The British professionalisation project achieved a unified professional association in 1970 and a code of ethics soon afterwards (Payne, 2002), associated with the formation of a large local government unified social work service in 1971. Similar developments emerged in many European countries, presaging a European social model of **welfare state** service provision.

Critiques of the professionalisation project developed in the 1970s. Toren (1969), in another 'trait' analysis, identified occupational groups, including social work, as 'semi-professions', which could never achieve full professional status because they were employed by **agencies** which had the right to direct them in their professional objective and practices. This analysis suggests that alternative types of professional occupations had emerged, rather than just one model, based on the template of individual professional independence. Freidson's (1970) sociological work on the medical profession produced evidence of the critique of professions in this influential group. Marxist analysis (Parkin, 1979) argued that professions thus seek exclusionary 'closure' and usurp or take over the roles of connected or overlapping occupational groups.

The risk of such developments of professionalisation is that it creates inflexibility in service provision, and Illich, Zola, McKnight, Caplan and Shaiken (1977) argued that professions were 'disabling', because by limiting access to expertise in dealing with important aspects of their lives, they limit the freedom of patients and clients as individuals to make their own decisions and of communities to pursue their interests. Writers such as **Wootton** (1959) and Brewer and Lait (1980) argued in the UK, supported by the claims of **evidence-based practice**, that social work's knowledge base did not support its claims of expertise. During the 1980s, the impact of **functional analysis** of social work roles and **new public management** reinforced doubts about the professionalisation process in social work, and **neoliberal** thinking added to this a withdrawal by the state from financing social welfare provision. Consequently, there were arguments for deprofessionalising social work, with **McDonaldisation** of practice into a **Fordist** form of industrialised less-skilled practice. Dressel (1987) argued that one of the factors in social work deprofessionalisation is the high proportion of women social workers. As the demands of neoliberal policies deprofessionalised the labour process of social work, they furthered the subordination of women; arguably the subordinated position of women facilitated this process.

In North America, professionalisation continued with an increase in **counselling**-style and psychotherapeutic professional practice, established social work roles in **mental health** and strong regulation of social work education and professional accreditation strengthened the professional status of social work. There was criticism (for example, by Specht & Courtney, 1994) at the end of the twentieth century, however, that this **privatisation**, in both senses of the term, led social work to lose its mission for social change and improvement. In the UK (Brand, 1999), and in much of Europe, the position is more ambiguous, since, although social work and its education is regulated, that regulation is dominated by governments. Because the primary roles of social work lie in government provision, the adverse industrialising and deprofessionalising effects of shifts towards neoliberal and new public management thinking continue to affect the professional position of social work. In the UK, however, there have been moves to reprofessionalisation in response to criticism of **proceduralisation** in child safeguarding and the public sector generally. Experiments in **social entrepreneurship** (Le Grand, 2007) and changing organisational culture to support professionalised practice are examples (Cross, Hubbard & Munro, 2010).

Progressivism is the idea that situations, or aspects of them, progress, either

naturally or by actions pushing them forward. It may also be applied to an understanding of both human beings and societies, that they naturally, or by the influence of various social processes, develop progressively. Issues may arise with progress and related ideas such as **change** and development. Social workers are often concerned about the assumption, either by **agencies** or **clients**, that situations should make progress and how progress will be defined in this case. Alternatively, it may be assumed that interventions are required to help progress.

Progressivism is also a philosophical and political idea, and is associated with a political movement in the USA around the turn of the twentieth century, during which social work was emerging as a **professional** group. In the USA, social work is sometimes seen as an aspect or creation of progressivist policies concerned with progress in society.

Psychoanalysis is a system of psychological theory and psychiatry and related

cultural and historical thought, which had a profound influence on thinking about the mind and on social work. It was devised by Sigmund **Freud** around the turn of the twentieth century, and developed by him and his many followers and detractors.

There are three important elements of psychoanalytic theory:

- Developmental theory.
- Structural theory.
- Treatment theory.

The developmental theory is a **stage** theory, proposing that people develop through stages of their lives. This emphasis in psychoanalysis on early infancy and parenting – particularly mothering, as the source of stability, or of future psychological disturbance if difficulties are not suitably resolved – is the source of important strands in social work thinking, in particular **attachment** theory. Examples are involvement in the child guidance movement, the importance of the social work role in researching and creating social histories, including events in infancy and childhood, and the tendency to theorise stages in clients' life events as the source of personal and social difficulties.

The structural theory describes metaphorical structures in the psyche. There is an undifferentiated 'id', a collection of drives and feelings that are dynamic, that is, they push the person into interacting with the outside world to meet psychological as well as physical needs. Through those interactions, the mind learns to control and manage the id so that a child's behaviour becomes acceptable to the people around them. This learning creates the 'ego', a rational aspect of the psyche which manages interactions with the outside world. As children develop language and social interactions, they begin to incorporate into their minds the ideas of powerful people in their world, often their parents, about appropriate behaviour. This forms a sort of consultant in the

P

mind, the 'superego', which guides the ego about moral and practical ways of managing relationships with other people. The structural theory assumes that most mental activity is unconscious, with people never becoming aware of the many forces affecting their behaviour and ways in which thoughts and ideas dangerous to mental stability can be repressed in the unconscious by **defence mechanisms**.

The treatment theory helps patients to achieve **insight** into the workings of their unconscious mind through introspection and reflection, which then allows the ego to manage previously poorly understood internal pressures. The psychoanalyst encourages patients to talk about things about their life and experiences, while collecting and interpreting evidence about the structures and processes going on in the patient's mind. This treatment process is one of the sources of the **non-directiveness** of **traditional social work** practice.

Further Reading

Borden, B. (2009). *Contemporary psychodynamic theory and practice*. Chicago, IL: Lyceum.

Psychodynamic theory
describes theories of behaviour and helping that derive from a wide range of **psychoanalytic theory**. The term 'psychodynamic' is used because the underlying psychoanalytic theories believe that people's internal mental processes (the 'psyche') motivate and thus have an impact on people's behaviour, directing and managing how they respond to internal thoughts. They are thus the dynamo that gives energy to behaviour and social interaction: we act like we do because of the way we think. Psychodynamic ideas were a prominent influence on social **casework** in the US from the 1930s, and in the UK from the 1950s, coming under attack in the 1960s from the developing social sciences, in particular **radical theory** and **learning theory** (Yelloly, 1980). Important theories that were explicitly psychodynamic were the original iteration of **crisis intervention**, as well as **ego, diagnostic, functional, problem-solving** and **psychosocial** theory. Contemporary theories deriving from psychodynamic ideas include **attachment, relational** and **therapeutic community** practice.

Psychologisation
involves seeing behaviour and social relations as the product of the mental processes and thinking of the people involved. This emphasises their personal **agency** and responsibility, rather than broader social factors, such as political and social movements or poverty.

Psychosocial theory
in social work proposes the importance of bringing together both psychological and social knowledge to understand and intervene with people

receiving health and social care services. In medical care, and particularly in palliative care and other forms of care for long-term conditions, psychosocial care refers to working to reduce the psychological and social consequences of a condition or treatment. A criticism of this formulation is that it often leads to **individualisation** and **psychologisation**, by emphasising emotional and psychological rather than social issues. One of the arguments for social work as a separate discipline and profession is its insistence on the inclusion of the social in such organisational arrangements.

In social work, psychosocial theory refers to Florence Hollis' formulation of **psychodynamic** social work practice, which she developed during the 1950s and '60s building on **diagnostic** theory. In its earliest comprehensive presentation (Hollis, 1964), it brought together Hollis' empirical research on classifying casework interventions with the traditional diagnostic focus on the **person-in-situation**, that is, looking at individuals' psychology and relevant social factors. Both of those elements limit and enable them. These ideas are used to create an analysis of 'treatment procedures' with an account of 'psychosocial study', **diagnosis** and choosing treatment objectives and procedures.

The casework procedures that Hollis identified are:

- Sustaining, direct influence and ventilation.
- Reflective discussion of the person-in-situation.
- Reflective consideration of dynamic and developmental factors.

Later editions of Hollis' book incorporate elements of **systems** theory after this became a feature of US social work practice. Its final edition, by Woods and Hollis (1999), while retaining many features of Hollis' original psychosocial theory, became a broader general introductory text.

P

Q

Quality is a concern in several aspects of social work, as follows:

- Quality of life conceptualises **holistically** the way of life of clients within their environments, but the complexity of measuring the interacting factors makes it difficult to evaluate how successful social work services are in achieving it.
- Quality of practice or service provision similarly involves complex judgements about defining and evaluating practice. Social work theory is only one aspect of the many factors involved in understanding social care service provision and social work practice, and is difficult to separate from political and social objectives, and resource issues.
- Quality is an issue in **marketisation** since in markets there is always a trade-off between price and quality. Theoretically, people will pay more for higher quality, providing incentives to traders for service improvement. But in an imperfect market, traders may covertly reduce quality to increase profits. Market information and regulation seek to reduce this problem, but it is hard for consumers to judge quality in complex professional services which depend on coordination and professional standards. Market competition may lead to fragmentation of provision among competing providers, and driving prices down through competition may lead to poorly understood reductions in quality.

A **quasi-market** is a public service organised to gain the claimed benefits of cost-restraint and quality improvement provided by competition between providers in a market. Mechanisms are established to mimic purchasing and providing in a market, and to regulate the market processes. In the UK social care system, various systems have used social work theoretical ideas to do this since a quasi-market was established in the mid-1990s, including **care management**, a form of American **case management**, and **self-directed care.**

R

Race is sometimes used as a term to refer to a group of people or a population of an identifiable ethnicity, as in 'race relations', 'race riot' or 'racial minority'. Its use goes back to a time when people from Asian, African, Black or Caribbean peoples were seen as of a different and inferior 'race' from Caucasian, European and white peoples. Since all human beings are biologically of one race, most social scientists refer to **ethnicity**, which emphasises cultural, historical and genetic identities of a population group rather than physical characteristics from genetic heritage. **Critical race theory**, mainly used in the USA, reflects the historical connection of 'race' with **slavery** and focuses on understanding Black perspectives and white **privilege**.

Racism and **institutional racism** is discrimination against people and social groups because of their race, a term that refers to **ethnicity** associated with distinctive physical features allied to culture, language or religion different from a majority population. Institutional racism is a pattern of governance and organisation in social institutions that incorporates attitudes, assumptions, conventions, expectations and social structures into their mode of operation which lead them to discriminate against devalued ethnic groups that lack the social **privileges** of the majority ethnic group. Racism is common among individuals and within social groups, and influences important institutions in society, raising professional concern to combat social injustice caused by it and the resulting barriers to personal and social achievement. This has led to the development of **anti-discriminatory** and **anti-oppressive** practice as significant elements in social work, both to combat racism itself and the personal and social consequences of it as they affect clients and the social groups that clients come from.

Radical practice theory See **Critical practice**, **Marxism**.

Rawls, John (1921–2002) was an American political philosopher, with **liberal** views, who was concerned with people's **freedom** to pursue their own beliefs and interests, with democracy legitimising actions to maintain a stable, **pluralist** liberal society that allows that freedom. His writings on **justice** influenced the policy environment in which governments provide for social needs. His liberal views of freedom led him to see justice from an 'original position' where we would have no knowledge of individuals' and groups' existing power, mitigated by the '**difference**' principle that the powerful rich should give preference to the needs of the powerless poor.

Reciprocity is passing privileges or resources between individuals or groups as an exchange, each person or group responding to the other. In law, it affirms agreements or **contracts** between people, implying **fairness** and **equality**. Reciprocal relations also balance **individualism**, combating selfishness and promoting **inclusivity** in social relations. Consequently, a lack of reciprocity may lead to **dependent, discriminatory** and **oppressive** relationships. It is also an important element in **caring** and **helping** relationships; returning past care may occur over time, for example an adult reciprocating care given by a parent when that parent needs care as an older person. A high degree of reciprocity in community relationships is one of the factors in **social capital** that assists **resilience** in the face of adversity (Kirmayer, Sehdev, Whitley, Dandeneau, & Isaac, 2009), for example in **family support** (Canavan et al., 2016). **Eco** practice implies reciprocity between humans and the environment: as people have an impact on the **environment**, they also provide for the environment's sustainability.

Reciprocity may be important to successful practice, particularly where, as with disabled clients, **helping** may be seen as demeaning. It may also generate ethical concerns for practitioners. Conventional social expectations and some political philosophies may assume that care or services should be reciprocated by clients with gratefulness or social compliance. Social work values, however, do not require reciprocation or appreciation of the social worker from clients (Leighton et al., 1982).

Recognition is identifying an idea, a person or a thing from its known characteristics, and from previous experience. Recent debate conceptualises social processes, in which recognising the social implications of injustice or relationship loss may help to reverse adverse social reactions. There are two main positions, but debate (Fraser & Honneth, 2003) suggests that both positions are complementary, so that both interpersonal and **social justice** practice may use recognition ideas.

- The **critical** social philosopher Axel Honneth draws on **psychoanalytic** theory, particularly Bowlby's **attachment theory** and Winnicott's view that secure child development derives from human interaction. Honneth focuses more on building social self-confidence, self-respect and self-esteem, so that interpersonal recognition in human relations is created in society. This position has proved attractive to social workers (Garrett, 2018a: 190–3); for example, Thomas (2012) has argued that recognition is a useful way of understanding the value of children's participation in decision-making in social work.
- The feminist philosopher Nancy Fraser (2000) argues that recognition should be a response to social injustice or problems with adopting a social group's human rights. If the injury to human rights or injustice is recognised and responded to in an **authoritative** way, people affected may be helped to deal with the personal consequences of the injustice. Redistributive **social justice** actions would constitute a political recognition of and reparation for such injustices, while interpersonal recognition, for example of gender oppression through **identity politics**, does not achieve this.

Further Reading

Garrett, P. M. (2018). *Social work and social theory: Making connections* (2nd ed.). Bristol: Policy Press.

The **reconceptualisation movement** in Latin American social work was a Marxist-influenced philosophy, critical of capitalism, contesting personal change as a strategy to meet the needs of people in **poverty** and experiencing **racism**. It sought community **empowerment** through processes like **Freire**'s ideas of **conscientisation** and participatory action research. When authoritarian dictatorships suppressed this movement, community work concentrating on protecting human **rights** and developing local strengths through education were important social work strategies (Saracostti, Reininger & Parada, 2012).

Recovery is a movement or practice theory in **mental health**, derived from mental health patients or survivor movements which promote service users' leadership in care provision for people recovering from mental illness. Mental health **activism** developed these ideas, influencing American mental health services during the 1980s and 1990s (Adame & Leitner, 2008). **Peer support** by recovering patients for each other has been shown to help recovery for both supporter and patient. Many Western governments, including Ireland, New Zealand, the UK and the USA, developed policies favouring recovery in the twenty-first century (Watts & Higgins, 2017).

Criticism of recovery is of two kinds. One view contests recovery's lack of ambition in not aiming for positive mental health, a 'cure', rather than simply improvement in some capacities for normal living. This burdens patients, carers, community and family with long-term disability and stigma. Against this, the recovery view argues that demanding too much also places an unrealistic burden on the patient and steady progress towards improvement may be motivating. The other criticism is the way in which it encourages an **anti-psychiatry** distance from effective medical psychiatric treatment.

Recovery from mental illness implies moving towards or achieving a mental state that someone prefers to their condition of illness. It looks back to past attainments and regaining some of the capacity that the mentally ill person previously benefited from. In this way, it challenges assumptions in early psychiatry that complete recovery from major or psychotic mental illness was not possible. Later experience and research found that individuals improved at least in the remission of symptoms; sometimes the illness is described as 'burned out'. This may lead to decreased medication, and a decline in social disabilities so that living independently and working became possible for many (McCranie, 2010: 473–4). Recovery thus became associated with improvements in at least some aspects of the **quality** of life.

R

Seeing recovery as a process through which people move contests a therapeutic or **medicalised** view of recovery as treatment coming from an external source leading to a cure. During the recovery process, people use their internal resources to acknowledge being socially disabled but nevertheless move towards achieving a new sense of **self** (Deegan, 1995). This might include '... the development of new meaning and purpose in one's life as one grows beyond the catastrophic effects of mental illness' (Anthony, 1993: 527). These conceptions are related to **strengths** theory; Rapp and Goscha's (2012) strengths practice in mental health was reformulated as 'recovery-oriented' in its later iterations.

Tew et al.'s (2012) literature review of social factors in recovery from mental illness identifies the importance of working with **families** and **communities**. They suggest this forms a proactive agenda for mental health practice in social work. Frost, Tirupati, Johnston and Conrad's (2017) review of the literature makes a helpful distinction between **psychosocial** intervention and rehabilitation aims in setting service requirements for an integrated recovery-oriented service:

- Psychosocial interventions promote hope, recovery, self-**agency** and social **inclusion**.
- Rehabilitation interventions achieve improvements in daily functioning, working with the service user on restoration of skills and competencies and active community reconnection.

This recent professional analysis incorporates recovery movement ideas into service planning and management for professional and user-led mental health services and emphasises the social aspect of mental health.

Reflection is the process of examining and thinking about situations that we are involved with and being able to change our future behaviour as a result. It is important in **attachment** practice theory and also in professional education and practice, as follows:

- Attachment theory and practice evaluates and works with attachment figures' **attunement** to the emotions and reactions of people they are caring for. Part of this is mentalisation, the capacity to build a mental picture of how others see you and compare it with how you see yourself. Being able to reflect on our relationships with others is an important aspect of our capacity to care for others successfully.
- Reflection on experiences and changing our professional responses is an important part of professional development in occupations such as teaching or helping people, and a methodology has been built up for doing so; see **Critical reflection**. This is connected with the interpersonal and research processes of **reflexivity**.

Reflexivity is a process in which you interact with others taking account of your understanding of their concerns and perceptions, and they do likewise. You all also facilitate the others in expressing their **frames** of reference about the situations with which

you are concerned. As you do this, the interaction influences and responds to every-one's knowledge and understanding of the behaviour and reaction within the situation. Thus, the interaction becomes **intersubjective**. This means that everyone involved is a **subject**, a **self-directed** actor, in the process, and all your subjective experiences and interpretations are part of what goes on. In social work therefore, the practitioner does not do social work to clients, families or communities, but each participant in the social work influences how the **process** moves. All the participants define and express the social work, and the social worker is as influenced as everyone else involved.

Reflexivity is the outcome of a successful **dialogical** process, in which the interaction is equally open to the expression of all participants' perceptions and reactions. This concern with bringing together openly the external and internal dialogues of the participants originates in **feminist** thinking. Reflexivity is also associated with successful **critical reflection** in practice and with developing **participation** in research about disabled people's and women's issues.

Five types of reflexivity are:

- Introspection, in which each participant looks at their own thoughts and the as-yet-unthought-about elements of others' thoughts that they become aware of.
- **Intersubjective** reflection, in which participants work together to reflect on the meaning of the concepts they are using and to deconstruct the social processes that are going on among them.
- Mutual collaboration, perhaps particularly relevant in **multiprofessional** work or where carers or clients are 'expert' in their condition or community. This is about sharing interpretations and creating new ideas building on each other's thoughts.
- Social critique, using ideological commitment or processes of **critical thinking** to interrogate what is taken for granted in the situation.
- Ironic **deconstruction** in which you take away the privileges of existing conventions and explore unexpected ambiguities. 'We can't do that? Why not – because daddy will think we're bad girls?' (Finlay, 2003: 6–16).

Reframing is a family therapy technique, widely used in social work practice and derives partly from **Goffman**'s sociological '**frame analysis**'. Reframing starts from the reality that everyone limits the perspective they have on situations they are involved with. Our own concerns and interests draw a boundary around the issues and personalities that we look at. Reframing involves looking at the situation from a different point of view. For example, a father may see a teenage daughter's hostility to her mother as lack of respect and sullen behaviour perhaps connected with hormonal change. But this frame does not permit him to look more widely at principled disagreements between both parents and the daughter about appropriate behaviour and interests for young women. Shifting his frame of reference might enable all three to have a more constructive joint response to changing attitudes in the family. A social worker might help with reframing by discussion of possible alternative perspectives, or by working with the family members to experiment with behaviour changes that might alter or broaden perspectives.

Reid, William J. (1928–2003) was an American social work academic who made influential contributions to practice theory with the creation, with Laura Epstein, of **task-centred practice** (Reid & Epstein, 1972b). He also made significant contributions to promoting effectiveness in practice through research, including leadership in an 'empirical practice movement' (Reid, 1994; Witkin, 1996) and wider analysis of social work effectiveness (Reid & Hanrahan, 1982; Reid, Kenaley & Colvin, 2004), leading to the important **evidence-based** practice movement.

Relational practice is an important twenty-first century theory of practice, building on **psychodynamic** ideas. It focuses on how people can better manage themselves in relationships with others. Relational practice starts from engaging in and fostering helping relationships with a client or clients. This connects with earlier theory centring social work on **relationship**.

Ruch's (2018a: 27–8) statement of the main understandings informing relational social work are as follows:

- All professional intervention includes human behaviours and professional relationships.
- Human experience is enriched but complicated by conscious and unconscious emotions affecting rational thought.
- Internal and external worlds are inseparable parts of human experience.
- Social work encounters are each unique, responding to individuals' circumstances.
- Collaborative client–worker relationships channel interventions, emphasising the use of **self**.
- **Respect** for individuals' uniqueness involves practising in **inclusive** and **empowering** ways.

In relational practice (Freedberg, 2009; Goldstein, Miehls & Ringel, 2009; McColgan & McMullin, 2017; Ruch, 2018b; Ward, 2018), early relationships, powerful feelings, anxiety and uncertainty are made visible by being mirrored in the client–practitioner relationship through transference and countertransference. Issues are tackled through boundary-setting, containing emotions and anxieties in a safe environment. This balances clients' and workers' self-autonomy with their affective connection. Safety enables curiosity about, and exploration of, life experiences that are not fully known. The use of self involves accepting that in professional encounters awareness of core elements of our personal identity interact with others to influence our interactions with others. Those elements include political, spiritual, professional and personal attitudes and experiences.

Interactions therefore inevitably involve appropriate self-disclosure about clients' and workers' lives and feelings. **Intersubjectivity** means that emotional reactions to the world are jointly experienced in the relationship. This is achieved through workers' **attunement** to and **empathy** with clients' lives. Such approaches may be challenging to implement in practice agencies managed within **neoliberal** economic policies, but may contribute richness to otherwise prosaic interventions (Froggett, 2002; Marshall, 2017).

Further Reading

Ruch, G., Turney, D. & Ward, A. (Eds.) (2018). *Relationship-based social work: Getting to the heart of social work* (2nd ed.). London: Jessica Kingsley.

Relationship was theorised as an important aspect of social work practice from the 1930s onwards, identifying a specifically social work approach to **helping** others, and distinguishing the social work relationship **psychodynamic** ideas about psychotherapy. Consumer research (e.g. Glastonbury, 1976; Howe, 1993; Huxley, Evans, Beresford, Davidson, & King, 2009) shows that good **quality**, **respectful** relationships are valued by clients as **helpful**. Contemporary practice continues to see effective worker–client relationships as essential. Examples are Rapp and Goscha's (2012) account of **strengths** practice,

Relationship is important in social work practice theory for two main reasons. First, one person influencing another requires an interpersonal relationship; it cannot be done at a distance (Perlman, 1957: 64–83). Ideas about relationship analyse important characteristics of social work helping processes. Second, relationship is important in social work because social workers often deal with people's difficulties in relationships with others. The social work helping relationship engages directly in those difficulties as they occur by modelling and offering options for alternative ways of relating (Irvine, 1952). For example, if clients or families feel oppressed by people in **authority**, social workers can model, in the helping relationship, the use of their official and professional powers. In this way, people experience how to relate positively to people in authority (Studt, 1959).

Early accounts of social work (Cannon, 1913; Richmond, 1965[1917]) do not emphasise relationship. Robinson (1930) argued that the period 1920–30 saw a shift from a focus on the individual to relationship in the theorisation of social work. Elements of relationship in casework are summarised in **Biestek's** (1961) important text. Rejecting friendship, contact, sympathy, rapport and transfer as descriptions of social workers' relationships with clients, he saw the purpose of relationship as helping clients with their psychosocial needs and problems, by creating an atmosphere in which clients can engage with practitioners. Relationships focus, first, on attitudes, defining the direction that the client wants to move in. Second, these interact with emotions, the conscious excitement to act, brought about by stimuli in the client's life. The relationship moves as clients' needs interact with practitioners' sensitive responses and clients' awareness of practitioners' sensitivity and understanding. Seven principles for relationship define how the worker creates it:

- **Individualisation**, recognising a client's uniqueness, and therefore adapting interventions to clients' specific needs.
- The purposeful expression of feelings, enabling them to be recognised and dealt with.
- Controlled emotional involvement, practitioners' sensitivity and responsiveness to clients' feelings.
- **Acceptance**, dealing with clients as they are, enabling them to reveal themselves.
- Non-judgemental attitudes, avoiding evaluations of clients' attitudes, standards and actions and setting aside their responsibility for causing problems.
- Clients' **self-determination** in making choices as part of their work together.
- Confidentiality, preserving secret information about clients.

While some of these principles are ethical responsibilities or **values** in social work, Biestek sees them instrumentally, as necessary to creating a successful helping relationship.

A Marxist critique of this focus on interpersonal relationships in social work is that it prevents us acknowledging that all relationships are conditioned by economic relationships, which our practice then fails to tackle (Rojek et al., 1988: 50).

Feminist social work accounts of relationships from the 1980s focus on the value of women's relationships with each other in working on matters of emotional welfare (Dominelli & McCleod, 1989: 88–9), and a **dialogic** style, in which workers and women clients engage in interactions between equal participants, fostering awareness of shared interests, rather than between a worker with professional status and a less influential client (1989: 131–54). Feminist writing identifies the importance of workers' and clients' identities as women, and the organisational context in which sharing is facilitated and women's identities are valued (Hooyman, 1991; Kravetz & Jones, 1991; White, 2006); this idea may be extended to shared interests in any practice context. Milner (2001: 5) stresses that a **narrative** and **solution** approach is open to accepting a range of clients', and particularly women clients', experiences, a focus on present and future rather than past lives and a focus on behaviour rather than emotions. This challenges the focuses of relationship theory in the 'traditional' psychodynamic history of social work thinking on relationship.

Further Reading

Biestek, F. P. (1961). *The casework relationship*. London: Allen and Unwin.

Religion is belief or faith in a transcendent being or beings, existing beyond and exceeding ordinary human experience, which exercises influence on humanity and nature. Important world religions are **Buddhism**, **Christianity**, Judaism and **Islam**

and there are many faiths with fewer adherents. Religion is a form of socially organised **spirituality**; religious institutions have wide social functions. Different religious traditions are important as influences on social work theory and values and because religious organisations provide social care services and sometimes social work. Significant forms of social work originated in Christianity and Judaism in Western cultural traditions, and have had a considerable influence on social work professional practices and values. Many public and other social care agencies pursue explicit secularism to reduce the direct impact of practitioners' religious beliefs on potentially diverse populations. The continuation of this influence from Western religion is part of cultural imperialism, and because these ideas are woven into all social work means we cannot disentangle Christianity from any practice. Other Indigenous and religious traditions have also begun to influence social work for particular population groups or in particular nations or regions, but this does not remove the impact of Western religions on social work everywhere.

Representation arises in social work in two ways:

- Social workers representing clients' interests through **advocacy** and other means both within their own agency and also to other organisations.
- Representation as presenting a picture of ourselves, the social work profession and perhaps more importantly, of clients and communities to colleagues. Social workers do this, for example, in case conferences, court proceedings, meetings, reports, social histories. While this is relevant to advocacy and also to **narrative** techniques, the picture represented of clients through words and in unspoken ways may be something that the practitioner is less aware of. How the practitioner presents themselves may also influence others in the way they understand and react to social work practice.

Residential care or residential work is providing care and therapeutic services and accommodation together. Although not usually included in the idea of **modality**, residential work practice could reasonably be regarded as a form of social work. Clough's (2000) typology of residential care theory covers theories of the residential world, of the function and task of residential care work, of intervention and of residential homes as systems.

Applying practice theories in residential care work requires adapting them to the special characteristics of work in the social organisation of an institution in a **place**, a specific location separate from ordinary life. Practice theories that focus on residential care work include:

- **Group care**, seeing the care home as a location for **groupwork**.
- Life space or **milieu** therapy focusing on learning to live with others and the practitioner in a shared living space.

- Reality therapy (Glasser, 1965), seeing care homes as a location for preparing people to make choices in their lives about how to meet their needs for power over their lives, love and belonging, independence and autonomy, fun and satisfaction and survival needs.
- **Social pedagogy**, seeing care homes as a location for activity through which people learn about successful social relations with others, both peers and helping professionals.
- **Therapeutic community** theory, seeing the management of life and regime of the care home as the focus of psychological development and social skills learning.

Resilience (UK) or resiliency (US) means, in psychology and social work, the capacity to recover from adverse circumstances. It may refer to individuals, families or communities or wider social processes. Greene (2012), for example, presents resilience as an explanation of human behaviour helpful to social work practice, and describes research in social work as identifying **strengths** that allow a child to emerge from a history of abuse or neglect, or adults from a history of mental illness and social disruption. Reflecting a developmental psychology view of resilience, which explores interactions between children and others, Gilligan (2004) analyses three elements of resilience in children as **processes** that generate positive **adaptation** when someone faces adversity. This process involves the creation of relationships with key people, providing a **secure base**; this aspect of his analysis derives from **attachment** theory. A sociological critique proposes that while lack of resilience is produced by social factors such as **poverty** and **inequality**, most theoretical analysis from a psychological perspective does not address the social factors in causation. People at risk are expected to accommodate to social risks, rather than the social factors being addressed in preventive interventions (Garrett, 2018b; Park, Crath & Jeffrey, 2020). The **individualisation** of psychological conceptualisations of resilience is thus inadequate to account for resilience in collectives. Walsh (2016: 4–7), from a family perspective, criticises the idea of the 'rugged individual', suggesting that resilience comes from cooperation and mutual **support**. Similarly, Canavan et al. (2016) see resilience in **family support** as about developing skills in negotiating support in systems surrounding a family.

Kirmayer et al.'s (2009) account using resilience ideas from materials science identifies three strengthening ecological mechanisms: preventive buffering, reduces the impact of stresses; 'self-organisation', a complex adaptive systems idea, maintains important functions; ecological recovery, however, involves 'transition' to a new state, a concept also picked up in **eco** social work practice theory.

Resistance. Various conceptions of resistance influence social work theory:

- The intuitive understanding is that some people will not accept social work intervention either at all, or of particular kinds, or in particular matters, or at particular times, and will therefore refuse cooperation with social workers.

- The **transtheoretical model of change** and **motivational interviewing** contest these ideas, proposing that people take time to make changes in their lives, and this should not be judged as a psychological failing. A generous and helpful response from agencies may help them decide and act on thoughts about change.
- In **motivational interviewing**, 'rolling with resistance' proposes that where clients are not yet ready to make changes they may 'push back' against suggestions for change from people in authority, including the social worker. Rolling with resistance involves listening to the client's reasons for being unable to change, accepting them and then helping to overcome them. You shift the focus and reframe the issues that clients have (Hohman, 2016: 99–113).
- **Psychodynamic theory** identifies resistance as a defence mechanism. It arises because of important thoughts about reality that are repressed when the client is unable emotionally to accommodate them in their rational thinking. This view of resistance is different from other senses of the term because clients are unaware of its happening; their unconscious mind is the obstruction. Practitioners would help clients gain **insight** into why they are unable to make progress and explore alternative actions that avoid anxieties that prevent them from acting as rationally they would like.
- A **radical** conception of resistance, deriving from **Marxist** thought, refers to situations in which oppressed people are helped to become conscious of pressures to conform with the interests of capitalist elites and work collectively to resist those pressures, for example by campaigning or other **activism**. Contemporary social movements extend resistance from class-based activism to broader community activism, by helping groups to identify and take action where social pressures are forcing them into something that lies outside their beliefs. Social workers would help individuals find others who share consciousness of their oppression. They would enable groups to identify and raise their concerns, helping people to take control of improving their situation through working.
- Community conceptions of **resilience** propose that resilience often arises from experiences of resistance to some kind of assault on the humanity of community members, leading them to organise and build community structures to achieve resilience.
- **Foucault's** concept of resistance is connected with his analysis of power and domination (Howarth, 2000: 82–3). He contests the Marxist and Weberian views of **power** and domination. The Marxist sees power as domination of oppressed people from above. **Weber** is concerned with the way that **bureaucratic** and other structures of authority and power form a rational logic that becomes part of the accepted assumptions about how we should act. Foucault challenges this, pointing to the reality that as soon as force or structural inertia affects us, resistance is natural, even universal. **Oppression** is never total; people find their ways of avoiding it and identifying and building resistance is part of **anti-oppressive practice** (Baines, 2017a). Social work theory needs to theorise non-compliance and possible responses to it.

R

Respect, and respect for persons, is an important value in social work

practice, although Plant (2009[1970]: 23) argues that it is not specific to social work, but 'a presupposition of [all] morality ... the property of any morally engaged person'. Respecting someone has become, in the twenty-first century, a daily demand for treating a person, their opinions and their individual and collective **identity** as of value to us. We value both their 'generic self', that is, the merits that all or most human beings have, and the 'idiosyncratic self', the aspects of identity that are special to this individual (Downie & Telfer, 1969: 19).

How do we carry out this respect? Downie and Telfer (1969: 23–30) argue that this means having two sets of behaviour. First, we have a particular attitude towards another person, experiencing a shared feeling with them, conscious of them as a person and being concerned for them and their experience of life. Second, we form principles of action in how we treat people, in public and private morality. As a result, public services and individual social workers must behave respectfully. So must other people in their interpersonal relationships. These principles involve seeing people as equals, in brotherhood and sisterhood and valuing the ends that they seek for themselves. Similarly, respect implies treating people as ends in themselves, rather than acting towards them as a means to an end.

The concept is connected to impartiality, a refusal to be swayed in our actions or decisions by irrelevant considerations, which calls on **Enlightenment** views that value rationality as an important human value.

Types of respect that may be distinguished include the following:

- Recognition respect is acknowledgement by ourselves or others that something or someone is worthy of respect.
- Appraisal respect is differences in the extent and way in which we communicate respect.
- **Self-respect** is also important and follows similar lines (Banks & Gallagher, 2009: 118–20).

Further Reading

Banks, S. & Gallagher, A. (2009). *Ethics in professional life: Virtues for health and social care* (pp. 111–23). Basingstoke: Palgrave Macmillan.

Richmond, Mary Ellen (1861–1928) is considered one of the pioneers

of social work, through her leadership in the American charity organisation movement of the late nineteenth and early twentieth centuries, particularly in Baltimore. One major work formulated the extensive collection of social information about a family, as the basis of a **holistic diagnosis** (Richmond, 1965[1917]). A later account of **social casework** (Richmond, 1922), derived from case studies in local agencies, focuses more strongly on relationship. Robinson (1930) sees 'Social Diagnosis' as an account of the period's holistic sociological casework, being supplanted by relationship ideas drawing primarily on psychoanalysis. Thus, Soydan's (1999) analysis of her work within the history of ideas in social work classifies it as a focus on movement from practice to theory, the micro to the macro.

Rights See **Human rights**.

Risk is the likelihood that an adverse event will occur; concern about risk is a response to **ambiguity** and uncertainty. Webb (2006) connects its theoretical importance to **modernity**, the post-**Enlightenment** focus on rationality, and the **neoliberal** emphasis on regulation of the state's participation in the **social**. Beck (1992), the sociological source of this analysis, shows how this privileges the interests of capital to operate freely, without economic resources being used to reduce risk for people whose lives are made precarious.

As a result of these processes, social work as a profession becomes regulated, part of which is enforcement of **technical rational** processes in **new public management**, to manage actions and decisions. Such processes include mechanisms such as developing, researching and implementing risk-management technologies for analysis and control of risks. Professional accounts (Titterton, 2005; Taylor, 2017) therefore emphasise the legal source and practical means of managing risk taking. A particular concern has been to manage child safeguarding, mental health risks of violence against the public or suicide, and risks of disabled and older people's physical frailties leading to social costs. This has led to **proceduralisation** to control professional discretion leading to social expenditure (Parton, 2005, 2014). An example is the emphasis on risk in **signs of safety** even though this is a **solution** and **strengths** approach to children safeguarding. These movements connect with clients' psychological need for security and contest the idea of management of **discretion** through professional processes such as **critical reflection** and supervision.

R

Various responses contest these developments. One approach is to reassert **profession-alisation** of **discretion** and **judgement** as more flexible in dealing with complexity (Cross et al., 2010; Munro, 2011). Kemshall's (2010) more complex accounts of risk management suggest that 'responsibilising' a client or practitioner as a 'rational actor' without resources to accept the responsibility to use rational techniques in the absence of analysis of the constraints and pressures in which the risk is 'situated', requires a range of both flexible and technical means of managing risk. Another response is to assert the importance of **security** in social structures and interpersonal and social relations.

Further Reading

Taylor, B. J. (2017). *Decision making, assessment and risk in social work* (3rd ed.). London: Sage.

Role, an aspect of **structural-functional** theory in sociology, is the idea that we may identify positions that people occupy in social relations and social structures. Shared understanding of these positions derives from social expectations of the people around them in connected positions. Questioning of limitations in structural-functional theory has led to a decline in the influence of role theory. The idea of role continues in use, however, because it expresses responsibilities attached to designated roles in organisations, and distinguishes some sets of responsibilities in organisations from others, for example in job descriptions and in multiprofessional settings. In 2019, for example, the English government published an extensive report on 'new social work roles' in mental health, designating social work as a 'key profession' in mental health services (Bayliss-Pratt, 2019).

Roles may be:

- Ascribed, that is, given by a person or organisation; for example, job roles given by employers, and by acceptance among other employees and clients.
- Achieved, that is, gained as actions and events occur; for example, parental roles when children are born and cared for.

Interactions between people in their roles create expectations that form social structures contributing to social cohesion and certainty in behaviour and relationships. Sticking to roles helps people to have greater certainty about how others will react than if expectations are unclear. Working to clarify people's understanding of their roles and other people's expectations of them in social situations helps to deal with anxiety, fear and insecurity, whereas permissiveness may be unhelpful (Varley, 1968: 365).

Critique of using role concepts is similar to concerns about structural-functional theory. It assumes that an established social structure of relationships in society leads to people's functions in relationships being broadly agreed. In culturally and socially diverse societies, people may have different expectations of others, so there is no certainty in role expectations. Also, structures may be in flux preventing agreement and stability in roles.

Goffman's dramaturgical role theory (1968) suggests, in a theatrical analogy, that all role-based actions contain elements of **performance**, 'impression management' behaviour designed to demonstrate attention to and achievement of the task required of a person. Consequently, performance is not a characteristic of the person but something all people do in taking on a role, and people are not 'performers' as a matter of personality. People's performance often participates in a '**team**' effort in which people cooperate to maintain an impression of action relevant to the task. Performances take place in particular **places** appropriate to the performance, and where roles are discrepant, containing conflicts or confusions, people retreat 'off-stage' to reconstruct their teamwork, or to engage in 'back-stage' behaviour not relevant to the impression they want to give of task completion. In public (Goffman, 1972), teams generate supportive interchanges to show how they are performing in the task and remedial interchanges if observers or other participants in the activity are gaining the wrong impression of what they are doing.

The element of performance in roles also has ethical implications: does performing a role mean that the person disappears, that there is nothing of the human being in the performance of the role? In many activities, for example in relationships between clients and social workers, both personal and role-based elements are present. The humanity of the social worker, avoiding impersonality, is essential to forming a professional relationship in practice and to being, ethically, a social worker in relationship with a client. Moreover, it must always be expected by an **agency** or other organisation relevant to practice, such as a court of law, and is an aspect of the professional judgement of the practitioner. Therefore, performing professional roles always blends personal and impersonal elements (Downie, 1971: 134–8).

The following entries outline some ideas about role that have been helpful in social work practice.

Role ambiguity arises where it is unclear what role a person is occupying in a social situation, or people involved in the situation have differing expectations of the role.

Role complementarity theorises (Spiegel, 1957) that roles are patterned within cultures, so that much role-based behaviour is unthinking; this emerged in family work, but may also be applied in organisations or elsewhere.

Role conflict is the idea that roles held or viewed by individuals may cause difficulties when they conflict.

Role distance is a way of managing relationships to deal with role ambiguity or conflict; while people accept a role, they demonstrate by their behaviour that they are not fully committed to it (Ruddock, 1969: 14–15).

Role set is a concept in sociology devised by Robert K. Merton (1968[1949]: 41–3). It proposes people maintain several roles in their lives associated with positions in a social structure, often in different spheres, whose interactions may be identified and analysed. A social worker, for example, has roles in private life as child and parent, as an employee of the social **agency** where they work, as **carer** or **helper** of clients, as colleague of foster carers, informal caregivers and team members, as an ethical practitioner, as an **authority** figure for clients and in **surveillance** of social behaviours. Although all these roles and others go together, elements of them may conflict. For example, a caring role with a client may conflict with responsibility for ensuring that the client behaves appropriately, for example preventing them from ill-treating their spouse or children.

S

Safeguarding is the contemporary theorisation of the social work role in protection against abuse. While it involves **relationship** practice, it integrates actions, interventions and policies by agencies according to legal official procedures into professional practice (Lawson, 2017). The critique of safeguarding as a social work role revolves around the history of **proceduralisation**, particularly in child safeguarding and the way in which **neoliberal** econo-mics and **new public management** in children's services have led to a withdrawal from preventive and supportive services and a failure to provide the range of care services and personal support that underlies the assumptions of safeguarding policy.

Further Reading

Parton, N. (2014). *The politics of child protection: Contemporary developments and future directions.* Basingstoke: Palgrave Macmillan.

Salomon, Alice (1872–1948) was a German feminist activist and leading social work educator, who founded and became first president of what became the International Association of Schools of Social Work. She saw **social justice** as an important aim of social work, a precondition of which is the same **rights** for both men and women, people from all social classes and all minorities and disadvantaged groups. She believed all human beings to be **interdependent**, opposed **individualism** and considered mutual aid a 'law of life' (Kuhlmann, 2001: 67).

Schön, Donald S. (1930–1997) was an American educationalist and manager, associated with the Massachusetts Institute of Technology. He was influential in social work and a wide range of other professions, in the development, with Chris Argyris (Argyris & Schön, 1974), of ideas of **reflection** in professional knowledge development and practice.

Security is an issue in many aspects of social work:

- Many views of **need** place physical and psychological security as an important human need. Increasing insecurity in employment and family life due to economic and social flexibilisation in complex **globalising** societies requires mechanisms to build trust, and social work may be one of those mechanisms. Economic and employment security as a basis for security in personal relationships and social behaviour informs the centrality of poverty and financial pressures in social work.

- In **helping** relationships, clients need to be secure in knowing that they will be helped and how and why the social worker is acting as they are. Clients' **autonomy** and control of their lives contributes to that, for example in **bereavement** and **crisis intervention**.
- Insecurity and **risk** are important social issues in contemporary society (Beck, 1992), and affect social workers' actions and responsibilities. This is crucial in practice because feeling insecure prevents people from working on difficulties.
- Providing security in childhood is seen as an important social objective of parenting, and in social work with children and families. **Attachment** practice, for example, seeks a **secure base** and replacement attachment figures to strengthen security.
- Laing's concept of 'ontological security' in **anti-psychiatry** proposes that people who are insecure in how they think of their **being** think differently about their relationships with others than people who are secure about their **identity**.
- **Existential** and **humanistic** practices give significant importance to both emotional and physical security.

The **self** is an important concept in many systems of philosophy and psychology, referring to an aspect of people's **being** which distinguishes them from others. Since the **Enlightenment**, understanding of the self has been a crucial aspect of being a helping professional, and exploring the self is consequently significant in critical reflection and supervision (England, 1986; McBeath & Webb, 1997). Working on the self is not entirely internal, however, because it is created by external interactions.

- Mead's (1934: 144–64) **symbolic interactionism** proposes that understanding of the world comes from conversations and interactions with others; we create symbols of our understandings. This is true also of our self. As we develop, we organise our internal conception of our self (the 'I'), but we also create an organised view, a symbol in our mind, of others' attitudes and reactions towards us (the 'me'). Self-consciousness arises when we become aware in ourselves of the reactions to our self that we awake in others, and we make use of the symbol of that understanding of our self in acting. The self is **reflexive** in this way acting on and reacting to people and things outside the person.
- Self psychology in psychoanalytic thought (Kohut, 1971, 1977) sees the self as a structure within the psyche that is constituted in relationships with others around the individual. This is done through mirroring, feeling that we are accurately perceived by others, idealising, connecting with a calming wise person, and twinship, experiencing a sense that we share some of our characteristics with others (Zimmerman et al., 2019). People need **affirmation** or validation from others so that they can develop a construction of their self that allows them to interact satisfactorily. Thus, self psychology rejects psychological **individualisation**, and sees the self as **intersubjective**.

- Rogers' (1961: 108–24) **person-centred** practice theory focuses on the development of **being**. Macdonald's (2017) recent presentation of it distinguishes between the 'actual self', the individual's conception of it, 'perceived self', as seen by others, and the 'ideal self', the actualisation of the self that the individual is aiming for. Rogers argues for practitioners to aim for **equilibrium** between these views of the self.
- **Giddens** (1994) claims that the self is a reflexive project undertaken by individuals reconstructing in their minds a **narrative** trajectory of the importance to their conception of their own **identity** of aspects of their personal history.
- **Foucault** saw the self as formed by the history of social events and practices created by human knowledge and **action**. All practices, including professional practices, link to and shape the self through **dialogue** within relationships; it is not individual but an extension of the social relations that form it (Chambon, 1999: 52–3). **Globalisation** extends the range of relations forming our self, in interactions with **ambiguous** and complex ideas reflecting different cultures (Hermans & Hermans-Konopka, 2010). 'Technologies of the self', among which is social work, are ways in which people make changes in their self. Doing so also brings them in touch with the governmentality exercised within society by such helping professions (Foote & Frank, 1999: 157–64). An example of this is **bereavement**, when grief and mourning require people to actively change their self, usually helped by family and friends, occasionally by professionals, all of whom bring influences from wider social structures into the process.

Self-actualisation is a **humanistic** theory concept, building on the work of Abraham Maslow. His analysis suggests that there is a hierarchy of human **needs**, with people prioritising meeting basic needs for nutrition and personal relationships. Once they are **secure** in such matters, people seek self-actualisation, to make progress towards fulfilling their human capacity to the greatest possible extent – 'peak experience' (Maslow, 1971: 162–3). This implies not perfection but experiences that help people towards moral or personal attainments. The critique of this concept is that it implies that people have deficits and can never be satisfied, always searching for some 'real' self, rather than the self that they have managed to achieve. Also, seeking self-actualisation may be inward-looking, even selfish, rather than concerned about others or social developments. Giddens (1994: 253–4) argues that self-actualisation implies a focus on time: what was different in the past that leads to the project for changing the present for an improved future? This involves a balance of opportunity and **risk**, letting go of the now to become something that you do not fully know. For social work, there is also the question of whether we should always encourage or push people to try to self-actualise, when they do not want to commit energy to future goals. In answer to these points, it can be argued that **ethical** practice would enable people to identify their achievements, satisfactions and **strengths**, as well as possible future aims. Social work might also aim to help people think about how to contribute to **social change** or interpersonal achievements as well as being inward-looking.

Self-advocacy See Advocacy.

Self-determination has been regarded in social work as an important ethical and practice principle, although this is controversial and ideas of **participation** and **self-direction** have sometimes been preferred (Biestek & Gehrig, 1978). Keith-Lucas (1975[1963]: 44) describes it as 'non-interference except in essentials', suggesting also that social workers should have a **liberating** role, helping clients to understand cultural, psychological and social factors that may get in the way of **freedom** to act.

Freedom to act may be limited by the social structures set by the impositions of government, such as bureaucratic processes, legal requirements and organisational constraints. Contemporary society is not laissez-faire in its expectations of its citizens, neither in authoritarian nor in democratic societies. Whittington (1975) notes, as well, that social work intervention is itself part of the paraphernalia of social conformity. Another critique of self-determination comes from **Foucault**'s ideas of governmentality and discipline. By learning, through technologies such as social work, to develop power over themselves, people incorporate into their understanding knowledges from society, influencing but not determining their actions.

Biestek and Gehrig (1978), in the classic historical account of self-determination in the USA, argue that socio-economic conditions affect the way in which self-determination was implemented in different periods; this is a warning to social workers committed to freedom in all periods of history. For example, in the 1920s, though the principle was acknowledged, social workers in the US accepted constraints on clients' freedoms to generate public support for their work. In the economic depression of the 1930s, clients were unlike the destitute of previous decades and received more respectful treatment.

Self-determination continues to be a concern for contemporary developments of social work theory, being important for example in **motivational interviewing**, and by implication in many **counselling** and psychotherapeutic forms of **helping**, such as **narrative, solution** and **strengths** practice, which all provide for a high degree of client control of any social work interventions and for freedom to go their own way. An important development of self-determination is ideas such as **co-production** and self-direction. These are differently focused, however, on control of service provision, rather than independent decision-making within the relationship with the practitioners, which is the main emphasis in self-determination.

Further Reading

McDermott, F. E. (Ed.) (1975). *Self-determination in social work: A collection of essays on self-determination and related concepts by philosophers and social work theorists*. London: Routledge and Kegan Paul.

Self-direction is the idea that human beings have the capability and right to decide on their actions without influence from others and from social influences. This concept is integral to **individualism** (Lukes, 1973), the related idea that individual human beings should be **respected** as having value and worth in themselves. Self-direction in this philosophical sense, because it is treated as a human right, is stronger than the **self-determination** in social work, which is merely a practice convention.

Self-direction is also part of governmentality in **Foucault's** (Chambon et al., 1999) social philosophy. This idea suggests that by developing knowledge, relationships and social skills that permit us to self-direct our lives, we come to be governed by the understanding that we have gained, which inevitably comes from wider influences in society, and therefore controls our direction through the hidden and informal **power** relations that have created these forms of knowledge.

Self-direction is an element of the aims of person-centred care in UK adult social care; this is unrelated to Rogers' **person-centred** practice. Originated by an independent agency, In Control, active during the early twenty-first century in the development of personalisation policy in UK adult social care (Gardner, A., 2014: 12), it operationalises **participation** policies. Self-direction contributed to defining clients' budgets for providing care services as part of managing 'direct' payments; this term refers to the UK implementation of the international movement towards 'cash-for-care' policies. It enables clients to achieve a greater degree of control of service provision. An example of **neoliberal** and **new public management** thinking, using economic incentives as part of public sector service provision, it was particularly strong in Scottish social care policy following the Social Care (Self-directed Support) (Scotland) Act 2013.

Further Reading

Pearson, C., Ridley, J. & Hunter, S. (2014). *Self-directed support: Personalisation, choice and control.* Edinburgh: Dunedin.

Self-efficacy is a psychological concept, originally developed in research on treatment of phobias by Bandura (1977b). It proposes that people's belief that they can do something affects the extent to which they can succeed, and has influenced virtually all psychological **helping** procedures, including social work. As a result, practice often tries to increase people's self-confidence that they can achieve what they aim for, especially in personal relations or in changing organisations, and this is an important motivating idea in **solution** and **strengths** practice.

Self-respect is a form of respect, seeing oneself as worthy of being valued as a human being for the characteristics we possess. Three types may be identified, related to the types of **respect** we might have for others:

- Human self-respect is a recognition of our own human worth.
- Appraisal self-respect is celebration of and pride in our achievements as a person, a form of **self-affirmation**, affirming the self.
- Status self-respect is the valuation of our worth by others (Banks & Gallagher, 2009).

Semiotics (earlier called semiology) is the study of signs and symbols in communication in social relations. This is important to social work, which uses communication extensively, because it explains how, as people steeped in our culture, we attach **meaning** to things.

While it has a long history and was part of Peirce's **pragmatist** philosophy, semiotics has become important in the **linguistic turn** in the social sciences in the later twentieth and early twenty-first centuries. It is a postmodernist development of some ideas of de Saussure, a French theorist of the early twentieth century. The argument is that words are nothing in themselves, merely 'signs' of an idea or object that our culture has attached them to. But it is useful to think about the process of 'signification', how we attach our word-signs to things. I can see a house opposite; everyone knows what a 'house' is, the signification 'house' distinguishes it from the apartments and garden sheds that I can also see. But other ideas are contained in this word. Domestic, perhaps, personal, private, safe, solid, respectable, a place that centres its residents in our community? Something that brings the English husband, Russian wife and teenage son who live in that building together; they go out with somewhere to come back to? Then, some social work creates significations. For example, Golding's (2008) **attachment** theory-based 'house' model of parenting, a picture of a house with safe haven on the ground floor, parenting with PACE (playfulness, acceptance, curiosity and empathy) built on that on the next floor, and behaviour management in the roof space. Using an ordinary domestic concept to represent a practice approach shows how our culture 'signifies' house, connecting the idea of house and ideas about parenting. All words have significations attached, and when we analyse them, we can see how they carry cultural signs.

Saussure's ideas underlie social theorisation about how our signs and signification show how words **construct** how we think about the world, and how the human and physical characteristics we find in the world come to have significance attached to them.

S

Sen, Amartya Kumar is an Indian economist and philosopher, a Nobel Prize winner in economic sciences (1998), who has worked in the UK and the USA. He is important in social work for his ideas about **poverty**, for example that the extent of famines is not natural, but created by the failure of governments to react quickly and strongly enough. He is also known for his work on development economics and **social development** (Sen, 2001). Moreover, he made an important contribution, based on that work, to theories of **justice** (Sen, 2009).

Sheffield, Ada Eliot (1869–1943) was an early American social worker who
made significant early contributions to the understanding of **case records** and clients' social
history as a social work technique (Sheffield, 1920), and to the formation of groupwork as a
member of 'the Inquiry' (Siporin, 1986). Later, she was, against the **psychologistic** trend of
the time, an important researcher and commentator on the sociology of social work, who
emphasised the 'situation' as an important element of thinking about practice (Shaw, 2019).

Signs of safety is a practice approach in child protection work drawing on
positive psychology and **solution** practice, devised by two Australian social workers,
Andrew Turnell and Steve Edwards (1999), which has been adopted internationally. It
focuses on **family support** to achieve child safety, drawing on concrete prescriptions of
brief intervention practices, such as **task-centred** practice. The critique of the approach
is its structured and **proceduralised** processes, although this helpfully aims at clarity
and involvement for clients. Another critique is the use of **authority** and the priority
given to the child **safeguarding** objectives inconsistent with the therapeutic aims of
its **strengths** and **solution** practices. Against this, it offers a positive engagement with
opportunities for success in family life alongside protection and safety. Research in several
countries suggests that it can be implemented with many positive results, even where
family members deny abuse (Turnell & Murphy, 2020: 10–24).

There are three main principles of practice:

- Build effective working relationships between all professionals and family members
  involved.
- Foster a stance of inquiry and critical thinking.
- Focus on practitioners' and service users' descriptions of helpful practice rather than
  broad aspirations to solutions and strengths practice 2020: 5–7).

The most important basis of safeguarding is a **risk** assessment. Strengths are evidenced
positively by looking at protection over time, avoiding treating risk as a negative. Consequently, four domains of risk are assessed by looking for positives:

- What are we worried about? This covers past harm, future danger and complicating
  factors.
- What's working well? This concentrates on strengths and safety.
- What needs to happen? This plans for the elements of future safety, as a solution.
- These points lead to a judgement: where are we on a scale of 0–10? 10 equals enough
  safety to close the case, zero says that it is certain that the child will be (re)abused.

The assessment contains three elements, which must be carefully distinguished: gaining
information, information analysis and judgements. Cases that create anxiety generate
demands for excessive and intrusive information gathering, but analysis of dangers,
strengths and safety shows when there is enough information to make a judgement.

The assessment is presented in straightforward statements focused on specific, observable behaviours, in language that clients can understand, so that they can think it through for themselves. The plans for future safety often involve the use of **authority** in a nuanced way. This avoids arbitrary and non-participatory coercion by clearly explaining the reasons for authoritative interventions, connections with the court or **agency** requirements and not taking emotional or aggressive reactions personally (Turnell & Murphy, 2020: 32).

Assessment leads to a continuing assessment and analysis cycle in which the child, immediate family and others providing support interact with child safeguarding services, legal systems and extended professional networks to identify:

- Shared goals.
- A trajectory of action, with clear steps.
- Measurement scales of progress.

An action cycle is jointly created from this, involving:

- Listening to and involving the children. There are various tools for doing this, for example the 'My three houses' model: children picture houses of 'good things', 'worries' and 'wishes' in their lives. See **Semiotics**.
- Parents, support people and children carrying out an everyday plan to ensure wellbeing, safety and success.
- Establishing a permanent naturally connected **support network**.
- Regular checking by support people to ensure that the plan is permanent.

The assessment, and analysis and action plans continue interacting with each other, until the judgement is reached that the safety level is seven or better.

These processes lead to the creation and implementation of a 'safety' plan. This involves:

- Setting up a working relationship with the family.
- Devising a straightforward understandable description of the child protection concerns.
- Safety goals: parents need to know clearly what will satisfy the authorities.
- Bottom lines: how the goals will be achieved, mainly devised by the family.
- Involving a lifelong network.
- Negotiating the details: who will do what, when.
- Plans for jointly monitoring the family's reunification, if they are separated, and progress.
- Creating word and picture explanations: working on these portrayals of the process for the children helps everyone's clarity.
- Seeing the safety plan as a continuing journey, not a product for one time.

The signs of safety model envisages a careful training and reflection process for developing multi-agency and practitioner commitment to the programme.

S

Further Reading

Turnell, A. & Murphy, T. (2020). *Signs of safety comprehensive briefing paper* (4th ed.). East Perth: Resolutions. Retrieved from: www.signsofsafety.net/product/signs-of-safety-comprehensive-briefing-paper-2/ (frequently updated).

Slavery affects social work thinking in two ways:

- The historical slave trade operated mainly by European colonialists for economic gain in the Americas and West Indies, drawing slaves from Africa. This derived from assumed **ethnic** and **racial** hierarchies, which still affects the thinking of majorities in Europe and other countries of Western culture, and creates a continuing personal experience of slavery for people mainly drawn from Africa. It influences the widespread importance given to **African-centred practice** concerned with African culture and traditions in affected countries.
- Modern slavery and people trafficking as an important form of exploitation and a safeguarding issue in many societies.

The **social** describes a field of concern and study about societies, their organisation and how people experience them that places social understanding at the centre of conceptions of society. Thus, it contests the **individualising** tendency of psychological understanding of social relations. In conceptions of the social, people act within social relationships as **subjects**, experiencing themselves, therefore, as being **self-determining** in their actions and decisions in social relations, but within the social contexts and structures that both facilitate and limit their **agency**. They are also **objects**, people who are acted on by patterns of influence and power within the relationships in societies. Ideas and knowledge about the social draw primarily on sociology and social philosophy. Thinking about social work as concerned with the social contests the **psychologisation** of social work **assessment** and **intervention**.

Focusing on the social is an important feature of **social work** that distinguishes it from **counselling**, health professions and psychotherapy.

Social action is activism in political decision-making processes to achieve social change. There are broader accounts of social action in sociology, which see it as **actions** taken within social relationships for collective or shared purposes.

Many practice theories suggest that social action through activism is integral to social work's broad social improvement aims. This is true of **advocacy, critical, eco, empowerment, macro, radical, social development** and **structural** practice ideas.

But Fenton (2019) points to a problem. Social action requires an agenda, energy and time on top of the main **caring** and **helping** jobs social workers are employed for. Since many of them are employed in government, there is usually some legal or managerial limitation on their involvement in political decision-making, except through internal **advocacy**. And clients are also busy, **oppressed** and pressed people whose priorities for their social workers may lie elsewhere. The consequence is that although there is professional debate about taking social action, there are no specifically social work practice guides to taking such action in general. Practice theory is focused mainly on specific actions to achieve outcomes for particular social groups or social issues.

Experiencing the economic depression of the 1930s led some social workers to see social action as an essential element of social work. Harry Lurie (1939[1933]: 756), representing a social action strand in US social work (Shriver, 1987), called for social work to acknowledge 'the fact that basic economic factors are involved in many of the social problems of the dependent family and the individual'. Coyle (1939b: 566) argued that social workers should not 'continue to pick up the pieces without even attempting to stop the breakage'.

Individual practitioners or groups of them need to consider what their agency and the political process allow and expect of them. A hierarchy of social action is as follows:

- Do not be quiet. Raise injustice and ineffective services within the agency and in interagency and interprofessional practice. In turn, agencies have a duty to review and change processes to respond to and take up reasonable evidence from its workers with decision-makers who can make a difference. Collecting and presenting good evidence is therefore an important professional skill (Hoefer, 2019).
- Participate in social action recognised as part of your job, and find jobs that make it possible.
- Representative bodies of your employment and profession may provide a supportive channel for communication and influence.
- Social action in your private life can avoid actions against clients' or employers' interests.
- Democratic and other representative processes allow movement towards change.
- Social action in clients' interests is discredited by acting for producer interests, the influence, power and status of your **agency** or of social work.

Social capital is building influence and power through increasing the number and strength of social networks and relationships. This can achieve social stability or social change as much as economic resources such as money, property, or physical resources. There are three main sources of this idea:

- **Bourdieu** argues that people, individually and as part of social groups such as families, accumulate resources that give them power by building 'durable networks' of relationships through which they know and appreciate, and are known and appreciated by, other people and groups (Bourdieu & Wacquant, 1992: 119).

- Coleman (1988), an American educational sociologist, argues that people need to communicate, particularly to children and family members, their knowledge and understanding of the world by helping and supporting others in families, communities and general social relations.
- Putnam (2000) argued that **individualised** rather than collective activities were encouraged by contemporary economics and politics, at least in the USA.

Among the contributors to social capital in a community are social relationships, networks and **reciprocity**, shared norms and values, a culture of trust, collective **participation** and access to resources (Mignone & O'Neill, 2005).

Social care refers in general to the link between 'the social' and **care**. They are linked because caring takes place in social relationships and within social institutions that incorporate social expectations and values, such as caring professions, marriages and care homes (Payne, 2014).

Social care is the UK sector of the economy and services that make provision for social development and support; other countries refer to 'social services' or 'social work services'. The term distinguishes the wider range of work carried out in the sector from social work, when that became a regulated profession at the beginning of the twenty-first century. It has the advantage of emphasising the **caring** and direct service aspect of social provision rather than therapeutic help or **social change** and working with people affected by long-term conditions. It also has the advantage of making a political and linguistic link with 'healthcare', with the relevant government ministry being named the Department of Health and Social Care in 2018.

Designating a social care sector and social care workers potentially expresses the **deprofessionalisation** of social care practice, excluding a range of service provision from professional social work. A critique suggests that it is developing an alternative profession, rejecting the direction of social work professionalisation.

Early usages of the term 'social care' include the development by the Barclay Report (1982) on the role and tasks of social workers, of 'social care planning' as one of two elements of social work, the other being **counselling**. Another early usage was the establishment in 1985 of the Social Care Association, drawing most of its membership from the former Residential Care Association, a professional association of residential care workers seeking to extend its influence in day and home care. The distinction between social work and a social care 'sector' gathered pace and logic in the 1990s as a substantial sector of for-profit residential, day and home care developed, and the UK government formalised a **quasi-market** for care services. The conceptualisation of 'social care' is therefore partly a creation of the **marketisation** and **privatisation** of UK social provision, in its turn an aspect of **neoliberal** economic and political thinking.

Further Reading

Payne, M. (2014). Social care and social justice. In M. Reisch (Ed.), *The Routledge international handbook of social justice* (pp. 398–408). Abingdon: Routledge.

Social change See Change.

Social construction See Constructionism.

Social development (SD) is a social work practice theory, drawing on

and contributing to **community development** ideas. Midgley (1993, 1995) identified three main forms of activity, similar to early formulations of **community work**:

- 'Individualist' strategies aiming at **self-actualisation, self-determination** and self-improvement of individuals within social institutions or **communities**.
- 'Collectivist' strategies concerned with building organisations.
- 'Populist' strategies using small-scale activities in local communities.

Contemporary SD theory contests the **individualisation, medicalisation** and **psychologisation** of Western social work. It emerges from theory informing the work of international development agencies, often associated with the United Nations. It formulates practice at a **macro** level, creating programmes of local social provision humanising and extending economic development.

Practice in Asia and Africa rejects these global development aims, however, and reflects regional priorities. Many concerns, nonetheless, are widely shared and generate a consistent perspective, as follows:

- Tan, Chan, Mehta and Androff (2017), in Southeast Asia, conceptualise SD's focuses as workforce and migration issues, welfare services and the role of women as caregivers and in the workforce, and development of community organisations and **capacity-building**.
- Patel (2015), in a South African perspective, places **globalisation**, technological change and economic and social integration driving both demands and opportunities to find new ways of addressing human needs for social welfare and address social issues that achieve human wellbeing, security and **social justice**, with different regions taking alternative courses.

- Desai's (2015) Asian perspective sees SD as emerging from different countries' alternative ways of responding to the diversity of spiritual and social issues they face.
- Pawar (2017), in the context of economic development in many Asian countries, argues that SD philosophies are relevant to both developed and developing countries, balance social, economic and ecological issues, focus on structural inequality and aim for peace-building and international cooperation.

Patel (2015: 125–6) identifies five main themes of this practice:

- A rights-based approach.
- Interrelating economic and social development to generate human **capital**.
- Democratic and **participative** strategies.
- Pluralistic involvement, including state and non-state actors alongside individuals, families, households and communities.
- Overcoming divisions between micro and macro practices.

Social exclusion See Exclusion.

Social justice is fair and equal relations between individuals and groups in society. Justice is about doing what is considered morally right, expressing **fairness** and impartiality in decisions between people, providing systems for adjudicating and enforcing fairness in society and in particular eradicating inequalities. Social justice, between social groups and institutions, is a complex, contested concept depending on cultural and social traditions of morality and on social relations (Reisch, 2014). The International Federation of Social Workers' (2014a) Global Definition of Social Work claims social justice as the first of social work's central principles, rather than an objective of practice.

Important views on justice are those of **Rawls** (1999), **Fraser** (2000) and **Sen** (2009). In Rawls' position, individual liberty requires that everyone should have an equal right to basic liberties such as freedom of expression, liberty of conscience and **religion**, and free choice of occupation and the right to work. Economic and social **inequalities** must also be provided for by **equal** opportunities and by adherence to the **difference** principle. This proposes that where social inequalities exist, the least advantaged should gain the most benefit from them. Rich people, to use their wealth in society, must contribute to the levelling up of the poorest. Fraser's argument is that redistribution of resources to achieve social justice should be a political objective as a recognition of and reparation for injustices. Sen emphasises procedural social justice, reducing injustices wherever we find them. We should do this by rationally thinking through issues that we come up against that seem to involve justice and arriving at a practical view about what we think is fair in the specific instances we are dealing with. Sen (2009: 225–317) argues that in doing so, we must always examine the strengths that are present in the institutional position of people affected by injustice and in the cultural and social possibilities in their lives, so that we work against both individual unfairness and structural oppression.

In social work practice, social justice is implemented by a variety of professional arrangements. Both individual fairness and social justice require detachment from organisational, personal and professional interests, and this also requires contestability: the chance to present your case and have it heard properly. The organisation and professionals need resources and training to provide just systems. Some outcomes may also require restoration of losses, including psychological losses, due to injustice, and transformational justice, which achieves change as a result of any adjudication that takes place. An example is where an organisational failing has led to loss, and people's response is to seek evidence that 'it will never happen again'; that means real and transparent change (Banks & Gallagher, 2009: 161–73). Social work is implicated in these as a profession that provides services to the public, implying that its practices are just and fair, and because it contributes to institutions that might compensate for injustices in decision-making, or unjustly distributed resources.

One longstanding social injustice arises from social stratification due to class divisions in many societies, and consequent economic inequalities and social immobility. **Poverty** and the related health inequalities are known to be socially determined. **Intersectionality** suggests that social injustice on grounds of **age**, **disability**, **ethnicity**, gender, religion, sexuality and **spirituality** are equally connected.

Watts and Hodgson (2019) identify four approaches to social justice within social work:

- Distributive justice, achieving fair and equal distribution of benefits, resources, rights and opportunities through fair and just functioning of publicly accountable **institutions**.
- **Autonomy** and rights, supporting people to act freely as moral agents with **dignity**, worth and recognising their **human rights** with personal and social **identities**.
- **Participation** and democracy, increasing spaces for participation and democratic decision-making and inclusion in public discourse.
- Critical, critiquing and challenging domination and **oppressive** relations embedded in economic and political **structures**.

S

Social learning theory is an element of cognitive behavioural therapy

devised originally by Bandura (1977a). It proposes that cognitive or thinking processes based on social experience and relationships mediate between stimuli and responses in traditional learning theory, so that people learn behaviours by experience and observation, particularly of people who are models. This incorporates educational and social strategies into behaviour change methods, making CBT more relevant to social work.

Important techniques include **modelling** and encouraging imitative behaviour. You persuade someone whom the client trusts to demonstrate a desired behaviour. Then you help clients to rehearse it in safe surroundings, and then to practise it in ordinary social surroundings. Similarly, social skills training, often done in **groups**, helps people rehearse skills in relating to others, and allows group members to support each other in practising the skills in real life. 'Assertiveness training' is used to help people learn the balance between being too **aggressive** in dealing with social problem and being too accepting of other people's incursions on their goodwill. Social skills training has been an important basis of help for people with intellectual disabilities or offenders in learning to live in community settings.

Social movements theory refers to sociological analysis of **alliances** of activist groups and people seeking widespread social change on a global scale using broad ideological concepts, such as environmental sustainability and women's **equality**, that gain widespread interest. Their breadth and global spread also engage commitment among social workers, leading to alliances between social workers' groups and other activist networks. That commitment interacts with ideologically founded theoretical developments in social work, such as **eco** and **feminist** practice.

Social pedagogy is a practice theory and range of professional services based on German, Nordic and Polish philosophy widely practised in mainland Europe, and the dominant social profession in some countries. Other similar social professions include cultural animation or education and social education. These social professions theorise practice as education rather than, as in social work, as processes of assistance and helping or psychological improvement or therapy. Consequently, social pedagogy is a forward-looking or positive practice theory, rather than being problem-based or therapeutic. It would therefore also be available to the whole population, rather than focusing on people in poverty or in working-class families and communities. For example, social pedagogy is part of post-school care in some Nordic countries where a high proportion of young people participate in 'wrap-around' pre- and post-school collective provision to facilitate their parents' employment.

The German philosophers Diesterweg and Mager (Hämäläinen, 1989, 2003; Lorenz, 1994: 91–7; Charfe & Gardner, 2019: 17–31) were early influences on the theory, arguing that people in poverty benefit from education and support to participate in democratic and social structures. Practice focuses on **activity** as a common 'third world' within which people experience and develop the links between their internal personal world or personal **identity** and their social world, their community environment (Kasca, 2015: 52–4). This develops skills in **participation** in local democratic structures and in wider social relations. As in **critical** and **macro** practice using **Freire**'s ideas, learning takes place within activities in a shared setting in which people develop tools for analysing social situations, learning from communication and interaction in the social contexts of these activities, to be able to explore and understand processes that lead them towards **action**. Marynowicz-Hetka (2019a, 2019b), drawing on Polish traditions, sees social pedagogy as an action science, in which shared social activity enables people to bring together analyses of social issues from multiple social science perspectives. This helps them meet social objectives such as living in harmony and contributing to society (see **Balance**), and particularly to local communities. Similarly, the Swiss writer Staub-Bernasconi (2003) sees social work as transdisciplinary, incorporating a range of perspectives for exploring how we should act in response to social problems in ways that enhance human rights.

Stephens (2013: 6), with a Nordic perspective, identifies four elements of social pedagogy, as follows:

- Developing people's personas, nurturing individual potential and achievement, and reducing the impact of conflicts that create **boundaries** between people.
- Working through assistance with personal **development**, especially in communication skills.
- Educational development.
- A universal ethos, or 'haltung' (Eichsteller & Holthoff, 2011; Kasca, 2015: 19), empowering individuals within their settings to become good individuals in a good society. This means unconditional respect for other people, empowerment to achieve **self-direction** in people's lives, improved confidence, self-belief, skills and greater **autonomy** in action (Kasca, 2015: 20).

The concept 'head, heart and hands' comes from the work of the Swiss educational-ist Pestalozzi (Charfe, 2019: 18–20). 'Head' is knowledge, 'heart' is deep, unconditional respect for humanity, and 'hands' represent practical use of shared **activity** to promote inclusion and participation in society. Interpersonal communication skill develops dialogues in supportive relationships, how to deal with conflict, and how to operate in democratic and emancipatory ways in organisations (Cameron & Moss, 2011).

These ideas are used in community education and residential care settings, particularly for children, but also in activity-based work in care homes for people with intellectual disabilities and mental illnesses and for older people. These ideas are present in social work in the UK, particularly in youth work. Many countries integrated it with social work, but were suppressed by **individualism** and **psychologism** in mainstream social work (Smith & Whyte, 2008).

Further Reading

Charfe, L. & Gardner, A. (2019). *Social pedagogy and social work*. London: Sage.

Social problems theorise some social relationships, behaviour or events as problematic in society because they are incompatible with important social values to the extent that interventions are needed to restore commitment to those values. Different conceptions of the processes exist, as follows:

- Nineteenth-century 'social pathology' views saw social effects of industrialisation and urbanisation as damaging to normal society, creating a sort of social illness that needed to be 'cured' by **intervention**.
- Social disorganisation views saw society becoming disorganised, with social norms breaking down and leading to conflict. The answer was city planning and effective public services.
- Value conflicts were a concern from the 1930s to the 1950s, as ideological and political conflicts around fascism, Nazism and communism led to social conflict.
- Deviance perspectives in the 1950s and '60s saw groups such as teenagers as rebelling against traditional values.
- **Labelling** theory raised questions about who defines problems and whether they are legal or moral transgressions or illnesses. Alcoholism and drug abuse are examples.
- **Critical** perspectives take a Marxist position, that deviance is a rational response to class conflict, social division and social **inequality**.
- **Social construction** perspectives explore the processes by which a condition of society becomes defined as a social problem; an important feature is 'claims-making' by particular social groups that have an interest in changing the behaviour or social reactions to the behaviour (Rubington & Weinberg, 1995).

These ideas link to **moral panics** and **stigma**. One critique of social problem views is that the characteristics of individuals, families and social groups are defined as problematic, rather than societies being organised to allow distress, inequalities and **poverty** to exist.

Further Reading

Rubington, E. & Weinberg, M. S. (Eds.) (1995). *The study of social problems: Seven perspectives* (5th ed.). New York: Oxford University Press.

Social reproduction theory focuses on the process that reproduces a society's social relations from one generation to the next, reproducing also social structures, such as social classes and **family** relationships. This idea, from **Marxist** sociology, problematises **socialisation**. Who does this, using what social processes and with what social outcomes? **Bourdieu** questions how ideas in society become authorised ways of thinking in people's habitus and fields. Marxist theory focuses on reproduction of the capitalist system as a whole: social institutions such as the family and education prepare people for their position as capitalists or workers, and establish norms of behaviour that prevent social mobility and retain the power of capitalist elites. This questions women's positions in the domestic sphere reproducing family life and child development cultures and the devaluation of their right to participate in work. Other issues are how the pension system frustrates a good quality of life as people age, and how discriminatory attitudes to disability and LGTBQ+ sexuality are replicated in society.

What about social work's part in social reproduction? It plays a role in child development and childcare for marginal groups or where difficulties appear, and in doing so reproduces current patterns of relationship and **power**, so children in public care leave care for working-class jobs, rather being able to pursue high-paying careers. Does social work reinforce the reproduction of **oppressive** power relations? Or does it contest present social assumptions, for example for LGTBQ+ people? Does its practice promote social change and social mobility, or stultification of social relationships? What are the assumptions about disability, work and position of retired people? Does it promote ageism, disablism, sexism, homophobia, **racism** in the way it helps people?

Systems theory has an alternative interpretation: that **complex adaptive systems** do not reproduce, but can adapt to generate non-linear changes, through feedback loops as energy moves around a system, thus offering opportunities for change.

Further Reading

Bhattacharya, T. (Ed.) (2017). *Social reproduction theory: Remapping class, recentering oppression.* London: Pluto.

Social role valorisation is a development, by Wolfensberger (1983), of ideas of **normalisation**. He focuses on how people with intellectual disabilities are devalued, and therefore what is accepted as 'normal' in caring provision damages the goals and strategies of care for devalued people. He argues, therefore, that services should conceptualise what is valued in ordinary social life and seek to provide services that achieve these valued characteristics.

Further Readings

Race, D. G. (Ed.) (2003). *Leadership and change in human services: Selected readings from Wolf Wolfensberger.* London: Routledge.

Website of the International Social Role Valorization Organization: https://socialroleval-orization.com.

S

Social work is:

Practice **actions**, associated with an occupational or professional group, informed by a discipline, an organised body of knowledge, research, skills and values.

The nature of social work is contested; any account of social work requires us to recognise balances and tensions in views about it. The term 'social work' is regarded as universal by international social work bodies, and as including other occupational groups and disciplines present in some countries. But several social professions emerge from national cultural traditions and service structures. **Social pedagogy** (in France, 'social éducateur') is a recognised profession interwoven with social work. In Africa and Asia, **social development** is a more important practice than the practice with individuals and families that most people associate with 'social work', although both are present.

The term 'social work' emerged at the end of the nineteenth and beginning of the twentieth century in the USA and also came into use in the UK during this period. At first, it referred to any practical helping activities with people affected by **poverty** and other social **disadvantages**; this usage persisted into the 1930s. The term distinguished such work from social reform and social research; all these fields contributed to a ferment of efforts to achieve social improvement at the turn of the twentieth century. As paid jobs began to develop, 'social work' gradually became established as the most common term for helping, including the following:

- Assistance, implying **helping**, not taking a leading position, and in some Latin languages 'waiting on', serving.
- **Caring**, helping others by being kind to and concerned about them and providing practical and intimate care in times of need.
- **Development**, implying growth and improvement.
- Education, implying a process of growing understanding; this is often referred to in European languages as 'formation'.
- Service, implying working for or on behalf of someone, not on one's own behalf or to one's own advantage; this is connected with **altruism** and **humanitarianism**.
- Work, implying **action** and **activity**.

Widely accepted roles for social work are as follows:

- **Counsellor**, or **caseworker**.
- **Advocate** on behalf of poor and socially excluded people.
- Partnership working together with disadvantaged or disempowered individuals and groups.
- **Assessor** of risk or need, associated with **surveillance**, a role that may conflict with counselling.
- **Care manager**.
- Agent of social control (Asquith, Clark & Waterhouse, 2005).

These roles were carried out in varying ideological contexts, as follows:

- Welfarism, social democratic paternalism.
- **Professionalism**, stressing the expertise and authority of the professional.
- Consumerism, with the service user as a consumer.
- **Managerialism**, privileging managerialist and economic concerns.
- **Participationism**.

My own, constructionist, account of social work identifies a tension between aims of social improvement but, on the other hand, using mainly interpersonal practice inconsistent with that broad objective. Three objectives interact. They are derived from alternative political positions: individualist–reformist (social democratic), socialist–collectivist (socialist) and reflexive–therapeutic (neoliberal). These are represented in the Global Definition as, respectively, empowerment and liberation, social change and development, and social cohesion objectives (Payne, 2021[1990]). In this view (Payne, 2006a), each social work act, each practitioner's professional position, each **agency's** interpretation of its role and each political view of social work represents an interaction between these objectives, shifting between emphases among them.

Further Reading

Payne, M. (2006). *What is professional social work?* (2nd ed.). Bristol: Policy Press.

Social work theory comprises sets of ideas for explaining, exploring and

understanding social work and its practice. It forms part of and draws on social science, on the humanities and on cognate areas of professional theory. The most significant social science areas are psychology, social policy and sociology, with economics and political science also influential. The most significant area of the humanities is philosophy, with some influence from linguistics. Significant areas of influential professional theory and knowledge derive from education, law, management, medicine and nursing.

Formal, informal and tacit theory are relevant (Sibeon, 1990). Formal theory derives from research and scholarship, reported in academic and professional books and journals, and published also in information and news media and through electronic media such as podcasts and websites. Informal theory is not codified through formal publication; it derives from experience of life and social work practice and shared in a **discourse** among managers and practitioners in the course of their work. Tacit theory is informal theory that cannot easily be conceptualised and formulated.

There are three main forms of theory about social work:

- Theory about the aims and nature of social work.
- Practice theory, which analyses and prescribes systematic ways of doing social work.
- Theories of the 'client world', which analyse data and ideas about the experiences and lives of clients served by social workers (Sibeon, 1990).

Practice education requirements in social work education generate theories offering prescriptions for appropriate practice, particularly in Anglophone countries influenced by **empiricist** and **pragmatist** philosophies.

Social work practice theory reflects a tension between empiricist and **interpretivist** views of human and social relations. The empiricist position seeks universally relevant objective evidence explaining the causation of behaviour and social structures to establish effective social work interventions. The interpretivist position claims that human self-awareness and social **diversity** mean that all behaviour and social structures derive from human perception and cultural, historical and social contexts from which they emerge, so that evidence can only be provisional. The interpretivist argues that empiricist evidence cannot deal with the **emergent** properties of many human and social situations, while the **objectivist** argues that the interpretivist fails to seek evidence of continuities and patterns in human life. Munro and Hardie (2019) argue that this dichotomy is overdrawn, and attributes such as evidence about particular issues and situations, and disagreements about interpretation and personal matters, can be more precisely delineated and evaluated to establish evidence that can be agreed for many practical purposes.

Solution practice theory is a positive psychology therapy devised by

Steve de Shazer and colleagues. It looks forwards to solutions, therefore, rather than backwards at people's problems and troubles. It connects with social construction ideas that **discourse** and **language** about social situations can reconstruct people's behaviour and perceptions. Solution practice does this by a positive focus on clients' futures, **disrupting** clients' expectations of an emphasis on their behavioural or **social problems**. Ideas of future possibilities are used to change the present. This contests the **psychodynamic** emphasis on insight into past experience and building **support** through such concepts as **attachment** or **relational** help and the **cognitive behavioural** emphasis on changing specific problem behaviours. The idea of 'discrepancy' in **motivational interviewing** practice uses comparisons with the future to motivate present change.

Critiques of the approach suggest that focusing on solutions implies that problem-based ideology underlies the approach, inconsistent with the positive psychology aims of using it. Since asking for help with problems is intuitive to many people, constantly redirecting their thinking towards solutions can seem irritatingly false, simply renaming problems 'challenges'. Critics also suggest that the clinic- or office-based **individualistic** approach is demanding for people experiencing very severe social stresses, and assumes it is up to them to manage external difficulties, **oppressions** and social **inequality** and injustice, rather than focusing on **social change**. It would be possible to work on solutions that involve social change and working together with others, but that is not the main focus of techniques. Solution practice calls on strengths ideas, since it aims to build **resilience** and strengths, and to some degree encourages doing so in cooperation with others, but developing family and community resources is not as important as building personal **coping** skills. Another criticism is the risk of focusing on insubstantial 'dreams' for the future. This may prove difficult with administrative and legal responsibilities, for example devising less than ideal care packages for clients or families, or managing conflict around safeguarding responsibilities. Solution theory answers these points by suggesting that non-therapeutic aims misuse the techniques. Precise analysis of problems and potential solutions also avoids this issue. Turnell and Edwards' (1999) '**signs of safety**' approach to child protection, which has a solution ideology, also emphasises the importance of starting from the position that the responsibility is to maintain the child's safety. Therapeutic actions, for example with parents, have to be within that context. This point can adapt solution practice as part of other responsibilities.

Since solution practice is disruptive, it is important to help clients shift from a problem-oriented view of their situation, and build 'co-construction' by working together to reconstruct their intentions. Practitioners listen carefully to clients' accounts of how they tried to deal with the problem to identify patterns of behaviour. Patterns involve things that regularly happen before and after a problem occurs. As with externalisation in **narrative** practice, problems happen to clients, they themselves are not problems. Doing this **affirms** their strengths and motivation. An important aspect of this is to look for exceptions, occasions when the problem doesn't happen or doesn't have unfortunate consequences. The aim is to try to repeat patterns of events that prevent or ameliorate the problem.

The original approach to the solution method is a conventional clinic- or office-based series of discussion sessions, with the client trying out various options in **in vivo** work, **activities** or exercises as part of their daily lives.

Solution practice can be used flexibly with other techniques. Parton and O'Byrne (2000) integrated it into a range of other positive psychology approaches, emphasising its social **construction** ideology. Greene and Lee (2011) devised a solution approach that emphasises strengths and also calls on **narrative** practice. This involves using the narrative techniques as part of the process of exploration of clients' situations and finds solutions through re-storying. Shennan's (2014) practical account of solution practice emphasises the communication elements of the approach, and shows how the questioning technique can be used to disrupt people's established ways of thinking about their problems in many situations, without invoking a full-scale solution-focused intervention.

Further Reading

Shennan, G. (2014). *Solution-focused practice: Effective communication to facilitate change.* Basingstoke: Palgrave Macmillan.

Space See **Place**.

Spirituality is beliefs, feelings and faiths concerned with transcendence, the sensitivity to an existence beyond and exceeding ordinary understanding. In social and healthcare provision, using the term acknowledges the importance of transcendence in many people's experience, while retaining a secular position in providing professional services. Making **meaning** is an important aspect of many conceptions of spirituality, including **existentialist** and **humanistic** ideas and therapies such as Frankl's 'logotherapy'. The idea of spirituality is used to accept and work with people's allegiance to **religion**, without commitment to any particular belief or faith. Because of the secular position of public services and generalist provision in many countries, spirituality has been neglected in social work practice (Canda, Furman & Canda, 2019) and formulation of theory has been limited. Recent accounts, however (Holloway & Moss, 2010; Dudley, 2016), identify the importance of practitioners being sensitive to the importance of spiritual issues in clients' lives and being competent to help with spiritual issues. This may be particularly important at times of significant transition in people's lives, such as in **bereavement**, childbirth and at end of life.

Practitioners distinguish spirituality from 'spiritualist' beliefs. Spiritualism claims that a spirit exists connected with but separate from the person, and some people believe that it is possible for a spirit to survive death and communicate with living survivors.

Further Reading

Crisp, B. R. (Ed.) (2017). *Routledge handbook of religion, spirituality and social work*. Abingdon: Routledge.

Stage theories propose that an aspect of life or practice may be understood as a series of phases or points in a continuing process. They arise in several aspects of social work:

- Stages in child or human development, such as **psychoanalytic** development theory and Erikson's stage theory of human development.
- Stages in the process by which an issue develops, for example Kübler-Ross' stages of bereavement and the **transtheoretical theory of change**.
- Stages in the development and resolution of crises in **crisis intervention**.
- Stages in models of intervention, such as stages of **advocacy**.

Stage models may clarify and formalise steps in complicated or lengthy processes, making them easier to explain to clients. It also makes them easier to retain in the practitioner's mind.

The critique of stage models focuses on hidden assumptions. First, they may assume that a set of factors progress (an example of theoretical **progressivism**) when they are relatively stable. Alternatively, they may assume that progression is natural, whereas it only occurs in particular circumstances. An example of these problems is Worden's (2010) argument that working with bereavement may require taking actions to ensure that people make progress in dealing with issues that they face. Stages of **group** or **team** development are another example of this issue. Transfers from laboratory research describing development in small groups were interpreted to apply to the behaviour of groups that are work teams (Tuckman, 1965; Tuckman & Jensen, 1977), whereas the element of **task** in a work role may mean that no progression takes place or that it is not required.

Stage theories may also oversimplify complex processes, such as cycles or spirals in progression or various elements progressing at different rates. Similarly, a stage model may bring together different aspects of a situation when greater differentiation might be appropriate. Alternatively, the theory that stages exist may lead social workers to assume that factors they find in a situation are part of the stage, rather than exploring how they developed.

Steady state is a systems theory conceptualisation of **equilibrium**, used in later formulations of **crisis intervention** and **ecological systems** practice. A steady state is progress through life, in which people can **cope** with difficulties and disruptions in their social stability. That steadiness is assumed as the normal way of life, reminds us that these are social order or social cohesion practice theories, which operate on the assumption that the structures of society form an ordered and secure basis for life and social relations.

Stigma, originally a mark or a stain, denotes the existence of a human characteristic that people see as a flaw; the characteristic may be visible or invisible. In history, invisible stigmatised characteristics have sometimes been marked by a physical marker on people, such as a badge or tattoo. Examples are people receiving poor relief in the UK or Jewish people in Nazi Germany. This has also been achieved by uniform clothing in a prison or workhouse. Stigmatising characteristics lead to emotional reactions in people with the characteristic and those who perceive it in someone else. **Goffman** (1964) explored how people with known or perceptible 'spoiled identities' sought to manage their behaviour or appearance to 'pass as normal' or cover their stigmatised characteristic.

Stigma is not, however, only a characteristic or element of the individual that they must deal with, because people are seen as **'other'**, and social relations create the devaluation of the characteristic that the stigma represents. Parrott with Maguinness (2017: Ch. 6) point out that social processes create the stigma of **poverty**, because **liberal** and **neoliberal** thinking requires incentives for people to work in devalued occupations. Stigma is thus a socially damaging approach to social relations because stigmatised people are disadvantaged in achieving socially approved objectives such as creating families or stable social relationships or finding housing or work. Stigma thus excludes people unhelpfully, damaging the economy and social fabric. Educating the public to achieve better integration becomes more difficult, and society and social workers have to expend effort and resources compensating for its social disadvantages. It also excludes positive discussions about the value of stigmatised characteristics, such as migration or the positive aspects of some drug use, such as cannabinoids.

S

Social work is associated with stigma because it developed from nineteenth-century services such as the Poor Law in many European countries to respond to poverty. It also has to deal with social problems such as criminality, infectious disease associated with poor social conditions, such as tuberculosis, and, particularly in the USA, immigration by 'outsiders'.

Dealing with stigmatised people has an effect on services: there are fewer efforts to maintain the humanity and quality of services; people try to avoid using them, so they do not apply for them or demand improvements in services; and the services are discriminated against as compared with universal services. Social workers may need to deal with people who avoid applying for their services despite need, or resist intervention because of perceived stigma for all these various reasons. One aspect of helping people, therefore, may be explaining rights, reducing the visibility of service provision, working to offer as much choice and control as possible, and avoiding authoritative or intrusive interventions with care.

Strengths practice aims to identify and build clients' personal and social strengths, including resources within their social **networks** such as family and community. In this, it contests the problem-based perspective of many social work practices. From the turn of the twenty-first century, strengths ideas, always present in social work, have gained a higher profile, and emphasised social aspects of positive psychology concepts such as **construction** and **solution** perspectives.

Saleebey's (2013) edited text had a strong impact. Rapp and Goscha's (2012) mental health text, with a good research base, offers a coherent and strong practice prescription, combined with **recovery** theory. Strengths-based practice is connected with solution practice and both are linked to the **signs of safety** approach in child protection and safeguarding.

Using the strengths concept fits well with broader social work values. Research validation with other client groups (Blundo, Bolton & Lehmann, 2019) adds to Rapp and Goscha's (2012) mental health research. Critique of strengths theory focuses on the vagueness of the concept, deriving from its idealistic stance and emphasis on community support in Saleebey's presentation.

Another criticism has been its adoption by official agencies and practitioners. Oliver and Charles (2014), researching child protection practice, found five different interpretations of strengths practice, enhancing the therapeutic **relationship**, supporting **self-determination**, identifying and working with clients' internal and external resources, working on a balanced understanding of clients and 'enacting firm, fair and friendly practice' (2014: 22). Only the last of these fully implemented strengths theory; others achieved only partial implementation and often presented difficulties in balancing child safety with help. Under-resourcing of client safety plans in the self-determination approach often led to unreasonable attempts to 'responsibilise' clients without enough support. This has also been an issue in the UK, where strengths ideas have been encouraged in adult social care services (Fox, 2013). Some practitioners have gained the sense that the managerial aim of using this model is to avoid committing resources to agencies' service provision by encouraging clients first to seek community resources; it may thus serve a **neoliberal** policy objective of restraining public expenditure.. There is a history here, since UK adult services in the 1990s twisted the positive features of American **case management**, by adopting a restricted model of practice, called **care management**, over-emphasising the assessment phase as a rationing instrument. It appears that the relationship development features of strengths practice have been vitiated with the same intent.

Rapp and Goscha (2012) discuss principles informing a theory:

- Setting out desired outcomes, such as **quality** of life, sense of competence, life satisfaction and **empowerment**.
- Identifying the features of living niches, which determine quality of life, such as living arrangements, opportunities for leisure, work, education and social relationships. People should not feel trapped in unsatisfactory niches.
- Identifying individual strengths required to improve quality of life: aspirations, competencies and confidence.
- Identifying environmental strengths required: tangible resources and services, worthwhile social relationships and opportunities.

The individual and environmental strengths define niches that are appropriate for clients.

American strengths practice theory is not the only source of strengths ideas in social work. Resources also come from cultural and social **capital** and the accumulation also of economic capital and other resources during the **life cycle**, for use in later life. **Bourdieu**, for example, argues that older people construct a lifestyle and standard of living from contemporary cultural ideas, and cultural and social capital form the structures of their lives, more so than economic and class distinctions (Gilleard & Higgs, 2020: 32–5). Social work practice therefore needs to explore the cultural and social expectations that form people's life preferences and build on these, rather than accepting that care is defined by the packages of services available in health and social care provision. Seligman's (2017[2002]) positive psychology, similarly, is an important social science source, proposing that people construct their own preferences and judgements about care provision and help.

S

Further Reading

Rapp, C. A. & Goscha, R. J. (2012). *The strengths model: A recovery-oriented approach to mental health services* (3rd ed.) New York: Oxford University Press.

Structural-functionalism in sociology was influential from the 1950s to the '70s, associated with Robert K. Merton and Talcott Parsons. It theorises that social structures persist because they perform functions that maintain a coherent social order within a society. Examples are organisations and social institutions such as childrearing, marriage, policing, schools and work. This concept should not be confused with **functional theory** in social work.

Structural practice is a **critical** practice theory, associated with Canadian writers Maurice Moreau (1979, 1990) and Bob Mullaly, with co-authors (Mullaly & West, 2018; Mullaly & Dupré, 2019). It theorises the role of social structures in **oppression**, aiming to redirect their impact on people experiencing **poverty** and oppression. As a conflict perspective, it counterposes the interests of oppressed peoples and people with **power**, requiring struggle for social **change**. The main structures of concern are inequalities because of social class divisions and oppressive social relations. Other critical practice theories include structural issues, but achieving **social change** to respond to structural issues is the main focus here.

The starting point is structural analysis of issues that practitioners deal with. Individual and intrapsychic work repairs damage from structural oppression, but the aim is to move on to identify structural issues that created individual and family problems. All practice focuses on **inequalities** that discriminate against people through class, gender, race, age, ability and other issues. Individual problems always emerge from social issues, which always lead to individual expressions of their impact, but practice looks back from these individual expressions to their structural sources. Responses only to the individual oppression 'blame the victim' and will not lead to a long-lasting resolution. Practice explores the interaction of structures, **ideologies** or belief systems and consciousness of how individual and social changes link together. Thompson's (2016) personal-cultural-social (PCS) model of **discrimination** identifies interactions in different arenas of concern, but all these aspects interact; they are not a linear progression from the more to less individual, but are constantly interacting factors of constant social change. Small changes accumulate until the point at which a more extensive or radical change becomes apparent.

Dialectical analysis of forces of social change see that social conflicts contain contradictions, binary oppositions that disclose an issue that can be worked on to achieve more extensive change. For example, domestic violence between intimate partners usually demonstrates male privilege, assumptions that men's violence expresses masculinity, and discloses issues about how, in families, men maintain that **privilege** and oppress women in childcare and domestic roles. To help, practitioners need to explore and understand the **intersections** of issues about family, financial oppression, **gender**, privilege and violence and move onwards to create some practical changes. Furthered by similar practitioners in similar situations, such changes will begin to transform over time the conceptions that generate this issue in people's lives. Continually disentangling contradictions in people's ideas about family and violence, making sense of them, helps that progress along; simply dealing with practicalities does not make that broader progress. Through such analyses, structural practice answers the central contradiction of social work in trying to achieve social change through individual actions.

Structural practice centres on oppression and social structures that create oppression because of inequalities in society. An important element is privilege assumed by social groups that leads to unthinking oppression through following conventional social structures.

The main critique of structural practice, as with **critical, Marxist** and **radical** practice, is the neglect of individual and personal needs in favour of wider social interventions. The response to this is that individual and psychological interventions neglect the main sources of the difficulties that such interventions are designed to meet. It proposes that interventions of any kind should work in the direction of responding to those wider sources of social conflict. Inevitably, therefore, this requires understanding of those structural sources so that our work does not perpetuate them and progresses towards dealing with them.

Structural psychodynamic theory is the metaphorical account
in **psychodynamic** theory of the structures, for example the ego, id and superego, that influence the mind's impact on behaviour. The id is an inchoate collection of drives, which generate energy that pushes the mind to take action to meet the id's needs; it is the dynamo of the human mind. As it comes up against external realities, however, the ego finds ways of taming the id's pressures to fit better with the demands and restrictions of external reality. As this process continues, people learn social rules by which the ego can manage internal drives to fit in with social expectations, creating a superego, supervising the ego. Many such social rules come from a child's parents' expectations, but as life develops outside, the other sources of authority also become important, this may include education and social work. The transactional analysis formulation (Pitman, 1983) of these structures as an internal parent–adult–child offers a tongue-in-cheek metaphor for this structure – the parent is the superego, the adult is the ego and the child is the id.

S

Structuralism is a French sociological theory and social philosophy proposing
that 'deep structures' can be identified in society influencing social relations; it is contested by post-structuralism, an important '**post**' idea..

Study was the precursor to **diagnosis** in social work practice theory until the 1960s,
later replaced by **assessment**. During the 1960s, **crisis intervention** and **systems** theory led to comprehensive study of clients' histories and situations in all social work being displaced by a stronger emphasis on relevance and salience of issues to the practice theory used (Germain, 1968).

The **Subject**, referring to people, conceptualises them as active participants in social relations, with **agency** in those relations, not as being done to by others. See **Object** for a discussion of the **balance** between someone being an object and a subject in particular situations or in general.

Support conceptualises an objective and procedure in social work; it implies helping people find a way of bearing the weight of their troubles. **Ego psychology** strengthened support as an objective that differentiated social work from traditional psychoanalytic practice focused on internal psychological difficulties (Bandler, B., 1963).

Progressivist critique of the concept complains that agencies and other professions refer people to social work agencies for 'support' without clear objectives, and social workers also undertake support without clear aims for moving forward. The ideas in use described good intentions rather than specific actions. Briar and Miller's (1971: 26) critique of **diagnostic** or **traditional** social work, for example, says:

> Supportive treatment is essentially palliative. It attempts to return the client to the state of functioning that was present prior to the eruptive stress … perhaps with a few new strengths and resistive capacities … [S]upport is ambiguously and unsystematically defined. It is exhortative rather than prescriptive; it is defined by intent rather than procedure.

As conceptualisation of support developed during the 1970s and '80s, four types of support were distinguished:

- **Affiliational**, enabling people to feel bound to and valued by another person or group.
- Informational, providing information about resources and training in skills to deal with current challenges.
- Emotional, enabling people to express feelings and reflect on emotionally difficult events in one or more relationships.
- Instrumental, providing financial aid or practical services (Compton, Galaway & Cournoyer, 2005: 259).

Similar forms of support are identified as useful within agencies, organisations and in **teamwork**.

Support **needs**, once defined through social work **assessment**, might be provided by the social worker directly, or by enabling clients to identify people in their existing social networks to provide one or more of these forms of support and helping potential supporters to do so.

A significant stream of practice grew from the preventive psychiatry of Caplan and Parad to develop support **networks**, either for specific clients, or more commonly as projects for groups of clients experiencing similar difficulties.

Helpful concepts from the intellectual and physical disabilities and mental health fields include 'supported living' and 'active support' deriving from the **disabled living**, **ordinary housing** and **ordinary living** movements proposing **normalisation** for various client groups. Supported living (deriving from mental health services) provides an independent lifestyle, but with wraparound services that check up on clients, helping them feel safe because someone reacts when they experience a difficulty. Clients need to know there is a 'ring of confidence' around them, as the toothpaste ads have it. Person-centred active support (deriving from work with people with intellectual disabilities) emphasises a **social pedagogy** approach: every moment has potential, little and often graded assistance, and maximising choice and control (Beadle-Brown, Murphy & Beadshaw, 2017).

Surveillance refers to a practice of watching people carefully, and implied in the

idea is the sense that this is being done to reinforce authoritative control over an unaware individual or population. In a more complex way, this is an important idea in **Foucault's** social philosophy. He suggests that bio-power is a form of social power in which people are managed as part of the population of a society by control of their **bodies**. An obvious technology is managing drivers' behaviour in public using traffic cameras. Where there are extreme concerns about people's characteristics or behaviour, society sets up institutions that provide surveillance, such as psychiatric hospitals or prisons, which explicitly control personal and social behaviour by limiting access to a wide population and by watching current behaviour and preventing it from having dangerous effects. Social workers are often part of such institutions, to try to improve inmates' behaviour and circumstances and to help people discharged from them.

Less obviously, societies manage important areas of personal and social lives by surveillance, even if this behaviour is partly or mostly in private. For example, our sexuality is partly about our **self**, but that self is expressed in private and public behaviour which is to some extent controlled by setting social expectations of behaviour towards others and is managed by everyday surveillance by the people around us as we relate to them. If we deviate from expected behaviour, we might fear investigation for domestic or sexual abuse, and awareness of others' surveillance is a limiting factor in how we decide to behave. More extreme surveillance might arise when a social worker is called upon to investigate, since we know that this might lead to legal processes or public revelation. Not only actual surveillance, but concern or expectations about it become factors that manage our behaviour.

Social work, then, is involved in a variety of forms of surveillance. While this provides security for clients, the people around them and the public, it requires social work to consider the interaction of surveillance in helping organisations and their own work, and the role of social work in surveillance.

Symbolic interactionism is a perspective in social psychology initiated
by the work of G. H. Mead (1934), drawing on **pragmatist** ideas, which has influenced ways of thinking about human **reflexivity**, and **postmodern** and **social construction** ideas about human behaviour. It connects also with ideas about mentalisation in **attachment** theory.

The starting point is a claim that all human social interaction involves exchanging symbols, mainly in the form of language. Through **language**, we gain access to other people's ideas. People generate symbols which represent the meaning that they attribute to events and actions. Symbols give meaning to social objects, which arise from experiencing interactions between people (and other organisms) and the environment. An element of pragmatist philosophy is the view that we explore and learn about things in practical ways to generate understanding. By experiencing how people interact with their environment we can come to an understanding of a social object, and represent it in a symbol. 'Social acts' are social objects, so we can share our practical exploration of the world by creating and using with others our symbols about their behaviour. For example, if we share wide swings in mood using the symbols 'mental illness' and 'manic depression', we create different symbolic interactions from the same behaviour than if we used the symbols 'creative energy' and 'excitement'. Through their interactions, people take up and act using the social attitudes of communities and groups they are members of, both actual groups they are in contact with and wider social attitudes cutting across society, for example through social media.

Blumer (1969) developed symbolic interactionism to examine human interactions in detail, and how this was affected by their social context. We should explore the contexts in which different activities and behaviours arise and patterns of social relations to understand how people are interpreting the social situations around them. For example, if we see clusters of issues, such as offending or violence in public housing estates, this should sensitise us to explore what aspects of these estates are interacting with human needs and creating the issues we are concerned about.

Later work in interactionism, for example **Goffman**'s work examining social behaviour in detail, and ethnomethodology, makes clear the importance of looking at the particularities of how patterns of behaviour are created by the social demands of the situations that clients and the people around them face.

Further Reading

Roberts, B. (2006). *Micro social theory*. Basingstoke: Palgrave Macmillan.

Systems theory is a practice theory based on biological theorisations that
everything, both in natural and social worlds, consists of elements in interaction with each other; they form links to create a system. Larger supra systems contain smaller meso or mezzo systems, which in turn contain still smaller micro systems. Human bodies, for example, contain nervous and circulatory systems made up of neurons and blood vessels in turn consisting of molecules and atoms. Social systems might consist of individuals, in a living unit such as a family, in a community or other **place**-based system.

Systems are characterised by transforming or using energy as it passes among the elements within a boundary. Closed systems cannot pass energy across the boundary, and so use up the energy supplied by their components. The battery in a toy, for example, runs down as it feeds the toy's actions. Entropy, this running down process, is natural: all animals, for example, eventually die. Social systems are open systems, however, and can receive inputs of energy across the boundary, such as activity, knowledge, information and resources such as finance or nutrition. These create **actions** within the social system, a throughput of energy, and become an output, such as changed activity, transformed resources and waste. For example, a body receives input of food and drink, transforms them in the digestive system into energy for the body's use, and output such as defecation and sweat and personal achievements. Another example: a social system such as a family receives input through the wages of earners; throughput consists of bringing up children, pursuing family activities; and output consists of social relations and achievements as a family. A characteristic of social systems is that they have synergy, and can create their own energy through creativity emerging from the relationships between their elements, which continues to power them.

Systems ideas includes different types of theory, as follows:

- **General systems** theory provides the set of ideas and terminology to explain how the wide variety of systems work; it is therefore very generalised. Its intellectual source is von Bertalanffy's (1971[1950]) account. It was picked up and promoted by Hearn (1958, 1969), achieving wide international impact in social work on the publication of texts by Goldstein (1973), Pincus and Minahan (1973) and Siporin (1975). These ideas gained influence because of contemporary interest in systems views of families within family therapy (for example, Walrond-Skinner, 1976). It also offered a view of social work that integrated sociological analysis without adopting a Marxist or socialist stance. This meant that it was inclusive of the previously dominant psychodynamic perspectives (Payne, 2002). Advantaged in influence by offering an integrative (Goldstein, 1973; Roberts, 1990) perspective, systems ideas had their strongest impact at a time when large generic public sector social work agencies were being established in the UK and other parts of the world.
- **Ecological** or **eco systems** theory draws on the work of Bronfenbrenner (1979) theorising child and human development through systems. Rather than

concentrating on interactions within a system, as general systems theory does, it focuses on interactions between systems and their immediate environment and shows how social systems develop and strengthen internal and external links. It was influential because it helpfully connected with the **person-in-situation** perspective in **traditional social work**. Ecological systems also theorised an interest in **networks** to provide **support systems** at a time when **deinstitutionalisation** policies required a greater concentration on community interaction.

- Complex **adaptive** systems theory is a development of systems theory that explains how large and complex systems adapt (Hudson, 2010, 2019). One of the criticisms of general and ecological systems ideas is that it is hard to understand how the many elements of large systems interact with each other; the impacts on each other are too variable to follow. Large systems demonstrate patterns in the way they operate, and **chaos** and **complexity** theory brings these into focus.

Wakefield's (1996) extensive critique of systems theory in social work identifies four arguments for it: it allows (unlike many psychological theories of behaviour) the analysis of non-linear explanations and processes, it broadens the range of issues explored in assessment, it can integrate alternative explanations of behaviour and social relations, and it includes social factors more clearly than **traditional social work**. All systems theory has several flaws:

- It describes rather than explaining.
- It does not help you decide what to do or where to intervene.
- It is a generalised theory that is hard to apply to specific situations.
- It is overinclusive, making it hard to focus.
- It overstates the importance of stability, the **steady state, integration** and **adaptation**.
- It emphasises slow and **progressive change**, for example through feedback loops, rather than radical change.
- Systems practice emphasises sustaining systems, and tries to prevent entropy, but some systems, for example strife-torn families or racist social groups, should be destroyed.
- It uses a complex technical language for simple social processes and encourages a jargon.

Practice involves identifying, exploring and understanding systems relevant to clients and their situations. Pincus and Minahan (1973) specify four systems to consider:

- The change agent system – social workers and organisations they work in.
- The client system – clients and people involved with them.
- The target system – people whom the change agent system changes.
- The action system – people and agencies that the change agent system works with.

Compared with many forms of social work, this analysis connects with the reality that social work usually involves more people than just a client and a practitioner. And, although the emphasis is on change, systems ideas do not assume that the client has to be changed: this may be any of the systems they are involved with. Luhmann's (1995; Schirmer & Michailakis, 2019) account of German systems ideas focuses on complexity in systems. While we can never fully understand all the elements and linkages in a complex system, it is helpful to see how the system organises those elements, how they interact and communicate, and how they differentiate their functions within the system. Practice here looks at communication to identify how different parts of a family or community take on different roles or styles of behaviour.

Consequently, systems practice theorises indirect work, changing people around the client or invoking other agencies. Work with **support systems** therefore developed from systems ideas in social work.

Systems ideas helpfully emphasise that social work is concerned with many systems, while other professions focus primarily on individuals. For example, teachers focus on their pupils, and counsellors, doctors, nurses and psychotherapists on their specific clients or patients. To these professions, families, communities and social systems are a background to their main work, and their ethics focus on their responsibility to their client, patient or pupil. Social workers can use systems ideas to show how they are different in working with wider aspects of clients' situations.

T

Task in social work refers to a variety of issues, as follows:

- **Activities** that clients undertake, as in **task-centred** practice, to assist them in making **progress** in resolving issues that they sought social work help with. This idea is contested by practice theories such as **motivational interviewing** and **solution** practice, which see mental or psychological preparation or engagement as required for effective change.
- **Actions** that people take in order to complete a phase of life or to deal with a particular situation, for example Worden's (2010: 38–53) 'tasks of mourning' in grief counselling. He argues that the concept of task is more active than phase or **stage** theories.
- Tasks of social work practice or the profession were subjected in the 1970s to **functional analysis** by dividing up overall social work activities into a series of roles or tasks. A report by the British Association of Social Workers (1977) used this research to distinguish the characteristics of qualified social work by arguing that some of these tasks required the undertaking of a social work qualification, whereas other tasks could be undertaken by social care staff without qualifications. The tasks limited to the qualified social worker in this analysis were: diagnostician, planner, counsellor, attitude/behaviour changer, consultant and director, all described in the context of interpersonal practice.

Task-centred practice provides for structured, short-term interventions on specific objectives defined by clients. Its clear, practical intervention model can be used in many situations. Because it is short term, it is acceptable to clients wanting quick results without intrusion in wider personal or family issues. It is also economical regarding time and resources. There have been criticisms that this means it may be overused by agencies to manage demand and avoid responsibilities for **social change**. Proven effectiveness for different purposes and being easy to explain to clients, managers and politicians contribute to social work and agency **accountability**. Criticisms have been made of its over-formal use of **contracts** and that it is an over-simplified form of **cognitive behavioural therapy**.

Task-centred practice was devised as a **casework** model by American social work academics William J. Reid and Laura Epstein (1972a). Research validation in several countries (Reid & Epstein, 1972b) led to rapid acceptance, just as social work services were expanding, short of personnel and therefore needing to justify increasing expenditure with research-backed claims for effectiveness. Other US writers focused on applications in family and groupwork settings (Fortune, 1985) and following Reid's lead, as part of searching for empirical support for social work practice (Rzepnicki, McCracken & Briggs, 2012). In the UK, Doel (2009) and Marsh (Doel & Marsh, 1992; Marsh & Doel, 2005; Marsh, 2015) became influential interpreters adapting elements of the original model; for example, eschewing 'contracts', with their legalistic implications, in favour of the more informal 'agreements'.

The ground-breaking study of the task-centred treatment model (Reid & Epstein, 1972a), carried out in Chicago, identified seven target problems that task-centred casework would help with:

- Interpersonal conflict.
- Dissatisfaction in social relations.
- Relations with formal organisations.
- Role performance.
- Social transition.
- Reactive emotional distress, that is, distress about some event in people's lives.
- Inadequate resources.

Further research and practice experience identified a wide range of problems that task-centred practice may be helpful with – many examples are given in Reid's (2000) practical manual.

An important element is helping the client to identify problems that they need or want to tackle, and prioritising them, 'scanning the headlines' (Doel & Marsh, 1992) of their lives. The work then focuses on one or a limited number of problems, selected because of their importance, or for easy attainment to demonstrate rapid progress to doubtful clients. Later accounts emphasise identifying clients' goals as end points to assess priority, distinguishing goals from problems (Tolson, Reid & Garvin, 2003: 73–4, 84–5).

Brief duration and time limits build on practice research showing that most change occurs early in intervention. Specifying tasks allows clients to be clear about how to tackle their problems. Practitioners can also clarify the client's motivation, how feasible the task is and its desirability. Sub-tasks and multiple tasks can be established, and in later work (Reid, 1992), the value of interlocking tasks for client and worker, and others involved, so that they are motivated by others' tasks depending on completing their actions. Practice requires systematic communication and responsiveness to clients' and others' expressions of commitment, doubts and motivation (Reid & Epstein, 1972a: 121–38; 176–91).

An important feature of this approach is its focus on client **self-determination** in setting priorities and tasks, and active client **participation** in planning and taking action. Later research (Reid, 1978, 1992) showed that the worker's active participation and taking on tasks can also be motivating for clients.

Later research also showed how the service may be integrated into longer term social work responsibilities. The original formulation was for a service responding to identifiable problems presented by applications from clients for help. In an ongoing case, for example where family work involving child safeguarding is continuing, it was possible to have interludes for tackling suitable problems. Then the work returns to other interventions. Contracts could also be chained; success with one problem might encourage further contracts to tackle the next priority, then others.

Doel and Marsh downplayed the formality of what they called agreements, and Tolson et al. (2003: 86) suggested that the evidence of the need for formality was mixed. They recommended experimentation to work out what was relevant to the agency's work or to particular clients. Social workers can informally sketch out potential points for an agreement on paper, flipchart or chalkboard or use joint work on a computer screen, emails, texts, video conferencing and other IT options. Such an approach is consistent with contemporary ideas of **co-production** in practice, by clients and practitioners working together.

Another critique of task-centred practice (Gambrill, 1994) is that, probably like other brief interventions, it only deals with selected problems as a minimal response to deep-seated social issues. Dealing with issues that clients can identify may conceal resource-poor social provision and political and professional failure to deal with poverty and social inequality underlying the problems that task-centred practice responds to. It is easy for agencies to say they are doing something, without making inroads into more substantial social issues.

Some commentators argue that task-centred practice is a simplified, 'dumbed-down' version of cognitive behavioural therapy, not allowing for the behavioural understanding required to tackle more complex psychological difficulties. Against this view, it is an easy-to-explain way of tackling the kind of problems presented to social work agencies, just as important as psychological therapies, and some critics of social work (for example, **Barbara Wootton**) think the practical issues often presented by clients should be taken at face value and worked on, rather than looking for psychological problems that clients have not presented.

Further Readings

Marsh, P. & Doel, M. (2005). *The task-centred book*. London: Routledge.

Tolson, E. R., Reid, W. & Garvin, C. D. (2003). *Generalist practice: A task-centered approach* (2nd ed.). New York: Columbia University Press.

Technical assistance programmes during the period from 1945 to 1970 were **social development** strategies, providing international support to

developing countries. The main focuses were public assistance, child health and welfare, and social security developments (Murase, 1955). The programmes were supported by the United Nations and the USA as part of policies during the Cold War to encourage liberal democratic regimes. They were important for financing the transfer of social work ideas, particularly the American model of casework practice, from Western countries to countries in Africa, Asia and South America. Social work was used by the USA and Western countries as an acceptable and practical way of promoting democratic political values. These programmes therefore constitute one of the sources of concern about post-colonial imposition of Western cultural and social values on Indigenous cultures, and led to movements for the **decolonisation** of theory in social work.

Technical rational or **technicist practice** refers to social work that emphasises theory validated by scientific research and organised into 'scripted sequences of techniques that have been experimentally demonstrated to accomplish a specified goal' (Polkinghorne, 2004: 3). To take this quotation apart, practice is technical, and perhaps excessively so, if it emphasises techniques, rather than judgement and reflection, specifying and achieving goals confirmed by research, leading to **manualisation** and **proceduralisation** of sequences of actions.

Theory is sets of connected ideas used for explaining, exploring and understanding something. See also **Social work theory**, which covers formal, informal and tacit theory.

Therapeutic alliance theorises the process of engagement with clients in individual work that aims to improve their social functioning. It is more than an agreement or contract; it aims to establish a shared sense of endeavour to tackle and resolve the issues that arise in the **case**.

Therapeutic community theory refers to a theory of practice used in hospitals, prisons and residential care mainly in the fields of drug misuse, mental illness and children with emotional and behavioural difficulties. The aim is to create a democratic regime usually set and managed by a regular meeting of all residents and staff. The original ideas grew from **psychodynamic** theory used in Second World War **groupwork** experiments, but as it developed in diverse environments several other theoretical influences were felt. This included ideas of belonging, **social learning theory**, promoting **agency**, **empowerment** of the **self** and **self-efficacy** through experiential **community** and **group activity**. It also involved efforts to promote democratisation in a communal, open, permissive regime with a flattened hierarchy of authority to enhance residents' self-discipline.

Three types of theory are as follows:

- Planned environment therapy, based on work with young people with emotional and behavioural disorders.
- **Milieu therapy**, mainly an American practice, a relevant concept based on the idea of helping people use their 'life space' to understand interactions between individuals and within groups (Millar, 2018). It also used ideas from Lewin's (1951) **field** theory, which aims to plot and work on forces in the social environment of the client.
- Therapeutic community theory, deriving from Maxwell Jones' (1968) work in psychiatric hospitals.
- Psychologically informed planned environments (PIPEs) are a programme for offenders with difficult-to-treat personality disorders or other serious behavioural difficulties operated in UK prisons and similar institutions. The programme involves structured psychological treatment using groupwork.

Criticism of the theory refers to the lack of clarity in particular theories; 'therapeutic community' is an umbrella term. Another criticism is that success often relies on the charisma of innovative leaders. This has been particularly so in the organisation of residents' meetings and other mechanisms which may be open to hidden agendas of, or manipulation by, leaders and staff.

Further Reading

Pearce, S. & Haigh, R. (2017). *The theory and practice of democratic therapeutic community treatment.* London: Jessica Kingsley.

Time is an issue in various aspects of social work:

- Mead's (1929) view of time is that everything about the past or future emerges in the present; the past is reinterpreted by connections with the present; the future emerges from present trends. In social work, practice involves assessing and exploring **narratives** given by clients or others to contribute to present interventions, or **solutions** and hopes for the future are always moulded by views of the present. In practice, we ask how the present recreates the past or extends towards the future.
- Time was a distinctive element in **functional** practice, linking with Mead's points. Taft (1962[1949]) refers to transference, not as searching the past to explain current behaviour, but clients recognising that they want to live differently from the past in the present and future; in contemporary theory, clients naturally have a **solution**-focused stance.
- Tsang (2008) argues that time is integral to practise **wisdom** and distinguishes 'kairos', qualitative time as felt by participants in events, from 'chronos', quantitative

time as counted by clocks. Awareness of clients' time pressures 'to get this done', 'to take time' is an important part of practice, and in many situations doing things at the 'right' time is an important aspect of success in practice.

Timms, Noel (1927–2018) was a prolific British academic, a pioneer in consumer research (Mayer & Timms, 1970), and pre-eminent in UK writing on social work philosophy and ethics from the 1960s to '80s.

Tokenism is a superficial acknowledgement of an injustice or oppression, or cursory reaction to it, with the aim of seeming fair. Token responses fail to repair damaging consequences, and do not make changes in behaviour or procedures that ensure that social justice is achieved or restored in the future. In Dominelli's (2012b) typology of **empowerment**, for example, tokenism is the most minimal empowering practice response.

Tongan social work refers to Indigenous concepts relevant to social work from this Polynesian island, explored in the work of Mafile'o (2004) and others. Mafile'o and Vakalahi (2018) argue that, like many areas of the Pacific, Tonga is the source of a diaspora across Southern Asia and beyond. The cultural spread has led to a need for social work to recognise and work with cultural traditions on which people in such migrations rely. This is a well-documented example of **Indigenist** thinking taken up and widely documented within a social work context to inform practice.

The **community** and the collective are important in Tongan, as in many **Indigenist**, social work analyses. Exploring **community work**, using Tongan concepts, Mafile'o (2004) argues that practitioners need to be internal to the community, sourcing solutions at the community level with collectivity as a strength. As with other Indigenist analyses, seeking out culturally distinctive structures for intervention is important. Mila-Schaaf (2006), exploring possibilities for social work in the Pacific, argues the relationships within the collective rather than with individuals, social work's basis in collective cultures working **holistically** rather than **individualistically**. Tofuaipangai and Camilleri (2016) use the Tongan concept of fatongia (obligation) to make a critique of the asymmetrical **neoliberal** concept of conditionality. They argue that Tongan obligation must be freely entered into, like a gift, and enforces a balanced mutuality of duties and responsibilities.

Total institutions is a concept associated particularly with the work of Erving **Goffman**, American sociologist, and his 'Asylums' (Goffman, (1968[1961])), a study of patterns of life in long-stay psychiatric institutions. A total institution is a treatment setting that provides on one site all or most of the requirements for living, including

T

housing, leisure, social interaction and work. Long-stay psychiatric hospitals are the classic total institutions, but the term might also be applied to monasteries, nunneries, prisons and children's homes. Goffman's (1968[1961]: 11) definition emphasises structures of interaction: '… a place of residence and work where a large number of like-situated individuals, cut off from the wider society for an appreciable period of time, together lead an enclosed, formally administered round of life'. The enclosure, exclusion from everyday life, period of residence and formal regime create interacting life worlds for staff and patients, in which there are institutional ceremonies and formalised patterns of behaviour and communication, but also a hidden 'underlife' of relationships that are delinquent or even a sign of **resistance**, because they do not respect the formal requirements of the institution. People adapt to the social characteristics of this enclosed place, and this unfits them for engagement in ordinary social life. Thus, **deinstitutionalisation** for people in long-stay mental healthcare requires not only finding housing for people outside the hospital, but enabling them to live in a completely different life world.

Traditional social work describes social **casework** practice, typical of social work agencies in the 1950s. It used psychodynamic theory focused on helping individual clients and their families adjust to conventional social expectations of behaviour or deal with problems of living. It did not exclude, but did not prioritise, groupwork with similar aims and community work that sought people's participation in improving social provision and living arrangements. 'Traditional social work' is a coinage of radical social workers in the 1960s onwards to describe the kind of social work they sought to displace with a broader range of activity and a stronger commitment to **social change**.

Transformation in **justice**, in organisations and in practice is a change that demonstrably moves in a new direction or changes the frame of reference within which things are done. The idea, often connected with **emancipation**, requires defining in what ways the change significantly alters previous patterns of behaviour. Transformational change is often an objective of **critical**, **radical** and **structural** practice.

The **transtheoretical model of change (TTM)** is a theory of behaviour **change** (Prochaska & DiClemente, 1983; Prochaska, DiClemente & Norcross, 1994), which suggests that behavioural and personal change is not rationally governed, but goes through a series of **stages**, most of which take place before any change is achieved. These include pre-contemplation, contemplation and preparation before an **action** phase. The model provides for a phase of maintaining progress, relapse from changes that have not yet fully stabilised, and a termination phase as someone shifts from the change process to everyday life. **Self-efficacy** is an important aspect of change outcomes.

TTM is helpful to social work by emphasising that change is difficult, not wholly rational and therefore requires help. Relapses are also highlighted, so they can be prepared for and dealt with. It also makes clear that mental preparation is required; **activity** is not a sign that movement is taking place, as for example **task-centred** practice assumes. TTM is the underlying model of change used in **motivational interviewing,** responding to critiques that TTM does not explain helping processes. Other criticisms (Littell & Girvin, 2002) are that it is derived from smoking cessation, and uses in drug abuse emphasise the difficulty of motivating people to change addictive behaviour; it may not transfer to other behaviour change aims or to **social change**.

An important element of TTM is that it theorises change as taking place in **stages**. A meta-analysis of research studies (Cahill, Lancaster & Green, 2010) showed that practice using stage-based theories of change was no more effective than non-stage-based theories.

Trauma means a distressing event or injury. In medicine it refers to any physical injury, but the psychological and social work usage refers to experiences that have powerful emotional effects to the extent that they damage the future functioning of the individual, particularly where there are complex factors. Post-traumatic stress disorder (PTSD) is a mental illness caused by involvement in or seeing disasters such as road accidents, violent death, wars or other extreme events. There may be dreams or flashbacks to the experiences and serious anxiety and depression.

Troubled families See **Problem families**.

T

U

The **underclass** conceptualises the idea that there is a devalued residual population in many societies that forms a 'class' separate from the working class of Marxist thought. Charles Murray (1990), writing towards the end of the ascendency of UK Conservative and US Republican governments, claims that physically deteriorating poor neighbourhoods provide a location for criminal, immoral, promiscuous, violent, welfare-dependent, work-evading and primarily young people, alien to **family** values. The critique of this view is that it diverts attention from structural problems which reduce employment for unskilled and young workers and exacerbates **poverty** and its impact on many working communities.

V

Values See Ethics.

Virtue ethics focuses on the character or way of looking at the world disclosed by the actions of moral agents, that is, people thinking about what is right when they take actions. The argument for this is that it seems logical that ethical behaviour should be based on ideas of what is right or good (Fenton, 2016: 67). Several religious traditions and some philosophical views follow virtue ethics. This view contests a **principle**-based ethics, which tries to establish rational rules of behaviour, which critics say leads to vague and generalised statements that do not give enough guidance in practice (Banks, 2012: 71–7).

Different types of virtue may be distinguished: intellectual, moral, physical and social virtues. The intellectual virtues identified by the Greek philosopher Aristotle are 'episteme' (knowledge), 'nous' (intelligence), 'phronesis' (prudence, practical wisdom) and 'techne' (art or skill). Moral virtues are probably the most relevant to social work and include care, respect for persons, trustworthiness, courage, integrity and justice. Physical virtues are health, beauty, strength, size and competitive prowess. Social virtues include politeness, sociability and wit (Banks & Gallagher, 2009: 61). Phronesis is sometimes debated in discourses about **constructionism**, **evidence-based practice** and practice **wisdom**.

A virtues ethicist concerned with social work looks both at whether someone displays moral virtues and connects them to traits such as commitment to **social justice**, good judgement or discernment in making decisions, moral courage to take actions that might be disapproved of by others, broad- or open-mindedness, professional or practice wisdom, responsiveness, stability, thoughtfulness and trustworthiness.

The criticism of this approach to ethics in social work is that many virtues might be relevant and there is no agreed list. Other difficulties are that they may be hard to define or describe, and they partly describe professional skills. A more philosophical objection is that when you examine them, they fall back to principles, that is, the virtuous person is someone who sticks to accepted professional principles. Thus, it might be argued that virtue ethics relies on principle-based ethics.

One issue is whether virtue is **holistic**, representing a person's character. Do you look for good people, rather than specific virtues? Banks and Gallagher (2009: Ch. 3) propose that virtues are complex and interact with each other, but are to some extent modular, that is, they operate separately in different situations. They suggest that we should see virtues and vices as paired to form a continuum from too much of one to too much of the other. Taking the example of **caring**, a deficiency of caring leads to the deficiencies of indifference or callousness, while an excess of caring leads to excessive or smothering concern. Other continua are: disrespectfulness, respect and servility; partiality, justice and indifference; unreliability, trustworthiness and punctiliousness; cowardice, courage and foolhardiness; superficiality, integrity and inflexibility (2009: 64). A social worker would aim for the mid-point, being aware of slipping inappropriately to either of the extremes.

Further Reading

Banks, S. & Gallagher, A. (2009). *Ethics in professional life: Virtues for health and social care*. Basingstoke: Palgrave Macmillan.

Voice is a useful concept in social work theory, as follows:

- **Accountability** structures increasingly provide for citizens, including social work clients, to have influence over services and professional responsibilities such as those of social workers, through having voice, the right to express views and giving feedback about services they receive.
- **Advocacy** practice may focus on representing the voice of people who are unable to represent themselves in decision-making forums or processes which affect their lives.
- **Anti-discriminatory** and **anti-oppressive** practices seek to draw on multiple voices to understand discrimination and oppression rather than drawing only on analysis or concerns from limited or single areas of exclusion or oppression.
- **Narrative** practice seeks to make manifest subjugated voices of people restricted from expressing their beliefs, experience, feelings or understanding about the world.

W

Weber, Max (1864–1920), a significant German sociologist, set many important directions in sociological thought. His work explored, through comparative analyses of culture and structures in different civilisations, how ideas and interests in any society create social structures that in turn set an ordered set of social relationships. For social work, his theories of **authority** and **bureaucracy** have been influential on thinking about social work organisations and **power** relations.

His analysis of Western civilisation claims that Western Europe was successful in building powerful capitalist economic systems because of the 'protestant ethic' of hard work and abstinence, and this established an important social order (Weber, 1930). This position contests the conflict perspective of **critical**, **Marxist** and **radical** theory, and also reveals the assumptions of a colonial mindset, which is contested in contemporary thinking by ideas that pay attention to the values of alternative traditional cultural and social structures, for example in **African-centred** and **Indigenist** perspectives on knowledge.

Further Reading

Gerth, H. H. & Mills, C. W. (Eds.) (1948). *From Max Weber: Essays in sociology*. London: Routledge and Kegan Paul.

Welfare refers, at its broadest, to 'doing well'. During the twentieth century, the term, sometimes as **social welfare**, came to describe services designed to help people in difficulties, again quite broadly. Ideas of the **welfare state** were used in the period of post-Second World War economic and social expansion to describe the wide responsibility of modern states for helping people in difficulties. The sense of 'welfare' has increasingly narrowed, so that now it often means financial assistance to people in **poverty**; if they need state help they are often described as 'on welfare' and the assistance is called 'welfare benefits'. The practice of advocacy in this field is often called **welfare rights** work.

Welfare rights is **advocacy** to help citizens claim their entitlements and apply successfully for discretionary assistance for benefits and financial or practical aid from public social security provision and charities. It may include assistance in dealing with debts and preventing problems arising from the enforcement of payments. Wootton (1959) and others argue that it is an important role for social work to help people with the financial and practical issues they face, and can prevent other family and social problems arising. Social care problems arise where financial stresses are considerable, for families with children, people with mental illness, people with disabilities who incur extra costs because of their condition, and older people. Responding to these difficulties is therefore logically part of social care provision.

In some public service systems, welfare rights is a specialised service because the administrative and legal knowledge required does not require the interpersonal skills of social workers. Social work, however, developed historically as provision for people in poverty, and all social work requires engagement with the 'money world' (Feldman, 1957) of clients with multiple problems. Resolving resource problems can also be helpful in gaining acceptance and develop trust to work on wider and more complex family issues. Many social work responsibilities connect to welfare rights issues, and because they involve services that meet people's accepted rights, this balances the more **discretionary** and judgemental elements of social work intervention.

Social workers find it useful to explore finance issues with individuals and families at particular times in their lives, as follows:

• When making major financial commitments, for example renting or buying living accommodation.
• When the family is expanding or contracting, for example marriage, childbirth, retirement or death.
• During periods of economic change, for example high unemployment or disaster.
• During major changes in life, for example in **caring** responsibilities, ill-health, migration or other change in **place**.

Further Reading

Bateman, N. (2006). *Practising welfare rights*. Abingdon: Routledge.

A **welfare state** is a country whose government accepts responsibility for the health and social welfare of its population through providing comprehensive services for education, healthcare, housing, social security and other social provision, usually including social work. Most states provide some services to provide security for people affected by economic and social pressures and to regulate the adverse human consequences of reliance on **liberal** economies.

The extensive development of social work services occurred from 1945 when, with the ending of the Second World War, many European countries began to make existing social provision more comprehensive. One historical question, therefore, is whether social work requires the presence of comprehensive welfare provision to develop. Is it a necessary aspect of comprehensive provision or a nice extra rather than a necessity?

A related political, and to some extent historical, question is whether there is a role for social work in a comprehensive welfare state. Views from the Left sometimes propose that comprehensive social provision supersedes helping roles. Because this was the position in communist regimes in Eastern European countries and in Soviet Russia, the historical question connects with the rapid reinstatement of social work after regime change. But this may also suggest that it is capitalist societies that require social work to mitigate the problems that **(neo)liberal** economic policy environments raise for marginalised social groups. Other views, for example **Wootton**'s (1959) arguments, suggest that guidance through the complexities of a comprehensive welfare state is required, and this is a suitable role for social work. Another contrary view is that interpersonal help with the stresses of life is valid, even if provision for material needs is sufficient.

Esping-Anderson's (1990) analysis of different types of welfare state influenced study of welfare states, and led to acceptance that there are a range of different types of welfare 'regime'. His approach mainly considers commodification, how much the market plays a role in service provision, and the comprehensiveness and social role of welfare state provision. His analysis focuses on pension rights and the labour market so later writers have explored wider elements of welfare states. The three types are:

- **Liberal**, with modest, mainly market-based, provision and few social rights.
- Corporatist, with stronger provision, acceptance of social rights, but family and class stratification is maintained.
- Social democratic, with universal, de-commodified provision, focusing on independence and guarantees of full employment.

The picture is more complex than these different types, but the analysis has led to considerable debate about the role of the state in social provision, and questions about comprehensiveness of provision and financing. Garland (2016) contends that there is considerable variation both between and within states that have significant welfare provision, and considerable variation and policy evolution over time, depending on changing social concerns.

Wisdom, often referred to as practice wisdom or professional wisdom, was in philosophy regarded as 'phronesis', an intellectual **virtue** concerned with prudence in making decisions. Five features may be identified (Devettere, cited by Banks & Gallagher, 2009: 78–9). The first is that practice wisdom becomes the primary element in decision-making. Deciding what will help people flourish, therefore, is more important than, say, morality, which some principled ideas tell us is good for people. The other four points are that practice wisdom is gained through deliberation (thinking things through, rather than intuitive), involves reasoning to distinguish good and bad practice, relies on experience and provides ethical norms for action. This last point makes clear that in practice, experience and **reflection**

W

are more important than theoretical prescriptions or systems to show us what will work to achieve appropriate aims, and should therefore set our approach to decision-making. Cheung (2016) argues that social work practice is often better based on the practitioner's intuition responding to the context than theoretical guidelines that do not connect with the situation they are facing. He proposes research, like Sheppard and his colleagues (Sheppard, 1995; Sheppard, et al., 2000; Sheppard & Ryan, 2003), into the decisions and thought processes used by practitioners. Practice wisdom might also be an important element of practice education in social work education, since this is a situation in which practice experience can be formulated and evaluated (Zuchowski, Hudson, Bartlett & Diamandi, 2014).

Various writers in social work such as Krill (1990) and Goldstein (1990, 2001) proposed a role for practice wisdom, to incorporate understanding from practice into formal theory. Goldstein (1990) argued that theories drawing on psychology and social science were alien to social work, and practice was better informed by a combination of practice wisdom, the humanities, and interpretive human sciences. Many ideas connect with seeing practice as an **art**, requiring creativity and imagination as well as social science knowledge, or that practice wisdom should be informed primarily by social work values such as social justice (Dybicz, 2004). My work on the practitioner a 'wise person' (Payne, 2007) argues that clients' expectations or perceptions of wisdom on issues that are unfamiliar to them are a characteristic of the social work **performance** within **helping** roles.

Two approaches to practice wisdom are as follows:

- Practice wisdom as an integrative mechanism, to bring together a range of sources of knowledge, both formal and informal, and apply them in practice situations (Klein & Bloom, 1995).
- Practice wisdom as an accumulation of experiences over time, that guides practitioners in work that they are regularly involved with (Collins & Daly, 2011).

Further Readings

Sheppard, M. (1995). Social work, social science and practice wisdom. *British Journal of Social Work*, 25(3), 265–93.

Cheung, J. C. S. (2016). Researching practice wisdom in social work. *Journal of Social Intervention: Theory and Practice*, 25(3), 24–38.

Wolfensberger, Wolf (1934–2011) was a German-born American psycho-logist, who also had a significant career role in Canada. He was a major figure in **deinstitutionalisation** of people with intellectual disabilities, and in the development of thinking about **normalisation**, originating the term **social role valorisation**.

Working through is a psychodynamic practice concept. It involves returning to examples of problem behaviour as they occurred during a client's life, exploring what happened and thinking about ways in which events and their emotional consequences might have been different; **narrative practice** may be analogous. In doing this, practitioners should beware of allowing constant repetition of depressing problem-talk; the aim is to get clients to think about alternatives and plans for the future.

Wootton, Barbara (Baroness Wootton of Abinger, CH) (1897–1988), was a much-honoured UK economist, doing work on equal pay, and magistrate dealing with youth offending. She argued that social workers were the 'first line of defence' (Wootton, 1959: 268) against deviance and social pathology. Wootton's (1959: Ch. 9) famous attack on 1950s **casework** argues that social work should forego behaviour change and other psychotherapeutic objectives, as excessively ambitious, and **ambiguous**, favouring an interventionist social work for the broader social good. **Professionalisation** (1959: 287–8) is an aggrandising pursuit of social status. She proposes that social workers should focus on guiding their clients through the complexities of the then-burgeoning **welfare state**.

W

References

Ad Hoc Committee on Advocacy (1969). The social work as advocate: Champion of social victims. *Social Work, 14*(2), 16–22.

Adame, A. L. & Leitner, L. M. (2008). Breaking out of the mainstream: The evolution of peer support alternatives to the mental health system. *Ethical Human Psychology and Psychiatry, 1*, 146–62.

Ahmad, B. (1990). *Black perspectives in social work*. Birmingham: Venture.

Ainsworth, F. & Fulcher, L. (1981). Introduction: Group care for children – concept and issues. In F. Ainsworth & L. Fulcher (Eds.), *Group care for children: Concept and issues* (pp. 1–15). London: Tavistock.

Alcoff, L. M. & Mendieta, E. (eds.)(2003). *Identities: Race, class, gender, and nationality*. Malden: MA: Blackwell.

Alternative Planning Group (2008). *Citizenship matters: Re-examining income (in)security of immigrant seniors*. Toronto: Wellesley Institute.

Anderson R. E. & Carter, I., with Lowe, G. R. (1999). *Human behavior in the social environment: A social systems approach* (5th ed.). New York: Aldine de Gruyter.

Anthony, W. A. (1993). Recovery from mental illness: The guiding vision of the mental health service system in the 1990s. *Psychosocial Rehabilitation Journal, 16*: 521–37.

Applegate, J. S. & Shapiro, J. R. (2005). *Neurobiology for clinical social work: Theory and practice*. New York: Norton.

Archer, M. S. (1996). *Culture and agency: The place of culture in social theory* (rev. ed.). Cambridge: Cambridge University Press.

Argyris, C. & Schön, D. A. (1974). *Theory in practice: Increasing professional effectiveness*. San Franciso, CA: Jossey-Bass.

Ariès, P. (1996[1962]). *Centuries of childhood: With a new introduction by Adam Phillips*. London: Pimlico.

Ashton, R. (2010). *How to be a social entrepreneur: Make money and change the world*. Chichester: Capstone.

Askeland, G. A. & Payne, M. (1999). Authors and audiences: Towards a sociology of case recording. *European Journal of Social Work 2*(1): 55–67.

Askeland, G. A. & Payne, M. (2017). *Internationalizing social work education: Insights from notable figures across the globe*. Bristol: Policy Press.

Asquith, S., Clark, C. & Waterhouse, L. (2005) *The role of the social worker in the 21st century: A literature review*. Edinburgh: Scottish Executive. https://www.webarchive.org.uk/wayback/archive/3000/https://www.gov.scot/Resource/Doc/47121/0020821.pdf.

Atchley, R. C. (1999). *Continuity and adaptation in aging: Creating positive experiences*. Baltimore, MD: Johns Hopkins University Press.

Atkin, A. (2016). *Peirce*. Abingdon: Routledge.

Austin, J. L. (1962). *How to do things with words*. Oxford: Clarendon Press.

Ayalon, L. & Tesch-Römer, C. (2018). Ageism: Concept and origins. In L. Ayalon & C. Tesch-Römer (Eds.), *Contemporary perspectives on ageism* (pp. 1–10). Cham: Springer.

Bachrach, P. & Baratz, M.S. (1970). *Power and poverty: Theory and practice*. New York: Oxford University Press.

Bailey, J. (1980). *Ideas and intervention: Social theory for practice*. London: Routledge and Kegan Paul.

Bailey, R. & Brake, M. (Eds.) (1975). *Radical social work*. London: Arnold.

Baines, D. (2017a). Anti-oppressive practice: Roots, theory, tensions. In D. Baines (Ed.), *Doing anti-oppressive practice: Social justice social work* (3rd ed.) (pp. 2–29). Halifax: Fernwood.

Baines, D. (2017b). Anti-oppressive practice: Neoliberalism, inequality and change. In D. Baines (Ed.), *Doing anti-oppressive practice: Social justice social work* (3rd ed.) (pp. 30–54). Halifax: Fernwood.

Baines, D. (2017c). Bridging the practice-activism divide: Advocacy, organizing and social movements. In D. Baines (Ed.), *Doing anti-oppressive practice: Social justice social work* (3rd ed.) (pp. 89–104). Halifax: Fernwood.

Baltes, P. B. & Baltes, M. M. (Eds.) (1990). *Successful aging: Perspectives from the behavioural sciences*. Cambridge: Cambridge University Press.

Bandler, B. (1963). The concept of ego-supportive psychotherapy. In H. J. Parad & R. R. Miller (Eds.), *Ego-oriented casework: Problems and perspectives* (pp. 27–44). New York: Family Service Association of America.

Bandler, L. (1963). Some casework aspects of ego growth through sublimation. In H. J. Parad & R. R. Miller (Eds.), *Ego-oriented casework: Problems and perspectives* (pp. 89–107). New York: Family Service Association of America.

Bandura, A. (1977a). *Social learning theory*. Englewood Cliffs, NJ: Prentice-Hall.

Bandura, A. (1977b). Self-efficacy: Toward a unifying theory of behavioral change. *Psychological Review, 84*, 191–215.

Bandura, A., Ross, D. & Ross, S. A. (1961). Transmission of aggression through imitation of aggressive models. *Journal of Abnormal and Social Psychology, 63*(3), 575–82.

Banks, S. (2004). *Ethics, accountability and the social professions*. Basingstoke: Palgrave Macmillan.

Banks, S. (2012). *Ethics and values in social work* (4th ed.). London: Red Globe.

Banks, S. & Gallagher, A. (2009). *Ethics in professional life: Virtues for health and social care*. Basingstoke: Palgrave Macmillan.

Barbalet, J. M. (2001). *Emotion, social theory, and social structure: A macrosociological approach*. Cambridge: Cambridge University Press.

Barclay Report (1982). *The roles and tasks of social workers*. London: Bedford Square Press.

Barise, A. (2005). Social work with Muslims: Insights from the teachings of Islam. *Critical Social Work, 6*(2), 73–89.

Barker, R. L. & Briggs, T. L. (1968). *Differential use of social work manpower: An analysis and demonstration study*. New York: National Association of Social Workers.

Barker, R. L. & Briggs, T. L. (1969). *Using TEAMS to deliver social services* (Manpower Monograph 1). Syracuse, NY: Syracuse University Department of Social Work.

Barnes, M. (2012). *Care in everyday life: An ethic of care in practice.* Bristol: Policy Press.

Barnes, M., Brannelly, T., Ward, L. & Ward, N. (Eds.) (2015). *Ethics of care: Critical advances in international perspective.* Bristol: Policy Press.

Barry, M. & Hallett, C. (1998). *Social exclusion and social work: Issues of theory, policy and practice.* Lyme Regis: Russell House.

Bartlett, H. (1961). *Analyzing social work practice by fields.* New York: National Association of Social Workers.

Bartlett, H. (1970). *The common base of social work practice.* New York: National Association of Social Workers.

Bartoli, A. (Ed.) (2013). *Anti-racism in social work practice.* St Albans: Critical Publishing.

Barton, W. T. (1959). *Institutional neurosis.* Bristol: John Wright.

Bateman, N. (2006). *Practising welfare rights.* Abingdon: Routledge.

Batsleer, J. & Humphries, B. (2000). *Welfare, exclusion and political agency.* London: Routledge.

Bauman, Z. (2000a). *Liquid modernity.* Cambridge: Polity.

Baumann, Z. (2000b). *A meeting with Zygmunt Bauman* [video]. Oslo: Oslo University College.

Bayliss, E. (1987). *Housing: The foundation for community care.* London: National Federation of Housing Associations.

Bayliss-Pratt, L. (2019). *New roles in mental health: Social workers task and finish group.* London: Health Education England.

Beadle-Brown, J., Murphy, B. & Bradshaw, J. (2017). *Person-centred active support* (2nd ed.). Brighton: Pavilion.

Beardshaw, V. & Towell, T. (1990). *Assessment and case management: Implications of the implementation of 'Caring for People'* (Briefing Paper 10). London: King's Fund Institute.

Beck, U. (1992). *Risk society: Towards a new modernity.* London: Sage.

Beck, U. & Beck-Gernsheim, E. (2001). *Individualization: Institutionalized individualism and its social and political consequences.* London: Sage.

Becker, H. S. (2018[1963]). *Outsiders: Studies in the sociology of deviance.* New York: Free Press.

Beckett, C., Maynard, A. & Jordan, P. (2017). *Values and ethics of social work* (3rd ed.). London: Sage.

Ben-Ari, A. & Strier, R. (2010). Rethinking cultural competence: What can we learn from Levinas? *British Journal of Social Work, 40*(7), 2155–67.

Bennett, S. & Nelson, J. K. (Eds.) (2010). *Adult attachment in clinical social work: Practice, research, and policy.* New York: Springer.

Béres, L. (2014). *The narrative practitioner.* Basingstoke: Palgrave Macmillan.

Beresford, P. & Croft, S. (1986). *Whose welfare? Private care of public services.* Brighton: Lewis Cohen Centre for Urban Studies.

Beresford, P. & Croft, S. (1993). *Citizen involvement: A practical guide for change.* Basingstoke: Palgrave Macmillan.

Berger, P. L. & Luckmann, T. (1971[1966]). *The social construction of reality.* Harmondsworth: Penguin.

Berlin, I. (1969). *Four essays on liberty.* Oxford: Oxford University Press.

Bernstein, S. (ed.) (1965). *Explorations in group work: Essays in theory and practice.* Bristol: Bookstall Publications.

Bernstein, S. (ed.) (1970). *Further explorations in group work.* Bristol: Bookstall Publications.

Bertens, H. (1995). *The idea of the postmodern: A history.* London: Routledge.

Bettmann, J. E. & Friedman, D. D. (Eds.) (2013). *Attachment-based clinical work with children and adolescents.* New York: Springer.

Bieling, P. J., McCabe, R. E. & Antony, M. M. (2006). *Cognitive-behavioral therapy in groups.* New York: Guilford.

Biestek, F. P. (1961). *The casework relationship.* London: Allen and Unwin.

Biestek, F P. & Gehrig, C.C. (1978). *Client self-determination in social work: A fifty-year history.* Chicago, IL: Loyola University Press.

Bion, W. R. (1961). *Experiences in groups and other papers.* London: Tavistock.

Blair, T. (2006). Our nation's future: Social exclusion. *British Political Speech: Speech Archive.* Retrieved from www.britishpoliticalspeech.org/speech-archive.htm?speech=283.

Blaug, R. (1995). Distortion of the face to face: Communicative reason and social work practice. *British Journal of Social Work, 25*(4), 423–39.

Blood, I. & Guthrie, L. (2018). *Supporting older people using attachment-informed and strengths-based approaches.* London: Jessica Kingsley.

Blumer, H. (1969). *Symbolic interactionism: Perspective and method.* Berkeley, CA: University of California Press.

Blundo, R., Bolton, K.W. & Lehmann, P. (2019). Strengths perspective: Critical analysis of the influence on social work. In M. Payne & E. Reith-Hall (Eds), *Routledge handbook of social work theory* (pp. 216–23). London: Routledge.

Boehm, W.W. (1961). Social work: Science and art. *Social Service Review, 35*(2), 144–52.

Boone, K., Roets, G. & Roose, R. (2019). Social work, participation, and poverty. *Journal of Social Work, 19*(3), 309–26.

Boone, M. S. (Ed.) (2014). *Mindfulness and acceptance in social work: Evidence-based interventions and emerging applications.* Oakland, CA: Context.

Boone, M. S. (2014). Introduction: Mindfulness and acceptance in social work. In M. S. Boone (Ed.), *Mindfulness and acceptance in social work: Evidence-based interventions and emerging application* (pp. 1–18). Oakland, CA: Context.

Bourdieu, P. (1980). *The logic of practice.* Stanford, CA: Stanford University Press.

Bourdieu, P. (1991). *Language and symbolic power.* Cambridge: Polity.

Bourdieu, P. & Wacquant, L. J. D. (1992). *An invitation to reflexive sociology.* Cambridge: Policy.

Bowell, T., Cowan, R. & Kemp, G. (2020). *Critical thinking: A concise guide* (5th ed.). Abingdon: Routledge.

Bowers, S. (1949). The nature and definition of social casework. *Social Casework, 30*(8), 311–17; 369–75; 412–7.

Bowlby, J. (1988). *A secure base: Clinical applications of attachment theory.* London: Routledge.

Bowles, W., Collingridge, M., Curry, S. & Valentine, B. (2006). *Ethical practice in social work: An applied approach.* Maidenhead: Open University Press.

Boyne, R. & Rattansi, A. (Eds.) (1990). *Postmodernism and society.* Basingstoke: Macmillan.

Brake, M. & Bailey, R. (Eds.) (1980). *Radical social work and practice.* London: Arnold.

Brand, D. (1999). *Accountable care: Developing the General Social Care Council.* York: Joseph Rowntree Foundation.

Brandon, D. (1989). The courage to look at the moon. *Social Work Today, 50*(50), 16–17.

Brandon, D. (1990[1976]). *Zen in the art of helping.* London: Arkana.

Brewer, C. & Lait, J. (1980). *Can social work survive?* London: Temple Smith.

Briar, S. & Miller, H. (1971). *Problems and issues in social casework.* New York: Columbia University Press.

Brieland, D., Briggs, T. & Leuenberger, P. (1973). *The team model of social work practice* (Manpower Monograph 5). Syracuse, NY: Syracuse University Department of Social Work.

Briggs, T. L. (1973). Identifying team functional roles and specializations. In D. Brieland, T. Briggs & P. Leuenberger, *The team model of social work practice* (pp. 16–25). Syracuse, NY: Syracuse Unievrsity School of Social Work.

British Association of Social Workers (1976). *The social work task.* Birmingham: British Association of Social Workers.

British Association of Social Workers (1977). *The social work task: A BASW working party report.* Birmingham: British Association of Social Workers.

Bronfenbrenner, U. (1979). *The ecology of human development: Experiments by nature and design.* Cambridge, MA: Harvard University Press.

Burford, G. & Hudson, P. (Eds.) (2017[2000]). *Family group conferencing: New directions in community-centered child and family practice.* Abingdon: Routledge.

Burrell, S. R. & Flood, M. (2019). Which feminism? Dilemmas in profeminist men's praxis to end violence against women. *Global Social Welfare, 6*(4), 231–44.

Butler, J. (1990). *Gender trouble.* New York: Routledge.

Butler, S. & Wintram, C. (1991). *Feminist groupwork.* London: Sage.

Butler-Mokoro, S. & Grant, L. (Eds.) (2018). *Feminist perspective on social work practice: The intersecting lives of women in the 21st century.* New York: Oxford University Press.

Cahill, K., Lancaster, T. & Green, N. (2010). Are stage-based interventions more effective than non-stage-based ones in helping smokers to quit? *Cochrane Database of Systematic Reviews 11.* Art. No.: CD004492. DOI: 10.1002/14651858.CD004492.pub4.

Cameron, C. & Moss, P. (Eds.) (2011). *Social pedagogy and working with children and young people: Where care and education meet.* London: Jessica Kingsley.

Cameron, N. & McDermott, F. (2007). *Social work and the body.* Basingstoke: Palgrave Macmillan.

Canavan, J., Pinkerton, J. & Dolan, P. (2016). *Understanding family support: Policy, practice and theory.* London: Jessica Kingsley.

Canda, E. R., Furman, L. D. & Canda, H. J. (2019). *Spiritual diversity in social work practice: The heart of helping* (2nd ed.). New York: Oxford University Press.

Cannon, I. M. (1913). *Social work in hospitals: A contribution to progressive medicine.* New York: Russell Sage Foundation.

Cannon, M.A. (1939[1933]). Recent changes in the philosophy of social workers. In F. Lowry (ed.), *Reading in social casework 1920–1938* (pp. 99–108). New York: Columbia University Press.

Caplan, G. (1965). *Principles of preventive psychiatry*. London: Tavistock.

Carey, M. (2019). Paradigm shift? Biomedical science and social work thinking. In M. Payne & E. Reith-Hall (Eds.), *Routledge handbook of social work theory* (pp. 68–80). London: Routledge.

Carkhuff, R. R. with Benoit, D. (2019). *The art of helping* (10th ed.). Amherst, MA: HRD Press.

Carpenter, J., Schneider, J., McNiven, F., Brandon, T., Stevens, R. & Wooff, D. (2004). Integration and targeting of community care for people with severe and enduring mental health problems: Users' experiences of the care programme approach and care management. *British Journal of Social Work, 34*(3), 313–33.

Cassidy, J. & Shaver, P. R. (Eds.) (2018). *Handbook of attachment: Theory, research and clinical applications* (3rd ed.). New York: Guilford.

Chambon, A. S. (1999). Foucault's approach: Making the familiar visible. In A. S. Chambon, A. Irving & L. Epstein (Eds.), *Reading Foucault for social work* (pp. 51–81). New York: Columbia University Press.

Chambon, A. S., Irving, A. & Epstein, L. (Eds.) (1999). *Reading Foucault for social work*. New York: Columbia University Press.

Charfe, L. (2019). Social pedagogical key thinkers. In L. Charfe & A. Gardner, *Social pedagogy and social work* (pp. 18–31). London: Sage.

Charfe, L. & Gardner, A. (2019). *Social pedagogy and social work*. London: Sage.

Cheung, A. B. L. (2002). The politics of New Public Management: Some experience from reforms in East Asia. In K. McLaughlin, S. P. Osborne & E. Ferlie (Eds.), *New public management: Current trends and future prospects* (pp. 243–73). London: Routledge.

Cheung, J. C. S. (2016). Researching practice wisdom in social work. *Journal of Social Intervention: Theory and Practice, 25*(3), 24–38.

Cigno, K. and Bourn, D. (Eds.) (1998). *Cognitive behavioural social work in practice*. Aldershot: Ashgate.

Clough, R. (2000). *The practice of residential work*. Basingstoke: Macmillan.

Cohen, S. (2002[1973]). *Folk devils and moral panics*. London: Routledge.

Cole, A. & Burke, C. (2012). *Guidance for practitioners from social care and health services in developing culturally competent practice*. London: Foundation for People with Learning Disabilities.

Coleman, J. S. (1988). Social capital in the creation of human capital. *American Journal of Sociology, 94*, S95–S120.

Collier, A. (1977). *R. D. Laing: The philosophy and politics of psychotherapy*. Hassocks: Harvester.

Collins, E. & Daly, E. (2011). *Decision making and social work in Scotland: The role of evidence and practice wisdom*. Glasgow: Institute for Research and Information in Social Services.

Compton, B. R., Galaway, B. & Cournoyer, B. R. (2005). *Social work processes* (7th ed.). Pacific Grove, CA: Brooks/Cole.

Cooper, D. (1970). *Psychiatry and anti-psychiatry*. London: Paladin.

Corcoran, J. (2006). *Cognitive-behavioral methods for social workers: A workbook*. Boston, MA: Allyn and Bacon.

Corcoran, J. (2016). *Motivational interviewing: A workbook for social workers*. New York: Oxford University Press.

Corrigan, P. & Leonard, P. (1978). *Social work practice under capitalism: A Marxist approach*. London: Macmillan.

Coyle, G. L. (1939a). Case work and group work. In F. Lowry (Ed.), *Readings in social case work 1920–1938* (pp. 558–64). New York: Columbia University Press.

Coyle, G. L. (1939b). Social workers and social action. In F. Lowry (Ed.), *Readings in social case work 1920–1938* (pp. 565–68). New York: Columbia University Press.

Craib, I. (1998). *Experiencing identity*. London: Sage.

Crawford, K., Price, M. & Price, B. (2016). *Groupwork practice for social workers*. London: Sage.

Crenshaw, K. (1995). Mapping the margins: Intersectionality, identity politics and violence against women of color. In L. M. Alcoff & E. Mendieta (Eds.), *Identities: Race, class, gender and nationality* (pp. 175–200). Malden, MA: Blackwell.

Critcher, C. (2016). Commentary: Moral panics yesterday, today and tomorrow. In C. E. Cree, G. Clapton & M. Smith (Eds.), *Revisiting moral panics* (pp. xvii–xxxvi). Bristol: Policy Press.

Cross, S., Hubbard, A. & Munro, E. (2010). *Reclaiming social work: London Borough of Hackney Children and Young People's Services*. London: Human Reliability/London School of Economics and Political Science. Retrieved from: https://secure.toolkitfiles.co.uk/clients/28663/sitedata/files/Eileen-Munro.pdf.

Crow, G. & Marsh, P. (1998). *Family group conferences in child welfare*. Oxford: Blackwell.

Cumming, E. & Henry, W. H. (1961). *Growing old: The process of disengagement*. New York: Basic Books.

Dalley, G. (1988). *Ideologies of caring: Rethinking community and collectvism*. Basingstoke: Macmillan.

Dalley, G. (1992). Social welfare ideologies and normalization: Links and conflicts. In H. Brown & H. Smith (Eds.), *Normalization: A reader for the nineties* (pp. 100–11). London: Routledge.

Dalrymple, J. & Boylan, J. (2013). *Effective advocacy in social work*. London: Sage.

Davies, B. & Challis, D. (1986) *Matching needs to resources in community care*. Aldershot: Gower.

Davies, H. & Kinloch, H. (2000). Critical incident analysis. In C. Macauley & V. Cree (Eds), *Transfer of learning in professional and vocational education* (pp. 137–50). London: Routledge.

Davies, M. (1985). *The essential social worker: A guide to positive practice* (2nd ed.). Aldershot: Wildwood House.

Dean, H. (2020). *Understanding human need* (2nd ed.). Bristol: Policy Press.

Deegan, P. (1995). Coping with recovery as a journey of the heart. *Psychiatric Rehabilitation Journal, 19,* 91–7.

Deindl, C. & Brandt, M. (2017). Support networks of childless older people: Informal and formal support in Europe. *Ageing & Society, 37*(8), 1543–67.

Derrida, J. (1982[1968]). Différance. In J. Derrida, *Margins of philosophy* (pp. 1–28) (Tr. A. Bass). Brighton: Harvester.

Desai, M. (2002). *Ideologies and social work: Historical and contemporary analyses.* Jaipur: Rawat.

Desai, M. (2015). *Social development in Asia: Diversity and implications.* Jaipur: Rawat.

Dixon, L. (2000). Assertive community treatment: Twenty-five years of gold. *Psychiatric Services, 51*(6), 759–65.

Doel, M. (2009). Task-centred work. In R. Adams, L. Dominelli & M. Payne (Eds.), *Critical practice in social work* (2nd ed.) (pp. 169–77). Basingstoke: Palgrave Macmillan.

Doel, M. & Lawson, B. (1986). Open records: The client's right to partnership. *British Journal of Social Work, 16*(4), 407–30.

Doel, M. & Marsh, P. (1992). *Task-centred social work.* Aldershot: Ashgate.

Dominelli, L. (2012a). *Green social work: From environmental crises to environmental justice.* Cambridge: Polity.

Dominelli, L. (2012b). Empowerment: Help or hindrance in professional relationships. In P. Stepney & D. Ford (Eds.), *Social work models, methods and theories: A framework for practice* (2nd ed.) (pp. 214–35). Lyme Regis: Russell House.

Dominelli, L. & McCleod, E. (1989). *Feminist social work.* Basingstoke: Macmillan.

Donne, J. (1624). Meditations 17. In J. Donne (1999), *Devotions on emergent occasions/Death's duel* (p. 103). New York: Vintage.

Douglas, T. (1979). *Group processes in social work: A theoretical synthesis.* Chichester: Wiley.

Douglas, T. (1993). *A theory of groupwork practice.* Basingstoke: Macmillan.

Dowie, J. & Elstein, A. (Eds.) (1988). *Professional judgment: A reader in clinical decision making.* Cambridge: Cambridge University Press.

Downie, R. S. (1971). *Roles and values: An introduction to social ethics.* London: Methuen.

Downie, R. S. & Telfer, E. (1969). *Respect for persons.* London: Allen and Unwin.

Doyal, L. & Gough, I. (1991). *A theory of human need.* Basingstoke: Palgrave Macmillan.

Dressel, P. (1987). Patriarchy and social welfare work. *Social Problems, 34*(3), 294–309.

Dudley, J. R. (2016). *Spirituality matters in social work: Connecting spirituality, religion, and practice.* Abingdon: Routledge.

Dupré, M. (2012). Disability culture and cultural competency in social work. *Social Work Education, 31*(2), 168–83.

Dustin, D. (2007). *The McDonaldization of social work.* Aldershot: Ashgate.

Dybicz, P. (2004). An inquiry into practice wisdom. *Families in Society, 85*(2), 197–203.

Eichsteller, G. & Holthoff, S. (2011). Conceptual foundations of social pedagogy: A transnational perspective from Germany. In C. Cameron & P. Moss (Eds.). *Social pedagogy and working with children and young people: Where care and education meet* (pp. 33–52). London: Jessica Kingsley.

Ekman, P. (1992) Are there basic emotions? *Psychological Review, 99*(3), 350–3.

Elder, G. H., Johnson, M. K. & Crosnoe, R. (2003). The emergence and development of life course theory. In J. T. Mortimer & M. J. Shanahan (Eds.), *Handbook of the life course* (pp. 3–19). New York: Kluwer.

Emerson, E. (1992). What is normalization? In H. Brown & H. Smith (Eds.), *Normalization: A reader for the nineties* (pp. 1–18). London: Routledge.

England, H. (1986). *Social work as art: Making sense for good practice.* London: Allen and Unwin.

Epstein, L. & Brown, L. B. (2002). *Brief treatment and a new look at the task-centered approach* (3rd ed.). Boston, MA: Allyn & Bacon.

Erikson, E. (1965). *Childhood and society* (2nd ed.). London: Hogarth Press.

Esping-Anderson, G. (1990). *The three worlds of welfare capitalism.* Cambridge: Polity.

Esquao, S. A. & Strega, S. (2015). *Walking this path together: Anti-racist and anti-oppressive child welfare practice* (2nd ed.). Halifax: Fernwood.

Esterson, A. (1972). *The leaves of spring.* Harmondsworth: Penguin.

Faatz, A. J. (1985[1953]). *The nature of choice in casework process.* Chapel Hill, NC: University of North Carolina Press.

Fairclough, N., & Fairclough, I. (2018). A procedural approach to ethical critique in CDA. *Critical Discourse Studies, 15*(2), 169–85.

Farmer, R. (2009). *Neuroscience and social work practice: The missing link.* Thousand Oaks, CA: Sage.

Farrelly, S., Szmukler, G., Henderson, C., Birchwood, M., Marshall, M., Waheed, W., Finnecy, C. & Thornicroft, G. (2014). Individualisation in crisis planning for people with psychotic disorders. *Epidemiology and Psychiatric Sciences, 23*(4), 353–9.

Featherstone, B. (2001). Where to for feminist social work. *Critical social work, 2*(1) [Online]. Retrieved from: https://ojs.uwindsor.ca/index.php/csw/article/view/5619/4592.

Feldman, F. L. (1957). *The family in a money world.* New York: Family Service Association of America.

Fenton, J. (2016). *Values in social work: Reconnecting with social justice.* London: Palgrave.

Fenton, J. (2019). *Social work for lazy radicals: Relationship building, critical thinking and courage in practice.* London: Red Globe.

Ferguson, I. (2019). The return of macro approaches in social work. In M. Payne & E. Reith-Hall (Eds.), *Routledge handbook of social work theory* (pp. 216–23). London: Routledge.

Ferguson, I., Ioakimidis, V. & Lavalette, M. (2018). *Global social work in a political context: Radical perspectives.* Bristol: Policy Press.

Ferguson, I. & Woodward, R. (2009). *Radical social work in practice: Making a difference.* Bristol: Policy Press.

Finch, J. (1989). *Family obligations and social change.* Cambridge: Polity.

Finch, J. & Mason, J. (1993) *Negotiating family obligations.* London: Tavistock/Routledge.

Fine, M. D. (2007). *A caring society? Care and the dilemmas of human service in the twenty-first century.* Basingstoke: Palgrave Macmillan.

Finlay, L. (2003). The reflexive journey: Mapping multiple routes. In L. Finlay & B. Gough (Eds.), *Reflexivity: A practical guide for researchers in health and social sciences* (pp. 3–20). Oxford: Blackwell.

Fish, J. (2012). *Social work with lesbian, gay, bisexual and trans people: Making a difference.* Bristol: Policy Press.

Fisher, B. & Tronto, J. C. (1991). Toward a feminist theory of care. In E. Abel & M. Nelson (Eds.), *Circles of care: Work and identity in women's lives* (pp. 35–62). Albany, NY: State University of New York Press.

Flexner, A. (2001[1915]). Is social work a profession? *Research on social work practice,* 11(2), 152–65.

Flowerdew, J. & Richardson, J. E. (2018). Introduction. In J. Flowerdew & J. E. Richardson (Eds.), *The Routledge handbook of critical discourse studies* (pp. 1–10). Abingdon: Routledge.

Fook, J. (1993). *Radical casework: A theory of practice.* St Leonards: Allen and Unwin.

Fook, J. & Gardner, F. (2007). *Practising critical reflection: A resource handbook.* Maidenhead: Open University Press.

Foote, C. E. & Frank, A. W. (1999). Foucault and therapy: The disciplining of grief. In A. S. Chambon, A. Irving & L. Epstein (Eds.), *Reading Foucault for social work* (pp. 157–87). New York: Columbia University Press.

Fortune, A. E. (1985). *Task-centered practice with families and groups.* New York: Springer.

Foucault, M. (1972). *The archaeology of knowledge and the discourse on language.* New York: Pantheon.

Fox, A. (Ed.) (2013). *The new social care: Strength-based approaches.* London: Public Service Hub.

Frankel, A. J., Gelman, S. R. & Pastor, D. K. (2019). *Case management: An introduction to concepts and skills* (4th ed.). New York: Oxford University Press.

Frankl, V. E. (2011[1948]). *Man's search for ultimate meaning* (rev. edn.). London: Rider.

Franklin, C. (1998). Distinctions between social constructionism and cognitive constructivism: Practice applications. In C. Franklin & P. S. Nurius (Eds.) *Constructivism in practice* (pp. 57–94). Milwaukee, WI: Families International.

Fraser, N. (1989). *Unruly practices.* Cambridge: Polity.

Fraser, N. (2000). Rethinking recognition. *New Left Review, 3,* 107–20.

Fraser, N. (2008). *Scales of justice: Reimagining political space in a globalizing world.* Cambridge: Polity.

Fraser, N. & Honneth, A. (2003). *Redistribution or recognition? A political-philosophical exchange.* London: Verso.

Freedberg, S. (2009). *Relational theory for social work practice: A feminist perspective.* New York: Routledge.

Freidson, E. (1970). *Profession of medicine: A study of the sociology of applied knowledge.* New York: Dodd, Mead.

Freire, P. (1970). *Cultural action for freedom.* Harmondsworth: Penguin.

Freire, P. (1972). *Pedagogy of the oppressed.* Harmondsworth: Penguin.

Freire, P. (1974[1967]). *Education: The practice of freedom.* London: Writers and Readers Publishing Cooperative.

Froggett, L. (2002) *Love, hate and welfare: Psychosocial approaches to policy and practice.* Bristol: Policy Press.

Frosh, S. (1987). *The politics of psychoanalysis: An introduction to Freudian and Post-Freudian theory.* Basingstoke: Macmillan.

Frost, B. G., Tirupati, S., Johnston, S. & Conrad, A. (2017). An integrated recovery-oriented model (IRM) for mental health services: Evolution and challenges. *BMC Psychiatry, 17*(2). DOI 10.1186/s12913-016-1939-8.

Frost, N., Abbott, S. & Race, T. (2015). *Family support: Prevention, early intervention and early help.* Cambridge: Polity.

Gabriel, N. (2017). *The sociology of early childhood: Critical perspectives.* London: Sage.

Gair, S. (2017). Pondering the colour of empathy: Social work students' reasoning on activism, empathy and racism. *British Journal of Social Work, 47*(1), 162–80.

Galper, J. (1980). *Social work practice: A radical approach.* Englewood Cliffs, NJ: Prentice-Hall.

Gambrill, E. (1994). What's in a name? Task-centered, empirical, and behavioral practice. *Social Service Review 68*(4): 578–99.

Gambrill, E. (2019). *Critical thinking and the process of evidence-based practice.* New York: Oxford University Press.

Garavan, M. (2013). Dialogical practice in social work – towards a renewed humanistic method. *Journal of Social Intervention: Theory and Practice, 22*(1), 4–20.

Gardner, A. (2014). Personalisation: Where did it come from? In A. Gardner (Ed.), *Personalisation in social work* (2nd ed.) (pp. 1–19). London: Sage.

Gardner, F. (2014). *Being critically reflective: Engaging in holistic practice.* London: Red Globe.

Garfinkel, H. (1967). *Studies in ethnomethodology.* Englewood Cliffs, NJ: Prentice-Hall.

Garland, D. (2016). *The welfare state: A very short introduction.* Oxford: Oxford University Press.

Garran, A. M. & Rozas, L. W. (2013). Cultural competence revisited. *Journal of Ethnic and Cultural Diversity in Social Work, 22*(2), 97–111.

Garrett, A. (1958). Modern casework: The contribution of ego psychology. In H. J. Parad (Ed.), *Ego psychology and dynamic casework* (pp. 38–52). New York: Family Service Association of America.

Garrett, P.M. (2013). Pierre Bourdieu. In M. Gray & S. A. Webb (eds), *Social work theories and methods* (2nd Ed.) (pp. 36–45). London: Sage.

Garrett, P. M. (2018a). *Social work and social theory: Making connections* (2nd ed.). Bristol: Policy Press.

Garrett, P. M. (2018b). *Welfare words: Critical social work and social policy.* London: Sage.

Gergen, K. J. (1994). *Realities and relationships: Soundings in social construction.* Cambridge, MA: Harvard University Press.

Gergen, K. J. (1999). *An invitation to social construction.* London: Sage.

Gergen, M. & Gergen, K. J. (Eds.) (2003). *Social construction: A reader.* London: Sage.

Germain, C. B. (1968). Social study: Past and future. *Social Casework, 49*(7), 403–9.

Germain, C. B. (1970). Casework and science: A historical encounter. In R. W. Roberts & R. H. Nee (Eds.), *Theories of social casework* (pp. 3–32). Chicago, IL: University of Chicago Press.

Germain, C. B. (1976). Time: An ecological variable in social work practice. *Social Casework, 57*(7), 419–26.

Germain, C. B. (1978). Space: An ecological variable in social work practice. *Social Casework*, *59*(9), 515–22.

Gerth, H. H. & Mills, C. W. (Eds.) (1948). *From Max Weber: Essays in sociology*. London: Routledge and Kegan Paul.

Gibson, F. (Ed.) (2018). *International perspectives on reminiscence, life review and life story work*. London: Jessica Kingsley.

Giddens, A. (1976). *New rules of sociological method*. London: Hutchinson.

Giddens, A. (1990). *The consequences of modernity*. Cambridge: Polity.

Giddens, A. (1994). The trajectory of the self. In L. M. Alcoff & E. Mendieta (Eds.), *Identities: Race, class, gender and nationality* (pp. 248–66). Malden, MA: Blackwell.

Giddens, A. (1998). *The third way: The renewal of social democracy*. Cambridge: Polity.

Giddens, A. (2000). *The third way and its critics*. Cambridge: Polity.

Gilleard, C. & Higgs, P. (2020). *Social division and later life: Difference, diversity and inequality*. Bristol: Policy Press.

Gilligan, C. (1993[1982]). *In a different voice: Psychological theory and women's development*. Cambridge, MA: Harvard University Press.

Gilligan, R. (2004). Promoting resilience in child and family social work: Issues for social work practice, education and policy. *Social Work Education, 23*(1), 93–104.

Gitterman, A. & Germain, C. B. (2008). *The life model of social work practice: Advances in theory and practice* (3rd ed.). New York: Columbia University Press.

Glasser, W. (1965). *Reality therapy: A new approach to psychiatry*. New York: Harper & Row.

Glassman, U. (2009). *Group work: A humanistic and skills building approach* (2nd ed.). Thousand Oaks, CA: Sage.

Glastonbury, B. (1976). *Paying the piper*. Birmingham: BASW Publications.

Glick, I., Parkes, C. M. & Weiss, R. S. (1974). *The first year of bereavement*. New York: Wiley.

Goffman, E. (1964). *Stigma: Notes on the management of spoiled identity*. Harmondsworth: Penguin.

Goffman, E. (1968[1961]). *Asylums: Essays in the social situation of mental patients and other inmates*. Harmondsworth: Penguin.

Goffman, E. (1968[1963]). *Stigma: Notes on the management of spoiled identity*. Harmondsworth: Penguin.

Goffman, E. (1968). *The presentation of self in everyday life*. Harmondsworth: Penguin.

Goffman, E. (1972). *Relations in public: Microstudies of the public order*. Harmondsworth: Penguin.

Goffman, E. (1974). *Frame analysis: An essay on the organization of experience*. Cambridge, MA: Harvard University Press.

Goldberg, E. M. & Warburton, R. W. (1979). *Ends and means in social work: The development and outcomes of a case review system for social workers*. London: Allen and Unwin.

Golding, K. S. (2008). *Nurturing attachments: Supporting children who are fostered or adopted*. London: Jessica Kingsley.

Goldstein, E. G., Miehls, D. & Ringel, S. (2009) *Advanced clinical social work practice: Relational principles and techniques*. New York: Columbia University Press.

Goldstein, H. (1981). *Social learning and change: A cognitive approach to human services.* Columbia, SC: University of South Carolina Press.

Goldstein, H. (1973). *Social work practice: A unitary approach.* Columbia, SC: University of South Carolina Press.

Goldstein, H. (Ed.) (1984). *Creative change: A cognitive-humanistic approach to social work practice.* New York: Tavistock.

Goldstein, H. (1990). The knowledge base of social work practice: Theory, wisdom, analogue, or art? *Families in Society, 71*(1), 32–43.

Goldstein, H. (2001). *Experiential learning: A foundation for social work education and practice.* Washington, DC: Council on Social Work Education.

Goleman, D. (1996). *Emotional intelligence: Why it matters more than IQ.* London: Bloomsbury.

Goleman, D. (2007). *Social intelligence: The new science of human relationships.* London: Arrow.

Gonzales-Prendes, A. A. & Cassady, C. M. (2019). Cognitive-behavioural therapy and social work practice. In M. Payne & E. Reith-Hall (Eds.), *Routledge handbook of social work theory* (pp. 193–204). London: Routledge.

Goode, E. & Ben-Yehuda, N. (2009[1994]). *Moral panic: The social construction of deviance.* Oxford: Blackwell.

Goodley, D. (2017). *Disability studies: An interdisciplinary introduction* (2nd ed.). London: Sage.

Gorey, K. M., Daly, C., Richter, N. L., Gleason, D. R. & McCallum, M. J. A. (2003). The effectiveness of feminist social work methods: An integrative review. *Journal of Social Service Research, 29*(1), 37–55.

Graham, M. (2002). *Social work and African-centred worldviews.* Birmingham: Venture.

Gray, M. & Lovat, T. (2008). Practical mysticism, Habermas, and social work praxis. *Journal of Social Work, 8*(2), 149–62.

Gray, T. (1991). *Freedom.* Atlantic Highlands, NJ: Humanities Press.

Greenberg, J., Solomon, S. & Pyszczynski, T. (1997). Terror management theory of self-esteem and cultural worldviews: Empirical assessments and conceptual refinements. *Advances in Experimental Social Psychology, 29,* 61–139.

Greene, G. J. & Lee, M. Y. (2011). *Solution-oriented social work practice: An integrative approach to working with client strengths.* New York: Oxford University Press.

Greene, R. R. (2012). Human behavior theory: A resilience orientation. In R. R. Greene (Ed.), *Resiliency: An integrated approach to practice, policy and research* (2nd ed.) (pp. 1–28). Washington, DC: National Association of Social Workers.

Greenwood, E. (1957). Attributes of a profession. *Social Work, 2*(3), 45–55.

Griffiths, M. (2017). *The challenge of existential social work practice.* London: Palgrave.

Gutiérrez, G. (1973). *A theology of liberation.* Maryknoll: Orbis.

Gutiérrez, L. M. (1994). Beyond coping: An empowerment perspective in stressful life events. *Journal of Sociology and Social Welfare, 21*(3), 201–19.

Haber, D. (2006). Life review: Implementation, theory, research, and therapy. *International Journal of Aging and Human Development, 63*(2), 153–71.

Hadley, R. & Hatch, S. (1981). *Social welfare and the failure of the state.* London: Allen and Unwin.

Hadley, R. & McGrath, M. (Eds.) (1980). *Going local – Neighbourhood social services.* London: Bedford Square Press.

Hadley, R. & McGrath, M. (1984). *When social services are local: The Normanton experience.* London: Allen and Unwin.

Hadley, R. & Young, K. (1990). *Creating a responsive public service.* Hemel Hempstead: Harvester Wheatsheaf.

Haight, B. (1995). Reminiscing: The state of the art as a basis for practice. In J. Hendricks (Ed.), *The meaning of reminiscence and life review* (pp. 21–52). Amityville, NY: Baywood.

Haines, N. (1966). *Freedom and community: A study of social values.* London: Macmillan.

Hall, C., Juhila, K., Matarese, M. & van Nijnatten, N. (Eds.) (2014). *Analysing social work communication: Discourse in practice.* Abingdon: Routledge.

Hall, C., Juhila, K., Parton, N. & Pösö, T. (2003). *Constructing clienthood in social work and human services: Interaction, identities and practices.* London: Jessica Kingsley.

Hall, S., Held, D. & McGrew, T. (Eds.) (1992). *Modernity and its futures.* Cambridge: Polity.

Halmos, P. (1965). *The faith of the counsellors.* London: Constable.

Halmos, P. (1970). *The personal service society.* London: Constable.

Halmos, P. (1978). *The personal and the political: Social work and political action.* London: Hutchinson.

Hämäläinen, J. (1989). Social pedagogy as a meta-theory of social work education. *International Social Work, 32*(2), 117–28.

Hämäläinen, J. (2003). The concept of social pedagogy in the field of social work. *Journal of Social Work, 3*(1), 69–80.

Hamilton, G. (1951). *Theory and practice of social case work* (2nd ed.). New York: Columbia University Press.

Hamilton, G. (1952). The role of social casework in social policy. In C. Kasius (Ed.), *Social casework in the fifties: Selected articles, 1951–1960* (pp. 28–44). New York: Family Service Association of America.

Harlow, E. & Webb, S. A. (Eds.) (2002). *Information and communication technologies in the welfare services.* London: Jessica Kingsley.

Harris, J. (2003). *The social work business.* London: Routledge.

Hart, M. A. (2019). Indigenist social work practice. In M. Payne & E. Reith-Hall (Eds.), *Routledge handbook of social work theory* (pp. 268–81). London: Routledge.

Hartman, A. (1981). The family: A central focus for practice. *Social work, 26*(1), 7–13.

Havighurst, R. J. (1961). Successful aging. *Gerontologist, 1*(1), 8–13.

Hayden, C. & Jenkins, C. (2014). 'Troubled Families' programme in England: 'Wicked problems' and policy-based evidence. *Policy Studies, 35*(6), 631–49.

Healy, K. (2014). *Social work theories in context: Creating frameworks for practice.* London: Palgrave.

Hearn, G. (1958) *Theory-building in social work.* Toronto: University of Toronto Press.

Hearn, G. (Ed.) (1969). *The general systems approach: Contributions toward a holistic conception of social work.* New York: Council on Social Work Education.

Hermans, H. & Hermans-Konopka, A. (2010). *Dialogical self-theory: Positioning and counter-positioning in a globalizing society.* Cambridge: Cambridge University Press.

Heywood, C. (2001). *A history of childhood: Children and childhood in the West from medieval to modern times.* Cambridge: Polity.

Hick, S. F. (2009). *Mindfulness and social work.* Chicago, IL: Lyceum.

Higashida, M. (2019). *Developmental social work in disability issues: Research and practice for promoting participation in rural Sri Lanka.* Hyogo: Ashoka Disability Research Forum.

Hochschild, A.R. (2012[1983]). *The managed heart: The commercialization of human feeling.* Berkeley, CA: University of California Press.

Hodge, D. R. (2005). Social work and the house of Islam: Orienting practitioners to the beliefs and values of Muslims in the United States. *Social Work, 50*(2), 162–73.

Hodgson, D. & Watts, L. (2017) *Key concepts and theory in social work.* London: Palgrave.

Hoefer, R. (2019) *Advocacy practice for social justice* (4th ed.). New York: Oxford University Press.

Hoffman, M. L. (2000). *Empathy and moral development: Implications for caring and practice.* Cambridge: Cambridge University Press.

Hofstein, S. (1964). The nature of process: Its implications for social work. *Journal of the Social Work Process, 14:* 13–53.

Hohman, M. (2016). *Motivational interviewing in social work practice.* New York: Guilford.

Hollingsworth, A. (2019). The politics of intersectionality as location. In S. Nayak & R. Robbins (Eds.), *Intersectionality in social work: Activism and practice in context* (pp. 52–62). Abingdon: Routledge.

Hollinsworth, D. (2013). Forget cultural competence; ask for an autobiography. *Social Work Education, 32*(8), 1048–60.

Hollis, F. (1964). *Casework: A psychosocial therapy.* New York: Random House.

Holloway, M. & Moss, B. (2010). *Spirituality and social work.* Basingstoke: Palgrave Macmillan.

Hollway, W. (2006). *The capacity to care: Gender and ethical subjectivity.* Abingdon: Routledge.

Hooyman, N. R. (1991). Supporting practice in large-scale bureaucracies. In M. Bricker-Jenkins, N. R. Hooyman & N. Gottlieb (Eds.), *Feminist social work practice in clinical settings* (pp. 251–68). Newbury Park, CA: Sage.

Houston, S. (2001). Beyond social constructionism: Critical realism and social work. *British Journal of Social Work, 31*(6), 845–61.

Houston, S. (2013). Jürgen Habermas. In M. Gray & S. A. Webb (Eds.), *Social work theories and methods* (pp. 13–24) (2nd ed.). London: Sage.

Howarth, D. (2000). *Discourse.* Buckingham: Open University Press.

Howe, D. (1993). *On being a client: Understanding the process of counselling and psychotherapy.* London: Sage.

Howe, D. (2005). *Child abuse and neglect: Attachment, development and intervention.* Basingstoke: Palgrave Macmillan.

Howe, D. (2008). *The emotionally intelligent social worker.* Basingstoke: Palgrave Macmillan.

Howe, D. (2011). *Attachment across the lifecourse: A brief introduction.* Basingstoke: Palgrave Macmillan.

Hudson, C. G. (2010). *Complex systems and human behaviour.* Chicago, IL: Lyceum.

Hudson, C. G. (2019). Theory on systems, complexity and chaos. In M. Payne & E. Reith-Hall (Eds.), *The Routledge handbook of social work theory* (pp. 181–92). Abingdon: Routledge.

Hugman, R. (2005). *New approaches in ethics for the caring professions.* Basingstoke: Palgrave Macmillan.

Humphreys, C., McCarthy, G., Dowling, M., Kertesz, M. & Tropea, R. (2014). Improving the archiving of records in the out-of-home care sector. *Australian Social Work, 67*(4), 509–24.

Huxley, P., Evans, S., Beresford, P., Davidson, B. & King, S. (2009). The principles and provisions of relationships: Findings from an evaluation of support, time and recovery workers in mental health services in England. *Journal of Social Work, 9*(1), 99–117.

Iacovetta, F. (1998). Parents, daughters and family-court intrusions into working-class life. In F. Iacovetta & W. Mitchinson (Eds.), *On the case: Explorations of social history* (pp. 312–37). Toronto: University of Toronto Press.

Ife, J. (2012). *Human rights and social work: Towards rights-based practice* (3rd ed.). Port Melbourne: Cambridge.

Illich, I., Zola, I. K., McKnight, J., Caplan, J. & Shaiken, H. (1977). *Disabling professions.* London: Marion Boyars.

Imbrogno, S. & Canda, E. R. (1988). Social work as an holistic system of activity. *Social Thought, 14*(1), 16–29.

International Federation of Social Workers (2014a). *Global Definition of Social Work.* Retrieved from: www.ifsw.org/what-is-social-work/global-definition-of-social-work/.

International Federation of Social Workers (2014b). *Global social work statement of ethical principles.* Retrieved from: www.ifsw.org/global-social-work-statement-of-ethical-principles/.

Irvine, E. E. (1952). The function and use of relationship between client and psychiatric social worker. In E. Younghusband (Ed.) (1966), *New developments in casework* (pp. 88–94). London: Allen and Unwin.

Irvine, E. E. (1956). Transference and reality in the casework relationship. In E. Younghusband (Ed.) (1966), *New developments in casework* (pp. 108–23). London: Allen and Unwin.

Jack, G. & Gill, O. (2013) Developing cultural competence for social work with families living in poverty. *European Journal of Social Work, 16*(2), 220–34.

James, R. K. & Gilliland, B. E. (2017). *Crisis intervention strategies* (8th ed.). Boston, MA: Cengage.

Javadian, R. (2007). Social work responses to earthquake disasters: A social work intervention in Bam, Iran. *International Social Work, 50*(3), 334–46.

Jin, K. (2010). Modern biological theories of aging. *Aging and Disease, 1*(2), 72–4.

Johnson, Y. M. & Munch, S. (2009). Fundamental contradictions in cultural competence. *Social Work, 54*(3), 220–31.

Jones, M. (1968). *Social psychiatry in practice: The idea of the therapeutic community.* Harmondsworth: Penguin.

Jordan, B. (1975). Is the client a fellow citizen? *Social Work Today, 6*(15), 471–5.

Jordan, B. (1979). *Helping in social work*. London: Routledge and Kegan Paul.

Jordan, B. with Jordan, C. (2000). *Social work and the third way: Tough love as social policy*. London: Sage.

Jordan, W. (1975). The rise and fall of local authority family casework in Great Britain. *International Social Work*, 19(5), 36–45.

Kabat-Zinn, J. (1990). *Full catastrophe living: Using the wisdom of your body and mind to face stress, pain, and illness*. New York: Delacorte.

Kane, R. (1982). Lessons for social work from the medical model: A viewpoint for practice. *Social Work*, 27(4), 315–21.

Kane, R. A. (1975). *Interprofessional teamwork* (Manpower Monograph 8). Syracuse, NY: Syracuse University Department of Social Work.

Karls, J. M. & O'Keefe, M. E. (Eds.) (1994). *Person-in-environment system: The PIE classification system for social functioning problems*. Washington, DC: NASW Press.

Kasca, M. (2015). *Social pedagogy: An invitation*. London: Jacaranda Development.

Katz, J., Holland, C., Peace, S. & Taylor, E. (2011). *A better life: What older people with high support needs value*. York: Joseph Rowntree Memorial Trust.

Katz, S. (2000). Busy bodies: Activity, aging and the management of everyday life. *Journal of Aging Studies*, 14(2), 135–52.

Kazi, M. A. F. (2003). *Realist evaluation in practice: Health and social work*. London: Sage.

Keith-Lucas, A. (1972). *Giving and taking help*. Chapel Hill, NC: University of North Carolina Press.

Keith-Lucas, A. (1975[1963]) A critique of the principle of client self-determination. In F. E. McDermott (Ed.), *Self-determination in social work: A collection of essays on self-determination and related concepts by philosophers and social work theorists* (pp. 43–52). London: Routledge and Kegan Paul.

Kelly, G. (1955). *The psychology of personal constructs* (2 vols). New York: Norton.

Kemp, S. P. (2010). Place matters: Toward a rejuvenated theory of environment for direct social work practice. In W. Borden (Ed.), *Reshaping theory in contemporary social work: Toward a critical pluralism in clinical practice* (pp. 114–45). New York: Columbia University Press.

Kemshall, H. (2010). Risk rationalities in contemporary social work policy and practice. *British Journal of Social Work*, 40(4), 1247–62.

Kirmayer, L. J., Sehdev, M., Whitley, R., Dandeneau, S. F. & Isaac, C. (2009). Community resilience: Models, metaphors and measures. *International Journal of Indigenous Health*, 5(1), 62–117.

Klass, D., Silverman, P. & Nickman, S. (Eds.) (1996). *Continuing bonds: New understandings of grief*. Washington, DC: Taylor and Francis.

Klein, W. C. & Bloom, M. (1995). Practice wisdom. *Social Work*, 40(6), 799–807.

Kohut, H. (1971). *Analysis of the self*. New York: International Universities Press.

Kohut, H. (1977). *Restoration of the self*. New York: International Universities Press.

Kramer, R. M. & Specht, H. (1969, 1975, 1983). *Reading in community organization practice* (1st, 2nd & 3rd edns.). Englewood Cliffs, NJ: Prentice-Hall.

Kravetz, D. & Jones, L. E. (1991) Supporting practice in feminist service agencies. In M. Bricker-Jenkins, N. R. Hooyman & N. Gottlieb (Eds.), *Feminist social work practice in clinical settings* (pp. 233–49). Newbury Park, CA: Sage.

Kreitzer, L. (2012). *Social work in Africa: Exploring culturally relevant education and practice in Ghana*. Calgary: University of Calgary Press.

Krill, D.F. (1990). *Practice wisdom*. Newbury Park, CA: Sage.

Krill, D. F. (2014). Existential social work. *Advances in Social Work, 15*(1), 117–28.

Krill, D. F. (2017). Existential social work. In F. J. Turner (Ed.), *Social work treatment: Interlocking theoretical approaches* (6th ed.) (pp. 166–90). New York: Oxford University Press.

Krumer-Nevo, M. & Sidi, M. (2012). Writing against othering. *Qualitative Inquiry, 18*(4), 299–309.

Kuhlmann, C. (2001). Historical portraits of important European leaders in social work: Alice Salomon (1872–1948) – Germany. *European Journal of Social Work, 4*(1), 65–102.

Laing, R. D. (1965). *The divided self: An existential study in sanity and madness*. Harmondsworth: Penguin.

Laing, R. D. (1971). *Self and others* (2nd ed.). Harmondsworth: Penguin.

Laing, R. D. & Esterson, A. (1970). *Sanity, madness and the family*. Harmondsworth: Penguin.

Laslett, P. (1996). *A fresh map of life: The emergence of the third age* (2nd ed.). Basingstoke: Palgrave Macmillan.

Lavalette, M. (Ed.) (2011). *Radical social work today: Social work at the crossroads*. Bristol: Policy Press.

Lavalette, M. & Ferguson, I. (Eds.) (2007). *International social work and the radical tradition*. Birmingham: Venture.

Lawler, J. (2013). Critical management. In M. Gray & S. A. Webb (Eds.), *The new politics of social work* (pp. 98–115). Basingstoke: Palgrave Macmillan.

Lawson, J. (2017). The 'making safeguarding personal' approach to practice. In A. Cooper & E. White (Eds.), *Safeguarding adults under the Care Act 2014: Understanding good practice* (pp. 20–39). London: Jessica Kingsley.

Layous, K. & Lyubomirsky, S. (2014). The how, why, what, when, and who of happiness. In J. Gruber, & J. T. Moskowitz (Eds.), *Positive emotion: Integrating the light sides and dark sides* (pp. 473–95). Oxford: Oxford University Press.

Le Grand, J. (2007). *Consistent care matters: Exploring the potential of social work practices*. London: Department for Education and Skills.

Lee, J. (1997). The empowerment group: The heart of the empowerment approach and an antidote to injustice. In J. K. Parry (Ed.), *From prevention to wellness through group work* (pp. 15–32). New York: Haworth.

Lee, J. A. B. (2001). *The empowerment approach to social work practice: Building the beloved community* (2nd ed.). New York: Columbia University Press.

Lee, J. A. B. & Hudson, R. (2017). Empowerment approach to social work treatment. In F. J. Turner (ed.). *Social work treatment: Interlocking theoretical perpsectives* (pp. 142–65). New York: Oxford University Press.

Lee, M. Y., Ng, S.-M., Leung, P. P. Y. & Chan, C. L. W. (2009). *Integrative body-mind-spirit social work: An empirically based approach to assessment and treatment*. New York: Oxford University Press.

Leighton, N., Stalley, R. & Watson, D. (1982). *Rights and responsibilities: Discussion of moral dimensions in social work*. London: Heinemann.

Leonard, P. (1984). *Personality and ideology: Towards a materialist understanding of the individual*. London: Macmillan.

Leonard, P. (1993). Critical pedagogy and state welfare: Intellectual encounters with Freire and Gramsci, 1974–86. In P. McClaren & P. Leonard (Eds.), *Paulo Freire: A critical encounter* (pp. 155–68). London: Routledge.

Leonard, P. (2004). The uses of theory and the problems of pessimism. In L. Davies & P. Leonard (Eds.), *Social work in a corporate era: Practices of power and resistance* (pp. 3–15). Aldershot: Ashgate.

Levitas, R. (1998) *The inclusive society? Social exclusion and New Labour*, Basingstoke: Macmillan.

Lewin, K. (1951). *Field theory in social science*. New York: Harper.

Lewin, K. (2010[1958]) *Resolving social conflicts and field theory in social science*. New York: American Psychlogical Association.

Lindsay, T. & Orton, S. (2014). *Groupwork practice in social work* (3rd ed.). London: Sage.

Lister, R. (1998). Citizenship on the margins: Citizenship, social work and social action. *European Journal of Social Work, 1*(1), 5–18.

Littell, J. H. & Girvin, H. (2002). Stages of change: A critique. *Behavior Modification, 26*(2), 223–73.

Loewenberg, F. M. (1968). Social workers and indigenous nonprofessionals: Some structural dilemmas. *Social Work, 13*(3), 65–71.

Lonsdale, S., Webb, A. & Briggs, T. L. (Eds.) (1980). *Teamwork in the personal social services and health care: British and American perspectives*. London: Croom Helm.

Lorenz, W. (1994). *Social work in a changing Europe*. London: Routledge.

Luhmann, N. (1995). *Social systems*. Palo Alto, CA: Stanford University Press.

Lukes, S. (1973). *Individualism*. Oxford: Blackwell.

Lukes, S. (2005[1974]). *Power: A radical view* (2nd ed.). Basingstoke: Palgrave Macmillan.

Lupien, S. J. & Wan, N. (2004). Successful ageing: From cell to self. *Philosophical Transactions of the Royal Society of London, 359*, 1413–26.

Lurie, H. L. (1939[1933]). Case work in a changing social order. In F. Lowry (Ed.), *Readings in social case work 1920–1938* (pp. 755–763). New York: Columbia University Press.

Lynch, K., Baker, J. & Lyons, M. (Eds.) (2009). *Affective equality: Love, care and injustice*. Basingstoke: Palgrave Macmillan.

Lynch, K., Kalaitzake, V. & Crean, M. (2020). Care and affective relations: Social justice and sociology. *Sociological Review. Retrieved from:* https://doi.org/10.1177%2F0038026120952744.

MacCallum, G. C. (1967). Negative and positive freedom. *Philosophical Review, 76*(3), 312–34.

Macdonald, S. J. (2017). Humanistic psychology: The stairway to Athena. In L. Deacon & S. J. Macdonald (Eds.), *Social work theory and practice* (pp. 48–57). London: Sage.

Macdonald, S. J. & Deacon, L. (2019). Disability theory and social work practice. In M. Payne & E. Reith-Hall (Eds.), *Routledge handbook of social work theory* (pp. 435–47). London: Routledge.

MacFadden, R. J. (2017). Social work practice in the time of neuroscience. In F. J. Turner (Ed.), *Social work treatment: Interlocking theoretical approaches* (6th ed.) (pp. 496–512). New York: Oxford University Press.

MacNeil, H., Duff, W., Dotiwalla, A. & Zuchniak, K. (2018). 'If there are no records, there is no narrative': The social justice impact of records of Scottish care-leavers, *Archival Science*, *18*(1), 1–28.

Mafile'o, T. & Vakalahi, H. F. O. (2018). Indigenous social work across borders: Expanding social work in the South Pacific. *International Social Work*, *61*(4), 537–552.

Mafile'o, T. A. (2004). Exploring Tongan social work: *fakafekau'aki* (connecting) and *fakat‑kilalo* (humility). *Qualitative Social Work*, *3*(3), 239–57.

Marmot Review (2010). *Fair society, healthy lives: Strategic review of health inequalities in England post-2010*. London: Marmot Review.

Marsh, P. (2015). Task-centred practice. In J. Lishman (Ed.), *Handbook for practice learning in social work and social care: Knowledge and theory* (pp. 211–24). London: Jessica Kingsley.

Marsh, P. & Doel, M. (2005). *The task-centred book*. London: Routledge.

Marshall, J. (2017). Relationship-based social work in family and childcare practice. In M. McColgan & C. McMullin (Eds.). *Doing relationship-based social work: A practical guide to building relationships and enabling change* (pp. 44–60). London: Jessica Kingsley.

Marshall, M. (1996). Case management: A dubious practice. *British Medical Journal*, *312*: 523.

Marshall, M. & Tibbs, M. A. (2006). *Social work and people with dementia: Partnerships, practice and persistence*. Bristol: Policy Press.

Marshall, T. H. & Bottomore, T. B. (1992[1949]). *Citizenship and social class*. London: Pluto.

Marx, A. J., Test, M. A. & Stein, L. L. (1973). Extrahospital management of severe mental illness: Feasibility and effects of social functioning. *Archives of General Psychiatry*, *29*, 505–11.

Marynowicz-Hetka, E. (2019a). The social pedagogy dimension of social work activity. In M. Payne & E. Reith-Hall (Eds.), *Routledge handbook of social work theory* (pp. 282–93). Abingdon: Routledge.

Marynowicz-Hetka, E. (2019b). Social pedagogy: Comprehending activity in the field of social practice, [English] summary. In E. Marynowicz-Hetka, *Pedagogika społeczna: Pojmowanie aktywności w polu praktyki* (pp. 329–39). Łodz: Wydawnictwo Uniwersytetu Łódzkiego.

Maslow, A. (1971). *The farther reaches of human nature*. New York: Viking.

Mathbor, G. M. (2007). Enhancement of community preparedness for natural disasters: The role of social work in building social capital for sustainable disaster relief and management. *International Social Work*, *50*(3), 357–69.

May, R. (1983). *The discovery of being: Writings in existential psychology*. New York: Norton.

Mayer, J. E., & Timms, N. (1970). *The client speaks: Working class impressions of casework*. London: Routledge and Kegan Paul.

Mayo, M. (2009). Community work. In R. Adams, L. Dominelli & M. Payne (eds) *Critical practice in social work* (2nd ed.) (pp. 125–36). Basingstoke: Palgrave Macmillan.

McBeath, G. & Webb, S. A. (1991). Social work, modernity and postmodernity. *Sociological Review, 39*(4), 171–92.

McBeath, G. B. & Webb, S. A. (1997). Community care: A unity of state and care? Some political and philosophical considerations. In R. Hugman, M. Peelo and K. Soothill (Eds.), *Concepts of care: Developments in health and social welfare* (pp. 36–51). London: Arnold.

McCaughan, N. (1978). Continuing themes in social group work. In N. McCaughan (Ed.), *Group work: Learning and practice* (pp. 22–31). London: Allen and Unwin.

McCold, P. & Wachtel, B. (2012). *Restorative policing experiment: The Bethlehem Pennsylvania police family group conferencing project.* Eugene, OR: Wipf and Stock.

McColgan M. & McMullin, C. (eds.) (2017). *Doing relationship-based work: A practical guide to building relationships and enabling change.* London: Jessica Kingsley.

McCormick, M. J. (1954). *Diagnostic casework in the Thomistic pattern.* New York: Columbia Unievrsity Press.

McCranie, A. (2010). Recovery in mental illness: The roots, meanings, and implementations of a 'new' services movement. In D. Pilgrim, A. Rogers & B. Pescosolido (Eds.), *The SAGE handbook of mental health and illness* (pp. 471–89). London: Sage.

McGee, R. (2020). Rethinking accountability: A power perspective. In R. McGee & J. Pettit (Eds.), *Power, empowerment and social change* (pp. 50–67). Abingdon: Routledge.

McLeod, J. (2013). *An introduction to counselling* (5th ed.). Maidenhead: Open University Press.

McNamee, S. & Gergen, K. J. (eds) (1992). *Therapy as social construction.* London: Sage.

McTighe, J. P. (2018). *Narrative theory in clinical social work practice.* Cham: Springer.

Mead, G. H. (1929). The nature of the past. In G. H. Mead (2011) *G. H. Mead: A reader.* (Ed. F. Carriera da Silva) (pp. 204–11). Abingdon: Routledge.

Mead, G. H. (1934). *Mind, self, and society: From the standpoint of a social behaviorist.* Chicago, IL: University of Chicago Press.

Merton, R. K. (1968[1949]). *Social theory and social structure* (rev. ed.). New York: Simon and Schuster.

Meyer, C. H. (Ed.) (1983). *Clinical social work in the eco-systems perspective.* New York: Columbia University Press.

Midgley, J. (1981). *Professional imperialism: Social work in the third world.* London: Heinemann.

Midgley, J. (1984). Social welfare implication of development paradigms. *Social Service Review, 58*(2), 181–98.

Midgley, J. (1993). Ideological roots of social development strategies. *Social Development Issues, 15*(1), 1–13.

Midgley, J. (1995). *Social development: The developmental perspective in social welfare.* London: Sage.

Mignone, J. & O'Neil, J. (2005). Social capital and youth suicide risk factors in First Nations communities. *Canadian Journal of Public Health, 96* Suppl 1, S51–4.

Mikulincer, M. & Shaver, P. R. (2016). *Attachment in adulthood: Structure, dynamics, and change* (2nd ed.). New York: Guilford.

Mila-Schaaf, K. (2006). *Vä-centred social work: Possibilities for a Pacific approach to social work practice. Social Work Review, 18*(1), 8–13.

Millar, J. (2018). Working in the life space. In J. Lishman, C. Yuill, J. Brannen & A. Gibson (Eds.), *Social work: An introduction* (2nd ed.) (pp. 325–36). London: Sage.

Miller, C., Freeman, M. & Ross, N. (2001). *Interprofessional practice in health and social care: Challenging the shared learning agenda.* London: Arnold.

Miller, W. & Rollnick, S. (2013). *Motivational interviewing: Helping people change* (3rd ed.). New York: Guilford.

Milner, J. (2001) *Women and social work: Narrative approaches.* Basingstoke: Palgrave.

Milner, J., Myers, S. & O'Bryne, P. (2015). *Assessment in social work* (4th ed.). London: Palgrave.

Mishra, R. (1981). *Society and social policy* (2nd ed.). London: Macmillan.

Moreau, M. J. (1979). A structural approach to social work practice. *Canadian Journal of Social Work Education, 5*(1), 78–94.

Moreau, M. J. (1990). Empowerment through advocacy and consciousness-raising: Implications of a structural approach to social work. *Journal of Sociology and Social Welfare, 17*(2), 53–68.

Morén, S. and Blom, B. (2003). Explaining human change: On generative mechanisms in social work practice. *Journal of Critical Realism, 2*(1), 37–61.

Morgaine, K. & Capous-Desyllas, M. (2015). *Anti-oppressive social work practice: Putting theory into action.* Thousand Oaks, CA: Sage.

Morgan, D. H. J. (1996). *Family connections: A introduction to family studies.* Cambridge: Polity.

Morgan, D. H. J. (2011). *Rethinking family practices.* Basingstoke: Palgrave Macmillan.

Morgenshtern, M. & Yu, N. (2020). Who owns the case record? Client access to case records in Canadian social work practice. *International Social Work, 63*(3), 337–50.

Morley, C. (2016). Promoting activism through critical social work education: The impact of global capitalism and neoliberalism on social work and social work education. *Critical and Radical Social Work, 4*(1), 39–57.

Morris, J. (1993). *Disabled lives: Community care and disabled people.* Basingstoke: Macmillan.

Morrison, T. (2007). Emotional intelligence: Emotion and social work: Context, characteristics, complications and contribution. *British Journal of Social Work, 37*(2), 245–63.

Mullaly, B. (R. P.) & Dupré, M. (2019). *The new structural social work: Ideology, theory and practice* (4th ed.). Don Mills: Oxford University Press.

Mullaly, B. (R. P.) & West, J. (2018). *Challenging oppression and confronting privilege: A critical approach to anti-oppressive and anti-privilege theory and practice* (3rd ed.). Don Mills: Oxford University Press.

Mullender, A., Ward, D. & Fleming, J. (2013). *Empowerment in action: Self-directed groupwork.* Basingstoke: Palgrave Macmillan.

Munro, E. (1998) *Understanding social work: An empirical approach.* London: Athlone.

Munro, E. (2011). *The Munro review of child protection: Final report: A child-centred system* (Cm 8062). London: TSO.

Munro, E. & Hardie, J. (2019). Why we should stop talking about objectivity and subjectivity in social work. *British Journal of Social Work, 49*, 411–27.

Murase, K. (1955). Some considerations for programs of social and technical assistance. *Social Service Review*, *29*(3), 241–6.

Murphy, Y., Hunt, V., Zajicek, A. M., Norris, A. N. & Hamilton, L. (2009). *Incorporating intersectionality in social work practice, research, policy and education.* Washington, DC: NASW Press.

Murray, C. (1990). *The emerging British underclass.* London: Institute of Economic Affairs.

National Association of Social Workers (2015). *Indicators for cultural competence in social work practice.* Washington DC: National Association of Social Workers.

Nayak, S. & Robbins, R. (Eds.) (2019). *Intersectionality in social work: Activism and practice in context.* Abingdon: Routledge.

Needleman, J. (2017). Nursing skill mix and patient outcomes. *British Medical Journal Quality and Safety*, *26*, 525–8.

Neimeyer, R. (Ed.) (2001a). *Meaning reconstruction and the experience of loss.* Washington, DC: American Psychological Association Press.

Neimeyer, R. (2001b) The language of loss: Grief therapy as a process of meaning reconstruction. In Neimeyer, R. (Ed.), *Meaning reconstruction and the experience of loss* (pp. 261–92). Washington, DC: American Psychological Association.

Neimeyer, R. (2005) Grief, loss and the quest for meaning: Narrative contributions to bereavement care. *Bereavement Care*, *24*(2), 27–30.

Neimeyer, R. and Anderson, A. (2002) Meaning reconstruction theory. In N. Thompson, Ed.), *Loss and grief* (pp. 45–64). Basingstoke: Palgrave.

Newman, J. (2002). The new public management, modernization and institutional change: Disruptions, disjunctures and dilemmas. In K. McLaughlin, S. P. Osborne & E. Ferlie (Eds.), *New public management: Current trends and future prospects* (pp. 77–92). London: Routledge.

Nylund, D. (2006). Critical multiculturalism, whiteness, and social work: Towards a more radical view of cultural competence. *Journal of Progressive Human Services*, *17*(2), 27–42.

O'Brien, M. & Penna, S. (1988). *Theorising welfare: Enlightenment and modern society.* London: Sage.

Oham, C. & Macdonald, D. (Eds.) (2016). *Leading and managing a social enterprise in health and social care.* London: Community Training Partners.

Oliver, C. & Charles, G. (2014). *Strengths-based practice in child protection.* University of British Columbia, Department of Social Work.

Oliver, M. (1983). *Social work and disability.* Basingstoke: Macmillan.

Oosterom, M. (2020). Power and agency in violent settings. In R. McGee & J. Pettit (Eds.), *Power, empowerment and social change* (pp. 169–81). Abingdon: Routledge.

Opie, A. (1993). The discursive shaping of social work records: Organisational change, professionalism, and client 'empowerment'. *International Review of Sociology*, *4*(3), 167–89.

Opie, A. (2003). *Thinking teams/thinking clients: Knowledge-based teamwork.* New York: Columbia University Press.

Papell, C. P. & Rothman, B. (1966). Social group work models: Possession and heritage. *Journal of Education for Social Work*, *2*(2), 66–73.

Parad, H. J. (Ed.) (1965) *Crisis intervention: Selected readings*. New York: Family Service Association of America.

Park, Y., Crath, R. & Jeffrey, D. (2020). Disciplining the risky subject: A discourse analysis of the concept of resilience in social work literature. *Journal of Social Work, 20*(2), 152–72.

Parker, G. & Lawton, D. (1994). *Different types of care, different types of carer: Evidence from the General Household Survey*. London: HMSO.

Parker Follett, M. (1998[1918]). *The new state: Group organization the solution of popular government*. University Park, PA: Pennsylvania State University Press.

Parkes, C. M. & Prigerson, H. G. (2010). *Bereavement: Studies in adult life*. London: Penguin.

Parkin, F. (1979). *Marxism and class theory: A bourgeois critique*. London: Tavistock.

Parrott, L. with Maguinness, N. (2017). *Social work in context: Theory and concepts* (pp. 78–96). London: Sage.

Parton, N. (1985). *The politics of child abuse*. Basingstoke: Macmillan.

Parton, N. (2005). *Safeguarding childhood: Early intervention and surveillance in a late modern society*. Basingstoke: Palgrave Macmillan.

Parton, N. (2014). *The politics of child protection: Contemporary developments and future directions*. Basingstoke: Palgrave Macmillan.

Parton, N. & O'Byrne, P. (2000). *Constructive social work: Towards a new practice*. Basingstoke: Macmillan.

Patel, L. (2015). *Social welfare and social development* (2nd ed.). Cape Town: Oxford University Press.

Pawar, M. (2017). Social development in Asia and the Pacific: Major trends and issues. In N. T. Tan, S. Chan, K. Mehta & D. Androff (Eds.), *Transforming society: Strategies for social development from Singapore, Asia and around the world* (pp. 53–67). Abingdon: Routledge.

Pawson, R. & Tilley, N. (1997). *Realistic evaluation*. London: Sage.

Payne, M. (1989). Open records and shared decisions with clients. In S. Shardlow (Ed.), *The values of change in social work* (pp. 114–34). London: Tavistock/Routledge.

Payne, M. (1999). The moral bases of social work. *European Journal of Social Work, 2*(3), 247–58.

Payne, M. (2002). The role and achievements of a professional association in the late twentieth century: The British Association of Social Workers 1970–2000. *British Journal of Social Work, 32*(8), 969–95.

Payne, M. (2006a). *What is professional social work?* (2nd ed.). Bristol: Policy Press.

Payne, M. (2006b). Teambuilding: How, why and where? In P. Speck (Ed.), *Teamwork in palliative care: Fulfilling or frustrating?* (pp. 117–36). Oxford: Oxford University Press.

Payne, M. (2007). Performing as a 'wise person' in social work practice. *Practice, 19*(2), 85–96.

Payne, M. (2009). Understanding social work process. In R. Adams, L. Dominelli & M. Payne (Eds.), *Social work: Themes, issues and critical debates* (3rd ed.) (pp. 159–74). Basingstoke: Palgrave Macmillan.

Payne, M. (2011). *Humanistic social work: Core principles in practice*. Chicago, IL: Lyceum.

Payne, M. (2012) *Citizenship social work with older people.* Bristol: Policy Press.

Payne, M. (2014). Social care and social justice. In M. Reisch (Ed.), *The Routledge international handbook of social justice* (pp. 398–408). Abingdon: Routledge.

Payne, M. (2017). *Older citizens and end-of-life care: Social work practice strategies for adults in later life.* London: Routledge.

Payne, M. (2020). *How to use social work theory in practice: An essential guide.* Bristol: Policy Press.

Payne, M. (2021 [1990]). *Modern social work theory* (5th ed.). London: Red Globe.

Pearson, G. (1973). Social work as the privatized solution of public ills. *British Journal of Social Work, 3*(2), 209–27.

Pease, B. (2001). Developing pro feminist practice with men in social work. *Critical Social Work, 2*(1), 1–8 [Online]. Retrieved from: https://ojs.uwindsor.ca/index.php/csw/article/view/5620/4593.

Percy-Smith, J. (2000). *Policy responses to social exclusion: Towards inclusion?* Maidenhead: Open University Press.

Perlman, H. H. (1957). *Social casework: A problem-solving process.* Chicago, IL: University of Chicago Press.

Pettit, J. (2020). Transforming power with embodied practice. In R. McGee & J. Pettit (Eds.), *Power, empowerment and social change* (pp. 68–82). Abingdon: Routledge.

Pierson, J. (2002). *Tackling social exclusion.* London: Routledge.

Pilling, D. (1992). *Approaches to case management for people with disabilities.* London: Jessica Kingsley.

Pinch, S. (1994). Labour flexibility and the changing welfare state: Is there a post-Fordist model? In R. Burrows & B. Loader (Eds.), *Towards a post-Fordist welfare state* (pp. 201–22). London: Routledge.

Pincus, A. & Minahan, A. (1973). *Social work practice: Model and method.* Itasca, IL: Peacock.

Pitman, E. (1983). *Transactional analysis for social workers.* London: Routledge and Kegan Paul.

Plant, R. (2009[1970]). *Social and moral theory in casework.* Abingdon: Routledge.

Polkinghorne, D. E. (2004). *Practice and the human sciences: The case for a judgment-based practice of care.* Albany, NY: State University of New York Press.

Pollitt, C. (2002). The new public management in international perspective: An analysis of impacts and effects. In K. McLaughlin, S. P. Osborne & E. Ferlie (Eds.), *New public management: Current trends and future prospects* (pp. 274–92). London: Routledge.

Popple, K. (2015). *Analysing community work: Theory and practice* (2nd ed.). Maidenhead: Open University Press.

Powell, J. L. (2013). Michel Foucault. In M. Gray & S. A. Webb (Eds.), *Social work theories and methods* (pp. 46–62) (2nd ed.). London: Sage.

Prior, V. & Glaser, D. (2006). *Understanding attachment and attachment disorders: Theory, evidence and practice.* London: Jessica Kingsley.

Prochaska, J. O. & DiClemente, C. C. (1983). Stages and processes of self-change of smoking: Toward an integrative model of change. *Journal of Consulting and Clinical Psychology, 51*, 390–5.

Prochaska, J. O., DiClemente, C. C. & Norcross, J. C. (1994). *Changing for good.* New York: Avon Books.

Puig de la Bellacasa, M. (2017). *Matters of care: Speculative ethics in more than human worlds.* Minneapolis, MN: University of Minnesota Press.

Putnam, R. D. (2000). *Bowling alone: The collapse and revival of American community.* New York: Simon and Schuster.

Ragab, I. A. (2017). Has social work come of age? Revisiting the authentization debate 25 years on. In M. Gray (Ed.), *The handbook of social work and social development in Africa* (pp. 33–45). Abingdon: Routledge.

Rani, S. V. (2001). Impact of liberalisation on women's health in the marine food export processing industry. *Indian Journal of Social Work, 62*(4), 603–17.

Rapp, C. A. & Goscha, R. J. (2012). *The strengths model: A recovery-oriented approach to mental health services* (3rd ed.) New York: Oxford University Press.

Rawls, J. (1999). *A theory of justice* (rev. ed.). Cambridge, MA: Harvard University Press.

Ray, M., Bernard, M. & Phillips, J. (2009). *Critical issues in social work with older people.* Basingstoke: Palgrave Macmillan.

Reamer, F. G. (2018). *Social work values and ethics* (5th ed.). New York: Columbia University Press.

Reder, P., Duncan, S. & Gray, M. (1993). *Beyond blame: Child abuse tragedies revisited.* London: Routledge.

Reeser, L. C. (1991). Professionalization, striving, and social work activism. *Journal of Social Service Research, 14*(3–4), 1–22.

Reeser, L. C. (1992). Professional role orientation and social activism. *Journal of Sociology and Social Welfare, 19,* 79–94.

Reid, K. E. (1981). *From character building to social treatment: The history of the use of groups in social work.* Westport, CT: Greenwood.

Reid, W. J. (1978). *The task-centered system.* New York: Columbia University Press.

Reid, W. J. (1992). *Task strategies: An empirical approach to clinical social work.* New York: Columbia University Press.

Reid, W. J. (1994). The empirical practice movement. *Social Service Review, 68*(2), 165–84.

Reid, W. J. (1997). Long-term trends in clinical social work. *Social Service Review, 71*(2), 200–13.

Reid, W. J. (2000). *The task planner: An intervention resource for human service professionals.* New York: Columbia University Press.

Reid, W. J. & Epstein, L. (1972a). *Task-centered casework.* New York: Columbia University Press.

Reid, W. J. & Epstein, L. (Eds.) (1972b). *Task-centered practice.* New York: Columbia University Press.

Reid, W. J. & Hanrahan, P. (1982). Recent evaluations of social work: Grounds for optimism. *Social Work, 27,* 328–40.

Reid, W. J., Kenaley, B. D. & Colvin, J. (2004). Do some interventions work better than others? A review of comparative social work experiments. *Social Work Research, 28*(2), 71–81.

Reisch, M. (1998). The sociopolitical context and social work method, 1890–1950. *Social Service Review, 72*(2), 161–81.

Reisch, M. (2014). Introduction. In M. Reisch (ed.). *Routledge international handbook of social justice* (pp. 1–6). Abingdon: Routledge.

Rex, J. (1997). Multiculturalism in Europe and North America. In W. W Isajiw (Ed.), *Multiculturalism in North America and Europe: Comparative perspectives on interethnic relations and social incorporation* (pp. 5–33). Toronto: Canadian Scholars' Press.

Rhodes, M. L. (1985). Gilligan's theory of moral development as applied to social work. *Social Work, 30*(2), 101–5.

Richmond, M. E. (1922). *What is social case work? An introductory description.* New York: Russell Sage Foundation.

Richmond, M. E. (1965[1917]). *Social diagnosis.* New York: Free Press.

Riggall, S. (2012). *Using counselling skills in social work.* London: Sage.

Ritzer, G. (1996). *The McDonaldization of society – An investigation into the changing character of contemporary social life.* Thousand Oaks, CA: Pine Forge.

Robb, M., Montgomery, H. & Thomson, R. (Eds.) (2019). *Critical practice with children and young people* (2nd ed.). Bristol: Policy Press.

Roberts, A. R. (2005). Bridging the past and present to the future of crisis intervention and crisis management. In A. R. Roberts (Ed.), *Crisis intervention handbook: Assessment, treatment, and research* (3rd ed.) (pp. 3–34). New York: Oxford.

Roberts, R. (1990). *Lessons from the past: Issues for social work theory.* London: Tavistock/Routledge.

Robertson, G. K. (2014). Transitions in later life: A review of the challenge and opportunities for policy development. *Working with Older People, 18*(4), 186–96.

Robinson, V. P. (1930). *A changing psychology in social case work.* Chapel Hill, NC: University of North Carolina Press.

Rogers, C. R. (1961). *On becoming a person: A therapist's view of psychotherapy.* London: Constable.

Rogowski, S. (2013). *Critical social work with children and families: Theory, context and practice.* Bristol: Policy Press.

Rojek, C. (1986). The 'subject' in social work. *British Journal of Social Work, 16*(1), 65–77.

Rojek, C., Peacock, G. & Collins, S. (1988). *Social work and received ideas.* London: Routledge.

Ronen, T. & Freeman, A. (Eds.) (2007). *Cognitive behavior therapy in clinical social work practice.* New York: Springer.

Ronnby, A. (1992). Praxiology in social work. *International Social Work, 35*(3), 317–26.

Ronnby, A. (2013). We need the community. *Azarbe, 2,* 21–31.

Rose, A. M. (1964). A current sociological issue in social gerontology. *Gerontologist, 4*(1), 46–50.

Rose, M. A. (1991). *The post-modern and the post-industrial.* Cambridge: Cambridge University Press.

Rothman, J. (2018). *Social work practice across disability* (2nd ed.). New York: Routledge.

Rowe, J. W. & Kahn, R. L. (1987). Human aging: Usual and successful. *Science, 237,* 143–9.

Rowe, W. S. (2017). Client-centered theory and the person-centered approach: Values-based, evidence-supported. In F. J. Turner (Ed.), *Social work treatment: Interlocking theoretical approaches* (6th ed.) (pp. 34–53). New York: Oxford University Press.

Rubington, E. & Weinberg, M. S. (Eds.) (1995). *The study of social problems: Seven perspectives* (5th ed.). New York: Oxford University Press.

Ruch, G. (2018a) The contemporary context of relationship-based practice. In G. Ruch, D. Turney & A. Ward (Eds.), *Relationship-based social work: Getting to the heart of social work* (2nd ed.) (pp. 19–35). London: Jessica Kingsley.

Ruch, G. (2018b). Theoretical frameworks informing relationship-based practice. In G. Ruch, D. Turney & A. Ward (Eds.), *Relationship-based social work: Getting to the heart of social work* (2nd ed.) (pp. 37–54). London: Jessica Kingsley.

Ruddock, R. (1969). *Roles and relationships*. London: Routledge and Kegan Paul.

Rzepnicki, T. L., McCracken, S. G. & Briggs, H. E. (Eds.) (2012). *From task-centered to evidence-based and integrative practice: Reflections on history and implementation*. Chicago, IL: Lyceum.

Sakamoto, E. (Ed.) (2012). *The roles of Buddhism in social work: Vietnam and Japan*. Hanoi: University of Social Sciences and Humanities, Vietnam National University/Chiba: Shukutoku University/Tokyo, Japan College of Social Work.

Saks, M. (1995). *Professions and the public interest: Medical power, altruism and alternative medicine*. London: Routledge.

Saleebey, D. (Ed.) (2013). *The strengths perspective in social work practice* (6th ed.) Boston, MA: Pearson.

Sands, R. G. & Nuccio, K. (1992). Postmodern feminist theory and social work. *Social work, 37*(6), 489–94.

Saracostti, M., Reininger, T. & Parada, H. (2012). Social work in Latin America. In K. Lyons, T. Hokenstad, M. Pawar, N. Huegler & N. Hall (Eds.), *Routledge international handbook of social justice* (pp. 466–79). Abingdon: Routledge.

Saulnier, C. F. (1996). *Feminist theories and social work: Approaches and applications*. New York: Haworth.

Saunders, J. A. Haskins, M. & Vasquez, M. (2015). Cultural competence: A journey to an elusive goal. *Journal of Social Work Education, 51*, 19–34.

Sawyer, E. & Burton, S. (2016). *A practical guide to early intervention and family support: Assessing needs and building resilience in families affected by parental mental health problems or substance abuse*. London: Jessica Kingsley.

Scheff, T. J. (Ed.) (1999[1984]). *Being mentally ill* (3rd ed.). Abingdon: Routledge.

Schirmer, W. & Michailakis, D. (2019). *Systems theory for social work and the helping professions*. Abingdon: Routledge.

Schön, D. A. (1983). *The reflective practitioner: How professionals think in action*. New York: Basic Books.

Schön, D. A. (1987). *Educating the reflective practitioner*. San Francisco, CA: Jossey-Bass.

Schore, J. R. & Schore, A. N. (2011). Clinical social work and regulation theory: Implications of neurobiological models of attachment. In S. Bennett & J. K. Nelson (Eds.), *Adult attachment in clinical social work: Practice, research, and policy* (pp. 57–75). New York: Springer.

Scott, M. (1989). *A cognitive-behavioural approach to clients' problems*. London: Tavistock/Routledge.

Seebohm Report (1968). *Report of the committee on local authority and allied personal services.* London: HMSO.

Seligman, M. (2017[2002]). *Authentic happiness: Using the new positive psychology to realize your potential for lasting fulfilment.* London: Brearley.

Sen, A. (2001). *Development as freedom.* Oxford: Oxford University Press.

Sen, A. (2009). *The idea of justice.* London: Allen Lane.

Sennett, R. (2003). *Respect: The formation of character in an age of inequality.* London: Penguin.

Sevenhuijsen, S. (1998). *Citizenship and the ethics of care: Feminist considerations on justice, morality and politics.* London: Routledge.

Shakespeare, T. (2000). *Help.* Birmingham: Venture.

Shakespeare, T. (2006). *Disability rights and wrongs.* Abingdon: Routledge.

Shapiro, B. Z. (1991). Social action, the group and society. *Social Work with Groups, 14*(3/4), 7–21.

Shardlow, S. (1995). Confidentiality, accountability and the boundaries of client–worker relationships. In R. Hugman & D. Smith (Eds.), *Ethical issues in social work* (pp. 65–83). London: Routledge.

Sharry, J. (2007). *Solution-focused groupwork* (2nd ed.). London: Sage.

Shaw, I. (2019). 'Let us go then, you and I'– Journeying with Ada Eliot Sheffield. *Qualitative Social Work, 18*(1), 116–38.

Sheffield, A. E. (1920). *The social case history: Its construction and content.* New York: Russell Sage Foundation.

Sheldon, B. (2011). *Cognitive-behavioural therapy* (2nd ed.). London: Routledge.

Shemmings, D. & Shemmings, Y. (2011). *Understanding disorganized attachment: Theory and practice for working with children and adults.* London: Jessica Kingsley.

Shemmings, D. & Shemmings, Y. (Eds.) (2014). *Assessing disorganized attachment in children: An evidence-based model of understanding and supporting families.* London: Jessica Kingsley.

Shemmings, D. & Shemmings, Y. (2019). Contemporary attachment theory: How can it inform social workers? In M. Payne & E. Reith-Hall (Eds.), *Routledge handbook of social work theory* (pp. 160–70). London: Routledge.

Shennan, G. (2014). *Solution-focused practice: Effective communication to facilitate change.* Basingstoke: Palgrave Macmillan.

Sheppard, M. (1995). Social work, social science and practice wisdom. *British Journal of Social Work, 25*(3), 265–93.

Sheppard, M., Newstead, S., di Caccavo, A. & Ryan, K. (2000). Reflexivity and the development of process knowledge in social work: A classification and empirical study. *British Journal of Social Work, 30*(4), 465–88.

Sheppard, M. & Ryan, K. (2003). Practitioners as rule using analysts: A further development of process knowledge in social work. *British Journal of Social Work, 33*(2), 157–76.

Shor, I. (1993). Education is politics: Paulo Freire's critical pedagogy. In P. McClaren & P. Leonard (Eds.), *Paulo Freire: A critical encounter* (pp. 25–35). London: Routledge.

Shriver, J. M. (1987). Harry Lurie's assessment and prescription: An early view of social workers' roles and responsibilities regarding political action. *Journal of Sociology and Social Welfare*, 14(2), 111–27.

Sibeon, R. (1990). Comments on the structure and forms of social work knowledge. *Social Work and Social Sciences Review*, 1(1), 29–44.

Sim, S. (Ed.) (1998). *The Icon critical dictionary of postmodern thought*. Cambridge: Icon.

Simpson, A., Miller, C. & Bowers, L. (2003). The history of the Care Programme Approach in England: Where did it go wrong? *Journal of Mental Health*, 12(5), 489–504.

Siporin, M. (1975). *Introduction to social work practice*. New York: Macmillan.

Siporin, M. (1986). Group work method and the Inquiry. In P. H. Glasser & N. S. Mayadas (Eds.), *Groupworkers at work: Theory and practice of the 80s* (pp. 34–49). Totowa, NJ: Rowman & Littlefield.

Smalley, R. E. (1967). *Theory for social work practice*. New York: Columbia University Press.

Smith, G. (2005). Green citizenship and the social economy. *Environmental Politics*, 14(2), 273–89.

Smith, M. (2011). Reading Bauman for social work. *Ethics and Social Welfare*, 5(10), 2–18.

Smith, M. & Whyte, B. (2008). Social education and social pedagogy: Reclaiming a Scottish tradition in social work. *European Journal of Social Work*, 11(1), 15–28.

Smith, Y. & Spitzmueller, M. C. (2016). Worker perspectives on contemporary milieu therapy: A cross-site ethnographic study. *Social Work*, 40(2), 105–16.

Solomon, B. B. (1976). *Black empowerment: Social work in oppressed communities*. New York: Columbia University Press.

Solvang, I. M. & Juritzen, T I. (2020). Between empowerment and discipline: Practicing contractualism in social work. *Journal of Social Work*, 20(3), 321–39.

Soydan, H. (1999). *The history of ideas in social work*. Birmingham: Venture.

Specht, H. & Courtney, M. (1994). *Unfaithful angels: How social work has abandoned its mission*. New York: Free Press.

Spector, M. & Kitsuse, J. I. (2017[1977]). *Constructing social problems*. Abingdon: Routledge.

Spencer, M. S. (2017). Microaggressions and social work practice, education, and research. *Journal of Ethnic and Cultural Diversity in Social Work*, 26(1–2), 1–5.

Spiegel, J. P. (1957). The resolution of role conflict within the family. *Psychiatry*, 20, 1–16.

Spivak, G. C. (1985). The Rani of Sirmur: An essay in reading the archives. *History and Theory*, 24(3), 247–72.

Starkey, P. (2000). The feckless mother: Women, poverty and social workers in wartime and post-war England. *Women's History Review*, 9(3), 539–57.

Staub-Bernasconi, S. (1992). Social action, empowerment and social work – an integrative theoretical framework for social work and social work with groups. *Social Work with Groups*, 14(3–4), 35–51.

Staub-Bernasconi, S. (2007). *Soziale Arbeit als Handlungswissenschaft*. Bern: Haupt.

Staub-Bernasconi, S. M. (2003). Social work as a transdisciplinary science of social problems and social action – program and educational practice. In C. Labonté-Roset, E. Marynowicz-Hetka & J. Szmagalski (Eds.), *Social work education and practice in today's*

Europe: Challenges and diversity of responses (pp. 37–54). Katowice: European Association of Schools of Social Work, Jagiellonian University, University of Łódz, University of Silesia.

Stein, H. D. (1963). The concept of the social environment in social work practice. In H. J. Parad & R. R. Miller (Eds.), *Ego-oriented casework: Problems and perspectives* (pp. 65–88). New York: Family Service Association of America.

Stephens, P. (2013). *Social pedagogy: Heart and head.* Bremen: Europäischer Hochschulverlag.

Stroebe, M. & Schut, H. (1999). The dual process model of coping with bereavement: Rationale and description. *Death Studies, 23*(3), 197–224.

Stroebe, M., Schut, H. & van den Bout, J. (Eds.) (2013). *Complicated grief: Scientific foundations for health care professionals.* Abingdon: Routledge.

Studt, E. (1959) Worker–client authority relationships in social work. In E. Younghusband (Ed.) (1966), *New developments in casework* (pp. 167–83). London: Allen and Unwin.

Taft, J. (1962[1937]). Time as the medium of the helping process. In V. P. Robinson (Ed.), *Jessie Taft, therapist and social work educator: A professional biography* (pp. 305–24). Philadelphia, PA: University of Pennsylvania Press.

Tamburro, A. (2013). Including decolonization in social work education and practice. *Journal of Indigenous Social Development, 2*(1), 1–16.

Tan, N. T., Chan, S., Mehta, K. & Androff, D. (Eds.) (2017). *Transforming society: Strategies for social development from Singapore, Asia and around the world.* Abingdon: Routledge.

Taylor, B. J. (2017). *Decision making, assessment and risk in social work* (3rd ed.). London: Sage.

Teare, R. J. & McPheeters, H. L. (1970). *Manpower utilization in social welfare: A report based on a symposium on manpower utilization in social welfare services.* Atlanta, GA: Social welfare Manpower Project, Southern Regional Education Board.

Teater, B. (2014). *An introduction to applying social work theories and methods* (2nd ed.). Maidenhead: Open University Press.

Tew, J., Ramon, S., Slade, M., Bird, V., Melton, J. & Le Boutillier, C. (2012). Social factors and recovery from mental health difficulties: A review of the evidence. *British Journal of Social Work, 42*(3), 443–40.

Thayer, H. S. (1970). Introduction. In H. S. Thayer (Ed.), *Pragmatism: The classic writings* (pp. 11–22). New York: New American Library.

Thomas, N. (2012). Love, rights and solidarity: Studying children's participation using Honneth's theory of recognition. *Childhood, 19*(4), 453–66.

Thompson, N. (2016). *Anti-discriminatory practice* (6th ed.). London: Palgrave.

Thorne, B. (1992). *Carl Rogers.* London: Sage.

Thorpe, C. (2018). Pierre Bourdieu: Symbolic violence and self-exclusion. In C. Thorpe, *Social theory for social work: Ideas and applications* (pp. 107–23). Abingdon: Routledge.

Tice, K. W. (1998). *Tales of wayward girls and immoral women: Case records and the professionalization of social work.* Urbana, IL: University of Illinois Press.

Timms, N. (1983). *Social work values: An enquiry.* London: Routledge and Kegan Paul.

Timms, N. (1989). Social work values: Context and contribution. In S. Shardlow (Ed.), *The values of change in social work* (pp. 11–23). London: Tavistock/Routledge.

Titterton, M. (2005). *Risk and risk taking in health and social welfare*. London: Jessica Kingsley.

Tofuaipangai, S. & Camilleri, P. (2016). Social policy, social work and fatongia: Implications of the Tongan concept of obligation. *Aotearoa New Zealand Social Work, 28*(1), 60–67.

Tolson, E. R., Reid, W. & Garvin, C. D. (2003). *Generalist practice: A task-centered approach* (2nd ed.). New York: Columbia University Press.

Toren, N. (1969). Semi-professionalism and social work: A theoretical perspective. In A. Etzioni (Ed.), *The semi-professions and their organization: Teachers, nurses, social workers* (pp. 141–95). New York: Free Press.

Torino, G. C., Rivera, D. P., Capodilupo, C. M., Nadal, K. L. & Wing Sue, D. (2019). Everything you wanted to know about microaggressions and didn't get a chance to ask. In G. C. Torino, D. P. Rivera, C. M. Capodilupo, K. L. Nadal & D. Wing Sue (Eds.), *Microaggression theory: Influence and implications* (pp. 3–15). Hoboken, NJ: Wiley.

Tosone, C. (2009). Psychodynamic model. In A. Gitterman & R. Salmon (Eds.), *Encyclopedia of social work with groups* (pp. 55–7). New York: Columbia University Press.

Towell, D. (Ed.) (1988). *An ordinary life in practice*. London: King Edward's Hospital Fund for London.

Trevithick, P. (2012). Groupwork theory and practice. In P. Stepney & D. Ford (Eds.), *Social work models, methods and theories* (2nd ed.) (pp. 236–54). Lyme Regis: Russell House.

Tripp, D. (1994). Teachers' lives, critical incidents, and professional practice. *Qualitative Studies in Education, 7*(1), 65–76.

Tripp, D. (2012[1993]). *Critical incidents in teaching: Developing professional judgement*. Abingdon: Routledge.

Tronto, J. C. (1993). *Moral boundaries: A political argument for an ethic of care*. New York: Routledge.

Truell, R. & Jones, D N. (n.d.). *The global agenda for social work and social development: Extending the influence of social work*. Retrieved from: www.ifsw.org/wp-content/uploads/ifsw-cdn/assets/ifsw_24848-10.pdf.

Tsang, N. M. (2008). Kairos and practice wisdom in social work practice. *European Journal of Social Work, 11*(2), 131–43.

Tuckman, B. W. (1965). Developmental sequence in small groups. *Psychological Bulletin, 63*, 684–99.

Tuckman, B. W. & Jensen, M. A. C. (1977). Stages of small-group development revisited. *Group and Organization Studies, 2*(4), 419–27.

Turnell, A. & Edwards, S. (1999). *Signs of safety: A solution and safety oriented approach to child protection casework*. New York: Norton.

Turnell, A. & Murphy, T. (2020). *Signs of safety comprehensive briefing paper* (4th ed.). East Perth: Resolutions. Retrieved from: www.signsofsafety.net/product/signs-of-safety-comprehensive-briefing-paper-2/.

Turner, F. J. (Ed.) (2017). *Social work treatment: Interlocking theoretical approaches*. New York: Oxford.

Turner, S. G. & Maschi, T. M. (2015). Feminist and empowerment theory and social work practice. *Journal of Social Work Practice, 29*(2), 151–62.

Twigg, J. (2000). Carework as a form of bodywork. *Ageing & Society, 20*(4), 389–411.

United Nations (2007). *United Nations Declaration on the Rights of Indigenous Peoples.* Retrieved from www.un.org/esa/socdev/unpfii/documents/DRIPS_en.pdf.

United Nations (2020). *Sustainable Development Goals.* Retrieved from: www.un.org/sustain abledevelopment/sustainable-development-goals/.

van Ewijk, H. (2009). Citizenship-based social work. *International Social Work, 52*(2), 167–79.

van Harreveld, F., Nohlen, H. U. & Schneider, I. K. (2015). The ABC of ambivalence: Affective, behavioral, and cognitive consequences of attitudinal conflict. *Advances in Experimental Social Psychology, 52*, 285–324.

Varley, B. K. (1968). The use of role theory in the treatment of disturbed adolescents. *Families in Society: The Journal of Contemporary Social Services, 49*(6), 362–6.

Versey, H. S. (2016). Activity theory. In S. K. Whitbourne (Ed.), *Encyclopedia of adulthood and aging* (vol. 1, pp. 10–16). Chichester: Wiley.

von Bertalanffy, L. (1971[1950]). *General system theory: Foundations, development, application.* London: Allen Lane.

Wachtel, T. (2017[2000]). Restorative practices with high-risk youth. In G. Burford & P. Hudson (Eds.), Family group conferencing: New directions in community-centered child and family practice (pp. 86–92). Abingdon: Routledge.

Wakefield, J. C. (1996). Does social work need the eco-systems perspective? Part 1: Is the perspective clinically useful? *Social Service Review, 70*(1), 1–31; Does social work need the eco-systems perspective? Part 2: Does the perspective save social work from incoherence? *Social Service Review, 70*(2), 183–213.

Wakefield, J. C. (2013). DSM-5 and clinical social work: Mental disorder and psychological justice as goals of clinical intervention. *Clinical Social Work Journal, 41*(2), 131–8.

Walker, S. (2015). Family therapy and systemic practice. In J. Lishman (Ed.), *Handbook for practice learning in social work and social care: Knowledge and theory* (3rd ed.) (pp. 241–61). London: Jessica Kingsley.

Walrond-Skinner, S. (1976). *Family therapy: The treatment of natural systems.* London: Routledge and Kegan Paul.

Walsh, F. (2016). *Strengthening family resilience* (3rd ed.). New York: Guilford.

Walton, R. G. & el Nasr, M. M.A. (1988). Indigenization and authentization in terms of social work in Egypt. *International Social Work, 31*(2), 135–44.

Ward, A. (2018). The use of self in relationship-based practice. In G. Ruch, D. Turney & A. Ward (Eds.), *Relationship-based social work: Getting to the heart of social work* (2nd ed.) (pp. 55–74). London: Jessica Kingsley.

Warkentin, B. & Sawatsky, A. (2018). Points of discourse: Reconciling Christianity and social work through critical theory. *Social Work and Christianity, 45*(2), 57–67.

Wastell, D. & White, S. (2014). Making sense of complex electronic records: Socio-technical design in social care. *Applied Ergonomics, 45*(2), 143–9.

Watson, D. (Ed.) (1985). *A code of ethics for social work: The second step.* London: Routledge and Kegan Paul.

Watts, L. & Hodgson, D. (2019) *Social justice theory and practice for social work: Critical and philosophical perspectives.* Cham: Springer.

Watts, M. & Higgins, A. (2017). *Narratives of recovery from mental illness: The role of peer support.* London: Routledge.

Weale, A. (1980). Procedural fairness and rationing the social services. In N. Timms (Ed.), *Social welfare: Why and how?* (pp. 233–57). London: Routledge and Kegan Paul.

Webb, S. A. (2006). *Social work in a risk society: Social and political perspectives.* Basingstoke: Palgrave Macmillan.

Webb, S. A. (Ed.) (2017). *Professional identity and social work.* Abingdon: Routledge.

Weber, M. (1930). *The protestant ethic and the spirit of capitalism.* London: Allen & Unwin.

Weber, M. (1978[1910–14]). *Economy and society* (Eds. G. Roth & C. Wittich). Berkeley, CA: California University Press.

Weick, A. (1983). Issues in overturning a medical model of social work practice. *Social Work, 28*(6), 467–71.

Weick, A. (1986). The philosophical context of a health model of social work. *Social Casework, 67*(9), 551–9.

Wendt, S. (2019). Feminist ideas in social work. In M. Payne & E. Reith-Hall (Eds.), *Routledge handbook of social work theory* (pp. 361–70). London: Routledge.

Wendt, S. & Moulding, N. (Ed.) (2016). *Contemporary feminisms in social work practice.* Abingdon: Routledge.

Wetherall, M. (2012). *Affect and emotion: A new social science understanding.* London: Sage.

White, M. & Epston, D. (1990). *Narrative means to therapeutic ends.* New York: Norton.

White, S. (2006). Unsettling reflections: The reflexive practitioner as 'trickster' in inter-professional work. In S. White, J. Fook & F. Gardner (Eds.), *Critical reflection in health and social care* (pp. 21–39). Maidenhead: Open University Press.

White, S., Fook, J. & Gardner, F. (Eds.) (2006). *Critical reflection in health and social care.* Maidenhead: Open University Press.

White, S., Gibson, M., Wastell, D. & Walsh, P. (2020). *Reassessing attachment theory in child welfare.* Bristol: Policy Press.

White, V. (2006). *The state of feminist social work.* Abingdon: Routledge.

Whittington, C. (1975). Self-determination re-examined. In F. E. McDermott (Ed.), *Self-determination in social work: A collection of essays on self-determination and related concepts by philosophers and social work theorists* (pp. 81–922). London: Routledge and Kegan Paul.

Wilkinson, R. & Pickett, K. (2010). *The spirit level: Why equality is better for everyone.* London: Bloomsbury.

Wilks, T. (2012). *Advocacy and social work practice.* Maidenhead: Open University Press.

Willetts, D. (2010). *The pinch: How the baby boomers took their children's future – And how they can give it back.* London: Atlantic.

Willmott, P. with Thomas, D. (1984). *Community in social policy.* London: Policy Studies Institute.

Witkin, S. L. (1996). If empirical practice is the answer, then what is the question? *Social Work Research, 20*(2), 69–75.

Wolfensberger, W. (1983). Social role valorization: A new insight, and a new term, for normalization. In D. G. Race (Ed.) (2003), *Leadership and change in human services: Selected readings from Wolf Wolfensberger* (pp. 80–6). London: Routledge.

Wolins, M. (1969[1965]) Another view of group care. In P. E. Weinberger (Ed.), *Perspectives on social welfare: An introductory anthology* (pp. 286–98). New York: Macmillan.

Wong, Y.-L. R. (2014). Radical acceptance mindfulness and critical reflection in social work education. In M. S. Boone (Ed.), *Mindfulness and acceptance in social work: Evidence-based interventions and emerging application* (pp. 125–43). Oakland, CA: Context.

Wong, Y.-L. R. (2019). Mindfulness and social work. In M. Payne & E. Reith-Hall (Eds.), *Routledge handbook of social work theory* (pp. 256–65). London: Routledge.

Woods, M. E. & Hollis, F. (1999). *Casework: A psychosocial therapy* (5th ed.). New York: McGraw-Hill.

Wootton, B. (1959). *Social science and social pathology*. London: Allen and Unwin.

Worden, J. W. (2010). *Grief counselling and grief therapy: A handbook for the mental health practitioner* (4th ed.). Abingdon: Routledge.

World Health Organization (2003) *International consultation to review community-based rehabilitation*. Helsinki: World Health Organization. Retrieved from: https://apps.who.int/iris/bitstream/handle/10665/68466/WHO_DAR_03.2.pdf?sequence=1&isAllowed=y.

World Health Organization (2008). *Closing the gap in a generation: Health equity through action on the social determinants of health*. Geneva: WHO.

Wright, B. A. (1983). *Physical disability – A psychosocial approach* (2nd ed.). New York: Harper and Row.

Yeager, K. R. & Roberts, A. R. (2015). Bridging the past and present to the future of crisis intervention and crisis management. In K. R. Yeager (Ed.), *Crisis intervention handbook: Assessment, treatment and research* (4th ed.) (pp. 3–35). New York: Oxford University Press.

Yelaja, S. A. (1982). Values and ethics in the social work profession. In S. A. Yelaja (Ed.), *Ethical issues in social work* (pp. 5–32). Springfield, IL: Thomas.

Yelloly, M. A. (1980). *Social work theory and psychoanalysis*. Wokingham: Van Nostrand Reinhold.

Zimmerman, P.B., Paul, H., Rohde, A., Roser, K., Powell, G., Livingston, L. & Hagman, G. (2019). An introduction to intersubjective self psychology. In G. Hagman, H. Paul & P. B. Zimmerman (Eds.), *Intersubjective self psychology: A primer* (pp. 3–13). Abingdon: Routledge.

Zuchowski, I., Hudson, C., Bartlett, B. & Diamandi, S. (2014). Social work field education in Australia: Sharing practice wisdom and reflection. *Advances in Social Work and Welfare Education*, 16(1), 67.

Index